SOCIAL CHANGE IN THE MODERN ERA

Daniel Chirot
University of Washington, Seattle

UNDER THE GENERAL EDITORSHIP OF
Robert K. Merton
Columbia University

HARCOURT BRACE JOVANOVICH, PUBLISHERS

San Diego   New York   Chicago   Austin
London   Sydney   Toronto

D0073984

To Cynthia K.

ISBN: 0-15-581421-4

Library of Congress Catalog Card Number: 85-81730

Printed in the United States of America

PREFACE

I began this book as a revision of my *Social Change in the Twentieth Century*. But after reading and thinking about what I had written almost ten years ago, I realized that I had changed my mind about so much of the earlier material that it would be necessary to write a new book.

First, I felt I should introduce the modern era with an explanation of why and how Western Europe came to dominate the world. This I have tried to do in Chapters 2 through 4. The obvious importance of science, technology, and what is generally called cultural history in explaining the rise of the West casts serious doubts on the theoretical framework—world system theory—used in my earlier book on social change. If this framework is useful in describing and understanding the Western-dominated world of competing capitalist empires at the start of the twentieth century, it is much less convincing in accounting for how that world came to be.

The middle parts of the book, Chapters 5 through 7, are those most similar and in some parts identical to the equivalent chapters in *Social Change in the Twentieth Century*. Chapters 8 through 10, however, are almost entirely changed. Part Three is about the contemporary world, and that world seems to me to be very different from the one I thought I saw in the 1970s. In the mid-1970s it was not yet obvious that the world economy was entering another cycle, repeating some of the experiences involving technological innovation that had occurred four times previously during the nineteenth and twentieth centuries. Now it is easier to see the direction of future change than it was a decade ago because the outlines of a new, "fifth" industrial cycle are more apparent.

In addition, the future role of both communist and Third World countries seems clearer than it did in the 1970s. These countries are unlikely to be as pivotal in determining future social change as once seemed possible, unless, of course, there is another great world war.

In Part Three, as in Part One, I found that world system theory was of limited use in explaining major trends in social change. The neo-Marxist vision of capitalism collapsing in the face of a joint challenge from socialist and peripheral or semiperipheral powers lacks plausibility in the 1980s and for the foreseeable future. In the immediate wake of political events in the early and mid-1970s, this was not always evident.

I should point out that it is possible to use sections of this book without being obliged to read others. A reader interested only in the twentieth century could begin with Chapter 5. Or, it would be possible to skip Part One entirely and begin with Chapter 6. Similarly, a reader wanting information about contemporary societies could read only Part Three. Although I think that the entire book has a theoretical consistency and that no section is superfluous, each section was written as an almost self-contained set of arguments and facts. The only exception to this is Chapter 5, which has as many connections to Part Two as it does to Part One.

One thing has not changed in the last ten years: I remain convinced that the study of social change limited to any single society or time, even a society as large and important as that of the United States today, is foolish and misleading. Societies exist in a world of complex interactions. No actors or groups of actors are islands that exist apart from these interactions. Furthermore, no change exists outside the history that preceded it. So it is only by studying social change within a global and historical context that it can be understood. What remains as true in the 1980s as in the 1970s is that too many students are not taught about social change in this way. Lacking a base for comparing their society and time with others, they remain as likely as ever to accept simplistic ideologies. Whether these ideologies are of the right or of the left, whether they are active or passive, it is equally disturbing to see how widely they are accepted. In 1986 as in 1977, I offer the material in this book in the hope that it will play a small role in fighting those simplifiers who rely on ignorance to peddle their false messages.

Acknowledgments

I would like to thank two friends and fellow social analysts for their helpful discussions and suggestions. Bruce Cumings of the School of International Studies at the University of Washington aided me by explaining how much he disagrees with my viewpoints and by teaching me the rudiments of Asian political economy. Bob Hefner, an anthropologist at Boston University, assisted by making me think about important moral issues.

Three other colleagues at the University of Washington were helpful in providing books, articles, and ideas about Asia: Michael Birt, Nicholas Lardy, and Elizabeth Perry.

Though I disagree with almost everything he writes, I still acknowledge an important debt to Immanuel Wallerstein.

In addition, I wish to thank Lee Bullock. Without her help I would certainly not have been able to write anything at all.

Finally, I am grateful to the staff at Harcourt Brace Jovanovich for encouraging me to try to sort out my ideas once again.

Daniel Chirot

CONTENTS

CHAPTER *1*

The Study of Social Change

*T*here are as many ways of studying social change as there are ways of studying societies. Economists, anthropologists, sociologists, demographers, literary critics, art historians, and many others bring their own special disciplines to bear in the examination of how and why social patterns and interactions have changed in the past, and what directions such changes might take in the future. Though the underlying assumption that humans have not undergone important genetic changes in the last few tens of thousands of years is widely accepted, it is perfectly obvious that the social settings in which they operate have been dramatically altered. They not only continue to change at a rapid rate, they also vary significantly from one society to another at any given time.

How is one to proceed to the study of change? How is one to pick the most significant changes that have occurred? Are there patterns that have repeated themselves? Are there specific institutions or parts of societies which so determine the lives of people that it is possible to understand social change by focusing on them rather than on the details of actual human lives? How far back into the past is it necessary to go in order to grasp the essence of contemporary social change?

No single approach can satisfy everyone. Mine is to claim that Yes, there are some master institutions that regulate human behavior; that there are a fairly small number of these; and that it is possible to study them in order to understand how they work. From such knowledge we can then develop an understanding of how other, more derivative parts of a social structure operate.

It is not enough to say that certain key parts of social structures are the master springs from which general social life flows, and that the study of how these parts change is the study of social change. Family structure, the organization of markets, the state, religious hierarchies, schools, the way in which elites have exploited the masses to extract surpluses from them, and the general set of values that govern society's cultural outlook are only a small and overlapping part of the long list of key institutions that have been called central.

I believe that in order to understand change, it is imperative to be comparative. There is no way of understanding the nature of the twentieth century without having a good idea of how Western civilization became so dominant in the preceding four centuries. There is no way of getting such an idea without being able to isolate the key ways in which Western Europe differed from other technologically and politically advanced civilizations. Such a comparison, if it studies the central aspects of societies, should provide a logical and satisfying answer to the question of how the West became dominant, and then suggest a model of what key institutions and comparisons need to be studied in order to understand twentieth-century change.

The first aspect of social structure that needs to be studied is class. Class positions are based on occupation, and they determine a good part of how various individuals perceive their interests. Peasants, merchants, bureaucrats, big landowners, manufacturers, factory workers, teachers, and all other occupational groups have a view of the world which is heavily, though certainly not entirely, determined by the work they do. Groups of occupations may have enough in common to form specific classes with joint political interests, though class boundaries are both more fluid and less inclusive than most Marxist theoreticians would suggest.

One of the key differences between various societies at any one time and within the same society over a long period of time is the various constellations of class forces which exist, and how these influence the distribution of political power. For example, in medieval China towns obtained much less independence than they did in Western Europe, and merchants and artisans consequently had less power and influence than they did in the West. This had far reaching consequences for the subsequent pattern of social change in both China and the West. Other comparative examples of equal importance exist within Europe itself, and even within individual countries over time. English class structure in the nineteenth century changed quite markedly as manufacturing became a dominant portion of the economy, replacing agriculture. This had major political effects as the nature of the English elite, and its interests, changed too.

A second crucial aspect of society is its way of perceiving itself, the world, and the universe. In part, this is derived from class structure, but not entirely. Historical tradition plays a role, as do political outcomes of major disputes and the events that make a society more or less successful in dealing with its problems. Law, religion, and science are products of a society's perception of itself, and they in turn influence the nature and direction of change.

It goes without saying that a society's economic structure must be understood and compared with others in order to have any grasp of how that society survives and changes. Economic structure is tightly bound to class structure, and the direction of economic change, growth, or stagnation is heavily influenced by a society's legal system, its religious outlook, and its notion of how natural phenomena operate.

Actually, it is almost impossible to separate all these things, and it is certainly foolish to assign the position of prime mover to any of them. They affect each other, and there can never be a final determination of what parts of the social structure "cause" change in others. The only way to determine the difference between cause and effect is to see what came before a certain type of change, and to find out whether or not similar prior events in other cases produced roughly similar outcomes.

There is nothing unique or original about the statements I have made so far, and were this book limited to this theoretical framework, there would be little reason to write it. But there is another element which must be added—one which is usually left out of most discussions of social change. That is the international or world-wide context in which societies exist and change, because this, along with internal factors, has an enormous influence on the direction and nature of change. This has been particularly true in the last five centuries.

Societies influence each other in many ways. They exchange goods and ideas, they make war or prepare their defenses for future war, and they may conquer or be conquered. These types of exchange and interaction, both peaceful and warlike, are obviously a major source of change. Powerful political units have always been able to take more from their neighbors than they returned, and the weak have always been subject to exploitation or extermination. It is therefore extremely important to understand what makes certain social structures particularly strong or weak.

→ Beginning in the late fifteenth century, however, there was a major change in the world. Western Europeans extended their reach far beyond Europe's borders, to America and to the coasts of Africa and Asia. Later, they came to dominate the entire world. In a sense, until the Western expansion, there had been several large "systems" of interlocked societies, but these had remained virtually autonomous from each other, with only limited contacts. After four centuries of European expansion, by the start of the twentieth century, there was only one system, one world, and the study of social change in this single global system must take that into account. ←

The key institution through which Western societies have regulated their interactions with each other and with outsiders has been the modern state. This, along with the capacity to make rapid technological and economic progress, distinguished Europeans from others until the late nineteenth and twentieth centuries, when the rest of the world learned to organize itself into a variety of modern states able to mobilize vast resources for international conflict.

To understand contemporary social change, it is necessary to know how the Western state came to be so powerful, how it gave Europeans an important advantage, and how the state has come to be the single most important institution in most contemporary societies. It can never be forgotten that the state's first, though certainly not its only, task is to control its territory and prevent its key resources from being exploited by others. The state governs a society and organizes it with the goal of meeting challenges to its power, ultimately by resorting to force if that is necessary. Until very recently all states were controlled by and organized for the benefit of a very small elite. These few organized the extraction of surpluses from the general population in order to maintain their own standard of living and protect their control over resources. The fact that in some Western states, and now in some non-Western ones as well, the state came to be seen as an instrument that exercises its power for the sake of the majority has not changed this definition. Even those states most concerned with the general well-being of their populations must see to it that outsiders do not steal their resources and that internally the population remains sufficiently well-organized and disciplined to defend the state.

The growing economic and organizational gap between Western societies and states and the rest of the world from about 1500 to 1900 allowed Europeans to dominate the world system that came into being during that time, and to exploit it to their advantage. By the early twentieth century this system had some well-established categories of societies with quite distinct roles to play in the world economy and in its political structure.

There were, on one hand, core societies. These were the relatively rich, industrialized societies organized into strong states. In them were the main scientific and manufacturing centers of the world. They were highly urbanized, and their economies were diversified. The European core, which included the United States by the second half of the nineteenth century, contained no more than one-sixth of the world's population in 1900. Its chief members, with the United States, were the United Kingdom, France, and Germany.

At the other end were the peripheral societies. They were poor, overwhelmingly rural and agricultural, and had little manufacturing. They were either organized into weak states, which were indirectly dominated by one or more core powers, or they were direct colonies of core states. About two-thirds of the world's population lived in such societies, including India, which was a colony of the United Kingdom, and China, which was theoretically independent but was actually a kind of international condominium largely controlled by outside powers. All of Asia except Japan, all of Africa, and all of Latin America and the Caribbean were part of the periphery which supplied primary products—agricultural and mineral—to the core in return for manufactured goods.

In between, about one-sixth of the world consisted of semiperipheral societies. These were either societies sinking into the periphery after a period as more central entities, like Spain and Austria-Hungary, or aspiring, rising societies attempting to enter the core, like Russia and Japan. In many ways, these were the most troublesome societies—beset with enormous internal social tensions, having large international ambitions, but faced with the rivalry of established core powers who both tried to use and control them.[1]

Even of the late nineteenth century, much less today, it is impossible to explain the relative backwardness and poverty of the majority of the world in terms of "traditionalism" or "failure to modernize." To be sure, in terms of the sixteenth century, it is reasonable to explain the relatively great dynamism of Europe and the stagnation of China, India, or the Islamic Near East in such a way, referring primarily to internal forces at work in these areas. But increasingly, as the European world system spread itself throughout the globe, non-Western areas became a part, though a peripheral part, of that system, and this played a major role in shaping their economies, societies, cultures, and politics. It is not that the rest of the world would be rich and industrialized if it had not been for the creation of a European world system, but that it would have evolved in a direction very different from the one it has actually taken. There is no way of understanding what has happened without reference to the entire world system, and in particular to societies' place in it. ←

This remains as true at the end of the twentieth century as in the beginning. No major social change occurs outside of the world context; and though the strengths and weaknesses of individual states and societies are largely determined by internal causes, it is the way these characteristics of societies interact with the world system that determines the direction, intensity, and speed of further internal changes. This is not simply true of peripheral societies, but of core and semiperipheral ones as well.

This is not to suggest that the world system of the late twentieth century is the same as the one of the nineteenth or early twentieth century. Quite the contrary is true. At what seemed then to be the very height of Western power and domination over the rest of the world, the system began to crack. World War I shook the West's faith in its rationality and produced the Communist revolution in Russia. World War II ended Europe's predominant position in world affairs, and the successor to Western Europe's position, the United States, was challenged by a strengthened and enlarged Soviet Union. Europe's colonies, one by one, broke their political, and in some cases, their economic ties with their old masters. States became stronger throughout the world, and many formerly peripheral or semiperipheral societies improved their ability to compete and to carry out social change among their people. Yet, a type of world system continues to exist, with core societies, peripheral ones, and semiperipheral ones. Whether or not this system will survive as economic and social change continue is a major question, but it would be folly to suppose that the world is likely to become any less interdependent or that social change will ever again occur in isolation from the world context.

The great social and ideological conflicts of the last part of the twentieth century are not new. Nationalism, socialism, and capitalism came into being in the centuries preceding ours, and their growth has much to do with the growth and subsequent partial diminution of the European world system. Religious and ethnic resistance to the influence of that world system are even older forces which remain as active today as ever. Knowing how they evolved over time in a global context is the only way to understand what they are doing now.

It follows from these introductory remarks that the organization of this book must be historical. Part One, Chapters 2 through 5, will explain the rise of a European world system and the reasons for and consequences of the Western domination of the world. Part Two, Chapters 6 and 7, will discuss the strains in the world system in the first half of the twentieth century, and the social changes produced by them. Part Three, Chapters 8 through 10, will deal with the second half of the twentieth century, and with the likely directions of social change in the near future.

Some questions that must be asked about the future are: How well will Western societies, particularly the United States, adapt to their relative decline? Will the inability of the old core to dominate the old periphery produce a serious internal crisis within the core? Will the established rich economies be able to maintain their prosperity? Will the strains of a changing world balance of power lead to social and political crisis? Which types of societies outside the old core will adapt best and prosper most in the changed global environment of the late twentieth century? Is communism a viable solution to the problems of change, or is capitalism still dynamic enough to provide answers? Is there a possible third solution, neither communist nor capitalist?

By a historical and comparative study of the key institutions and aspects of society which I have mentioned, I think it is possible to give tentative answers to these important questions. Though it would be impossible, and somewhat pointless, to discuss every major type of social change, I think that by focusing on the most important ones, it will be possible to get a sense of the future direction of change and to develop some idea of what the world of the early twenty-first century will look like.

Part One

THE RISE OF
THE WESTERN
WORLD

CHAPTER 2

The Advantages of Western Europe Before 1500

*T*he rise of the West did not happen quickly. It incubated for a full millennium between the fall of the Western Roman Empire in the fifth century and the burst of exploratory expansion that began at the end of the fifteenth. Without some quite accidental advantages, medieval Europe would not have emerged as the strong power it did. These advantages were chiefly geographic and political, and included a series of legal and religious developments which evolved from those.

Geography

That part of Western Europe between the Pyrenees Mountains and the Vistula's plain in Poland—an area which today includes most of France, England, the Benelux countries, Germany, Denmark, parts of southern Sweden, western Poland, and at least the Po Valley in northern Italy—has two climatic traits. It has cold, but not very cold, winters (the mean January temperature is between $-2°C$ and $+5°C$ except in the Alps and the Carpathian Mountains) and abundant precipitation which is spread more or less evenly throughout the year. The area does not require seasonal monsoons or large-scale irrigation to water its crops; it is rarely subject to severe droughts; yet the winters, while not unduly harsh, are cold enough to limit some of the parasites which, in the warmer parts of the world, prey on people and their domestic animals and cause endemic, debilitating diseases. This large northwestern European plain is the only major part of the world, except for the eastern United States, whose natural vegetation is broadleaf deciduous forest, a reflection of its temperate, well-watered climate. (It is possible that the northern Chinese plain around the Yellow River once harbored this kind of vegetation, but the rain there is seasonal, and the frequency of drought much greater than in Europe.)

The other major civilized high-density agricultural parts of the world either depend heavily on irrigation to supplement erratic rainfall, exist in tropical climates with more parasitic diseases, or both. In the past this was not a barrier to the creation of great agrarian states, but it proved to be a severe block to improving the standard of living of the population and accumulating enough capital once population densities reached the levels that obtained by the end of the first millennium A.D. Between about A.D. 500 and 1500 the populations of China and India roughly doubled, that of the Middle East remained about the same, and that of northwestern Europe more than tripled.[1]

Yet, despite this increase in population, northwestern Europe retained a land/animal and arable land/human ratio more favorable than the other major agrarian civilizations. The animal population was especially important because it provided labor for cultivation and meat products for food, both of which were in short supply for the masses of often overworked and sickly peasants of the Middle East, China, and India.[2] The greater food surpluses that could be produced in Europe and the relative absence of climatic catastrophes, or what was often worse in irrigated areas, the human destruction of its man-made waterworks, meant that there was less periodic destruction of human, animal, and physical resources which produce wealth. Over a millennium, Europe, or at least northwestern Europe, gained an advantage in the accumulation of human and animal capital which was far from inconsequential. This was particularly true after the spread of the heavy plow into northern France, England, the Low Countries, and Germany from the tenth century on, for this plow could handle and take advantage of the heavy forest soils of the area and improve drainage, which had previously been a problem.[3]

But climate was not northwestern Europe's only geographic advantage. It was also far from any warlike nomads, and neither its climate nor its vegetation was hospitable to the kind of predatory cattle-herding people who wandered through the immense Eurasian steppes, Arabia, and North Africa. In semiarid regions where overgrazing and the destruction of irrigation works can turn rich grain fields into desert in a generation, the harm done by such nomads is notorious. One study of Iraq, once the home of the first agrarian states in the world and the center of a long string of civilizations, indicates that from about A.D. 900 to 1500 the region lost at least 60 percent of its population as successive waves of Turks and then Mongols destroyed its arable land.[4] Almost all of China, all of the Middle East and North Africa, and much of India were at one time or another badly damaged by nomadic invasions. So were Eastern Europe and Russia. But the Eurasian steppe ends in Hungary (the Eastern Carpathians and the Transylvanian Plateau that separate Hungary from the Ukraine are not a serious barrier), and north of Castille the geography was no longer suitable for the Berber and Arab nomads who repeatedly invaded Spain. It was not only the distance, but the cold, wet, heavy forests of northwestern Europe which shielded it from invasion. Hungarian nomads raided Burgundy in the ninth and tenth centuries, just as Saracen pirates did. Neither settled there, and after the tenth century, they did not return. Later, it was more than luck that spared the Westerners from the Mongol raids. It is doubtful that the Mongols could have found in Germany the grazing lands and room to maneuver their cavalry and flocks that they found in the Ukraine and Hungary.[5] Again, Western Europe was subject to less catastrophic economic disruption, at least after the tenth century, than were other civilized parts of the world.

That is not to say that northwestern Europe was free of war, destruction, famine, or disease. But it was relatively better off, and this allowed it to accumulate more wealth. The only major catastrophe suffered by Western Europe in the millennium from 500 to 1500 was the Black Death which,

during 1350 to 1400, killed somewhere between one-fourth and one-third of
the human population. This episode, while accompanied by much bitter warfare (the so-called Hundred Years' War, which involved France, Spain, England, and the Low Countries), destroyed less material and animal capital than
did the Mongol invasions further east or the Bedouin invasions of North
Africa. In fact, by improving the land/human and animal/human ratio, the
Black Death actually enriched the survivors.[6] By 1500 Europe had recovered
from the damage and the sixteenth century was one of dynamic expansion.

Political Decentralization and the Power of the Towns

A different kind of geographic advantage helped Europe, too. Unlike China,
Western Europe has many small river valleys rather than two or three very
big ones. China, which held a technological lead over Europe until at least the
late fifteenth century, was far more easily unified after every episode in which
its central empire splintered. This was partly because there were only two
major river valleys to control, those of the Yellow and Yangzi. Under the Sui
and Tang dynasties, these were joined by a canal which brought rice to the
north. Communications were far easier than across Europe, and relative cultural homogeneity as well as political unity were simpler to maintain.[7]
    Nevertheless, Western Europe did maintain a certain cultural unity. It was
Christian, its educated classes wrote and read a common language, Latin, and
there existed similar institutions and habits across the continent. But to rule
over any one or two of the key, productive river basins did not confer such
power that the rest of Europe could then be brought under control. Because
there was no political union, individuals could flee religious and intellectual
persecution by moving from one area to another. Once Western Europe
crystallized into a number of distinct states, they were always in competition
with each other, and this stimulated some experimentation. It also meant that
after the rapid growth of trade in the eleventh century certain types of
movable capital could evade overtaxation and expropriation by the political authorities.
    It was not to the advantage of any of the great classical agrarian empires to
permit too much intellectual freedom which might question orthodox political
arrangements. Empires also tended to overtax visible wealth whenever possible. Their ruling aristocracies and court officials were primarily interested in
raising funds for their own consumption, and successful merchants were always a tempting target for bankrupt, wasteful rulers. History's most successful
agrarian empire, China, never succeeded in stopping all change, but it did
manage to prevent a class of independent capitalists and influential intellectual
nonconformists from shaking the foundations of society. Europe's less secure
petty kings and princes might have wished for such control; but when they
achieved it they never did so on a continental scale, and the economic ruin and
intellectual stagnation they therefore produced did only limited damage.

The most successful European agrarian empire after the fall of the Carolingian Empire in the ninth century was put together by the Spanish Habsburgs in the sixteenth. Where they ruled, they succeeded, in alliance with the Catholic Church, in crushing scientific progress, nonconformist religious thought, the mercantile middle class, and the kinds of unsettling social change that were rocking the rest of Europe. But they failed to gain control over northern Germany, Scandinavia, the northern Low Countries, France, Switzerland, and England. So while they managed to destroy the vitality of much of southern Europe, they failed to do so in northwestern Europe.[8] Had the Ming or Qing dynasties in China failed to unify China as the Habsburgs failed in northwestern Europe, it is quite likely that the first capitalist, industrialized societies would have developed in China, and it would have been the politically fragmented but strong Chinese who set out on the conquest of the world during the fifteenth to nineteenth centuries.

This is not a sufficient explanation, however, because outside of China none of the major agrarian empires managed to keep control over an entire cultural region for very long. Islam's unity was damaged when the Abbasids replaced the Umaiyads, and it was irretrievably shattered when the Abbasid Caliphate lost its political power. India between the time of Asoka and the Mughals was never close to being united under a single ruling house.

The political key to the West's eventual success was the rise of a strong and in some cases independent bourgeoisie in the Middle Ages.

The main reason for the collapse of Charlemagne's Empire in the two generations after his death in 814 was the absence of a strong taxation base for its rulers. Without enough money to pay its servitors, the Carolingians, instead, paid them in land, which quickly became so many private domains completely out of the control of the central authorities. The low level of trade, the shortage of cash, and the general poverty of the rural economy made financing a strong state impossible. Europe slipped into a nearly anarchic condition. Viking, Saracen, and Hungarian invasions compounded the problem by overwhelming the feeble resources of the Western monarchies. Protection by local lords became the only source of meager security. It was from this situation, and not so much from the earlier collapse of Rome, that feudalism arose.[9]

But the Western monarchies that succeeded the Carolingians did not disappear. Legitimized in part by the memory of Carolingian, and before that of Roman unity, and supported in its efforts to maintain internal peace by the Christian Church, the institution of kingship survived. In the eleventh century the invasions stopped, trade revived, and a series of important technological innovations allowed agricultural productivity to increase and new lands to be cleared. The population grew, and on this new material base, the monarchies began to rebuild their political power. From the start, the main contestants for power were the kings on one hand and the local lords on the other. In this long war, which in some cases was to continue into the seventeenth and eighteenth centuries, cities played a crucial balancing role. Merchants and town artisans had every interest in securing greater freedom from the control of local nobles and in preventing their interfering with trade. Consequently, the kings could use the fiscal and political support of the newly growing towns to help the slow consolidation of their power.[10]

Struggles between kings or emperors and their land-controlling local administrators are a common enough occurrence in almost all agrarian states to disprove the notion that this was a singular element in medieval Western Europe. Rather, it was the role played by the towns that was unique, and which, in the long run, was made possible by the inability to recreate a united European Empire.

Max Weber's insight on this issue has been confirmed by more recent historians. He wrote:

> The urban autonomy of varying extent, which was the specific characteristic of the medieval Occidental city, developed only because and insofar as the non-urban power-holders did not yet possess a trained apparatus of officials able to meet the need for an urban administration even to the limited extent required by their *own* interest in the economic development of the city. . . . The early medieval princely administration and courts did not have the specialized knowledge, continuity, and training in rational objectiveness which would have given it the capacity to order and direct the affairs of urban craft and commercial interests—affairs that were so far removed from the social habits and time consuming preoccupations of the knightly personnel of these bodies. The interest of the power-holders in the early period was only in money revenues. . . . The competition between non-urban powers, in particular the conflict of the central power with the great vassals and the hierocratic power of the church, came to the aid of the cities, especially since an alliance of any one of the contending powers with the money power of the burghers could provide it with decisive advantage.[11]

It was not that the kings or great nobles, whose powers were based on their control of vast amounts of rural land, trusted or liked the cities which were growing in their midst. They had no choice but to depend on them, and vie for their support. The cities, in return, could not gain power on their own, at least not far beyond their walls, because of the military preponderance of the rural elite. This was far more the case in northwestern than in southern Europe, where, quite exceptionally for the medieval Occident, the Italian city-states finally became the dominant political power.

The great French medievalist Marc Bloch said something similar when he wrote:

> In the last resort the collective independence which was the ideal of so many eager communities rarely went beyond varying degrees of limited administrative autonomy; but in order to escape the unintelligent restrictions of local tyrannies another course was available to the bur-

gesses which, although it might seem little more than a desperate remedy, was often proved by experience to be the most effective. This was to place themselves under the protection of the great royal or princely governments, guardians of law and order over vast areas. Their very concern for their finances gave these authorities—as they came to appreciate more and more—an interest in the prosperity of rich taxpayers. In this way again, and perhaps more decisively, the increasing power of the burgesses tended to undermine one of the most characteristic features of feudalism—the subdivision of authority.[12]

This does not mean that the early medieval Western towns were larger or more developed than the cities of that time in Byzantium, the Muslim world, India, or China. On the contrary, it was the very fact that they were, to begin with, less developed that shaped feudal society as a highly divided, rurally based political system. The division and rural base of power explain the rise of the Western city's autonomy between the eleventh and the thirteenth centuries.[13]

The political situation characterized by this three-cornered struggle—kings, feudal lords, and towns, with the latter starting in the weakest position—was complicated by the presence of the church. From the time of the late Roman Empire, the Christian Church established a network parallel to the Roman Imperial administration. It survived the fall of Rome, staffed in its upper echelons largely by the descendants of the Roman elite who managed to maintain their moral authority over the invading barbarians because of their literacy and their connection with the awesome memory of Rome's achievement.[14] Subordinated by the Carolingians, the church lapsed into ineffectiveness until it regained its autonomy in the tenth and, especially, the eleventh centuries when it challenged lay political power in the strongest of the European monarchies, Germany.

The long war between the popes and the German emperors ultimately ruined any prospect of German unity; and when it spread to Italy, had a similar effect there. Towns played an ambiguous role, using papal-secular conflict to gain their independence, particularly in northern Italy.[15] But even in France and England, the potential for church-state conflict gave the towns that much more leverage.[16]

In the end the complex political conflict between these parties led to the compromise which was so specifically Western European, the creation of a type of political structure called the *Ständestaat* (state of estates). This amounted to a partition of powers in the thirteenth and fourteenth centuries. Monarchs were recognized as legitimate heads of state. But lords, cities, and the church also retained a specific set of rights and duties, honorific statuses, and legal roles in the affairs of state. This was truer in the increasingly stable French, Burgundian (including the Low Countries), English, and Iberian monarchies than in Germany or Italy where the distribution of power did not lead to the revival of large unified states. But even in Germany where small local states developed, they went through a similar evolution. The new *Ständestaat* was more institutionalized than the feudal system, it had a specific territorial reference, and in effect provided for a constitutional division of powers.[17]

Few documents could better illustrate the beginning of such an arrangement than the Magna Carta of 1215, signed by John of England as the condition for the preservation of his throne against angry lords and the Church, which had been hostile to the attempt by English kings to take control of church matters.[18] This document was a detailed guarantee of the rights and privileges of the various estates far more concerned with the protection of elites against royal rule than with any principle of rights for the general population.[19] The calling of early English parliaments in the second half of the thirteenth century was addressed to these estates: magnates (large feudal lords), knights, churchmen, and representatives of the important towns. It was not an abstract respect for the rights of these estates that made Parliament an important institution, but the inability of kings to rule, raise taxes, and maintain internal peace without the help of the estates.[20]

England was not alone. The specific institutions varied in detail but not in essence throughout Western Europe. Almost eighty years before the calling of the first English Parliament, in 1188, Alfonso IX of Leon called a *consilio* with three estates representing the towns, nobles, and clergy. Later, a regular *cortes*, or parliament, was instituted in which the kings frequently used their alliance with towns against fractious nobles. Castile developed a *cortes* on the same model, and when Leon and Castile merged in 1250, the two *cortes* were also joined. Aragon had regional *cortes* in the thirteenth century, and after 1307, a national *cortes* met every other year. In France, too, there were regional and provincial councils of a similar nature, and in 1302 a national estates-general (this name was a later invention) was called largely to unite towns and nobles with the King of France, Philip the Fair, against the papacy which was trying to control the French church. Regional estates continued to meet in France, and in the fourteenth century towns gained considerable power in this way. In the fifteenth and sixteenth centuries, however, the national estates-general decayed, and the growing power of the kings virtually abolished it after its last meeting in 1615. In Germany, the independent principalities which were left after the collapse of the monarchy developed *Lantage* which were similar to estate councils elsewhere in Western Europe. In the Low Countries there were also such regional councils, and a Burgundian states-general met 160 times from 1464 to 1567, exercising great fiscal powers and defending the rights of towns and merchants. In Sweden a particular twist developed because of the relatively great strength of free peasants. They were represented in the parliament. In southern Italy, where towns did not gain the full independence of their northerly neighbors, there were, however, regional parliaments, and the one in Sicily played a considerable role in the fifteenth century. Poland, Hungary, and Bohemia also had medieval parliaments, but there, particularly in Hungary and Poland, the relatively lesser strength of towns and the correspondingly greater power of the landed nobility subverted these institutions and turned them into instruments of national dissolution as nobles blocked the emergence of powerful monarchical institutions.[21]

The institutionalization of the *Ständestaat* did not proceed smoothly. It was the result of almost continuous internal and interstate conflicts. Its ultimate beneficial results in strengthening the independence of towns and in providing a legal-constitutional basis for state power were neither anticipated nor necessarily desired by many of the participants in the conflicts who would have preferred to gain absolute power. But benefits there were: arbitrary government power was reduced; separation of powers between church and state was formalized; disruptive local feudal lords were controlled; highly specialized legal codes to regulate economic and fiscal exchanges were developed; and finally, there began to emerge a loyalty to state structures that went beyond faithfulness to any particular king or ruling house. This last development was the origin of nationalism in the most successful Western monarchies, France and England, and in the Netherlands and Sweden somewhat later.[22]

The *Ständestaat* did not survive throughout all of Europe. In the seventeenth and eighteenth centuries it was replaced by increasing royal control and absolutism in France. In Spain, absolutism developed even earlier, under the Habsburgs in the sixteenth century. In Central and Eastern Europe, where the *Ständestaat* compromise failed, those states which did develop, Prussia and Austria, were also absolutist. All the more was this the case in Russia. But in England, Sweden, and the United Netherlands, which broke away from Habsburg domination in a long war that began in 1572 and really ended only in 1648, the *Ständestaat* survived as a seeming anachronism. England's civil war (1642–1648) was a triumph of Parliament over the kings, and it is more than coincidence that it was precisely the Netherlands and England that led the way to Europe's seventeenth-century commercial revolution and rapid economic growth, while it was England that later became the first country to industrialize. What had seemed to be a seventeenth-century remnant of past political practices proved to be more flexible and conducive to progress than the newer, more centralized and bureaucratized ways of Europe's absolutist monarchs.

The full importance of the political compromise that produced, and in some cases nurtured, the *Ständestaat* becomes clear only if a corollary development is discussed, because it was this that led directly to the creation of social and cultural structures disposed to making rapid progress. This development was the religious and legal rationalization of life that took place in important parts of the West. In order to study this development we have to return to a period before the seventeenth century, to the earlier Middle Ages.

The Rationalization of Law and Religion

Institutional rationality means calculability. A clearly defined set of laws and procedures, stability of property relations, and governments bound by these make up a rational political system. An arbitrary and capricious government is the opposite of a rational one. The more a government relies on a set of established, codified procedures and the less it relies on the whim of a ruler, the more rational it becomes.

Cultural rationality is an analogous concept. It implies a drive to turn the human and nonhuman universe around each of us into a set of clearly understood, calculable objects and relations that behave according to a set of understood "natural" laws.

Economic rationality means that economic actors are willing and able to make reasonable predictions about their return on investments. Social and political systems which are arbitrary, or which do not guarantee property rights, or which do not protect key economic actors, are not conducive to economically rational behavior. This hardly means that in nonrational circumstances most people behave foolishly or illogically; only that predictability becomes so difficult that, to protect themselves, economic actors take measures that have little bearing on maximization of the productive powers of their investments. In a structurally rational environment, economic actors are freer to simply maximize their productivity to increase their profits.

One of the key requirements for an economically rational system is the presence and protection by the authorities of markets. Markets allow economic actors to compare values and to shift resources and goods in ways that will maximize return on investments. The more markets there are available, and the more information there is about them, the easier it becomes to calculate. Nonmonetized exchanges, in practice, are too cumbersome for this, but even where there have been highly monetized and extensive market networks, they cannot maximize economic rationality unless they are protected by the political power holders and unless rational market behavior is considered a suitable and legitimate form of behavior. In the history of the world, it has not been often that all these conditions have been met.

The rationalization of law and religion in Western Europe, combined with the increasing protection given to townsmen who embodied market and economic rationality, ultimately led to the creation of capitalist economic relations in northwestern Europe. It was then that the slowly accumulated wealth and relative geographic advantages of this part of the world were translated into decisive economic advances.

Rational law implies the possibility of impartial empirical validation of proof in the context of generally applicable procedural rules. For any given case the ethical issues of right and wrong are axiomatic, and it only remains to be shown what has actually happened so that events can be compared with the previously established standards of rightness. If the axioms change over time because of necessity, they do so slowly in rational legal systems. They adapt to changing social conditions, but that never eliminates the need to find the facts in any given case. Insofar as judges or juries are swayed by emotions, prejudice, or favoritism, they are considered to behave in a nonrational way. That much Western law retains the possibility of this kind of inappropriate behavior shows that perfect rationalization is impossible; but the ideal in the West has long tended away from the nonrational.

A rational legal system also requires the presence of a legal profession specially trained in procedural rationality and interpretation.

A rational legal system is important for the development of economic rationality because it can smooth commercial intercourse between widely divergent segments of society. When the rules are known and more or less impartially applied, it is possible for individuals and groups to calculate the probabilities of success more easily and to feel more confident that contracts and property rights will be enforced. Rational law protects from arbitrary confiscation, from unpredictable political interference with the marketplace, and from sudden changes in the rules which might turn a profitable activity into an unprofitable one for noneconomic reasons.

The history of legal rationalization in the West long antedates the Middle Ages. It goes back to the development of the Roman Republic's law and can be traced through the preservation and modification of that law in the late Roman Empire. Later, the same law was further modified by the Church in the Middle Ages, and extended to secular government, so that by the fifteenth and sixteenth centuries several European legal systems had become highly rationalized. Nevertheless, it must be recognized that every great agrarian civilization has developed more or less rational legal codes, and before specifying what was unique about the Western version some others must be examined.

In China, for example, a highly developed legal code was written in the second century B.C., and by the end of the second century A.D. the code, with its accompanying model case histories consisted of over 17,000,000 words. Later elaborations, particularly in the tenth and eleventh centuries, put Chinese law of that time substantially ahead of European law. But Chinese law was unevenly applied, and the vast majority of common people were not treated "equally under the law." The educated officials and gentry were subject to one set of laws, the impressively codified ones, and the masses to another, the disparate and unsystematized set of local customs. Though not entirely absent, commercial law was weakly elaborated in China. This stands in marked contrast to Rome, where, by the late Empire, commercial, as opposed to merely criminal and administrative law, was highly developed.[23]

Islamic law was also highly rationalized in some respects, and it blended its original religious inspiration with many elements of Roman Imperial law. But the separation of secular from religious law which occurred in the West because of conflict between common and canon law, and more deeply between secular and ecclesiastic authorities, never took place in Islam. Keeping the base of law in religion reduced the possibility of developing objective, practical laws in a variety of nonreligious spheres of life.[24]

The Byzantine Empire, which was the direct political descendant of Rome, and which inherited and further systematized Roman law in the sixth century, did not extend this development any further. There, too, the church and state became more tightly joined rather than separate. The empire remained unified long enough that no church-state conflict persisted. Rather, the state controlled the church and used it to its own ends, but in return, it used religious officials, dogma, and ritual to legitimize secular rule. Independent towns did not emerge, and in post-Justinian legal elaborations the distinction between secular and religious law was blurred.[25]

Indian law, whose roots are fully as ancient as Roman and Chinese law, was generally less systematized. J. Duncan M. Derrett has written that:

> The [Indian] texts are not concerned with many details of administration, agricultural and fiscal matters. They dilate on criminal penalties, and on penances; and theft figures in various guises, evidently a primary topic. The regulation of daily life in its infinite variety, especially commercial law, is eschewed.[26]

There are two sets of reasons for the development of rational law. All complex state structures need regularized procedures for administering their domain and for maintaining internal peace. The medieval Catholic Church, though it controlled only a small state as such, depended on a vast administrative apparatus that also required regularized legal codes and procedures. But the notion of law in such cases was always subordinate to the basic political and religious requirements of the authorities. The notion of law as something apart from direct religious or political interference carries rationalization further, and increases the possibility of basing decisions on purely impersonal criteria. Such an advance requires the existence of a class, or classes of people with considerable economic and political power, but without full power. It then becomes advantageous for this group to struggle for the establishment of a legal system that would protect its interests against political and religious rulers. This can be done precisely by insisting on the separation of law from religious and political considerations.

There have not been many instances of such a constellation of forces: strong but not ruling classes with an interest in rationalizing law and also wishing to preserve the state in which they existed. A typical outcome in most such cases was a disintegrative civil war, partition of the legal system into subsystems which did not overlap but dealt with each group as a distinctive entity, or civil war which ended with one group winning and crushing the legal rights of its opponents. The second possibility, of legal compartmentalization, explains the relative lack of legal unity in the Muslim Indian states which ruled non-Muslim populations throughout the late Middle Ages and early modern periods. It also accounts for a similar phenomenon in the Ottoman Empire. But disintegration or internal war which resulted in the establishment of a single coercive power was more common.

Weber suggests that the unusual rationalization of Roman law was part of the compromise achieved between lower-class plebeian citizens and the ruling elite in a long series of civil wars during the early Republic.[27] Similarly, the English Puritans in the seventeenth century also emphasized the need for rational law, and nineteenth-century European bourgeois made similar demands in order to protect themselves against forces they could not control but which could not overwhelm them, either. We find the same pattern today in

Third World countries subjected to arbitrary military autocracy; the educated middle classes, who do not rule but who are vitally important, demand an end to subjective laws and the enforcement of objective, rational standards.

Weber wrote that, "Formal justice is thus repugnant to all authoritarian powers, theocratic as well as patriarchic, because it diminishes the dependency of the individual upon the grace and power of the authorities."[28] The main reason for legal rationalization in the West, then, was the long, indecisive multisided political struggle between kings, nobles, the church, and the towns. The emergence of a kind of working truce institutionalized by the *Ständestaat* created the conditions for stable, rational legal rule which enhanced the possibility of rational economic behavior.

Religious rationality is a difficult concept to grasp because the demand for cold, logical proof and objectivity seems to be the opposite of faith. That is why in many religions self-induced trances through music, dance, fasting, drugs, or certain sexual practices are necessary to provide the celebrants with divine vision. Many major religions have stressed the opposite, rationality over induced ecstasy. But pushed too far from magic and ritual, and systematized too logically by theological specialists, faith in the divine risks has turned into either an ethic stripped of direct godly intervention or a radical skepticism about everything. The ancient Greek elite and a large portion of Rome's intellectual elite were pushed into precisely these positions, and it was the need to grapple with the skeptical philosophy of the ancient world that introduced such a strong rationalizing element into early Christianity.

The preservation of a distinct church hierarchy and a professional priesthood was also an important element in strengthening the rational component of medieval Christianity, but would not have resulted in such a strong push in that direction without the church-state split which characterized Western Christianity. After all, Byzantium, too, was Christian and had a church organization that was originally similar to that in the West. But in Byzantium, the maintenance of imperial control subordinated the church to the emperor and turned it into a political tool of secular politics. It was not until very late, in the dying days of the Byzantine Empire, that Eastern Christianity set out, once more, on the path of rationalization, at a time of disintegrating central authority. The revival of classical Greek learning and humanism in the fifteenth century, however, was accompanied by the final Ottoman conquest which destroyed the material basis for an independent Orthodox church.[29]

The tensions and lack of concordance between a religious promise and secular political events will drive religious thinkers to seek more logical and objective proofs of the meaning of the world, just as, at the opposite end, it will drive many ordinary people to escape into mysticism. But for the intellectual and rational element to thrive, it is necessary for it to retain a material base capable of supporting abstract speculative activity. The Western church in the Middle Ages existed in just such circumstances, again in large part because of the irremediable split and constant conflict between secular and ecclesiastic authorities.

In China, too, a rationalizing ethic was strongly developed, but it was the property of the Confucian bureaucratic intelligentsia whose ideal demanded service to the emperor and not to the separate development of theology. As Ronan and Needham have written:

> Confucianism became a cult, a religion based on a kind of hero-wor-ship and borrowing both from the cults of nature deities and ancestor worship. But since the conception of a priesthood was inimical to Confucian thought, the guardians and celebrants of the new religion were the local scholars and officials. The state religion of China which grew up from the beginning of the Imperial Age was something rather different. It involved the position of the emperor as the high priest of all the people, in which capacity the annual sacrifices at the altars of Heaven and Earth, the Sun and Moon, the Temples of Agri-culture, and so on, devolved upon him . . . it was not Confucianism.[30]

Ronan and Needham conclude their comments by calling Confucianism "a religion without theologians," one which was interested in human society alone, not in larger issues. This, as it happens, had an important effect on the development of natural science, because the Confucian intellectual elite had as little interest in that as in a systematic, rationalizing theology.

For practical purposes, at the level of the peasantry, Chinese religion re-mained remarkably unsystematic, a combination of various traditions and local cults, poorly integrated with each other. The secular success of the empire seems to have removed the felt need for religious rationalization which was so pressing in the divided West.

Islam, too, had a strong rationalizing element and was in this respect (as in many others) more advanced than Occidental Christianity in the early Middle Ages. There is little question that one of the spurs to Western rationalization in this domain, as in the rationalization of science and to some extent law, was its contact with the Muslim world through Spain and Sicily in the twelfth and thirteenth centuries.[31] But the material failure of Islam, the inability of its cities to defend themselves against nomadic invasions (and in Spain and Sicily against Christian conquest) destroyed the economic base on which further progress might have been made. The later, great Muslim Ottoman, Safavi, and Mughal empires were more traditional agrarian states where the priest-hood was largely, if not entirely, subjugated to the secular authority of the emperors. Though intellectual progress did not cease, much of the earlier impetus toward religious rationalization and toward the growth of learning in philosophy and science was lost.

Indian religions, whether early Buddhism, Jainism, or the varieties of Hin-duism, had one major aspect that affected their intellectual development. They were religions of withdrawal, of sanctification of other-worldly passivism. This led to the production of holy men, not to an active theology that tried to grapple with the problems of this world and their meaning.[32] Like the Chinese, as far as the masses of Indians were concerned, religion constituted a host of poorly integrated local cults, magical practices, and superstitions. This was typical of all peasants, whether in Europe, Africa, or Asia. If the intellectual and religious elite did not develop a rationalizing tradition, there was little opportunity for one to come from other groups. Indian religions seem to have made less progress in this respect than did Confucian philosophy or Islam.

The evolution of rational religion was never a question of purely internal progress within systems of religious thought. In Occidental Christianity a decisive role was played by the long-lived independence and growth of towns. Much as religious principles varied between civilizations, certain patterns reappeared over and over in many regions at various times. Any great religion holds many divergent strands within itself, and some strands tended to resemble each other across various religious traditions. This was due to the fact that even in different cultures and religions, people with similar occupations tend to develop similar ways of thinking.

Peasants, bound by custom to their small communities, have followed traditional magical religious practices devoid of ethical rationalism. It has happened that peasants pushed to revolutionary despair by excessive exploitation—unusual demands placed on them by their masters—have turned to radical messianic prophetic religions. Even then, in many cases, the recruits into such revolutionary movements have been more from the ranks of village and small-town artisans than from peasants as such. Their leaders have usually been heretical and marginal priests from the old religion, not peasant leaders.[33] Weber has written:

> The lot of the peasant is so strongly tied to nature, so dependent on organic processes and natural events, and economically so little oriented to rational systematization that in general the peasantry will become a carrier of religion only when it is threatened by enslavement or proletarianization, either by domestic forces (financial or seigneurial) or by some external political power.[34]

Peasants have generally lacked either the broad acquaintance with the outside world or the time and literary skills to be much preoccupied with theological issues. The repetitive, cyclical nature of agricultural tasks has produced practical religious and magical practices more concerned with obtaining good weather, fertility, and health than in abstract rationalization.

Warrior nobles, the most usual social elite in agrarian societies, have even less of a propensity to religious rationalization. As Weber explained:

> The life pattern of the warrior has very little affinity with the notion of a beneficent providence, or with the systematic ethical demands of a transcendental god. Concepts like sin, salvation, and religious humility have not only seemed remote from all ruling strata, particularly the warrior nobles, but have indeed appeared reprehensible to its sense of honor. . . . It is an everyday psychological event for the warrior to face death and the irrationalities of human destiny. Indeed, the chance and

adventures of mundane existence fill his life to such an extent that he does not require of his religion (and only accepts reluctantly) anything beyond protection against evil magic or ceremonial rites congruent with his sense of status, such as priestly prayers for victory or for a blissful death leading directly into the hero's heaven.[35]

This does not mean that Muslim or Christian medieval warriors lacked religious faith; it means that their faith was less concerned with problems of salvation and explanation of the inconsistencies of the world than with self-legitimation and glorification.

Government bureaucrats, whether in classical Rome or in China, developed their own rationalizing ethic, but as we have seen with the Confucian bureaucracy in China, its concerns were purely secular and social. Again, in Weber's words:

> The distinctive attitude of a bureaucracy to religious matters has been classically formulated in Confucianism. Its hallmark is an absolute lack of feeling of a need for salvation or for any transcendental anchorage for ethics. In its place resides what is substantively an opportunistic and utilitarian doctrine of conventions. . . .[36]

The situation is different with merchants and other townsmen. They have a particularly strong tendency toward religious rationalization.

> When one compares the life of a petty-bourgeois, particularly the urban artisan or the small trader, with the life of the peasant, it is clear that the former has far less connection with nature. Consequently, dependence on magic for influencing the irrational forces of nature cannot play the same role for the urban dweller as for the farmer. At the same time, it is clear that the economic foundation of urban man's life has a far more rational character, viz., calculability and capacity for purposive manipulation. Furthermore, the artisan and in certain circumstances even the merchant lead economic existences which influence them to entertain the view that honesty is the best policy, that faithful work and the performance of obligations will find their reward and are "deserving" of their just compensation.[37]

Weber places somewhat less importance on the religious rationality of the richer merchants who were inclined to practical, this-worldly religions. But for those who were still merchants and not yet trying to blend into the local landed aristocracy, much that Weber said about small merchants applied. Their lives were regulated by ledgers and accounts, whose elements could be rationally calculated and manipulated, and they had the time and education to think about the meaning of religion and the world.

The combination of the townsmen's natural propensity to rational regulation of their lives and the previously existing rationalizing tendencies of the Western Christian church produced a religious synthesis that would have been possible nowhere else: the systematizing, antimagical, logical tendency of late medieval Christianity combined with a strongly practical, this-worldly concern with personal salvation. This was the essence of the religious movements that began to shake Western Europe in the late fourteenth century, and that eventually culminated in the Reformation of the sixteenth century.

One might ask why the Chinese merchants and artisans, or those of the Muslim world or of India, did not develop similar religious ethics. The fact is that many did, but towns in these places did not achieve the internal autonomy of their counterparts in Western Europe. Their way of looking at the world could not play as important a role in the development of their civilizations' religious lives.

According to Mark Elvin, the Chinese case is particularly instructive. Chinese cities "played a limited role in pre-modern Chinese political history." Central imperial authority was maintained almost continuously, and the absence of political fragmentation gave the urban merchant class little leeway for greater independence. The bureaucratic elite were rotated from region to region, and there was little urban self-consciousness. Towns were not, of themselves, important cultural centers. Neither architecture nor art flourished in them, except in the imperial centers. In such towns that were always subordinated to the imperial authorities and to the ethical ideals of the bureaucracy, there was little opportunity for the religious rationality of the merchant and artisan class to achieve the decisive importance it did in Western Europe.[38]

The Economic Results of Rationality: The Birth of Capitalism

The rationalization of law and religion and the establishment of political systems that protected towns and their economies created an institutional setting favorable to economic growth. Economic specialists used to weighing the profitability of their activities, and able to make the best investment decisions, were able to retain control over their capital. It was this development that differentiated modern capitalism, which appeared in the late Middle Ages, from other, more common forms of economic activity. Speculation, trade, and the acquisition of profits by political means have been present in all agrarian societies, and probably long before that. It was much rarer to allow those who pursue profits on a regular basis and primarily by means of their investments—that is, those in business—to keep control of their capital and to remain primarily businessmen. Only in the West were townsmen, the bourgeois, allowed to retain considerable freedom of action for so long without being turned into landed aristocrats or imperial bureaucrats, or without having their capital confiscated.

Rationalization of law, and particularly religion, also created a cultural setting that legitimized and further encouraged capitalist rationality. The emphasis on the need for proof, on the value of what was efficacious, was entirely consistent with rational decision making in business activity. This was quite unlike the ethical system developed by agrarian nobles, court bureaucrats, or great monarchs for whom other, nonbusiness considerations were primary. Capitalist bourgeois were able to develop their own brand of rational religion in which success in their economic activities, in increasing their profits, became a kind of proof of their moral worth. Their moral as well as their physical universe could be turned into a vast ledger where accounts were carefully kept, and where everything could be measured and weighed as income or debits. Eventually this turned into a special version of Protestant Christianity, but even before the Reformation, it was an important way of looking at the world in key urban circles.[39] Furthermore, it fit into a previously existing and powerful strand of Western Christian thought. It therefore had more legitimacy than if it had been merely the way of thinking of money-hungry merchants and artisans.

None of this is meant to suggest that by about 1500 the majority, or even a very large portion of the people in Western societies, thought and behaved like rational bourgeois. Even today, a large percentage of the people who live in Western societies do not. Neither their economic nor their religious behavior fits the model described above. The point is that by 1500 there had been, for some 300 years or more, an important and growing segment of the population in a few towns of Europe who did think this way. They had key political and intellectual allies in governments and the church, and they were in the forefront of economic progress and growth. Able to benefit from the small material advantage accumulated by Europe, they led a revolutionary change that turned Western Europe into successful capitalist societies. But this change was to take another four centuries.

CHAPTER *3*

The Expansion of the Western World, 1500–1800

*U*ntil 1600, and in some respects until as late as the end of the seventeenth century, Europe was only slightly more advanced than the rest of the world. It could not yet make significant inroads into the Middle East, India, China, or Japan. The independence of its towns and its mercantile vigor had made Europe singularly expansive, but from the point of view of old, established civilizations, such as that of China, it was far from being a significant threat or a necessary model for emulation. Only in the Americas, where the rapid European conquest owed more to the natives' lack of immunity to Old World diseases than to anything else, did the West's expansion entirely overthrow the old order in the sixteenth century.[1] As for the Chinese, one of their seventeenth-century chroniclers wrote:

> The people we call Red-hairs or Red Barbarians are identical with the Hollanders and they live in the Western Ocean. They are covetous and cunning, are very knowledgeable concerning valuable merchandise, and are very clever in the pursuit of gain. They will risk their lives in search of profit, and no place is too remote for them to frequent. Their ships are very large, strong, well-built. . . . These people are also very resourceful and inventive. . . . If one falls in with them at sea, one is certain to be robbed by them.[2]

The great accomplishments of Western rationality, by that time, had been to make Westerners better sailors, merchants, and cannon makers.[3] These were not small advantages, however, even if the old civilizations of Asia could look at the Europeans as barbarians; and when combined with the accelerating economic, political, and scientific progress within the West itself, they set the base for the destruction of those old civilizations by the Red Barbarians.

Europe's Overseas Empires, 1500–1800

Europe may again be compared with China. Just as both had suffered from barbarian invasions and imperial collapse in the early part of the first millennium A.D., so both were subjected to severe plagues and depopulation, internal wars and political chaos, and a general social crisis 1,000 years later in the fourteenth century. From about 1300 to 1400, Western Europe's population fell roughly 30 percent, from about 55 million to less than 38 million. From about 1200 to 1400, China's population fell from some 115 million to about 75 million, a loss of roughly one-third.[4]

In China, recovery from the civil wars, famines, and plagues that marked the collapse of the Yuan Dynasty followed the pattern laid down before the crisis. Imperial unity was restored by the Ming; proper administration allowed a return to economic health and a renewed rise in population. From 1400 to 1600, China's population roughly doubled, a rate of increase as great as Europe's from 1450 to 1650.[5] An expansive, technologically advanced, united China could easily have been the first to create a great overseas empire, and even to expand to America through the Pacific Northwest. In fact, China began to create a sea empire in Southeast Asia and the Indian Ocean in early Ming times, about seventy years before the Europeans first entered the same waters. But these efforts came to nought. Fearful of the rising wealth of those involved in the Indian Ocean trade, the imperial bureaucracy forbade the continuation of ocean exploration. Also, the imperial government felt that long-distance trade routes opened the coast of China to pirate activity, and to the possibility that coastal people, in conjunction with pirates and other foreigners, would establish independent, threatening power bases. To avoid these troubles, and because the central state had no need to stimulate foreign trade or look for new sources of income, China cut itself off from ocean travel. Because the center was powerful enough to enforce its will on the southern coastal towns, the policy succeeded and left the Indian Ocean open to the Portuguese, and later to the Dutch, who built lucrative trading empires in it.[6]

In 1400, and perhaps as late as 1500, Chinese seamanship and cannon-making ability were superior to those of the West. After that, the balance changed quickly. Chinese skills atrophied from lack of use, and the Portuguese, Spanish, Dutch, English, and French began their conquest of all the oceans of the world.[7]

The analogy between Western Europe and China is interesting because the Chinese bureaucracy's perception of the dangers of overseas expansion proved to be perfectly correct. In Europe, the Atlantic coastal states were strengthened by the growth of transoceanic exploration. Both the political and social balance of power shifted, and eventually the old order was overthrown. The Chinese bureaucrats who prevented these changes in their own country missed only one point: The stagnation they imposed on themselves and their descendants would eventually, four centuries later, leave China open to devastating disruption by Westerners and their new ideas.

The Western tradition of maritime empires began in the Middle Ages in the Mediterranean Sea. Venice and Genoa, northern Italy's two greatest thalassocracies, and Catalonia in northeastern Iberia were the main thirteenth- and fourteenth-century island colonizers. Cash crops were grown for the European market with coerced native labor or imported slaves. The system of tropical and semitropical plantation economies, key naval bases strung out along trade routes, and the combination of mercantile and imperial domination over vast areas were well worked out before it began to spread beyond the Mediterranean in the fifteenth century.[8]

When the Italians began to circumnavigate Spain to reach the prosperous North Sea–Baltic trade network in the fourteenth century, they brought their knowledge of geography and finance, and of the institutions of their profit-oriented imperial rule, to the Atlantic coasts of Spain and Portugal. Nevertheless, the Iberian lead in the early drive to conquer the world is puzzling. Castile, the dominant Iberian power, was a society in which towns and merchants played a minor role while the church and aristocracy dominated. The prevailing ethos was a fanatically crusading spirit shaped by centuries of war against the Muslim states of Iberia and North Africa.[9]

Portuguese towns and merchants had relatively more power than their Castilian counterparts, but Portugal was also a cultural backwater with a feeble economy in the fourteenth and early fifteenth centuries.[10]

Iberia, however, was strategically placed next to the Atlantic. Its ports were ideal for catching favorable winds toward the south and west. Its coastal fishermen were experienced with the rough Atlantic weather.[11]

Also, in the fifteenth century, Portugal and Castile ran out of easy outlets for their crusading, anti-Muslim drive. Though it was not until 1492 that the last Muslim state in Iberia fell to the Castilians, Portugal had been shut out of expansion long before and had begun to build an overseas empire with the conquest of Ceuta in Morocco in 1415. J. H. Parry has written:

> The expedition to Ceuta was a genuine Crusade. . . . It was organized by King John I, partly in order to strike a blow against the Moors by sacking one of their principal harbors . . . partly to give his sons, who were candidates for knighthood, an opportunity to win their spurs in real battle rather than in the artificial fight of the tournament. . . . With the capture of Ceuta the crusading movement passed from its medieval to its modern phase; from a war against Islam in the Mediterranean basin to a general struggle to carry the Christian faith and European commerce and arms around the world.[12]

The curious thing is that the spirit and skills which animated the Iberian conquerors were fundamentally antagonistic to those of the townsmen and merchants who provided the commercial and scientific base without which the European conquests would have been impossible. The contradiction was to be the cause of Spain and Portugal's eventual failure to profit from their colonial ventures, but in the fifteenth century this was far from evident. It was not possible to separate crusading from greed, the promise of virtuous Christian and knightly honor from the base search for control of West African gold which had been coming into Europe from across the Sahara throughout the Middle Ages.[13] And when the Spaniards and Portuguese, often with Italian capital and expertise, developed plantation-slave economies on the Atlantic islands, it was an easy matter to reconcile this with the war for men's souls against paganism and Islam. Before Columbus's voyage, then, the Portuguese Madeiras, Azores, and São Tomé off the coast of Africa, and the Spanish Canaries had become major sugar producers, and the Guinea Coast was yielding gold to the Portuguese.[14]

With all this it is not surprising that a recently united Spain (Castile and Aragon, which included Catalonia, were joined by a marriage alliance in 1479), which had just eliminated the last Muslim kingdom in Iberia in 1492, should seek to catch up to its Portuguese neighbor in developing overseas colonies, bases, and trade routes. With the same geographic advantages, but with much greater resources, and with the help of Italian seamen and financiers, Spain sponsored Christopher Columbus and embarked on the conquest of America. A few years later, the Portuguese search for a route to the Indies around southern Africa finally paid off. Between 1497 and 1499, Vasco da Gama circumnavigated Africa, reached India, and returned to Portugal. Within the next fifteen years Portugal conquered an enormous oceanic empire that took control of the major trade routes of the Indian Ocean and became the source of the spice trade. A generation later, their traders reached China and Japan, and in Brazil they were beginning to plant sugar.[15]

Spain, too, moved quickly. The Aztec Empire of Mexico was destroyed by 1521. The Incas of the Andes were subjugated in 1533. The European diseases of smallpox, measles, and influenza—to which the American Indians had had no exposure, and therefore no immunities—did more to ensure Spanish victories than did firearms. However, the weaponry and organization of the Europeans allowed them to enslave the native populations and force large quantities of silver from American mines. This money, distributed through Europe by the Spanish Empire's purchases and wars, raised the European money supply and accelerated economic growth as well as inflation.[16]

But in the long run, neither Spain nor Portugal was able to profit from this extraordinary expansion. Portugal's sea empire skimmed a surplus off luxury trade; it did not alter production, or even the fundamental economic processes at work in Portugal itself. The Portuguese raised piracy to the highest level ever reached, but nothing more than that.[17]

Spain's failure was more dramatic. Using the riches of America to add to the wealth and economic power of Burgundy and the Low Countries (joined with Spain by a marriage alliance), Charles I (also called Charles V of the Holy Roman Empire) and his son Philip II tried to conquer Europe and put it under Habsburg control. Unlike little, weak Portugal, the Spanish Habsburgs controlled the most developed, urbanized parts of Europe in the Low Countries, significant parts of Italy and Germany, and the riches of America. But their effort to create a great Catholic empire drove the Dutch into revolt, ruined Italy, and bankrupted an overtaxed and internally underdeveloped Spain. Money spent to buy war supplies from the more advanced northern countries of Europe—and paid to mercenary armies in central Europe, the Low Countries, and Italy—neither stimulated Spanish progress nor provided a means for renewing the one-time windfall profits that came from the discovery of America. Spain sank into misery and despair, and by the seventeenth century, it was falling to the rank of a second-rate power unable to maintain its ambition to rule Europe.[18]

It cannot be doubted that the sixteenth-century expansion overseas accelerated European development, though it is not simply by measuring the growth of the money supply, of spices sold in Lisbon, or the number of emigrants sent abroad that this effect can be gauged. All such measurements come out looking too small. It is only when the entire, complex set of interactions is perceived as a whole new system of commerce and politics that its real impact can be appreciated.

The most important effect was the generation of surplus land and capital which greatly expanded the marginal profits of new economic activities by Europeans. In other words, it was not so much an absolute increase in profits and wealth that counted as the substantial opportunities for gain which came to those who engaged in activities related to the overseas expansion. For them returns were so large as to create a feeling of expansive confidence and opportunity and thus to support a new class of daring, innovative entrepreneurs. J. H. Elliott has put it this way: "Might it, then, be said that the discovery of the New World created an awareness of new economic opportunities, which itself provided a stimulus to change?"[19] Perception of opportunity accompanied a growing European arrogance and self-confidence which made the idea of other great feats seem possible.

A second and perhaps almost equally important effect of the expansion was to bring unexpected power and wealth to some states, beginning with Portugal and Spain, and thus making other European states eager to obtain similar advantages. The age of exploration ushered in a chain of competitive colonization efforts, wars, and accelerated state building in order to meet the challenge of other European states who tried to use their successes overseas to expand their power on the old continent.

One of the great advantages of Europe over China came to the fore at this point. There existed a European-wide culture in which learned men, traders, pilgrims, mercenaries, sailors, and statesmen moved with ease across political boundaries. But political lines were sharply drawn and fierce competition drove the various political units in Europe to try to attract the best talent that could be put to their use. Intolerant dogmatism pushed good minds, capital, and skilled men to other states and prevented stagnation. Thus it was that German printing techniques, Italian banking methods, Dutch cartography, Portuguese maritime experience, and the general explosion of learning, art, and science spread throughout Europe to help those who knew how to use them.

Portugal's success drove Spain to imitation. Spain obliged Francis I, King of France, to emulate Habsburg colonial triumphs. What France and Spain did, England had to try as well so as to ensure that it was not blocked from reaping the benefits of the expansion. The Dutch, as Habsburg subjects at first, and then as revolutionaries against the dogmatic Catholicism and extravagant taxation of the Spaniards, took the same path of exploration and international trade. Those European countries shut out of the race in the Atlantic by their geography were obliged to try to find their own "Americas" to expand and gain new sources of revenue against the growing Atlantic seaboard powers. The fever to explore and conquer was contagious, and the knowledge gained by one power quickly spread throughout the West, and even into parts of Eastern Europe.

The fact that internal Iberian economic and social structures did not progress as a result of colonial success left the way open to the more northerly Atlantic powers, the Netherlands, England, France, and to a lesser extent, Sweden, which expanded into the eastern Baltic and into northcentral Europe. C. R. Boxer's description of the differences between Dutch and Portuguese colonial policies in Asia captures the essence of the difference between the urban, merchant mentality of the north and that of the Iberian aristocrat:

> . . . the Portuguese, with their almost exclusive reliance on *fidalgos*, or gentlemen of blood and coat-armour, as military and naval leaders, were at a disadvantage compared with the commanders at the service of the Dutch East India Company, where merit and not birth was the main criterion for promotion.[20]

In America the Spaniards held on to their possessions, though their trade was gradually seized by the English, French, and Dutch. But the most productive parts of America came to be those exploited by these three northern powers, namely the Caribbean sugar islands, England's North American colonies, and the huge fur-producing inland empire developed by the French settlers of Quebec.[21]

The seventeenth century was a period of depression for the Mediterranean world, especially when compared with the exuberant growth of the sixteenth. The old pattern of excess population growth in boom times was followed by decline. But for the northwestern part of Europe, economic growth and colonial expansion continued.[22]

The Dutch colonial empire that was built in the first half of the seventeenth century in Asia was taken largely from the Portuguese. It included relatively little territory: parts of Java, the Moluccas, Ceylon, and the Cape of South Africa. Dutch trading posts, however, extended to Taiwan and Japan, and included bases on key sea routes that controlled points for the collection and exchange of valuable goods, especially pepper and spices.[23]

In the Atlantic the Dutch were less successful. They seized a large part of the sugar-producing lands of Brazil, some Caribbean islands, and a part of North America; but they were driven out of Brazil by the Portuguese and out of North America by the English. They also tried to take the Angolan Coast from Portugal, but failed. Nevertheless, they managed to capture a significant portion of the Atlantic trade, particularly the commerce in slaves being shipped from Africa to the American sugar plantations. But this was not what made them so important. Rather, as De Vries has put it:

The originality of the Dutch trading system that arose in the seventeenth century derived from long specialization of Dutch shipowners in bulk trades. As fishermen seeking employment for their vessels in the off-season, as captains in the employ of Antwerp merchants, and as Baltic traders in their own right, Dutch seafarers acquired unrivaled experience in economically transporting grain, salt, timber—even brick. When the Dutch expanded their horizons to deal in the rich trades of woolen cloth, silks, spices, and colonial goods, they were competing with seafaring traditions that had been accustomed to transporting high value–low volume goods. The Dutch specialization riveted their attention to the reduction of costs.[24]

De Vries goes on to describe the type of ship the Dutch built to reduce costs, lower the number of sailors required, and adapt ship-building techniques to a kind of high-volume mass production. In other words, the Dutch may have emulated Portuguese high-level, global piracy, but they also did much more: they turned a colonial overseas enterprise into a true capitalist search for maximization of profits through regular commercial enterprise and tight control of costs. It was particularly in the less glamorous Baltic trade that these virtues brought them impressive returns.

Because of the reduction in shipping costs, the Dutch could trade goods that had not before been profitable for long-distance trade. And with this, they were able to build the first truly global commercial network that could maximize profits by keeping their ships full with whatever goods were suitable for the regions in which they traveled. To their stores of spices, slaves, silks, and bullion, they could add cheap textiles, furs, fish, oil, rice or other cereals, fruit, wines, sugar, tobacco, or tea.[25]

The Dutch replicated the entrepot and colonial functions of late medieval Venice and Genoa. As the scope of Dutch trade expanded, so did the perfection of its banking, credit, insurance, and stock exchange—all inventions of the Italians, but now carried out on a much larger scale. All this, of course, required a relatively tolerant, town- and trade-oriented atmosphere, which was provided by Amsterdam's domination of the Netherlands and by its leading merchants' control of Amsterdam.[26]

But the Netherlands was a small country, no more populous than Portugal, and by the late seventeenth century, first England and then France, too, began to push aside the Dutch as Europe's foremost colonial power.

The eighteenth century saw what amounted to the first great world war, fought as a series of distinct but overlapping wars between France and England for mastery over the colonial territories and trade of America, Africa, and southern Asia. By then, however, the prizes being fought for were no longer merely trade routes and coastal enclaves but also two entire continental areas ripe for colonial exploitation—North America and India. France finally lost in America and Asia by 1763, but did not renounce its attempt to prevent England from dominating the world until 1815.

The consequences of the expansion of European colonialism may be gauged by looking at England's trade statistics in the eighteenth century (see Table 3-1). In the late seventeenth century England's primary export was still wool cloth. From 1660 to 1700 England's foreign trade increased by 50 percent, but the leading sector was reexports, mostly goods from India (cotton cloth) and America (tobacco and sugar) brought to England for resale to Europe. This was commerce on the Dutch pattern.[27] But in the eighteenth century there was a decisive shift. Trade with northwestern Europe (France, the German states, the Low Countries—that is, the most advanced parts of Europe) grew slowly, while trade with the Americas and the Indian colonies grew at an explosive rate. Reexports became less important and were replaced by an exchange of raw colonial products for manufactured English ones.

From the first to the ninth decade of the eighteenth century, the index of English exports (including reexports) went from 100 to 235, and of imports from 100 to 242. In the early eighteenth century, 54 percent of England's exports and reexports went to the Netherlands, Flanders, France, and the Germanies. In the period 1786–1790, that proportion fell to 27 percent. At the start of the century, 27 percent of England's imports had come from these countries; but by the end, only 9 percent were still coming from them. By the end of the century, England's three main sources of imports were the British West Indies, the East Indies, and its ruthlessly exploited European colony, Ireland. Following these were areas that were not (or were no longer) under British political control but that were raw-material and agricultural exporters rather than more advanced manufacturing countries: Russia, the United States, Italy, Spain, and Portugal. Well behind that group were the countries of France, Germany, and the Netherlands. The shift in trade would have seemed

TABLE 3-1

Index of Exports from and Imports to England, by Value, with 1706–1710 Average = 100[28]

	Exports		Imports	
	1746–1750	*1786–1790*	*1746–1750*	*1786–1790*
North America/ United States	353	763	258	325
Ireland	450	786	190	691
East Indies	593	2,174	231	800
British West Indies	227	436	212	548
Russia	—	—	163	1,132
Germanies	146	141	105	86
Netherlands	114	54	73	61

even more dramatic if technological progress in agriculture had not made England a net grain exporter throughout the first two-thirds of the eighteenth century. Only after 1765 did the growing urban population raise demand to such a level that grain exports ceased. And not until the nineteenth century did large amounts of grain begin to be imported.[29]

The transformation of English trade patterns was closely linked to England's ability to exploit its colonies much more thoroughly than could the Iberians or even the Dutch. More than piracy, more than the creation of a global trading network, the English were increasingly able to harness colonial production to their own domestic industry, and to stimulate their own progress through exchanges with the less-developed areas of the world.

Toward the end of the eighteenth century, English manufacturers learned to mass-produce cotton cloth with machinery that used raw cotton imports from tropical and semitropical areas. In return, the English began to send back increasing amounts of finished cloth.[30] This was the culmination of a long transformation. The European expansion was then turned, for the first time, into a tool of industrialization.

The eighteenth-century French pattern of trade was surprisingly similar to England's. Its industry grew almost as quickly as England's, and its foreign trade more quickly. Because France had begun the century at a lower level, it had not caught up by 1789. But, like England, its chief trading partner was its Caribbean slave-plantation empire in the West Indies, and had France managed to win the war against England for control of North America and India, it is quite possible that it would have industrialized first. With what eventually became a much smaller colonial market and catchment area for resources than England, however, France lost the race.[31]

While there can be no doubt that European expansion powerfully stimulated the economic growth and progress of a few Western countries, the effect on the non-Western people who were colonized was of a very different sort. The first big Spanish push into America broke the backs of the great American Indian civilizations and reduced the populations that survived to semi-Hispanicized peons, a sad condition from which many of their descendants have not yet escaped. In Portuguese Brazil and the Caribbean, the native Indians died out, or in the case of Brazil, fled into the back country, and black slaves who came mostly from the coastal hinterland of West Africa—from Senegal to Angola—came to make up most of the rural labor force. In both cases, whether the peons or slaves were Indians or blacks, colonial societies with small white elites were created, with a thin mulatto or mixed-blood middle class placed between the European lords on top and the despised, servile underclass on the bottom.[32]

In Africa, the effects of the slave trade were highly disruptive even though whites themselves did not penetrate far inland. Instead, they traded arms to the coastal Africans who raided inland villages for slaves who were then brought to the coast. A string of wars spread chaos into the interior, and this may account for the fact that from the fifteenth to the nineteenth century Africa's population did not grow.[33]

In North America, which was not brought into the European world until the seventeenth century, the effects of Western expansion developed more slowly, but were ultimately at least as drastic as in South America. On the eastern seaboard, the Indians were pushed out and exterminated as white settlers moved in, and in what became the southern United States, black Africans were brought in to work on the plantations. Further north and west, the effects of the fur trade spread guns, horses, disease, and alcohol throughout the continent, so that there were major upheavals in Indian societies even before the mass arrival of settlers in the nineteenth century.[34]

In Asia, the Western impact was weaker at first. The Iberian, and even the Dutch superiority was based on better ships and naval artillery, not on superior land armies. Only coastal points were touched initially, and the Asians had long been exposed to the same diseases as the Europeans, so that contact with whites did not raise mortality. But eventually, as Europe continued to make technological progress, Asia, too, underwent fundamental transformation. India, not deeply penetrated until the eighteenth century, had its economy gradually harnessed to that of England.[35] China remained practically untouched by the West, except for minor trade, until the nineteenth century. Japan, after extensive contacts with the Portuguese in the sixteenth century, closed itself to the West and retained only minimal contacts with the Dutch until well into the nineteenth century.

Exotic overseas areas were not the only ones touched by the Western expansion. Right next to England, Ireland was turned into a colonial society with a small class of English landlords ruling over the mass of Catholic Irish peasants. A bit further away, but still in Europe, the northern parts of Eastern Europe were deeply influenced by the West from the fifteenth century on. Cereal exports from this area were taken to the Netherlands by the Baltic Sea, and in return, manufactured imports from northwestern Europe were brought in. In the sixteenth and seventeenth centuries this trade strengthened the hand of the noble landowners, particularly in Poland, and gave them the economic power to overcome their kings and towns on one hand, and to enserf their peasants on the other. Poland's development perfectly mirrors that of Western Europe, but in the opposite direction. Towns and merchants lost power, the central state atrophied, peasants became more closely bound rather than freer, manufacturing declined, and Poland came to resemble Ireland or Latin America more than it did the free and growing societies of Western Europe.[36]

In fact, as Western power increased, it created a growing number of peripheral adjuncts to its economy. These were characterized by a strong landowning class, either native or imported from Western Europe, a serf or slave rural labor force, either native or imported from Africa, weak towns whose commercial lives were dominated by Western merchants, and weak central governments either directly ruled by Western power or else too weak to assert effective sovereignty. The economies of these peripheral societies remained overwhelmingly agricultural and they were harnessed as agricultural or mineral producers for the Western economies. This resulted in economic stagnation and vast human misery.

But in the most progressive Western areas, the core of the growing European world economy, which included the Netherlands, England, and France, a completely different pattern of development occurred. Importation of primary products and profits from the colonial trade combined with growing towns and technological innovation to permit increasing specialization and more complex production methods. Central states, able to use the growing tax base produced by prosperity, became stronger, and the local nobilities' power was curbed. Eventually, higher productivity led to higher wages. The freedom enjoyed in the towns spread, and politics became somewhat more humane. All this took a long time; but by 1800, the pattern was well set. The core and the periphery were heading in different directions, but they were very much part of the same, increasingly interconnected world.[37]

Clearly, Western success was not based exclusively on the subjugation of the rest of the world. It was the result of a long series of changes that began in the Middle Ages. On the other hand, Western expansion contributed to its economic growth, and to a profound, generally harmful effect on non-Western societies. In the nineteenth century, the penetration of the West into the rest of the world became much more intense, and the rate of economic and social change throughout the world greatly accelerated. It remains to be seen whether these changes continued along the same lines as those of the centuries that preceded 1800.

The Modern European State

Once states arose in agrarian societies, their rulers worked to strengthen their hold over their subjects in order to extract as many goods and as much labor as possible from them. This was simply because rulers made their living from such control, and generally a very good living indeed. The people were as vital a resource for rulers as land was for the peasant or sheep for the shepherd. People were the raw material of the ruling classes. William H. McNeill's insight on this is not farfetched, viewing rulers in agrarian societies as parasites whose success depended on milking their subjects just enough to maintain a high style of life and a sufficient number of armed retainers to keep themselves in power, but not so much as to bleed the population into a condition of weakness and decline.[38]

Achieving such a balance was difficult and dangerous. There were always more claimants to elite positions than there were open slots. Also, people were often unhappy about being milked, and care had to be taken to keep them under control. Outsiders coveted successful state structures, viewing them as legitimate objects of plunder. In a sense, almost no agrarian state was ever "strong enough." If it was able, it would conquer more territory to increase its ability to pay off its own troublesome nobles and officials and to obtain greater security from outside plunder. Large external gains could also lighten the amount that had to be squeezed from the original subject population, and could thus decrease the threat of revolt. But, of course, new conquests brought potentially troublesome new subjects into the state, created new enemies on the borders, and increased neighbors' covetousness.

This was more obviously the case in preindustrial societies than it is today, though to pretend that such statements are entirely inapplicable today would be naive. In agrarian societies it was assumed that the only way to enlarge a state's tax base was to conquer more subjects or physical resources. Economic growth, while always a recognized possibility, was also known to be slow and its limits narrow. Today it is understood that internal economic expansion may vastly increase a state's ability to finance itself; but this was not an idea that gained widespread credence, even in Europe, until the late nineteenth century, and among ruling elites it is an idea which, if it is accepted at all, is much more recent than that. In order to improve its ability to conquer new resources and subjects, however, a state had to establish greater internal mastery and an adequate, secure revenue base with which to construct its military machine.

Except for a part of the seventeenth century, China, from the late fourteenth until the early nineteenth century, was in a somewhat peculiar position for an agrarian civilization. Under the Ming and Qing dynasties it was a large, united state with no obvious competitors, and with only small gains to be made at the expense of its neighbors, which were much poorer and far from Chinese centers. Especially after the perfection of firearms under the Qing, holding off nomads, long the greatest threat to China, became a relatively simple matter. Within China itself, there were no competing political units to stimulate acquisitiveness.[39]

In India, or in the Middle East, as in Europe, the situation was quite opposite. Any state that failed to take into account the expansionary drives of its neighbors risked being outclassed, and its ruling elite could then be threatened with confiscation of their key resources, their lands and subjects.

Furthermore, in Western Europe in the fifteenth century, the conflict between church, kings, lords, and towns was far from being resolved. Local lords wanted to keep control of revenue collected from their lands; kings and emperors wanted it sent to their coffers; the church wanted to control revenue from its own lands and to draw more from all its Christian subjects; and towns wished to disburse as little as possible to outsiders. Nevertheless, Western European states in the fifteenth and sixteenth centuries had assets that those in other civilizations lacked: rapidly growing foreign trade and colonial holdings from which to draw substantial new revenues without overly exploiting their own populations; a rapidly developing technology to improve internal communications and provide weapons, such as heavy artillery, to bind together their territory against local revolts; and strong towns with financial experts to help them improve fiscal administration. There were even some states that could begin to draw on a growing loyalty toward the idea of the nation, a feeling which might have existed among widespread portions of the Chinese population, but which was quite alien to India and the Middle East. It was particularly in England and in northern France in the fifteenth century, and in the Netherlands in the sixteenth that such sentiments began to be important.

At this point it is necessary to understand a notable paradox. By the late fifteenth century the monarchies of Spain, England, and France were far stronger than they had ever been, in large measure because of the growing towns and the increased pace of commercial activity. Yet the chief instruments of military power were still armies led by agrarian nobles whose way of life, code of honor, and ambition were little changed from the Middle Ages. Monarchies had only recently, and in some cases still tenuously, brought them under control. The monarchs themselves were aristocratic landowners by behavior and temperament, not bourgeois clerks or merchants. They still saw wars and marriage alliances as the best way to strengthen their states. And their subjects, however much they had to be husbanded in order to keep them loyal, were still viewed primarily as objects to be taxed and used to uphold the king's honor, his dynastic ambitions, and the lavish way of life that he and his retainers expected as their due. It was therefore not surprising that the leaders of these newly strengthened states used their growing resources to set off on a royal chase to expand their domains at the expense of their neighbors even before their own nobilities had been brought under full control. The medieval regime in which each lord had sought to increase his base of subsistence by taking his neighbor's patrimony was simply raised to a higher level. The number of players decreased because of the consolidation of states, but the severity and frequency of wars did not diminish. Kings always needed more territories to increase their personal revenues, to buy off their nobles and soldiers, and to secure themselves against their equally ambitious fellow monarchs.

France began the modern age by throwing the English and Burgundians out of French royal territory, thus ending the long war over control of that territory which had been waged from the early fourteenth to the middle of the fifteenth century. Then, after internal consolidation, France invaded Italy in the late fifteenth century.

But the main actor in Europe soon came to be Habsburg Spain which, under Charles V, united a large part of the old Burgundian lands north and east of France and the Netherlands with the large parts of Germany and Austria already controlled by the Habsburgs. Spain itself controlled most of the New World and a large part of the western Mediterranean. In a series of wars, the Habsburgs forced the French out of Italy, took control of key parts and much of the land of that divided peninsula, and then of the Papacy itself. To gain legitimacy and to serve as the ideological cement of what was supposed to become a reunited Christian Empire, the Habsburg state became the champion of Catholicism, even though its biggest enemy remained Catholic France. The French could not defeat the Habsburgs, but they could hold them in check. Straining his resources to unite Europe, Charles V bankrupted Spain. His successor, Philip II, bankrupted it again, and his alliance with the Catholic Church pushed him into a crusade to destroy Protestantism. He provoked the richest part of his domain, the Netherlands, into revolt, and his ambitions finally ruined his country.[40]

Spain's adventure in the sixteenth century put immense pressure on the French and English to strengthen and rationalize their state structures in order to survive.

In France, the second half of the sixteenth century saw a relapse into internal civil war, this time in part on religious grounds between Protestants and Catholics, but primarily over control of the monarchy. The triumph of Henry IV of Bourbon at the end of the century allowed seventeenth-century France to begin constructing the most powerful monarchical apparatus in Europe. This was primarily the work of Henry's son, Louis XIII, and of Louis's chief minister, Richelieu, but it was continued and brought to fruition by Richelieu's successor, Mazarin, and by Louis XIII's heir, Louis XIV. In command of what had become the largest and richest kingdom in Europe, Louis XIV naturally set out to conquer what was left. He also became the model that other European monarchs tried to immitate, whether in architecture, style of dress, or political maneuvering.

The glorious absolutism of Louis XIV rested on three bases. The higher nobility was occupied by the expensive and time-consuming ritual at the magnificent court of Versailles and by permanent foreign wars. Nobles could advance their careers best by serving the king, particularly in the army. The second base, the bourgeoisie, was to pay taxes and loan money to the king for his costly adventures and way of life. Its most capable financiers were used to organize the fiscal affairs of the state. The third, and of course the largest base, was the peasantry, whose work and taxes provided most of the state's revenues. Its houses and animals were to be requisitioned by the army, its young men were to be impressed into military service, and if in the bargain the peasantry went hungry, that was of little consequence.

Charles Tilly, whose research on French social history has uncovered much new information, has described this very well.

> The impressment of a peasant's son for military service deprived a household of essential labor, and perhaps of a needed marriage exchange. The commandeering of an ox reduced the household's ability to plow. The collection of heavy taxes in money drove households into the market, and sometimes into liquidation of their land, cattle, or equipment. . . . We begin to understand that expanded warmaking could tear at vital interests of peasant households and communities. We begin to understand that conflicts of interest could easily align peasants against national authorities as well as against landlords. We begin to understand why local powerholders, with their own claims on peasant resources threatened, sometimes sided with rebellious peasants.[41]

So, along with the glitter of absolutism there was also the reality of increasing social strain, desperate peasant rebellion, and the gradual loosening of the compromise that had produced the *Ständestaat.*

To increase its tax base, the French state promoted taxable commerce as well, and engaged in the policy of mercantilism. This combined protection of domestic industries to raise productivity with an attempt to reduce internal trade barriers within France. Added to the pressure on peasants to go into the market to sell goods in order to pay their taxes, this policy certainly increased the scope of market forces and promoted economic rationalization. It also raised taxes, fed Louis XIV's ambitions, and further encouraged the wars which had been the reason for economic reforms in the first place. In other words, the appetite for military adventure and conquest further stimulated economic and political change, and was fed by economic progress. In the seventeenth and early eighteenth centuries, France was engaged in major foreign wars, from 1635 to 1659, in 1667 and 1668, from 1672 to 1679, from 1688 to 1697, and from 1702 to 1714. At one time or another, from 1635 to 1715, France was at war with most of the major powers in Europe, and was at peace for only twenty-seven years.[42]

The French state during this time greatly strengthened its bureaucratic machinery, primarily in order to maintain control over its population and to maximize tax revenues.[43] The cost for France was high, but the rest of Europe was obliged to follow as best it could simply to avoid defeat at the hands of the French. No matter that Louis XIV finally bankrupted France, as Charles V and Philip II had done to Spain in the previous century. For a while, Louis succeeded in dominating not only France but Spain, much of Italy, and what was left of the Spanish Netherlands (now Belgium). Then, in his last years, during the early eighteenth century, his life's work was undone. A grand European alliance united against him, and defeated him. He died having accomplished minimal territorial gains for France and leaving its economy and finances in ruin. Yet, he is remembered in French school books as France's greatest king, not as the one who ensured that France would fall behind England in the race for economic growth and progress.

For the rest of continental Western Europe, the years of French dominance and royal absolutism were a watershed. States and dynasties able to increase their tax base and control their finances built strong military machines and put great pressure on their neighbors. Those who could not adapt were dispossessed or saw their lands overrun. The Thirty Years' War (1618–1648), which initiated the period of intense warfare that dominated the seventeenth century, seemed to contemporary observers to be a war of religion fought between Catholics and Protestants. It was actually provoked more by the economic depression of the seventeenth century, which pushed kings and lords into a desperate scramble to find revenues for themselves, a search which became more imperative as external threats from powerful states became more acute.[44]

One of the most successful states to emerge from the Thirty Years' War was Sweden, whose conquests and depradations throughout Germany, Poland, the Baltic countries, and Russia spread the infection of military absolutism. Though Sweden itself was ultimately defeated, it left in its wake two powerful absolutist states which in turn eliminated Poland as a major power in central and eastern Europe.

Both Prussia and Russia shared important characteristics. Their nobles became royal officials. Peasants were enserfed and burdened with heavy obligations to pay lords and the state. The state itself became a military machine designed to provide rewards and new positions for the nobles who, in return, supported autocratic central rule. In both cases, cities were prevented from emerging as independent political forces, and political development took a direction different from that in states with a tradition of sharing power among estates.

In both Russia and Prussia, dynastic ambition and the creation of strong military bureaucracies to butress the absolutist state produced nations that placed the needs of their rulers' honor and the interest of their military officials above those of the rest of society.[45] The most successful state builders— Gustavus Adolfus of Sweden, the Great Elector Frederick William and Frederick the Great of Prussia, and Peter the Great and Catherine the Great of Russia—were, in a sense, mere imitators of Louis XIII and Louis XIV of France. But it was not a matter of choice. With the new resources placed in the hands of Europe's rulers by economic progress, those rulers who did not follow militaristic, state building policies, or who failed to carry them out successfully, lost their domain.

A somewhat different solution to the problem of absolutist aggression was found by England. Henry VII, who established the Tudor dynasty in the late fifteenth century, and his son Henry VIII built classical absolutist state machines. But, in the sixteenth century, England was a relatively small country compared with France or Spain, and at the same time it was protected from the continental absolutist wars by the sea. So it was neither able to have aggressive designs on the continent nor obliged to defend itself quite as ferociously. The Tudor monarchs built a strong navy, which was cheaper than a large army and could also be used for trade.[46]

Without a strong standing army the English kings and queens were unable to bring Parliament under full control or to centralize fiscal and bureaucratic power. Some, like Elizabeth I, adapted to these limits. The Stuart dynasty, which succeeded her in the seventeenth century, did not. This resulted in a civil war between the king, Charles I, and Parliament (1642–1648). Parliament's victory meant that the strengthening of the English state was not to be carried out by absolutist monarchs but by a ruling committee of landowners with strong interests in trade. Practicality and economic interests became more important determinants of English foreign policy than the dynastic pride and ambitions of a particular princely family.[47] This was a marked contrast to seventeenth- and eighteenth-century countries ruled by such grand families as the Habsburgs of Austria and Spain, the Bourbons of France, the Hohenzollerns of Prussia, the Vasas of Sweden, or the Romanovs of Russia.

Not only was the English state built on a different base than were the continental absolutist states, but because it was allied to, and in fact entwined with, mercantile interests, it developed a banking system that allowed it to mobilize far greater quantities of loans than even the French government. England was thus able to carry on its wars without resorting to ruinous taxation.[48] In this respect, it repeated the experience of the Dutch, who survived very nicely by retaining their *Ständestaat,* by paying more attention to business than to glory, and by preventing the emergence of a strong monarchy.

Nevertheless, even in England the primary task of the new state structure was to wage war. The modern states of Europe were not constructed for the "general welfare" of their populations, except for a very small ruling elite. Nor were they the result of any compact between rulers and people, except for the continuing role of the powerful estates in some countries. These too, however, were representative of small elites, not of the bulk of the population. These states were primarily instruments of violence to be used for selfish ends by a few people. This was not to change until the late eighteenth century when the American and French revolutions introduced new ideas of government into the Western world.

If the creation of the modern states of Western Europe was a function of the fiscal exigencies of war, so the two revolutions which began to change the nature of the state and of government were direct reactions against state measures to raise taxes in order to pay for wars. The English Parliament gradually attempted to raise taxes from its American colonies after the expensive Seven Years' War (1756–1763). That war, fought around the world between the French and the English for colonial mastery, was a great victory for the English. They decisively defeated the French in India and North America, and reduced the overseas French Empire to a few Caribbean islands and posts on the African and Indian coasts. But the English-speaking American colonists resisted efforts after the war to make them pay, and as Parliament saw the colonies as an area that should contribute more to the expenses of the English state, the decade after the war (called the French and Indian War in North America) saw increasing tensions between the colonists and the English.

The problem for the English was that their colonists in America had extended the English parliamentary tradition and created powerful local assemblies to govern themselves. In a land that lacked the old status divisions of Europe, in which there were no hereditary aristocratic nobles, no descendants of serfs, only a weakly established church hierarchy, and no powerful monarchical institutions except for the representatives of the distant and limited royal power in London, these assemblies went much further than any in Europe as real representatives of the middle classes and prosperous farmers. In the end, the assemblies revolted against England, and from 1775 to 1783, they defeated England and established the modern world's first republic with a government elected by a substantial portion, if not yet a majority, of its population.[49]

The French Revolution, which began six years later, in 1789, was connected to the American one in two ways. First, the Americans had received considerable French help in the later stages of their war against England, primarily because the French saw this as a way of regaining some of the losses they had sustained in the Seven Years' War. But the expenses of this war, piled on top of the other war debts and extravagances of the French monarchy, bankrupted France and caused a major fiscal and administrative crisis. Second, though certainly less important, was the fact that the establishment of a more or less democratic republic in America gave some Frenchmen the idea that such a reform might be desirable and possible in their own country. To understand this, however, it is necessary to return to the early part of the eighteenth century.

After the death of Louis XIV there was a noble reaction to his debilitating and humiliating regime. Though the nobility never regained anything close to the feudal power it had once possessed, it was able, with the help of allies in the church (which was also trying to protect its privileges and exemptions from taxes), to block every major attempt to further reform and rationalize fiscal policy. The monarchy of Louis XV and Louis XVI, faced with increasing debts and losses from its foreign wars, plunged into bankruptcy. Had the nobility and the church been forced to pay taxes, had administrative centralization proceeded in the same direction as under Louis XIV, and had important positions in the administration remained as open as before to talented men from the middle classes, the French government would have fared better. Why the eighteenth-century kings and royal administrators of France were less determined and able than those of the seventeenth century is not clear. Perhaps the dismal results and ruin brought to France by Louis XIV weakened the king's authority. The example of England, which was highly successful even though its kings were reduced to virtual powerlessness by Parliament, persuaded many French thinkers that absolutism was not an appropriate style of government. In the end, as the government of Louis XVI desperately tried to raise funds and find a solution, the nobility imagined that it had an opportunity to recapture its feudal position. This started the French Revolution.

France was a nation composed largely of peasants who feared that renewed noble power would impose ancient feudal dues on them on top of the existing taxes. It was also a nation with a large administrative bureaucracy whose members saw that their position would be gravely undermined if power were decentralized and seized by reactionary local nobles. These two classes, joined by the working and artisan classes in Paris which simply wanted to keep food prices within reasonable bounds and improve their low standard of living, made the revolution. On the other hand, the bourgeoisie so beloved by Marxist theoreticians as the makers of this upheaval, were less important. The high bourgeoisie, the financiers who had invested in government bonds, were not revolutionary at all, and there is little evidence that the merchant and manufacturing bourgeoisie were particularly revolutionary. Rather, at every step of the way, they tried to modify revolutionary ardor, and only went along with those changes that guaranteed that the nobility would not seize power.[50]

In 1789, the royal government called together the long abandoned Estates General, that assembly of estates which had been destroyed by the centralizing kings in the early seventeenth century. There seemed to be no other way to break out of the administrative and fiscal impasse that had led to bankruptcy. When news spread throughout the countryside that the nobles and churchmen were trying to control the assembly, a wave of rural uprisings took place.[51] It was at that moment that the lawyers and small bureaucrats who were the most radical element of the "third" estate (that is, neither nobles nor churchmen) took advantage of the situation. With the backing of the rioting Parisian mob and the fear of impending social and political collapse, they took control of the government. Their purpose was to sweep away the impediments to final centralization and rationalization of the fiscal structure of the state. This meant elimination of the remaining privileges of the nobility, of the church, and of the various local provinces which still retained important powers. Because the king, Louis XVI, clearly sympathized more with the nobles than with the revolutionary administrators who were actually carrying out the work of his ancestors, his powers were reduced, and eventually he was executed.[52]

The French Revolutionary State cleared the decks of ancient tradition, and created a more effective administration. But in the seeming chaos, the European powers saw an opportunity to gain an advantage by attacking what appeared to be a helpless country stripped of its noble officered army. The foreign threat was skillfully used to raise a large new popular army in the name of saving the French nation and the newly won rights of the people over feudal and royal privilege. This mass army, led by men picked for their skills rather than for their birth or royal connections, proved immensely more effective than the professional and mercenary forces used by the other European states. It beat back the rest of Europe, and from its ranks came one of its most brilliant young generals, Napoleon, who turned the gains of the revolution to his own end and established himself as the most absolutist French ruler of all. Administrative rationalization, a draft, a better taxation system, and for some time, genuine popular support and active French pride in France's revolutionary mission gave Napoleon the means to conquer Europe.

But no country in Western Europe has ever been big enough or strong enough to absorb the others, much less all of Central and Eastern Europe as well. Napoleon was finally defeated by a large coalition in 1814 and 1815. His methods and near success, however, repeated and intensified the effects on Europe which the equally fruitless attempts at universal empire made by the Habsburgs and Bourbons had produced. The other powers were obliged to initiate another round of administrative rationalization, of centralization, and to raise the level of popular participation and national consciousness in order to mobilize their people for the sake of their state's survival. From the French revolutionary and Napoleonic wars came the ideas of a universal military draft; of centralized school systems to teach nationalistic values and produce trained, capable bureaucrats; and, perhaps most critically, the idea that it was possible to arouse the masses for either destructive or constructive purposes. For the first time, popular will appeared as an important element in international relations.[53]

The effect of the French Revolution was not so much to bring democratic politics to Europe as to accelerate the formation of strong states and spread the idea of nationalism based on national languages and cultures.

There is a tendency to believe that all progress made in Europe from the fifteenth to the nineteenth century was interconnected and more or less continuous. This is a half-truth at best. The rise of absolutist states threatened the political looseness and intellectual freedom which underlay Western progress. On the other hand, it increased the size of markets and monetization of the economy because of governments' incessant demands for cash and supplies. Also, because no European state ever managed to establish its hegemony, parts of Europe always remained to shelter refugees and ideas from other, less tolerant parts. Finally, the political success of the Netherlands in the seventeenth century, and of England in the eighteenth and early nineteenth centuries, began to show that toleration for certain kinds of freedom of thought and commerce was as important an asset for national strength as strong armies. The near triumph of Napoleon further showed that nationalism was another major source of strength, and that this, in part, had to rest on a consensus within the population of any state that its rulers were legitimate and cared for the welfare of their subjects. In other words, the tendency of absolutism to create more autocratic and centralized states for the purpose of waging incessant war would not have yielded positive results if it had been more successful. Only the partial failure of absolutism and imperial militarism allowed economic and intellectual growth, without which the West would never have become so dominant in world affairs.

But to understand how that intellectual growth contributed so much to European success, it is necessary to move back in time to find the origins of something which eventually proved even more important than the growth of the modern state, namely the development of Western science.

Science

Western science is in many ways the crowning achievement of Occidental rationality. It is based on calculability, on proof, and on empirical observation in a way that no economy, legal or political structure, or religious ethic can be. It is, par excellence, the domain of highly trained specialists. It has also taken on a life of its own such that it can flourish in circumstances that would have been highly inimical to its spontaneous emergence. But in the beginning, it was a fragile growth that took root only because so many other developments in Western life were leading toward an increasing rationalization of social life. It was a combination of this generally heightened rationality and a measure of the intellectual toleration and material stability that characterized parts of the urban Occident that allowed science to progress.

Summarizing the work of Galileo, one of the three or four key thinkers of the scientific revolution of the seventeenth century, Stuart Hampshire has written:

> Galileo's magnificent achievements were based on two principles which have become the guiding principles of modern science: first, that in making statements and hypotheses about nature one must always appeal to observation and not authority; secondly, that natural processes can best be understood if they are represented in mathematical terms.[54]

In fact, there were two tendencies in seventeenth-century science which were not always easy to harmonize. And it is the unique achievement of the greatest minds of seventeenth-century Europe that they were able to bring them together. One of these scientific tendencies was the experimental orientation of Bacon and Hooke. The other was the more classical, purely logical orientation of Descartes. Bronowski has written:

> This union of two methods is the very base of science. Whitehead, who in his philosophy laid stress on it, dated the Scientific Revolution from the moment when Galileo and his contemporaries understood that the two methods, the empirical and the logical, are each meaningless alone, and that they must be put together.[55]

And, summarizing the monumental achievement of Newton in the late seventeenth century, Bronowski added:

> Here the logical outlook of Descartes is joined with the experimental passion of Bacon. . . .[56]

Why did this breakthrough not occur elsewhere, and particularly why not in China where, during the Song, the Jin, and the Yuan (Mongol) dynasties, from the tenth to the fourteenth centuries, extraordinary advances were made in empirical, experimental science as well as in mathematics? There, as in the West several centuries later, theoretical knowledge was accompanied by practical and mechanical progress in printing, manufacturing, warfare, and medicine.[57]

In the fourteenth century, however, the impetus to scientific progress seems to have withered in China. Partly this was due to the fact that the scientific and philosophical base of Chinese learning was very thin—relatively few scholars working in a few centers were responsible for maintaining it. Because, as Elvin put it, "The main driving force behind this renaissance of Chinese learning was the government,"[58] political disaster could quickly eliminate support for these activities. The small numbers engaged in them made it difficult for work to overcome such disruptions. The destruction of northern Song power by the Ruzhen from Manchuria had a dampening effect on the area that remained under the southern Song, perhaps because theoretical science and medicine had never developed in the south. The north remained an important center of scientific progress under the Ruzhen Jin dynasty and the Mongols who conquered them, but in the political and economic debacle of Mongol rule in the fourteenth century some of the most important aspects of a potential scientific revolution were killed. During the conservative Ming dynasty (1368–1644) this kind of work did not continue. In fact:

> By Ming times, there was no one left who could understand the more advanced positional algebra of the Jin Tartar and early Yuan periods; and this continued until the later seventeenth century. It seems plausible to explain it by the disruption of north China, both during the Mongol conquest, and during the wars when the Mongols were driven out in the middle of the fourteenth century. Above all, the motivation for the pursuit of advanced mathematics must have disappeared.[59]

It is possible to be more specific in comparing the fate of science in Ming China and in seventeenth-century Europe. One of the principal spurs to government financing of scientific research has always been the direct benefits anticipated from discoveries. In seventeenth-century Europe the growth of long-distance, sea-borne trade made more accurate navigation important, and the way to solve navigational problems was through improved astronomy. Government interest neither originated European astronomical studies nor provided the only spur to their pursuit. But it helped.[60]

It was astronomy that formed the basis of Galileo's and Newton's most important work. Newton in particular relied on a century of astronomical observation to formulate his theory of gravity. This was the only branch of human knowledge sufficiently removed from everyday life, yet furnished with enough precise, quantitative observations to allow scientific minds to conceive of a whole logical model of testable, mathematically interrelated properties.

In China, as we have seen, the early fifteenth century saw a burst of maritime growth and exploration a good century before they began in Europe. But after that, overseas shipping declined, and it even came to be forbidden to build large ships or engage in foreign trade.[61]

Chinese astronomy had always been somewhat restricted by government order because of its connection with "portents and the calendar."[62] In Song times, this limitation was not severe. But when combined with the facts that the absence of long-distance shipping did not spur the government to finance astronomical research, that there were few possible sources of innovation and research funding outside of government sponsorship, and that the highest ethical precepts of the Chinese educated classes did not place the study of natural science on a very elevated plane, this restriction was quite sufficient to prevent Chinese astronomy from making the decisive breakthroughs that were necessary to create a real scientific revolution.

In order to have the kind of progress that occurred in the West in the sixteenth and seventeenth centuries, it is necessary to have a growing number of specialists. As knowledge increases and it becomes more difficult for any single individual to remain in the forefront of all aspects of his field, the absence of growth in the number of researchers may kill a field before it goes very far. The great synthesizing geniuses such as Newton could never have accomplished their theoretical breakthroughs in isolation. No single or small number of human beings can personally accumulate enough knowledge to revolutionize science without the help of a large base of more prosaic research. Thus, the thinness of Chinese science, compared to the rapid growth of scientific interest in seventeenth-century Europe was critical.

A similar explanation can be used to show why Islamic science in the late Middle Ages failed to break through to higher levels. Quite simply, in the opinion of Hodgson, the multiplication of scientific specialists was unlikely to have occurred in declining urban economies.[63] And later, in the revived Muslim states, the alliance of church and state was too close. In the Ottoman Empire, for example, an important astronomical observatory was torn down by a superstitious vizier. Persecution of philosophical rationalists occurred, too, but it was not so much specific acts of repression that mattered as a whole religious way of thinking which considerably dampened intellectual speculation. In the seventeenth century, Ottoman science withered and fell hopelessly behind that of the West.[64]

The scientific revolution cannot be ascribed to single causes or events. The important, growing role of shipping in the West helped, as did astronomical and mathematical advances. The material prosperity of the towns, and the general growth of rationality in other aspects of social life also contributed. But there was more.

As with religious rationality, scientific advances were partly based on a new type of faith. Many of the scientists of the seventeenth century were Puritan Protestants deeply concerned with religion. "The Reformation," wrote Robert Merton about them, "had transferred the burden of individual salvation from the church to the individual, and it is this 'overwhelming and crushing sense of responsibility for his own soul' which explains the acute religious interest."[65] For the intellectual who was required to find his own salvation, but who maintained his faith in the rational order of God's way, it was important to find proof of that rationality in order to confirm the existence of God. Systematic scientific inquiry not only curbed "irrational" passions, but it could also exalt the glory of God by revealing His divine law.[66]

This tendency in Protestant, particularly Puritan Protestant, thought was the result of the profound doubt about religion which afflicted individuals forced back on their logic to save their souls. Newton, who was troubled by this problem, tried to use his discoveries to prove the existence of God. Earlier, Kepler had tried to use his astronomical findings to the same end.[67]

It was not only the Puritan mind which was beset by doubt. All thinking Westerners, confronted by a corrupt, fallible Catholic church and by endless church-state disputes and wars, were prey to doubts. In an age when it was difficult, and in most cases morally impossible, to give up faith, intellectuals had to recreate their own faith; and systematic scientific thought was one of the paths open to them.

Sixteenth- and seventeenth-century Christian churches of all varieties recognized the extreme danger of rational scientific thought and, wherever possible, attempted to crush it. Calvin's influence impeded scientific development in Geneva, and Luther "execrated the cosmology of Copernicus."[68] Jakob Huizinga firmly believed that Dutch science and learning progressed in the seventeenth century because the Calvinist church lost control over the universities, not because it was the official church.[69]

But it was only where a church's authority was firmly established, and allied to a powerful state, that intellectual conformity could be enforced. That took place most strikingly in areas under Habsburg and Catholic control. In Italy, Galileo's work was condemned, and he spent his last years under virtual house arrest.[70] The entire skeptical, scientific, secularizing thrust of the Italian renaissance was brought to a halt in the seventeenth century in Italy; though elsewhere, in parts of Europe that escaped Habsburg domination, its effects continued to spread. In Spain, the consequences of Habsburg-Catholic power were the most severe. As early as the mid-sixteenth century, the Inquisition had placed rationalizing works of learning in an Index of forbidden books. Contacts between Spanish students and other Occidental centers of learning were prohibited. By the seventeenth century, Catholic Spain had become an intellectual backwater, a position from which it is only slowly emerging in the twentieth century.[71] It is certain that if the Spaniards and the Catholic church had succeeded in regaining control over all the Netherlands, or over England, the scientific revolution would have died as it did earlier in China. Imperial intellectual hegemony and a united church and state can prevent the emergence of free thought, which was at the heart of the growth of scientific rationality in the Occident.

This does not yet close the debate. Just as the seeming correlation between Puritanism and capitalism led to a "Weber thesis" that tended to explain the latter by the former, so has the correlation between Puritanism and science led to a similar thesis proposed by Robert Merton.[72]

The historian and philosopher of science Thomas Kuhn has summarized it this way:

> After their initial evangelical proselytizing phases, it is claimed [by the Merton thesis], settled Puritan or protestant communities provided an "ethos" or "ethic" especially congenial to the development of science. Among its primary components were a strong utilitarian strain, a high valuation of work, including manual and manipulative work, and a distrust of system which encouraged each man to be his own interpreter first of Scripture then of nature. . . . [But] the main drawbacks of this viewpoint have always been that it attempts to explain too much. If Bacon, Boyle, and Hooke seem to fit the Merton thesis, Galileo, Descartes, and Huyghens do not. It is in any case far from

clear that postevangelical Puritan or Protestant communities existed anywhere until the Scientific Revolution had been under way for some time.[73]

Kuhn points to a solution. Puritanism was definitely closely associated with the Baconian or experimental tradition of science. But of the great mathematical theoreticians of the seventeenth century, only Newton fit the Merton thesis. Galileo, Pascal, Descartes, and many others did not.[74]

Western rationality, like Western capitalism, developed as part of a series of broad cultural, social, and political trends whose origins were not limited to or primarily located in Protestant settings. But certain varieties of Protestantism were themselves important parts of this movement, and where they were able to flourish without political or religious repression, rationality, too, could grow. Puritanism was associated with the more "practical" aspects of Western rationalization, and if the Weber and Merton theses are misleading when pushed too far, they are very useful in explaining some of what happened.

This leaves a final major issue: To what extent did the seventeenth-century scientific revolution influence economic growth? The answer, which may be surprising to most, is that it did not—or at least not very much. If anything, the influence ran the other way. Economic growth and increasing trade promoted scientific progress. But the great theoretical advances of Galileo, Newton, and others were of limited value in the economic sphere. Kuhn notes:

> . . . technology flourished without significant substantive inputs from the sciences until about one hundred years ago. The emergence of science as a prime mover in socioeconomic development was not a gradual but a sudden phenomenon, first significantly foreshadowed in the organic-chemical dye industry in the 1870s, continued in the electric power industry from the 1890s, and rapidly accelerated since the 1920s. To treat these developments as the emergent consequence of the Scientific Revolution is to miss one of the radical historical transformations constitutive of the contemporary scene.[75]

Despite this, there is little question that the scientific developments of the seventeenth century were important for the further progress of Europe. Bronowski explains it this way:

> Science did not bring about the Industrial Revolution. It did not even precipitate it, for science was quite out of touch with such work in the eighteenth century; and knew nothing that could help John Roebuck to make sulphuric acid in Edinburgh or Benjamin Franklin to fly a kite in a thunderstorm, or that most inspired of American adventurers Count Rumford to bore cannon in Munich. What Science did for these men, and for thousands like them in mines, at mills, and in workshops was to set their interests free. They no longer thought of the world as either settled or well taken care of. They saw the world

as man-made and ordered by man, and they saw the machine in every part of it.[76]

Later, when science and technology were brought together some two centuries after the scientific revolution, the indirect effects of the seventeenth-century's progress came to be felt very strongly by all of society. Kuhn has called this event a "second" scientific revolution, during which science became a regular profession supported by states and industries. This change was probably the single factor most responsible for the sudden acceleration of economic growth rates in the latter part of the nineteenth century, and science has become, in the twentieth century, an integral part of economic development. Of course, none of this could have occurred without the preparatory progress of the "first" scientific revolution.

Progress

By the end of the eighteenth century, the immense growth of European power throughout the world, the increase in knowledge about the natural environment, and the development of a self-conscious, objective branch of knowledge devoted to the study of societies, economies, and political systems had combined to convince the best-educated and most aware Westerners that even greater progress was possible. The eighteenth-century Enlightenment, particularly in England and France, produced the intellectual revolution, which has remained, however tattered, the fundamental base of Western thought since then.

In 1670 Spinoza had attacked the idea of monarchical absolutism; and in 1690, John Locke had suggested that royal authority should be based on a rationally derived contract between subjects and governments. The French Encyclopedists, led by d'Alembert and Diderot, produced a twenty-eight volume compendium of modern knowledge from 1751 to 1772. Its central theme was that human rationality was capable of producing a better organized world. In 1755 Jean-Jacques Rousseau wrote his discourse on inequality which laid the ideological base for the radical notion that the people should rule themselves and that neither the elite nor the king had any right superior to that of the commoners. In France, too, in the 1750s and 1760s, economists began to understand how wealth was produced, and why government attempts to distort market forces were more likely to decrease than to increase wealth. In 1776, the year of the American Revolution, the Scottish economist Adam Smith formalized the growing notion of the importance of letting markets determine the allocation of investments, products, and profits. His *Inquiry into the Nature and Causes of the Wealth of Nations* remains the classical statement on which modern economics is based.[77]

These intellectual developments were naturally connected to the growth of merchant and manufacturing interests that were hostile to the royal and aristocratic power which might impede their business and the enjoyment of their profits.[78] But they were more than that. After all, in less than three centuries the Western world had been deeply changed. If it remained true that most peasants, even in the West, were little aware of these changes, and that most of the world outside the West only dimly perceived any change at all, the number of educated, literate people, among them many in the new urban middle classes, was growing.[79] Such enlightened men were the leaders of the American Revolution, they were the principal ideologues of the French Revolution, they were advisers to the absolutist rulers of Central and Eastern Europe, and they were the proponents of reform in England.

But with all this, it turned out that the French Revolution produced an absolute ruler, Napoleon, more powerful and more ambitious than any of the seventeenth- and eighteenth-century kings. The states of Europe remained primarily machines for making war. If, in the nineteenth century, the Enlightenment's faith in the possibility of scientific and material progress was to be more than fulfilled, its faith in the power of human rationality to regulate its political affairs was to prove unjustified.

CHAPTER *4*

The European Century

*H*owever important the extent of material progress in the advanced parts of Western Europe before the nineteenth century, it would be dwarfed by the fantastic economic growth that was to follow. It would be appropriate, then, to try to establish a rough quantitative picture of the condition of those few relatively developed countries that were leading the way to further advances.

At about the turn of the nineteenth century, England and Wales's gross national product per capita per year (GNP/capita)—that is, the total amount of monetized goods and services produced—was about $900 (if measured in 1985 U.S. dollars).* This was higher than one century earlier, but by today's standards of rapid economic growth, it was not very much higher. The economic historian Simon Kuznets estimates that in the eighteenth century, England's per capita GNP increased by about one-third, so that in 1700 it was on the order of some $650 to $700.[1] By comparison, during the nineteenth century, GNP/capita in England would more than triple to about $2,800 per year. (Again, as in all other GNP figures to be given, the amounts have been transformed into 1985 U.S. dollars.)

England in 1800 had the best-developed economy in Europe and its highest standard of living. The Netherlands, though less industrialized, probably had close to the same standard of living; but France, the next richest country in Europe, appeared markedly poorer to contemporary observers.[2] Only the new United States of America, whose standard of living was as high or higher than England's almost as soon as its colonists became well established, had a higher

---

* GNP/capita per year is the most widely used measure of comparative economic development. Because it only takes into account those goods and services that reach the market, leaving out such important but unmeasurable items as work performed in a household by its members for their own consumption, it is not a good measure of the actual standard of living in less-developed economies in which a high proportion of production is not marketed. But because the more developed an economy, the higher is the proportion of its goods and services that are marketed and monetized, it is a good measure of the degree of economic development. When relatively highly monetized economies are compared, GNP/capita is also a good way of comparing real standards of living. But it is a mistake to think that in an economy with a GNP/capita of $10,000, an average inhabitant is in any real sense twenty times better off than one in an economy with a GNP/capita of only $500. Later, some alternative ways of calculating comparative standards of living will be presented. At this point, however, it is sufficient to point out that in almost any measurable material way, the average inhabitant of the $10,000 GNP/capita economy is much better off than the one in the $500 GNP/capita economy.

level of average wealth, but not by very much. Its GNP/capita was probably on the order of $950 per year.[3]

In 1981, of 125 countries for which the World Bank had data, a little over one-third, including China, all of South Asia, most of Southeast Asia, most of Africa south of Mediterranean North Africa, and some Latin American countries had GNP/capita figures lower than those of the United States and England in 1800. In all, in the early 1980s some 55 percent of the globe's population was living in economies less developed than those of England and the United States almost 200 years ago.[4]

In the middle of the nineteenth century, India's GNP/capita was about $160 per year, and though it may have been a bit higher or lower in 1800, it is unlikely to have been far from the $150 to $200 range. This gives some idea of the level of development of the largely peasant Asian civilizations of that time, and is probably very roughly equivalent to the level of economic development in Europe in the tenth century before the slow but significant growth that took place thereafter about A.D. 1000.[5]

In other words, even in 1700, England, the Netherlands, and some of the other most developed parts of Western Europe were far ahead of most of the rest of the traditional agrarian civilizations in terms of economic productivity and wealth. By 1800, the advantage had certainly grown, particularly in England. Then, over the next century, almost all of Western Europe and North America experienced a significant acceleration of economic growth while the rest of the world continued to stagnate, and this greatly increased the Western advantage. It is to this change, and its effects, that we now turn.

*

England's World, 1815–1873

The Industrial Revolution is usually said to have begun in England in about 1780. Indeed, from about 1760 to 1800 there was a major change in English textile production. Wool and linen were replaced by cotton cloth, which came to be manufactured in large-scale factories with machines. By the late 1780s some of these machines were already being powered by steam.[6] Not only could the speed of cloth manufacturing be increased, but its quality could be improved. The productivity of each worker grew quickly. This meant that prices could fall, and English cotton exports to other countries grew at a phenomenal rate. Because of this, industrial growth was not limited by the size of domestic English demand.

English consumption of raw imported cotton fluctuated between about 1,000 and 3,000 metric tons per year during the 1750s, 1760s, and 1770s. But it reached 14,000 metric tons in 1790, 24,000 in 1800, 56,000 in 1810, 54,000 in 1820, 112,000 in 1830, and 208,000 in 1840. From 1770 to 1840, cotton consumption doubled every ten years, despite the temporary dip in growth during the period 1810–1820.[7]

Putting people to work in the new factories was no easy task. The discipline demanded and the tedium experienced by the workers might have resulted in either a shortage of labor or pressure for higher wages. But the late eighteenth and early nineteenth century was a period of rapid population growth in the United Kingdom. From 1750 to 1830, population more than doubled, from 10.6 million to 24.1 million (including Ireland), an average yearly growth of about 1 percent. This population could not be accommodated in the rural areas, where improvements in agricultural methods eliminated the need for a growing labor force, and so people were forced into the towns and new industries where adaptation to the difficult requirements of the new work routines was simply necessary for survival. Because of the abundant and rapidly growing labor force, wages did not have to be high.[8]

That the population was growing in the United Kingdom is not, of itself, surprising. Many times in the past, growing prosperity had allowed the population to rise as death rates fell and new opportunities arose. But in England, something entirely new happened. As rural overpopulation was becoming a serious problem after a long period of economic growth, opportunities for new types of employment were invented, and the surplus population was gainfully absorbed. Population growth did not lead to the normal downward turn of the economic cycle. Whether in medieval Europe, in China, in the Middle East, or in India, such cycles in the past had always consisted of growth, prosperity, and population expansion followed by overpopulation, famine, economic and political instability, and a sharp rise in death rates. Now, however miserable the condition of England's new factory workers might have been, the old cycle was decisively broken, and catastrophe was averted.

But it is important to remember that by the 1820s and 1830s there was no assurance that this spectacular burst of progress was fundamentally different from what had occurred before. Only with hindsight can we tell that a new phenomenon had come into being, for much of the educated opinion prevalent at that time maintained just the opposite, that the old cycle was about to reassert itself.

Thomas Malthus had already predicted in 1798 in his *Essay on the Principles of Population* that the inevitable result of a rapidly rising population was economic and social catastrophe. David Ricardo, the most influential economist of his time, argued in 1817 in his *Principles of Political Economy and Taxation* that a rising population would tend to force up the price of food and make it increasingly scarce so that manufacturing and the cities would be ruined.

Far from appearing wrong, these views seemed farsighted in light of the short-term stagnation that followed the Napoleonic Wars in 1815, and even more so as the continuing technological improvements in the textile industry began to drive large numbers of workers, particularly more skilled craftsmen whose skills were becoming redundant, out of their jobs. Parts of the industry that had still relied on hand work disappeared and forced people into less remunerative and less independent positions or into outright unemployment and penury. Eric Hobsbawm explains:

The number of power looms in England rose from 2,400 in 1813 to 55,000 in 1829, 85,000 in 1833 and 224,000 in 1850, while the number of hand-loom weavers, still rising to a maximum of about a quarter of a million in the 1820s, fell to just over 100,000 in the 1840s, to a little more than 50,000 starving wretches by the middle 1850s.[9]

Then, too, the cotton industry's growth eventually began to run into problems even as it continued to expand. It was becoming obvious to manufacturers that their markets might not grow indefinitely. The higher demand for raw cotton was forcing up its price, but the selling price of finished goods tended to fall as markets became relatively filled. The falling rate of profits made it increasingly difficult for small manufacturers to keep up in the technological race to stay abreast of the latest labor-saving but increasingly expensive machines. These developments in England's most important industry, and the continued pressure of overpopulation on the land, produced the serious political crisis and social conflict of the 1830s and 1840s.[10]

What solidified the gains of the Industrial Revolution and the future success of England and other Western nations was that the age of textiles was followed by an even more intense and spectacular burst of progress, the "second Industrial Revolution" of railroads and iron.

The economic cycles of the industrial age are unlike those of the long agrarian age that preceded it. Innovations multiply around one another as a particular sector begins to produce substantial opportunities for profit. Feeding on each other, these innovations vastly increase productivity and demand for certain key raw materials. But increasing productivity and technical skill lowers prices of finished goods. Demand ceases to grow quickly because of relative saturation, and it becomes more costly to funnel new labor and raw materials into production. In other words, as happened with the cotton industry, after a while, the period of exuberant growth must be followed by diminishing returns on investment and a squeeze on the industry. Eventually, new investment begins to be frightened away, unemployment begins to rise along with bankruptcies, and the deck is cleared for a new phase. But aside from various short-term and highly irregular business cycles, long-term industrial waves do not necessarily produce absolute falls in economic activity. Investments and innovation shift out of old areas into new ones, and as "old" goods and techniques enter a relatively depressed or stagnant stage, new technologies, using newly important raw materials and exploiting new markets, come into being.[11]

In the case of the textile industry, those most hurt were the least progressive areas of this sector, those who had been able to work profitably in boom times, but who were now reduced to pauperism and technological marginality in the more demanding atmosphere. Because many of the individuals who suffered this fate had actually sustained themselves as semi-independent artisans proud of their status which seemed higher than that of the regimented factory workers, their fall was all the more shocking. Also, having been less uprooted than the factory workers, and having maintained a greater degree of traditional communal solidarity, they were better able to protest the economic changes destroying them. From about 1810 on into the 1840s, a whole series of protest movements shook England. Luddites tried to destroy the machines they held responsible for their ruin, and later, Chartists presented a set of revolutionary political demands that would have overturned the established way of running England's political life. There were waves of massive protest in 1811–1813, 1815–1817, 1819, 1826, 1829–1835, 1838–1842, 1843–1844, and 1846–1848.[12] By the 1840s the "first" industrial cycle was over and the rapid growth of the "second" was beginning to reduce the misery left by the decay of the "first."

This does not mean that the overall standard of living declined during this period, or even that the textile industry was destroyed. It remained a growing and important one. But it shrank as a proportion of England's total industrial output and exports, it ceased to be the most dynamic sector, and it no longer afforded spectacular opportunities for quick profits.[13]

What was happening in the 1820s, 1830s, and early 1840s was misunderstood by most observers at that time and errors about the crisis of that period have continued to misinform our understanding of each new analogous crisis that has arisen in industrial cycles ever since. Karl Marx's later studies of this period convinced him that investment in machines and technology was inherently unprofitable but essential to meet technological innovation by competitors. He came to believe that the only way to obtain profits was to take them out of labor's wages, so that as technology improved, wages would be forced ever lower in a desperate attempt to ward off collapse. He noticed that the crisis stage of the industrial cycle pushed small producers out of existence in favor of the larger ones who had enough resources to keep on investing and survive; but he concluded that, like the fallen artisans of the cotton industry, all these small producers would wind up as miserably poor factory workers. He then assumed that as a larger segment of the population was forced into factory work, the growing radicalism and organized protest that had occurred in this period would be repeated and intensified and eventually lead to a revolution and the overthrow of the capitalist industrial system. That this had not occurred at the end of the first industrial cycle did not mean it would not happen in later cycles as industrialization, and thus the gravity of each cycle increased. Marxists still interpret industrial cycles in this way, confusing what may indeed be happening in a leading sector of the previous industrial cycle with the industrial economy as a whole.[14] In fact, over a long period of time, neither profits nor wages have tended to fall; and new products, techniques, and markets replace the failing old ones.

But to take the precisely opposite viewpoint can be just as misleading. It is true that capital tends to flow into more dynamic sectors after the exhaustion of a particular cycle, and that as long as innovation continues, no particular "crisis" is really as final as it may seem to be to contemporaries. This hardly means that adjustment is easy. That the average standard of living may not fall much, if at all, during a crisis, does not negate the substantial amount of suffering and dislocation caused by massive industrial shifts. Markets do not adjust to such matters smoothly or painlessly. In England there was a real crisis, and the political order was threatened. If this did not produce a revolution, the same cannot be said for similar crises in some of the other Western countries involved in a closely related industrial cycle. In countries less stable, less prosperous, and less powerful than England, industrial cycles could and did produce more traumatic effects.

The invention and construction of railroads produced a deeper transformation than did the development of the textile industry. Railroads required more complex technology and a whole array of subsidiary industries, particularly in metallurgy, mining, and engineering. The railroads also spread the effects of modernity very quickly by creating the first rapid and cheap transportation system. Not only was a science-based technology first used on a large and impressive scale, but everyone, even in remote corners of Great Britain, saw it and was directly involved in its effects.[15]

None of this would have been possible in Britain without the prior advances in industry and technology. But the new scale of growth shows how this "second" Industrial Revolution deepened and extended the effects of the "first" and then went much further.

From 1820 to 1860 British* industrial production increased by 300 percent, coal output by 533 percent, output of pig iron by 1,500 percent, and the number of kilometers of railroad track laid went from nothing to 21,558.[16] In 1840, Great Britain produced 1.4 million metric tons of pig iron, 47 percent of the entire world's output. Its closest rival, France, only produced 0.35 million tons, the United States 0.3 million tons, and the countries that were going to make up the new Germany, only 0.2 million tons. By 1860, British pig iron production was up to 3.9 million tons, 49 percent of world production; while France produced 0.9 million tons, the United States 0.7 million tons, and Germany 0.5 million tons.[17] In 1840, too, Great Britain had 29 percent of all the world's railroad lines, exceeded only by the length of tracks laid in the much larger United States. It had more than five times as much as either France or Germany. By 1860, Britain's rail network still largely exceeded that of these other two European countries, both of which covered considerably more territory. (It should be noted, however, that the United States in 1850 had half of all the railroad tracks laid in the world.)[18]

What all this meant to the people of Britain can be summarized by a few dry statistics that actually show dramatic change from 1800 to 1860. Over

---

* Great Britain, or sometimes just Britain, leaves out Ireland, whereas United Kingdom refers to England, Wales, Scotland, and Ireland. Because Ireland was treated as a colony and was deliberately kept backward, it is better to treat Great Britain as the relevant entity, even though the entire political unit was and is still called the United Kingdom.

these six decades GNP/capita in Great Britain doubled to about $1,800 per year (in 1985 U.S. dollars). American GNP/capita remained higher at about $2,150, but France's in 1860 was about $1,300, Germany's $1,050, and a relatively poor Western European country like Italy had a GNP/capita of about $850.[19] In 1800 16 percent of Great Britain's population lived in its nine biggest cities. By 1860, 24 percent did, and these cities had grown in size from 1,671,000 people (of whom 1,117,000 lived in London) to 5,475,000 people (of whom 3,227,000 lived in London).[20] Great Britain by then was the most urbanized country in the world with over half its population living in cities or large towns, and London was by far the world's largest city.

In 1800, Great Britain was the only country in the world that had only a minority of its labor force employed in agriculture, some 34 percent still were, with 30 percent in industry, and 36 percent in services. By 1860, only 22 percent were in agriculture, 56 percent in industry, and 22 percent in services.[21]

If the United Kingdom was not quite the richest country in the world in terms of average wealth (the United States occupied that position), it was the most advanced in industry, in technology, and in social transformation from an agrarian to a modern society. It was also the most powerful nation in the world economy. Of total world trade in 1840, the United Kingdom was responsible for some 25 percent, France for 11 percent, Germany for 8 percent, and the more self-sufficient United States for only 7 percent. By 1860 this had hardly changed, with the British still responsible for a quarter of world trade.[22] Much of the industrialization going on in other Western countries was based on the export of British knowledge and skill, and to some extent, capital as well. This was particularly true of the United States which, though politically independent, remained a vital supplier of raw material and agricultural goods for England.[23]

In more human terms, these impressive numbers and facts can be translated into a set of statements describing a whole new way of life for a majority of the British. The ordinary working family was no longer, as in most of the rest of the world, peasant, but working in urban factories or shops or as servants to the growing middle classes. For many this meant migration from the countryside to a town, and for some, the loss of whatever independence they may have felt. For most, life in the growing towns was precarious. There were neither modern forms of social insurance nor the traditional forms of communal solidarity and support that had once been available. But for those who were healthy, there were employment opportunities and relatively decent wages.[24]

This transition, which may seem so normal to us today, was such a violation of what had been considered the ordinary way in which most humans lived that it took a long time for British society to adjust. Already in the late eighteenth century the authorities had tried to stop what they had seen as a dangerous tendency for people to migrate and leave the land. In 1795, the Speenhamland System had been passed by the representatives of the landowning gentry to provide relief to the rural poor on condition that they remain in their original home districts. This was meant to reduce movement, retain agricultural labor for the landowners, and alleviate what was seen as a serious problem of increasing rural misery. Of course, this could not work. As the growing population could not be employed on the land, and as the burden of relief rose, payment fell to miserable rates that could not keep the population in place. Further, the industrialists and urban middle classes, who were growing in number and economic importance as a result of the changes going on, were strongly opposed to any measure which blocked the emergence of a free labor market. But it was not until 1834 that this was finally accepted, and the poor laws were changed.[25]

It was at about this time, in the 1830s, that some of the major social and political consequences of industrialization came to be accepted by the English ruling classes, and that, through their flexible if antiquated Parliamentary system, they were able to accommodate themselves to it. In a dramatic but insightful passage, Karl Polanyi summarized this change by saying:

> The mechanism of the market was asserting itself and clamoring for its completion: human labor had to be made a commodity. Reactionary paternalism had in vain tried to resist this necessity. Out of the horrors of Speenhamland men rushed blindly for the shelter of a utopian market economy.[26]

It began to seem that for the first time it would be widely accepted that capital and labor should be entirely free of regulation, and that the resulting economic growth might alleviate the obvious social ills of industrialization. That this phase in political and economic thought would prove to be short-lived was not foreseen.

Much of the change was associated with the growth of the middle class. The growth of industry and expansion of commerce opened a large number of positions for those able to obtain sufficient education, or for those lucky and capable enough to take advantage of the new business opportunities. The bourgeoisie of the Middle Ages, indeed all of town life, had been tiny compared to what developed in the advanced nineteenth-century countries, particularly in Great Britain.

The most successful of the new entrepreneurs became immensely wealthy; and their sons, men like Robert Peel and William Gladstone, joined the old landed elite as part of the politically dominant class.[27] But on a much larger scale, those below them, the real middle class, also grew in wealth, power, and number. Its utilitarian, business-oriented, practical way of thinking and its dynamism lay at the heart of economic growth and created the basis for a new social ethos that enshrined bourgeois values. This, after all, was the hallmark of both nineteenth-century American and Victorian English social life: thrift, hard work, sexual self-control, a strong orientation to the protection and fostering of the nuclear family, and a devout but strictly compartmentalized and limited religiosity. If the rich above the middle class, and the poor below them failed to adhere to these values, society as a whole disapproved. Both at the very top of society, where Queen Victoria seemed to epitomize the bourgeois ideal, and among those poor who wished to better themselves, middle-class morality became the proper if not always followed model. What was so different about this was that it was the first time that bourgeois culture really had become so dominant rather than remaining, as it had been before the great growth of industry, the property of a small commercial and artisanal class.[28]

How large was this middle class in Great Britain? Eric Hobsbawm estimates that in 1871 it included no more than 200,000 households; at very most a million people, and probably somewhat fewer. In England and Wales it was no more than 4 to 5 percent of the population.[29] Perhaps in the United States it was somewhat larger, and there at least some considerable portion of the farming population was part of the independent middle class, too. It is likely that elsewhere in Europe, in the mid-nineteenth century, it was smaller than in Britain. Nevertheless, compared to the very small number of politically active, educated, and informed people in agrarian societies who were able to participate in the larger political system, this was a very large class, and one that increasingly demanded the right to have its opinions taken into account.

The social and political tensions of the first downturn of the industrial cycle produced a major political change. The British Parliament gave in to the pressure and in 1832 brought more of the middle class into the political system. The number of those permitted to vote was allowed to increase from some 435,000 to about 650,000 voters; that is, from about 2 percent to 3 percent of the population of the United Kingdom. As a proportion of adult males, the electorate increased from some 8 percent to close to 12 percent of the total. But it was not so much the increase in voters that was significant as the fact that for the first time the new industrial towns were given representation and the electorate ceased to be composed entirely of a small number of easily manipulated rural folk. The parliamentary system was adapted to take into account some of the social changes which had taken place. That this cooled political passions and dampened the pressure for revolution rather than increasing it taught the British ruling class a lesson and prepared the way for future gradual reforms of the same type.[30]

In 1867 a second reform was passed, this time to enfranchise a substantial portion of the urban working class, too. The electoral rolls were doubled to 2 million adult males; that is, about 8 percent of the total population of the United Kingdom, and about one-third of the adult males. If the largely disenfranchised Irish rural poor were excluded, after 1867 close to 40 percent of the adult British males had the vote—not universal suffrage, but a major step toward real mass political participation.[31]

The ability of the British to incorporate the rising demands, first of the middle class, and later in the nineteenth century of a portion of the working class, created the sense that Great Britain was so highly adaptable that it could avoid the revolutionary, violent lurches that characterized much of European continental politics. And though the notion that English history has always been gradual and relatively free of violence is false, it is true that in the nineteenth century, at a time of very rapid social and economic change, it did adapt rather more easily than other European countries.

Great Britain, then, was fortunate in many respects. A great naval and colonial power from the late seventeenth century on, relatively secure from invasion by land armies because it was an island, it also managed to avoid continental absolutism, which enabled its economy to grow more freely. Agriculturally progressive from the early modern period, and fairly well endowed with resources, it combined its political and natural advantages to produce the "first" Industrial Revolution, and then used its considerable strength and political stability to become the world's greatest power and dominate most of the nineteenth century. Only the United States, which inherited many of the political advantages and economic skills of the English, was in the same advanced category of development. But it was not until the very end of the nineteenth century that the United States ceased to be a purely regional power.

What the British did with their advantages was to create a global economic network of unparalleled size, strength, and complexity that was in many ways the precursor of the twentieth-century world system ultimately inherited by the United States.

More than any other Western industrializing power in the nineteenth century, Great Britain depended on foreign trade. Not only did the basic raw product of its "first" Industrial Revolution, cotton, enable it to maintain and raise its standard of living, but so, too, did an increasing amount of food and other primary products. The other side of the coin was that the rest of the world provided a huge market for its industrial exports. As shown in Table 4-1, Great Britain, both as a buyer and as a seller, had at its disposal much more than what was domestically available.

TABLE 4-1
Average Yearly Value of Foreign Trade by the United Kingdom (millions of pounds)[32]

	Imports	Index Value (base = 100)	Exports (including re-exports)	Index Value (base = 100)
1796–1800	47	100	44	100
1816–1820	60	128	51	116
1836–1840	83	177	59	134
1856–1860	183	389	149	339
1876–1880	382	813	256	582

Extraordinary as Britain's domination of international trade may have been, however, and productive as its factories were, it is evident that its exports did not match its imports. In fact, the unbalance tended to grow as imports regularly grew faster than exports. How did the British pay for this? From 1871 to 1875, when its average annual deficits were on the order of 65 million pounds, some 50 million pounds from earnings on investments abroad made up much of the difference. Also, revenues from what are called "invisible" exports (money paid for services such as shipping, insurance, and banking for which the entire world turned to London for expertise and security) were sufficiently large so that through most of the nineteenth century the United Kingdom was actually able to balance its international accounts or run a surplus.[33] What this means is that the British could not have sustained either their standard of living or their international power without their foreign investments to supplement their industrial economy.

But the United Kingdom's leading position was not simply maintained by industrial efficiency and financial wizardry, especially as the nineteenth century advanced and other countries in the West developed their own economic strength. Markets had to be kept open, foreign loans and investments had to be secured when they were threatened, and political forces throughout the world had to be manipulated. In a number of areas direct control had to be maintained or strengthened, particularly in that most valuable part of the British Empire, India, which provided a source of primary products, a significant market for exports, and a place for lucrative investments.

Losing control of the majority of its North American colonies in 1783 had taken away the most valuable part of the eighteenth-century British Empire. But Britain's final and decisive victory over the French when Napoleon's continental empire was destroyed in 1814 and 1815 cleared the way for the creation of an even vaster British imperial structure. In India, the French had already been largely pushed out in 1763, but now they ceased to be a maritime threat in any part of the world, and no other European power could come close to matching British naval strength. (In the first half of the nineteenth century, the number of British registered tons of shipping was equal to all of the rest of Europe put together.[34]

In Latin America, after making a half-hearted attempt to grab some Spanish territory, notably in Argentina, the United Kingdom limited itself to ensuring its trading rights. Eventually, that led it to a policy of siding with Latin American independence against Spanish and Portuguese control. The British fleet, British diplomacy, and, when necessary, direct aid to the independence movements helped achieve these ends. But at the same time, it was not in the British interest to have strong governments in Latin America, and through occasional naval blockades, commercial pressure, and direct interference, the United Kingdom contributed significantly to breaking up unifying schemes and weakening strong leaders. Two good examples were the subversive role played by them in helping to destroy the United Provinces of Central America in the 1830s, and in weakening the nationalist Argentine dictator Rosas (in which adventure they allowed the French fleet to play a major role) in the late 1830s and 1840s. In fact, the so-called Monroe Doctrine, in which the United States declared in 1823 that it would not tolerate European interference in the Americas, was enforced by and for the benefit of British interests throughout most of the nineteenth century.[35]

Though direct British investment in Latin America did not reach significant proportions until later in the nineteenth century, even in the first half, it provided a vital export market. Hobsbawm has estimated that about one-third of Britain's textile exports were going to Latin America, mostly to Brazil, in 1840, and that this market saved the prosperity of English cotton mills in this period.[36]

But the principal source of British trade in the region was with economies in which most of the labor on plantations that grew export crops for Europe consisted of African slaves. This was true, also, of the southern United States, which was Britain's main source of cotton. The United Kingdom had outlawed the slave trade in 1807 and emancipated the slaves in its colonies in 1838, largely for humanitarian reasons. This not only put its own West Indian colonies at a competitive disadvantage but also presented a serious moral dilemma. The British solution was to continue to press for an end to the trans-Atlantic commerce in slaves, but to steer clear of any local interference in the slave economies of the Spanish West Indies (Cuba and Puerto Rico), Brazil, or the United States. It even took a sympathetic stance toward the Confederacy during the American Civil War, though popular opinion supported the anti-slave North.[37]

The single biggest British overseas interest, however, was not in the Atlantic but in India. From the time of the Industrial Revolution to the mid-nineteenth century, a whole series of major political and economic changes took place in that colony. The British ceased to merely plunder it, but invested and developed systematic exchanges with the home country. They also rationalized their system of rule, extended their political control, and established a bureaucratic and fiscal system to properly exploit their territory. After the last great revolt against British rule was put down in 1857, the process was essentially complete.[38]

The social transformations brought about by the British were the result of these economic and administrative changes. A native landowner class was created from the remnants of the traditional court officials of pre-British political units. Peasants were systematically encouraged or forced to grow cash crops. Imports of English textiles seriously damaged rural artisans and created a large class of very poor landless folk. Caste lines were reinforced to maintain order.[39] But in the second half of the nineteenth century, the British also built Asia's largest rail network in India, and Indian industry began to develop. A sizable textile industry not only began to compete with British imports but also to export to other parts of Asia, and an iron and steel industry grew as well, controlled to a large extent by Indians rather than Englishmen.[40] In fact, the British had long known that one of the important benefits to be drawn from India was not simply direct exploitation but the control of India's trade with the rest of Asia.

As in much else connected with Western imperial expansion, the results were curiously mixed. Large groups among the colonized were severely injured by the West, but in the most successful cases of Western colonization, as in India, the nineteenth century saw some benefits accrue as well. Orderly administration and control of internal violence contributed to economic growth and a decrease in death rates in the colonies.

But some areas that were penetrated by Western economic forces, though not directly colonized, did not have the internal cohesion to resist the West's most nefarious effects or to organize administrative reforms to cope with the social disturbances caused by Western influences.

One of the more disgraceful and yet logical examples of the harm that British imperialism could perpetrate was the development of the opium trade between India and China. The British had discovered that though China had luxury goods, tea, and precious metals to export, it had little demand for manufactured British goods. But it did have a demand for opium, a product grown in India and one which British merchants began to bring into China in the late eighteenth century. By the 1820s, China's favorable trade balance with the West had been reversed, and it was losing significant amounts of silver, the base of its currency. This threatened the fiscal stability of the Chinese Empire. Opium addiction had become a severe social problem, and the corruption of local officials it caused, particularly in the area of Canton, the main port used by the British and other Westerners, was beginning to weaken administrative control. The trade was in any case illegal, and the government of China tried to stop it. This provoked the British into declaring war against China, the "First Opium War," from 1839 to 1842, at the end of which the British forced China to allow opium imports and give more privileges to Western merchants. The United Kingdom was also ceded Hong Kong as a permanent colony; five other ports were opened for foreign trade; and China was forced to pay an indemnity. Over the next decade, more concessions were forced from China, and Westerners, led by the United Kingdom, gained control over more of China's foreign trade. Further resistance by the Chinese government led to the "Second Opium War," from 1857 to 1860, which was actually over a much wider range of issues than just opium imports. The British and the French defeated China, and gained more concessions. By the end of the nineteenth century, not only had the central Chinese government become a virtual pawn of Western interests, but it is estimated that some 10 percent of the population had become opium addicts.[41]

The most active British diplomatic and military activities outside Europe were directed at the eastern Mediterranean which increasingly came to be the best route between England and India, and which was perceived as a choke point from which British supremacy in the East might be threatened. This issue first arose at the turn of the nineteenth century, when Napoleon tried to conquer Egypt to use it as a base from which to take India. His failure did not end the problem, particularly as Egypt came to be used as a transit point on the long sea voyage to India in order to cut time from the much longer trip around Africa. The importance of Egypt further increased with the construction of the Suez Canal, which was opened in 1869. The defense of this lifeline came to be called the "Eastern Question" and was connected to the interplay of conflicting forces in the area. On the one hand were the non-European powers, the Ottoman Empire and Egypt, and on the other, the growing Russian Empire, perceived as the United Kingdom's chief eastern rival, and France. Playing off the various parties against each other, the British eventually succeeded in limiting French power, in taking over the diplomatic affairs of the Ottoman Empire and preserving it against internal and external threats, in keeping Russian territorial gains within acceptable limits, and in entirely subverting Egyptian sovereignty and turning it into a virtual colony. A number of wars, chiefly the Crimean War of 1854 to 1856, and numerous naval actions, threats, and small interventions maintained British strength in the area. But this was done at a price. It created long-term antagonism against the United Kingdom among the other powers, it weakened local governments in the Near East, and it destroyed what little chance Egypt had of securing an independent and reasonably smooth transition into the modern world.[42]

This, then, was "England's world." It was a world in which the British pound sterling was the stable rock by which all other currencies were measured, in which English industrial progress and technology were the standards by which other manufacturers were judged, in which British diplomacy determined the fates of millions of unsuspecting "natives" outside Europe and decided the limits of international power exercised by the other Western powers, and in which British hegemony was ultimately backed by the strength of its economy and the force of its navy. But as in any hegemonic situation, it was also an unstable world because it was dependent on the fortuitous advantages that had made England the first industrial country, and it could not long survive if other powers reached or surpassed England's level of economic development. As soon as another big power learned to combine industrial progress with the kind of bullying tactics that had made the British so successful, British hegemony would be endangered, and what had been a stable world situation might quickly turn into a dangerously unbalanced one. In fact, this is precisely what happened in the last quarter of the nineteenth century and thus prepared the way for the unsettled, dangerous first half of the twentieth.

Nations, States, and Imperialism

A state that can rely on the loyalty of a large portion of its population can mobilize a larger portion of its human and material resources than can a state that needs to impose its control with force and is unable to draw on compliant subjects. If a population is nationalistic, if it believes that its primary political loyalty lies with the people within the boundaries of its state, so much the better for the state. But nationalism, which is now accepted as a normal characteristic of populations, is a fairly recent phenomenon that was not widespread, even in Europe, until the nineteenth century. It has only become common outside the West in the twentieth century.

Before the development of nationalism, the primary focus of political loyalty was a combination of the local community and the family. Peasants rarely felt they had much in common with their rulers or with others in their state, while nobles and royal ruling houses were primarily loyal to their extended families, their immediate patrons or retainers, and to the dynasties at the top of the social order. Beyond the village or town, the guild, the family or clan, the notion of loyalty to such an abstract political entity as "the state" was a rarity, and it was not uncommon for provinces to be bartered or split away from one state to another as part of a marriage price, to cut a political deal, or simply as the fruits of war. Being ruled by foreigners was not, of itself, either objectionable or a good cause for revolt unless the occupier taxed excessively or somehow persecuted the local population.

Much nineteenth- and twentieth-century history has been written to prove that the nations of today have long been struggling to gain independence and unity as cultural groups within their own state. The basic premise of a great deal of this literature is simply a carefully cultivated lie that is part of the effort of modern states to teach their subjects nationalism, particularly in school.

The cultural elements that define a nation to its people are a combination of language, religion, and common habits that have developed over time. But none of these is sufficient to create a feeling that those with a common culture deserve to have a state of their own, a state that by right ought to include most of the members of that cultural group, and exclude those who do not belong. First of all, definitions of appropriate cultural markers have always been unclear. If all Frenchmen want to be part of France, how about French-speakers who do not? How about people whose native language is not French but whose ancestors have been part of the French state for centuries? How about those who are not Catholic, those who are not Christian, those who are recent immigrants? And if the situation is less than perfectly clear for one of the oldest and most strongly established states in Europe, how confusing do such issues become in states with much more heterogeneous populations? Nevertheless, the nineteenth century saw the triumph in the West of the state that tried to become culturally unified, the "nation-state," and the spread of the ideology of nationalism beyond the West.

There are three ways in which nationalism grows. There may be, as in England and France over many centuries, a fairly stable state that gradually incorporates a growing number of elite persons into its administrative and economic networks so that among them a real sense of loyalty to the state, to a shared language, and to a way of thought creates a sense of nationhood. If economic development and the growth of a state bureaucracy spreads this sentiment to a growing middle class of officials, merchants, and townspeople who depend on large markets and support from the state to exist, then nationalism becomes more than simply the preserve of a small elite defending a ruling dynasty. By the end of the eighteenth century, such a form of nationalism existed in these two great European powers, and the French Revolution extended that feeling to an even greater number in France.[43]

A second, derivative way in which nationalism can develop is in reaction to foreign occupation, to bullying by a foreign power, particularly if that power is itself nationalistic and uses its nationalism to justify its aggressive behavior. The spread of French armies throughout Europe during the Revolutionary and Napoleonic wars did much to stimulate such reactive nationalism. But even without this, it would have spread as states tried to strengthen themselves by creating greater internal cultural unity in order to compete more successfully in the international arena. It was particularly in empires with many different linguistic and religious groups that such efforts could provoke nationalist reactions against the state as minority or relatively less powerful groups found themselves suddenly endangered by the effort to place another culture above theirs. Not peasants but aspiring officials, nobles, townsmen, and merchants who were thrown into a competitive disadvantage if they were from the less-favored culture became the nucleus of nationalist reactions. The most striking case was in the great, highly mixed Austrian Habsburg Empire that encompassed various Slavs, Romanians, Germans, Hungarians, and Italians in Central Europe. Once that empire began to try to create greater administrative and cultural unity on the basis of German culture, the others, beginning with the Hungarians, created their own nationalist myths and aspirations simply to fight back. The effort to unite such culturally disparate units was bound to fail and break up in bitter conflict.[44]

A third and closely related road to nationalism occurs when a people revolt because of over-taxation, or because a central empire finds itself too weak to rule, or simply because a local notable seizes an opportunity to become a sovereign prince, and a state is created with no unifying ideology. Before the nineteenth century such events often produced new states, but there was little perceived need to create nations. Since then, however, the leading states in the world, beginning with the Western ones, have been nation-states, and all new states, however they may have come into being, have tried to strengthen themselves by creating nationalism. This can be done by teaching it in school systems, by massive propaganda efforts, and by trying to arouse the population against "foreign" dangers. Such a process is very common in today's world.

Far from being a natural and spontaneous development, in most instances nationalism has been deliberately fostered to satisfy a state's needs. The primary instrument for that has been intellectuals working in schools and universities and governments; and in most cases, the spread of nationalism requires the growth of mass literacy as well as some loosening of traditional loyalties to local communities and families. Both the need for nationalism and the social conditions that foster it have flourished with modern economic growth. Migrations to towns, the increased capacity of governments to finance school systems, better communications, the birth of a class of specialized intellectuals, and the increasing ability of big powers to mobilize large parts of their populations to gain their ends have spurred nationalism.

In the eighteenth century some enlightened writers suggested that the causes of wars could be found in the nature of agrarian states ruled by tiny, grasping elites. Once these parasites were replaced by popular rule, suggested Rousseau, the reasons to make wars would vanish. The obvious failure of this vision led Karl Marx in the nineteenth century to explain the continuation of international conflict and war by blaming it on capitalism. In the past, wars had been fought so that kings and nobles might be able to seize more peasants to tax. Now, he claimed, they were fought to maintain profits. But if the capitalists could be overthrown, then war would end. This prophecy, too, fails to see that the fault lies in the nature of state structures. As long as these exist they will be composed of self-perpetuating administrative elites whose livelihood and self-respect depend on maintaining the independence and strength of their states against outsiders, and international conflicts will continue. Since powerful states can use their strength to enhance the economic position and prosperity of their people, weaker states will always have to try to strengthen themselves, while the strong ones work to maintain their positions. As there is no prospect for the end of a world organized on the basis of powerful state machines, there is no end to the prospect of intense competition between them.

It is possible to see how the infection of nationalism and competitive state-building not only continued throughout the nineteenth century, but also how it actually became more virulent and set the stage for a series of catastrophes that shaped the twentieth century.

For almost a generation after the fall of Napoleon the leaders of Europe tried to repress nationalism and revolutionary liberalism which demanded greater political democracy and economic freedom. Liberalism and nationalism had been closely associated during the French Revolution and were assumed to go together. Yet, the attempt at repression of these impulses did not obviate the need of European states to further centralize their governments in order to meet potential international competition. Nor did it eliminate their need to maintain and increase the loyalty of their populations in times of rapid and unsettling economic and social change. This became obvious in the crisis of the 1840s, when the full effects of the downward part of the first industrial cycle, that of textiles, spread through much of Western and Central Europe. In Great Britain the protest caused by economic distress was defused because the middle classes were granted some of their demands for greater political participation. In more autocratic continental states, such as Prussia, Austria, and even France, this was not the case. All of them were subjected to violent revolutionary outbreaks in 1848. The situation was further exacerbated where dissatisfied nationalistic grievances existed. In Italy and much of Germany the middle classes felt that their economic problems might be solved by national unity. In northern Italy, too, as in Hungary, there was resentment about Austrian rule.[45]

Except for France, the revolutions of 1848 were brought under control; yet, that example and the lessons of this period of upheaval eventually taught the conservatives that it was possible for them also to wave the flag of nationalism in order to legitimize themselves and retain power. Liberal reforms did not have to go very far to satisfy middle classes who did not want massive social change. A few political concessions that made them feel more integrated into the political process sufficed, and if combined with active nationalist rhetoric and assertive international behavior, it cooled their revolutionary ardor. The true social revolutionaries, the artisans and skilled workers who were being ruined by spreading industrialization, had no chance once they were abandoned by their middle-class allies.[46]

The most successful example of manipulation of nationalism for state ends was the career of Otto von Bismarck, first as chief minister of Prussia and then as German chancellor. He first came to power in 1862. In 1864 he arranged an alliance with Austria against Denmark, smashed the Danes, and annexed some of their territory. In 1866 he allied himself with Italy and gained France's neutrality as he turned against Austria and crushed its army. This made Prussia the dominant power in Germany. In 1870 Bismarck maneuvered France into a war which he used to unify Germany behind Prussia, and after overwhelming France in 1870–1871, he created a unified German Empire led by Prussia. He won over the German middle classes with his nationalism, destroyed the liberal political opposition with his successes, pacified the social revolutionaries by making limited reforms, and in the end allowed the old reactionary Prussian state elite to seize control over all of Germany. Though superficially somewhat democratized, the new Germany was actually dominated by the ethos of the Prussian military absolutist bureaucracy which then set the tone for the new German Empire. From 1871 on, this Germany was the chief continental European power, and as such, a growing menace to British world hegemony.[47]

German success caused further reverberations. France sought to atone for its defeat of 1871 by expanding its overseas empire in Africa and Southeast Asia, and this worried the British who saw their world trading hegemony threatened. Germany then entered the colonial game to keep up with France, and eventually to compete with England. Habsburg Austria, beset as it was with conflicting nationality problems, felt it necessary to expand to keep up with its rivals. It did this in the only possible direction, the Balkans. Russia, feeling threatened by the growth of German power and Austrian expansion, began a program of accelerated industrialization.

In Russia, as in Germany, it was the autocratic bureaucracy of the old monarchy that was in command of the process of change, not the new and more liberal middle classes, so the political effects of change were very different from those that occurred in America, England, and France. In fact, the last part of the nineteenth century demonstrated that a good way for backward economies to modernize, if they were ruled by solidly centralized autocratic states, was from the top down, by forced industrialization. In this way, such absolutist states as Russia and Prussia were able to keep up with their international competition, and Japan, a successful imitator of the European autocratic modernizers after 1867, followed the same path.

Whereas Europe in the first half of the nineteenth century had been relatively calm after the end of the Napoleonic wars, the second half of the century saw the gradual disintegration of the balance of power system put together by the anti-French alliance at the Congress of Vienna.[48] After the 1870s this instability turned into an increasingly desperate race for empire. Rising nationalism, spreading industrialization, and the prominence of a new, powerful Germany provoked all the major powers, as well as many minor ones, into intense international competition. It seemed as if those who failed to assure themselves of colonial empires might be doomed to second-class or even dependent status.

Though it may seem excessive to present a list of all the colonial acquisitions of the Western powers and Japan after 1860, such a list shows the dramatic nature of what happened, and the concentration of effort as the world was suddenly divided up among the advanced countries in little more than one generation (see Table 4-2). Aside from Latin America, which was economi-

TABLE 4-2
Seizure of Territories by Imperial Powers, 1860–1913[49]

Imperial Power	*Area Taken*	*Date*	*Comments*
Russia	Ussuri	1860	Taken from China, continuation of 200-year-old push by Russians into Siberia
United Kingdom	Lagos, Nigeria	1861	—
France	Vietnam and Cambodia	1862–1884	French move from south to north Indochina
Russia	Transcaucasia and Turkestan	1864–1895	Continues 18th century moves by Russia into Muslim Central Asia
United Kingdom	Malaya	1873–1914	Gradual seizure of Malay states, based on British control of Singapore and Penang coastal islands held since 1819 and 1786
United Kingdom	Fiji	1874	—

TABLE 4-2   Seizure of Territories by Imperial Powers *(continued)*

Imperial Power	Area Taken	Date	Comments
Austria-Hungary	Bosnia-Herzegovina	1878	Protectorate taken from Ottoman Empire, annexed in 1908
United Kingdom	Cyprus	1878	Taken from Ottoman Empire
France	Tahiti	1880	Under actual if not full legal control of France since 1841
France	Gabon and French Congo	1880–1888	French move inland from coastal bases established 1839–1849
United Kingdom	North Borneo	1881	British power originally established in neighboring Sarawak in 1841
United Kingdom	Egypt	1882	Follows growing British influence since 1850s
Italy	Eritrea	1882–1890	—
France	Tunisia	1882	French began to establish themselves in neighboring Algeria in 1830
France	Western Sudan	1883–1899	French move inland from Senegalese coastal positions first taken in 17th century
Germany	Southwest Africa	1884	—
Germany	Northeast New Guinea	1884	—
United Kingdom	Southeast New Guinea	1884	—
Germany	Togo	1884	—
United Kingdom	British Somaliland	1884	—
France	French Somaliland	1884	French move inland from coastal station established in 1862
Italy	Italian Somaliland	1884	Italians move inland from coastal station established in 1869
Spain	Rio de Oro	1885	—

(continued)

TABLE 4-2   Seizure of Territories by Imperial Powers *(continued)*

Imperial Power	Area Taken	Date	Comments
Spain	Spanish Guinea	1885	—
Germany	Cameroun	1885	—
United Kingdom	Southern Nigeria	1885	Lagos, on the coast of western Nigeria, became British colony in 1861
Belgium	Congo	1885	Personal property of Belgian King
France	Madagascar	1885	Protectorate. Full colony in 1896
Germany	Tanganyika	1885–1890	—
Germany, United Kingdom, France, and United States	Pacific Islands Marshalls New Hebrides Cook Samoa Gilberts Hawaii Marianas	1885–1900	The most important were the Hawaiian Islands taken by the United States
United Kingdom	Bechuanaland	1885	British move north from South Africa which they first took in 1795
United Kingdom	Upper Burma	1886	Coastal parts of Burma were taken by the British in 1826 and lower Burma in 1852
United Kingdom	Rhodesia	1888	Continuing expansion from South Africa
United Kingdom	Brunei	1888	Formal protectorate established over Sarawak at the same time
France	Interior of French Equatorial Africa	1888–1900	Expansion from Gabon and Congo
United Kingdom	Kenya	1888	—
France	Ivory Coast	1889–1890	French move inland from coastal positions established in 1843
United Kingdom	Uganda	1890	—
United Kingdom	Zanzibar	1890	Under de facto British control since 1860s

TABLE 4-2 Seizure of Territories by Imperial Powers *(continued)*

Imperial Power	Area Taken	Date	Comments
United Kingdom	Gold Coast	1890–1896	British move inland from coastal positions taken in 1821
France	Laos	1893	Completes French Indochinese Empire
Japan	Taiwan	1895	Taken from China
Italy	(Ethiopia)	1896	Italians defeated; Ethiopia remains the only independent African country except for Liberia, a protectorate of the United States
United States	Puerto Rico	1898	Taken from Spain
United States	Philippines	1898	Taken from Spain
United Kingdom, France, Germany, Russia, Japan	Chinese coastal cities	1898	The British began by seizing Hong Kong in 1841, but in 1898 there was a general scramble to take Chinese coastal cities as a prelude to a partition of China
United Kingdom	Sudan	1899	Reconquest of area previously controlled by Egypt
United Kingdom	Northern Nigeria	1900–1903	—
United Kingdom	Boer Republics	1902	Ends a long series of conflicts between British, who came to South Africa in 1795, and the original white colonizers, the Dutch Boers, who came in the middle of the 17th century
Japan	Korea	1905–1910	Japan defeats Russia to gain control in 1905. Annexation in 1910
United Kingdom and Russia	Zones of influence in Persia	1907	Prelude to partition which never occurred

(continued)

TABLE 4-2   **Seizure of Territories by Imperial Powers** *(continued)*

Imperial Power	Area Taken	Date	Comments
France	Mauritania	1908–1909	Joins North African and Western Sudanic French empires
France	Morocco	1912	Follows near war between Germany and France for control
Spain	Southern and Northern Morocco	1912	Assigned minor portions of Morocco in settlement
Italy	Libya	1911–1912	Taken from Ottoman Empire
Italy	Dodecanese Islands	1912	Taken from Ottoman Empire

cally colonized during this period but remained outside the political clutches of the Europeans because the British and Americans were still able to keep outsiders out, the only non-Western power which was fully spared was Japan. The others that retained a precarious independence did so only because they were border zones between competing Western powers. But aside from such marginal cases as Afghanistan in the mountains between Russia and British India, Thailand, which lay between French and English colonies, and Ethiopia, which managed to fight off the Italians, virtually no previously uncolonized African, Oceanic, or Asian area escaped. The British and French tended to expand from previously held coastal trading stations or old colonies, but both they and the others moved into entirely new territories as well.

Even this list does not fully convey the thrust of European and Japanese expansion during this period. In older colonies, particularly in British India and the Netherlands East Indies (Indonesia) the colonial powers extended and rounded out their holdings. The French did the same in Algeria. And the total amount of Western investment in non-Western areas expanded enormously as mines, plantations, railroads, and ports were built in the most promising parts of Asia, Africa, Oceania, and Latin America.

Why was this? Certainly, increasing competition among the European powers was one reason. Another was the example of the British, who seemed to have prospered while building the world's largest empire. Now that their hegemony was ending, others wanted to partake of the remaining spoils before it was too late. Then, also, there was the fact that the West's technological lead had continued to increase, and was now so huge that it seemed a fairly easy matter to annex vast foreign territories, even against the nearly universal wishes of local inhabitants.

In 1902 Hobson, the English liberal critic of imperialism, put forward a theory which was later taken over by Lenin, whose 1916 pamphlet, *Imperialism,* remains the chief Marxist work on the topic. The Hobson-Lenin argument goes as follows:

1. By the late nineteenth century the growth of capitalism in the core economies had led to the inevitable concentration of ownership of the economy into a few giant monopolies. While this process had its start in the middle of the nineteenth century, according to the theory, it did not mature fully until about 1900.

2. These giant monopolies came to be controlled by and to merge with large financial institutions (banks) which sought to maximize the return on their capital. These institutions were so big and rich that they effectively controlled the politics of the core states.

3. Maximization of profits, however, required constant economic growth, which in turn required ever larger amounts of raw materials. Raw materials, plentiful throughout most of the nineteenth century, were presumably becoming scarce in the later part of the century because of the tremendous growth of industrial capitalism.

4. The new investments in the core economies did not lead to maximization of profits because national wealth was too unequally distributed, and the working-class masses and the rural population did not have enough money to soak up increased production. In other words, demand was weak, and capital was over-abundant, and in order to maximize return on investments, capitalists had to invest abroad, or alternatively, convince their governments to increase demand by wasting huge sums on armaments.

5. This caused the financial monopolies in the core societies to engage in a series of desperate attempts to control new sources of raw materials and new markets in order to ensure the continuation of high profits. Quite quickly, this led to a division of the world among the four major capitalist powers and a few minor powers.

6. But all this had to lead to war. For by 1900, or certainly by 1910, the world had been "filled up," and there were no easy new colonies to take. The continued demand for cheap raw materials, for new markets, and the build-up in arms of the past several decades had to lead to a giant explosion.[50]

Were Hobson and Lenin right? The history of Western expansion in the nineteenth century supports their interpretation, at least to the point of showing that capitalist states were as predatory as old agrarian ones, and more efficient about their imperialism. Not only was their aggression directed against the non-Western world, but it was also part of an increasingly bitter

European competition that eventually led to the most destructive set of wars in history.

A look at the growth of foreign investments by the core economies outside their own borders further supports the notion that there was an enormous increase in the amount of available capital. The United Kingdom's foreign investments grew by 750 percent between 1855 and 1914 while its gross national product (in constant prices) was only increasing 260 percent. The growth of foreign portfolios by other major powers seems even more spectacular because unlike the United Kingdom they were not yet major exporters of capital before the 1870s and 1880s.[51] Lenin's estimate in *Imperialism* that the rate of growth of foreign investment by the major capitalist powers went up by about 500 percent in the forty years before 1914 may be slightly excessive but the general trend was sharply upward as he claimed.[52]

By 1914 the United Kingdom had 43 percent of all foreign investment (that is, investment by one country outside its borders, but including its colonies) held in the world; France had 20 percent; Germany had 13 percent; and the United States had 8 percent. The rest was held mostly by the minor, developed capitalist states, the Netherlands, Belgium, Switzerland, and the Scandinavians, though the Japanese were beginning to be serious outside investors by this time.

On the other hand, a look at the location of most foreign investment does not accord very well with the pattern of political imperialism of the last quarter of the nineteenth century. It was not in those parts of Asia or Africa, where most of the scramble for colonies was occurring, that the capitalist core powers held major investment positions. Rather, investments were largely in the older colonies, particularly those settled by large numbers of Europeans, and in the politically independent former colonies in America. Twenty-four percent of all foreign investment was in the United States (itself beginning to be a major exporter of capital) and Canada, and fully 35 percent of the United Kingdom's investment was in North America. Latin America held 20 percent of all foreign investments, and most of that was concentrated in Argentina, Brazil, and Mexico. Oceania, consisting almost entirely of Australia and New Zealand, contained 5 percent of all foreign investment. Europe, chiefly Russia, contained 26 percent of all foreign investment, and there the French were the primary holders of this investment, with the Germans second and the United Kingdom a distant third. Asia and Africa together held only 25 percent of all foreign investment, but 50 percent of Asia's investment was held by the British, and most of that in India, while another significant share was controlled by the Dutch in their old colony of Indonesia. The new Asian colonies held little foreign investment. As for Africa, it held only 9 percent of the world's foreign investment. Sixty percent was British, almost all of it in South Africa and Egypt. Most French African investment was in the old colony of Algeria. The vast new empires conquered by the Europeans in the last part of the nineteenth century and in the early twentieth century never provided much opportunity for markets, for profitable investments, or for meaningful returns of any kind on the military and administrative costs of seizing and running them.[53]

There can be no doubt, however economically irrational it may now seem, that the core capitalist powers took their imperialism very seriously, as if it were a matter of life and death. Indeed, in treating it as such, they made their nightmares a reality and pushed themselves into a frenzy of competition that eventually led to war. Table 4-3, which is a chart of expenditures for armaments by the major powers from 1875 to 1914, shows what happened.

The race to capture colonies was part of this general atmosphere which went far beyond mere economic rationality. This was particularly true in the new imperial powers, Germany and Japan, but even the United States, ostensibly the least imperialistic of the major powers, shared in this attitude. Theodore Roosevelt, among others, felt that the United States had to have its "place in the sun." A statement by a German in 1879 sums up this attitude, but it could have been written by any of the leading advocates of imperialism in the West or in Japan.

> Every virile people has established colonial power. . . . All great nations in the fulness of their strength have desired to set their mark upon barbarian lands and those who fail to participate in this great rivalry will play a pitiable role in time to come. The colonizing impulse has become a vital question for every great nation.[54]

The impulse for imperialism had four sources. One was that the elite in many of the most advanced states, even in England and the United States, still modeled themselves on the warlike landed nobles who had once ruled the agrarian empires. Matters of honor, virtue, and courage seemed to statesmen to hold an important role in the conduct of international affairs, as if states

TABLE 4-3
Expenditure on Arms: Growth, 1875–1914, with
1875 = 100[55]

	1875	1907	1913	*Average Growth per Decade (percent)*	*Average Growth in GNP per Decade (percent)*
United States	100	394	536	56	40
Germany	100	272	331	45	29
(base year 1881)					
United Kingdom	100	210	289	32	23
France	100	177	202	19	16
(base year 1873)					

were knights jousting or schoolboys competing for athletic trophies. In fact, much of the education of elite boys throughout the West was designed to teach precisely this kind of behavior. Japan, of course, was even closer to its agrarian past, and still dominated by an old aristocratic ethos.[56]

Second, there was no question that imperialism had paid off rather handsomely in the past. Its victory in the "first" great world war with France over control of overseas trade and colonies had positioned England for its economic successes in the first part of the nineteenth century. Though the new colonies might not yet yield much, one could never tell, and it seemed better to take what one could than to be relegated to inferiority in the future. It is probably correct to say that neither by education nor by inclination were the leaders of the major powers able to understand what really produced economic progress in the latter part of the nineteenth century, and they genuinely believed that empires were a key ingredient.

Third, there was the growing nationalism of the advanced powers. Growing middle classes, expansion of school systems, and the conscious use of nationalist mythologies to cement loyalty behind the various states had created a mass of citizens eager to push their governments into manly and honorable plunder of the rest of the world, and into aggression against their neighbors.

Finally, there was the fact that in 1873 there began a serious period of economic crisis, the downward part of the second major industrial cycle. Though this crisis was ultimately resolved through technological progress, for a time it did not seem that there was any other solution than to try to conquer new markets and sources of cheap raw materials and to engage in protective, restrictive trade policies.

Thus, a combination of cultural and economic pressures pushed the major powers of the world into the golden age of imperialism. At the end of that age, with the world filled up, with no new safe colonies to conquer, and with the tremendous weight of their arms buildup behind them, they had nothing left other than to turn on each other. In that sense, Lenin's theory of imperialism was correct even if it overemphasized the economic reasons and rationality of the entire process.

That it need not have been this way had men better understood the process of economic change can only be demonstrated by looking at the technological, scientific, and economic changes of the last part of the nineteenth century. From this perspective it is possible to see how greatly misled the statesmen of the period actually turned out to be.

Economic Growth, Technology, and Education

In 1873 the financial centers of the Western world were hit by a series of what were then called panics.[57] The one in the United States was symptomatic of what was wrong. Speculators had been loaning money for railroad construction on expectation of gaining rapid rewards. But though railroad construction was far from over, the peak boom years were, and too much capital was rushing in so that unsound projects were being financed. Railroads began to default on bonds in 1873, exposing investors to big losses. To take advantage of the imagined opportunities for big profits, speculators had been borrowing short-term money at high cost and loaning it to the railroads for the long term. Some tried to float bonds in Europe to cover their positions; but there, too, similar problems were developing. Finally, several major investment houses and banks went bankrupt, the New York stock market collapsed, and a full-fledged depression began.[58]

What followed in both the United States and Europe has sometimes been called the "Great Depression," and its ramifications continued for over twenty years, into the mid-1890s. Its effects seem to have been most severe in Germany, which experienced almost no economic growth from 1874 to 1883. But throughout the West, the financial effects were even stronger than the direct economic ones. Profits fell, and a long deflationary period of falling prices occurred. Particularly sharp was the drop in agricultural prices.[59]

This was actually the downward part of the second industrial cycle of railroads and iron, and was the period in which the "third" Industrial Revolution began, with the steel, chemical, and finally the electrical industries becoming the leading sectors for the rest of the century and into the early twentieth century. The major novelty of this third cycle was that for the first time it was highly dependent on the application of modern scientific discoveries rather than simply on inspired tinkering, and those countries that encouraged research and education were at an advantage.

For the more simple-minded Marxists, both those of that period and those who write about it now, the "Great Depression" of 1873–1896 was proof of the inherent contradictions of capitalism. The Western world, they claim, only saved itself by conquering a huge new empire from which to extract surplus labor and on which to dump excessive production. Therefore, the prosperity which returned by the end of the century was the result of imperialism's reactions to the crisis, and augured even worse crises in the future.[60]

There is enough truth in this supposition to make it impossible to dismiss. There did follow a desperate scramble for imperial conquests. In all the major powers, some important business interests were hurt, and governments were pressured to react by being more nationalistic and protective of their economies. As Peter Gourevitch has pointed out, the main outcome in international trade was the rise of steep protectionist tariffs,[61] a direct analogue to the increasingly short-sighted aggressiveness of the major powers in foreign affairs.

On the other hand, both governmental actions of that time and many analyses since then have missed the main point. Prices fell during this period because of increasing efficiency, particularly in transportation and agriculture. This was the pay-off to long years of investing in Europe itself, in North America, in Australia, and in Argentina, so that large-scale import of cheap cereals and meat became possible. The relative decline of the railroad boom was followed by the rapid rise of new, more productive industries, and consequently of better-paid work opportunities.[62] It was not the seizure of new territories in the jungles of North Borneo or the sandy wastes of the Sahara that made much difference, even though on a world map such areas loomed large.

Eric Hobsbawm points out that the 1870s were a real turning point for the standard of living of ordinary working-class Britons, precisely during the years of the "Great Depression." It was largely because of falling food prices and the general deflation that this occurred, and because new products became available that improved nutrition and general living conditions.[63] It was in the 1880s and 1890s, too, that for the first time, infant mortality, a key indicator of general well-being, began to drop (see Table 4-4). Available records indicate little if any progress in this area in the early and mid-nineteenth century, but a significant improvement after that, particularly in the continental part of Western Europe which had been worse off than England at mid-century. The infant mortality increase from the early 1850s to the early 1870s was probably largely due to better reporting of infant mortality, but in part it probably also reflected a drop in health standards as more people moved into the overcrowded urban slums of that period. If so, the small improvement from the early 1870s to the early 1890s would be all the more significant because industrialization and urbanization continued. The progress in the two decades that followed, of course, was much more dramatic, but it built on the progress that had preceded it.

Another clear indicator of the fact that economic growth did not stop, but merely slowed during the "Great Depression" is the average rate of overall economic expansion during those years (see Table 4-5). In the United Kingdom, France, and even more in Germany, the decades of the 1870s and 1880s

TABLE 4-4
**Average Yearly Infant (under one year old)
Mortality per 1,000 Infants**[64]

	England and Wales	France	Germany	Massachusetts *
1850–1854	143	160	292	131
1870–1874	154	185	307	170
1890–1894	149	170	224	163
1910–1914	109	120	163	117

* There are no available figures for the United States as a whole. Massachusetts was, however, much better off than much of the country, particularly the South.

TABLE 4-5
**Average Annual Rate of Economic Growth for
Twenty-Year Periods**[65]

	United Kingdom		France		Germany		United States	
	GNP	GNP/ Capita	GNP	GNP/ Capita	NNP*	NNP/ Capita	GNP	GNP/ Capita
1850/1854 to 1870/1874	2.2%	1.5%	1.9%	1.6%	2.9%	1.8%	—	—
1870/1874 to 1890/1894	1.7%	0.8%	1.3%	1.0%	2.1%	1.1%	4.4%	2.1%
1890/1894 to 1910/1913	1.9%	1.0%	1.1%	1.0%	2.9%	1.5%	4.1%	2.2%

* Net national product (NNP) is measured somewhat differently from gross national product, but its rate of change is virtually the same and it can therefore serve as a highly comparable index of economic growth.

were marked by a slower growth rate, and in Germany, by virtual stagnation for nine of these years. There is no evidence to indicate that this happened in the United States. What is more interesting about the data, however, is that German economic growth after 1883 was sufficiently rapid to make average 1870/1874 to 1890/1894 growth quite respectable. In the next two decades German average GNP/capita yearly growth was fully 50 percent higher than that of the United Kingdom and France. Yet, it was the United Kingdom that was the champion imperialist power of the era, both in its holdings of overseas colonies and in foreign investment; and though France was a distant second, it was markedly ahead of Germany in these areas. The United States, for its part, was only a minor imperialist power and overseas investor at this time, but it had its huge frontier to develop. In other words, the slowdown of the 1873 to 1896 period was not so dramatic as to threaten the still-growing capitalist economies. Standards of living improved during these years, and the return to a somewhat faster rate of growth (pronounced in Germany, slight in the United Kingdom, and nonexistent in France and the United States) in the 1890s could not have had any meaningful relationship to the imperial expansion of this period, whose fruits, if any, would have taken longer to mature.

This reality, however, was not self-evident, nor were the root causes of continued industrial change and economic growth, for in periods of financial panic, there is intense pressure on governments to act in dramatic and obvious ways. The fact that Western governments were increasingly subjected to middle-class and business interests, a sign of greater democracy, made them all the more likely to respond to such demands for rapid relief.

What, then, was the underlying reality? It can be grasped by looking at education statistics for the United States, Great Britain, France, and Germany in the early twentieth century. Though these figures post-date the period we are immediately interested in, they reflect the rather different types of educational systems which characterized these countries in the latter part of the nineteenth century.

In 1910, the first year for which complete data are available for all these countries, the primary school age population of France was 14 percent of the total population, of Great Britain 15 percent, of Germany 16 percent, and of the United States 20 percent. These figures are not dramatically different and reflect a difference in age structure more than in distinct policy. But if the number of secondary school and university students is compared to the number of primary school students, the startling picture shown in Table 4-6 emerges.

Germany, even more than the United States, was training a much larger number of secondary school students than were the other major powers, more than three times as many as Great Britain and more than four times as many as France, proportionately to their populations. The United States, while having a high, if not the highest ratio of secondary school students, was much more advanced than France or Germany in putting students through higher education. In those days, secondary education included substantial amounts of mathematics and science, and both Germany and the United States were far better supplied with technically skilled workers, engineers, and scientifically

TABLE 4-6
Education in 1910[66]

	Ratio of Secondary School Students to Primary School Students in 1910	Ratio of University Students to Primary School Students in 1910
Germany	0.0985 (= 9.85%)	0.0069 (= 0.69%)
United States	0.0605	0.0194
Great Britain	0.0295	— *
France	0.0223	0.0073

* Though there are no data for Great Britain at this time, it is unlikely it was more advanced than the other European countries. As late as 1930, Great Britain's university attendance ratio was less than two-thirds that of the United States in 1910.

literate populations than France and the United Kingdom. This was probably one of the main causes of the differential rates of economic growth, particularly when Germany is compared with the two other European powers, for none of them had the vast spaces and natural resources of the United States.

It went further than school systems. A look at the leading growth industries of the late nineteenth century shows how dependent they were on technological and scientific research, and how much further ahead the Germans were in these fields than the French or English.

The cutting edge of new industrial technology in the last quarter of the nineteenth century, the equivalent of the information and electronic industry 100 years later, was the chemical industry. If, following economic historian David Landes, one defines the chemical industry broadly and includes the advances made in metallurgy, the number of new technologies and materials available for manufacturing at this time or immediately before it makes an impressive list. The two most important were the Solvay process of alkali manufacture and the synthesis of organic compounds. The first was critical for the production of soap (a commodity that was coming into high demand with the new, higher standards of living and cleanliness to which the masses were becoming accustomed), textiles, and paper. The latter revolutionized dye-making for cloth. Scientific work leading to these advances took place mostly in Great Britain, France, Belgium, and Germany; but it was the Germans who systematically encouraged further research and development and became the leaders in the new chemical industry. By the early twentieth century, the organic chemical revolution was leading to a wide variety of new products—from better explosives to lacquers, photographic plates and film, artificial fibers, cellophane, and, in 1909, the first plastics, most of which were originally produced in Germany.[67]

The story of the development of the organic chemical industry is revealing. The first step was actually taken by an Englishman, William Henry Perkin, in 1856, though the first patents were taken out simultaneously by the English and Germans in 1869. By 1873 German production had surpassed Britain's in the key new product, alizarin. Between 1886 and 1900 the six largest German firms in this business took out 948 *British* patents, while the six largest British firms took out eighty-six. From the 1860s on, German polytechnics with government support were educating organic chemists, and at the University of Munich alone in 1871 there were fifty research students in the field while in all of the United Kingdom there was not a single university chair in organic chemistry.[68]

This was hardly a matter of spontaneous development, for in Germany the state, beginning with the independent states before unification and then the German imperial government after 1871, systematically fostered its technical and scientific schools and helped make the necessary connections between investment banks and industrialists in the new fields. The government also encouraged the formation of large firms and cartels to coordinate industrial development in key sectors. (This foreshadowed the role of the Japanese government in the continuing Japanese economic miracle of the latter twentieth century.) Samuel Lilley reached the heart of the issue when he wrote:

> In Britain three generations of 'practical men' had been making very good profits, and the role played by science in even a small proportion of these was far from obvious. The methods that had made Britain the workshop of the world could surely be expected to keep her so. Why take a risky gamble (as it would seem) on the brainstorms of labora-tory egg-heads? The Germans, on the other hand, had no hope of overcoming the disadvantages of a late start, except by maximum use of science and by concentrating, when possible, on industries based on science. Industrial leadership was put in the hands of scientists, not financiers; and even the banks had their scientific advisers.[69]

The world had changed since the first Industrial Revolution, but the British seemed unaware of this.

The other vital change in industrial structure in the last three decades of the nineteenth century was the development of the steel industry. Here, because of Britain's substantial and well-established lead in iron manufacturing, and because solutions to manufacturing steel were more a matter of adapting pre-viously known scientific principles than of making new discoveries, Great Brit-ain kept its lead longer. But as further advances in technology and mechaniza-tion of labor were made, the Germans and Americans pulled ahead.[70] In 1880, the United Kingdom was still the world's premier steel maker. In the next thirty years its production increased by a factor of 5.1, while that of Germany increased nineteenfold, and that of the United States twentyfold. By that time Germany produced twice as much steel as the United Kingdom, and the United States produced four times as much.[71]

Finally, in the last part of the century, an entirely new industry developed based on the use of electricity. Here, too, the Americans and Germans led, for the same reasons. In 1913 German electrical power output was almost twice as high as that of the United Kingdom and France put together.[72] And though the United States, a leader in the widespread use of electricity through the inventions of Edison and others, generated over three times as much electric power in 1912 as Germany, German output of electrical machinery was almost as big as that of the United States. In international trade, German exports dominated and were three times those of the United States.[73] This not only had implications for the improvement of energy production and distribution, but also for a host of related metallurgical, chemical, communications, and consumer industries as well as for the ultimate military potential of the indus-trial powers.

Table 4-7 consolidates some of the data discussed above and demonstrates the trends of the late nineteenth and early twentieth century.

But despite the increasingly obvious contributions of education, scientific research, and technological solutions to industrial and other economic prob-lems, the diplomatic and military race for imperial growth continued, even as

TABLE 4-7
Industrial Production, Key Indicators, 1870–1910[74]

	Steel (thousands of metric tons)				Sulfuric Acid* (thousands of metric tons)				Total Industrial Production Index, with 1870 = 100			
	U.K.	France	Ger.	U.S.	U.K.	France	Ger.	U.S.	U.K.	France	Ger.	U.S.
1870	334†	84	126	69	590	125§	75	—	100	100	100	100
1880	1,316	389	690	1,270	900	200‡	130	—	125	124	137	168
1890	3,636	683	2,135	4,344	870	—	420	—	157	143	210	284
1900	4,980	1,565	6,461	10,205	1,010	625	703	1,180¶	199	170	321	400
1910	6,776	3,413	13,100	25,752	1,082£	900£	1,727£	2,049∫	213	203	452	688

* Sulfuric acid production is an excellent indicator of the level of production of the chemical industry as a whole.

†, for 1871
‡, for 1878
§, for 1867
£, for 1913
¶, for 1899
∫, for 1909

the world was running out of new colonies to conquer, and long after profit-able new ones had been claimed. Combined with nationalism, this race made the great powers and many lesser ones behave as if such adventures and military posturing were a more important source of national well-being than basic development of human and industrial capital within their own territories. Thus, though it would be very difficult to demonstrate that their reasoning was entirely rational, the leaders of the Western world behaved as if they were obedient to the dictates of Marxist-Leninist theory, and plunged their miracu-lously growing, prosperous societies into a series of devastating wars.

The European World System

By the end of the nineteenth century the West had completed the construc-tion of what amounted to a vast world system encompassing all of the globe except for a few remote and thinly populated zones. Begun 400 years before at the start of the European expansion, this system had now reached its phys-ical limits. At the core it was dominated by four great powers: the United Kingdom, Germany, France, and the United States. There were also some other core societies, smaller, but equally developed and rather similar in social structure, culture, and level of industrialization.

The large periphery was dominated either directly, as colonies, or through investment and control of key sectors of its economies. The gap between the manufacturing, urbanized, wealthy core societies and the primary exporting, rural, poor, weak peripheral societies was immense, and seemed to Westerners at that time insurmountable. Even societies that were not directly ruled by the West, with the exception of Japan, were so subject to economic and political pressure from the West that they were at best merely semi-independent.

Between the core and periphery was that category Immanuel Wallerstein has called the "semiperiphery."[75] This consisted of societies that were eco-nomically and socially backward, but not as backward as most of the periphery (though we will discuss major exceptions to this in the next chapter). These societies were also organized into states powerful enough to play an interna-tional role, and they could not be pushed around as easily as the peripheral states. Some in the semiperiphery were rising new powers—Japan, Russia, and Italy. Others were declining old powers—Spain and Austria-Hungary. (The percentage of world population, by continent, in each category of country during the first decade of the twentieth century, is shown in Table 4-8. It gives a good idea of who controlled the system and to what extent.)

There remained some peripheral societies organized as decrepit empires. The Ottoman Empire and China were theoretically independent major states, but the former was being parceled out to outsiders, bit by bit, and the latter was being held up by the fact that no one had yet decided how to dismember it. Portugal, too, once a great empire, held on to bits of Asia and substantial

TABLE 4-8

Distribution of World Population in the First Decade of the Twentieth Century[76]

	Europe	Americas	Africa	Asia
Major Core	United Kingdom 10% France 9% Germany 13%	United States 52%	Colonies of the core: of the U.K. 50% of France 23% of Germany 7% of Belgium 6%	Colonies of the core: of the U.K. 34% of France 2% of the U.S. 1% of the Netherlands 5%
Minor core	6%	Canada 4%		
Semi-periphery	Austria-Hungary 11% Italy 8% Spain 4% Russian Empire (including Siberia) 31%		Colonies of Spain, Italy, and Portugal 7%	Japan and its colonies, Taiwan and Korea 7%
Periphery, the Balkans and Portugal	8%	The rest of the Americas, mostly independent but peripheral 44%	"Independent" periphery Liberia and Ethiopia 7%	"Independent" periphery China 44% Ottoman Empire 2% Others 5%
	100%	100%	100%	100%

territories in Africa, but it was so poor and weak and economically dependent on the United Kingdom as to be a peripheral society.

Most of the colonial holdings in the world were held by the major core powers, though the United States was a very minor holder of colonies. Two of the minor core powers, Belgium and the Netherlands, also held large overseas empires. The semiperipheral powers, particularly Russia and Japan, were vigorously expansionist at this time, and Italy was trying to be. Spain held pieces of its old empire and a few new African territories, while Austria-Hungary was trying to maintain its hold over its Balkan territories.

The figures from Table 4-8 are collapsed into a single chart in Table 4-9 to show the distribution of population in the world between 1900 and 1910. The four main core states and the three big semiperipheral states, seven powers in all, directly controlled 53 percent of the world's population, and indirectly controlled much of the remainder, particularly China.

The key fact about this world system was that it was not a united political unit, but rather one that was bound by trade and investment flows, and dominated by the few closely interacting, competing, and similar Western nation-states at its core. The diplomatic and military system of interacting independent states that had developed in Europe through the seventeenth and eighteenth centuries had now become the model according to which the entire world behaved. The cultural orientation of Europe that had grown for the thousand years before the twentieth century was now accepted as the dominant, if hardly the only one in the world. Science and technology harnessed by capitalist firms for the benefit of their profits seemed to be the only progressive and modern or even possible way of attaining Western levels of prosperity and power. The nationalist state appeared to be the best way of organizing

TABLE 4-9
**Division of the World's Population into Political
Categories, 1900–1910**

Core societies	15% (13% in the four main core societies)
Semiperipheral societies and their colonies	18% (15% in the Russian, Japanese, and Austro-Hungarian Empires)
Colonies of the core (not counting colonization within Europe)	28% (25% controlled by the four main core societies, and almost 20% by the United Kingdom alone)
Other peripheral (independent and semi-independent) societies	39% (about 25% in China)

societies, and of supporting the businesses on which each state's prosperity was based. If there were a few voices raised in opposition to the capitalist world system, both inside the core and outside, they were still weak and there was little indication that they might soon triumph in a number of areas, and thus threaten the entire system with collapse.

It seemed that a privileged few, the Westerners, had inherited most of the earth and now had it at their disposal to exploit, enjoy, and refashion as they wished. To Westerners in 1900 it was evident that they were superior beings who merited this distinction, and that it was impossible to change the situation which was certain to remain intact for centuries. Why they were so enormously wrong, and why the twentieth century would actually see the near elimination of the Western core's political monopoly, will be the topic of the remainder of the book. Knowing what happened in the remainder of the century, however, must not blind us to how imposing the structure of core rule looked in that first decade of the twentieth century.

CHAPTER 5

Social Structures in the Early Twentieth Century

*I*nternal class structures, or the distribution of power and wealth within particular societies, are related to the international distribution of power and wealth between societies. Class structures in core, semiperipheral, and peripheral societies tend to be distinct from one another, particularly in core and peripheral societies. This is true today, but it was even truer at the start of our century. The discussion that follows will be limited to roughly the first decade and a half of the twentieth century, and will begin with an examination of the pattern of stratification between the various countries in the world system of that time. Only after this will internal stratification patterns within the various types of societies be examined.

Core, Periphery, and Semiperiphery

Variation along three analytically distinct, though correlated dimensions defined societies' positions in the world system. First, there was sheer political and military power, the ability of a state to impose its will on others. The United Kingdom, with its great fleet, its string of colonies, and its advanced manufacturing and trading economy, was the world's strongest power in the years just before World War I. But it was far less dominant than it had been fifty, or even thirty years earlier. Rapidly growing Germany, with its larger population base, its more rapidly growing economy, and a larger army, was a serious competitor. The giant United States was potentially far stronger, though it had not yet entered the international arena as a first-class imperialist power. The fourth great power, France, was distinctly weaker than the first three, but its rich economy and overseas empire still made it important.

At the other extreme there were the colonies of the imperial powers, ranging from giant ones such as India and the Dutch East Indies, both of which were much bigger than the countries that ruled them, to insignificant dots of land with small populations, few resources, weakly developed economies, and no international role at all. Even big colonies, however, were not independent, and their people had no real power in the world system.

Between the big imperialist powers and colonial societies were a wide variety of independent and semi-independent states. Some, like China, Persia, or Thailand, were formally independent but without much international power because they had to follow the dictates of the great powers who were threatening to colonize them and carve them into occupied zones. Some of the Latin American states, or the Ottoman Empire, had somewhat more international influence, but still had very little freedom of action except in restricted local matters. Two minor European core states, Belgium and the Netherlands, had their own empires and some international standing, but they were limited by their small home populations. Other minor European core states were accepted as fully independent entities, but had little influence. On the other hand, some relatively more backward states in the semiperiphery were larger and could make up for their economic weakness by having strong governments capable of mobilizing considerable resources for diplomacy and war. Russia, Austria-Hungary, and Japan were certainly major powers that were feared and respected by their neighbors even if their economies were not on a par with the most advanced core societies.

International strength, then, was a function of a state's level of economic development, sheer size, and degree of internal cohesion. Giant China was an insignificant power because it was very poor and its government barely held the country together. Russia, though poor, had a sizable industrial base and a strong, well-organized government. Japan was particularly well-unified for a relatively poor economy, though by the twentieth century it had already made great progress toward industrializing itself.

The degree of economic development, though somewhat correlated to political and military power, must be treated as a distinct variable. The most developed economies of the world were highly industrialized and had less than half their labor force involved in agriculture. Moreover, they were diversified producers of a wide range of high-technology goods, and their productivity was great enough to give their populations high standards of living. The United States in the first decade of the twentieth century had an average yearly per capita GNP of about $4,450 (translated into 1985 U.S. dollars). The European core economies had yearly per capita GNP figures ranging from slightly below $2,000 to just below $3,000. Most of the rest of the world's per capita GNPs ranged from below $200 a year (India's was about $200) to just above $500 (Mexico's was about $540). The European semiperipheral economies—Russia, Italy, Spain, and Austria-Hungary—were richer than most peripheral economies but still much poorer than the core. (Italy's per capita GNP was about $970; Russia's $670.)[1]

Comparisons of the proportion of the labor force still involved in agriculture show that only one core economy, Sweden (at that time probably the poorest economy that could be placed in this category), with 55 percent, was the only one in which more than half the labor force was employed in agriculture. Among peripheral societies, on the other hand, most had 70 percent to 80 percent in agriculture. Only exceptional cases like Argentina (certainly the richest of the peripheral economies though still poorer than Sweden) had less than half their labor force in agriculture. Semiperipheral economies were highly variable, but on the whole they were still not yet sufficiently industrialized to have labor distributions very different from peripheral societies. Russia, for example, was still about 80 percent peasant, and even Italy was 59 percent peasant.[2]

The third dimension determining a country's position in the world system was actually a derivative of its level of economic development. Because an important school of economists, the Latin American "dependency theorists," identify this as the key variable in shaping peripheral and core economies, it needs to be explored in some detail.[3] The dimension in question is the degree to which an economy was dependent on primary (that is, agricultural or raw material) exports. As they developed, peripheral economies tended to become increasingly tied to the world market as primary exporters, and this sometimes seemed to block their development as more diversified, manufacturing economies. On the other hand, the rich core economies were highly diversified and industrialized, and at least the major core countries relied more on manufactured, high-technology exports than on unprocessed, low-technology, primary ones. Dependency theorists (the idea originated among Central and Eastern European economists who observed how their countries had become peripheral to the growing capitalist world economy, but it was fully developed in the mid-twentieth century by Latin Americans) saw this as an explanation for the continued poverty of the peripheral world. Primary-product prices, they claimed, tend to deteriorate over time relative to the prices of manufactured goods because manufacturing countries have greater power to set prices. Also, manufacturing requires greater labor skills and large capital investments, while primary products can be extracted with less-skilled, poorly paid labor. Thus, it is more difficult to start new manufacturing industries.[4]

It is true that the lower the technological input into any product (and not all agricultural or mineral products fit this category), the more volatile its price tends to be because it is relatively easier to shift production to new areas. There is no need to train skilled labor forces or make large new investments to start up production. Sudden new demand for a particular product, say coffee in the nineteenth century or rubber in the late nineteenth century, can cause prices to surge and an export boom to develop in the producing areas. But sooner or later production will spread to other areas, and because the relatively low-skill, under-capitalized export regions will be unable to shift production to other items, they will experience deep economic depression. Foreign investors, originally attracted by the boom in primary exports, will simply pick up and leave, and domestic capital will have no choice but to flee as well, or remain in the same, decreasingly lucrative type of production.

The Brazilian dependency theorist Celso Furtado has shown that when coffee prices fell, there was a long-run tendency for Brazilian coffee producers to grow even more coffee rather than switch to another product. They had no viable alternative. Overproduction then further depressed prices.[5] But had Brazil possessed a more balanced economy, as did the core countries, investors would have had a wide range of alternatives, and a skilled, adaptable labor force with which to work.

What happened to coffee, rubber, cotton, lumber, or any number of such products, could also happen to mineral exports, even though some of them required more skilled labor inputs. Generally, however, in peripheral economies, skilled labor for such production came in the form of foreign technicians and managers (that is, from core societies) while the physical labor was performed by low-paid, unskilled domestic workers. Mineral discoveries in other parts of the world, or the invention of substitutes, could cause a mining region to fall on sudden hard times. Then the domestic unskilled labor would be dismissed, and the foreign technicians would move to another part of the world, leaving the peripheral exporting region in ruins.

Historically, it is not true that primary products have tended to deteriorate in price relative to manufactured goods.[6] But that is almost beside the point, because sudden swings in primary-product prices leading to spectacular booms and busts are at least as damaging as long-range price deterioration to sound economic growth.

There were, of course, regions of core economies dependent on low-technology products, and they could suffer many of the same consequences. But at the very least they had some prospects of help from their governments, and some claim to relief, because they could apply domestic political pressure. But if the region in question happened to be part of a colony, or of a distant tropical peripheral state, there was little it could do to obtain help from those who dominated the world economy.

There is one more point. Economies that depended too much on primary exports also developed local elites whose position was based on control of these products. They then had an interest in maintaining their economy in the same condition. If the area in question was a colony, the colonial power would try to prevent the emergence of local industrialization in order to protect its home industries in Europe. But even if the area was part of an independent peripheral state, local elites making a living from the export trade and enjoying well-established connections with traders in core economies had every incentive to maintain export economies even in times of trouble. That was where their investments, knowledge, and power lay—not in risky new economic diversification ventures.

No one of these points might have been decisive on its own, but together they formed what became a classic syndrome, a vicious circle of dependent, export-oriented economic development that never seemed to produce permanent advances in the standard of living or in diversified industrialization. It was not primary production as such, or even dependency on a fairly small range of export products, that was dangerous. If agricultural production, as in the United States, was based on the latest sophisticated technological advances, farmers could adapt quite easily to shifts in the market. And if overall demand for agricultural labor decreased, as it did over time throughout the advanced parts of the world, there were alternative occupations in industry and service sectors. But if primary production was based on poorly paid, unskilled, low-technology production in an economy that had no other significant opportunities, primary export dependence could act as a block to economic development.

Taking all this into account, it is useful to include a country's relative degree of dependence on a few primary exports as a further indicator of its status in the world system. But this indicator, even more than the others suggested, must be used with caution.

Combining the various indicators discussed above, it is possible to construct a table showing how several major examples of core, peripheral and semiperipheral countries ranked. Table 5-1 summarizes the arguments made so far and gives a clearer picture of what these terms mean.

There are few surprises in this table. Though the United States, France, and Germany still had large agricultural populations by late twentieth-century standards, they were below 50 percent and falling at the time when most of the world still had over 70 percent of its labor force in agriculture. Argentina, an unusually rich and well-developed peripheral economy, stands out as an exceptional case; but outside the southern cone of Latin America, only core societies had such small agricultural labor forces.

As might be expected, semiperipheral societies produced mixed statistics. Russia was still heavily rural, but it was sufficiently industrialized to have a per capita GNP significantly higher than that of most peripheral economies. Because this industrial base was in such a huge country, it translated into a significant degree of international power for Russia. Japan, on the other hand, was quite a bit poorer than Russia but less rural and already much less dependent on primary exports. As in the case of Russia, its most significant trait was the internal strength and cohesion of its government, and even more than in Russia, the cultural unity and allegiance of its population. This made Japan a power greater than its economy might have suggested, and it also proved to be a major factor in allowing Japan to develop its own, diversified, technologically sophisticated industry as the twentieth century advanced.

The column on primary exports produces the most surprises. Rich, advanced Denmark was highly dependent on a few primary exports. But because it was so well developed in other ways, its agriculture was highly advanced technically, and it was able to industrialize internally for its own home market by using the profits of its agriculture. Denmark was not unique in this respect. The overseas English settler colonies of Australia, Canada, and New Zealand were very similar. They were rich, advanced, but highly dependent on primary exports. Australia's per capita GNP in the first decade of the twentieth century was $3,220, which made it the world's second richest country; and Canada's per capita GNP of $3,150 made it the world's third richest.[7] Despite the fact that both these countries were primary exporters and that much of their capital was still controlled by outsiders (mostly British), they were politically independent, had highly skilled, educated populations, significant domestic industry, and could be considered as minor core societies in most respects. They were, along with the Scandinavian countries, proof that dependence on primary exports does not, by itself, produce stagnant economies and poverty.

TABLE 5-1
International Stratification in the Early Twentieth Century[8]

Category	Country	Population in 1900 (in millions)	Percent of Labor Force in Agriculture in about 1900 (includes forestry and fishing)	Per Capita GNP, Yearly Average 1900–1910, in 1985 U.S. Dollars	Percent of Total Exports Made up of the Two Leading Primary Exports in 1913	Degree of International Power
Major core	Great Britain	37	9	2,810	8 (coal; no significant second)	very high
	United States	76	37	4,450	29 (cotton; petroleum products)	very high
	Germany	56	34	2,140	8 (coal; sugar)	very high
	France	38	43	2,480	7 (wool; wine)	very high
Minor core	Denmark	2.4	44	2,450	87 (meat; dairy products)	low
	Netherlands	5.1	33	2,310	19 (cereals; copper)	medium
	Sweden	5.1	55	1,710	34 (timber; iron ore)	low

Category	Country	Population in 1900 (in millions)	Percent of Labor Force in Agriculture in about 1900 (includes forestry and fishing)	Per Capita GNP, Yearly Average 1900-1910, in 1985 U.S. Dollars	Percent of Total Exports Made up of the Two Leading Primary Exports in 1913	Degree of International Power
Semiperiphery	Russia	129	78	670	51 (cereals; lumber)	high
	Japan	44	71	470	25 (silk; no significant second)	high
Rich periphery	Argentina	5	40	1,470	58 (cereals; meat)	low
Periphery	Brazil	18	73	420	79 (coffee; rubber)	low
	Egypt	10	71	440	87 (cotton; cotton seed)	very low
	Gold Coast (Ghana)	1.5	70 - 80	440	77 (cocoa; gold)	very low
	Dutch East Indies (Indonesia)	38	70 +	280	40 (sugar; petroleum)	very low

Only one more seeming anomaly needs to be explained. The Dutch East Indies (now Indonesia) exported a wider array of primary products than most other peripheral economies, so that its first two products only made up 40 percent of its exports. But its other exports were almost entirely limited to a fairly small number of tropical agricultural goods and minerals, so that its low number in that particular column is not as meaningful as it looks.[9]

The poverty, dependence, and lopsided development of peripheral societies perpetuated a problem which made it that much more difficult for them to break out of this pattern. They were poorly integrated, and in many instances their entry into the world economic system seemed to accentuate their regional and ethnic divisions. Primary exports tended to be limited to a particular geographic area or enclave where they grew well, or where they existed as mineral deposits. In physically large peripheral economies, such as those of Latin America or the Dutch East Indies or some of the large African colonies like the Belgian Congo, this meant that investments from the core went exclusively toward developing the mines or plantations of a particular enclave, as well as the transportation systems to those areas, but that little or nothing was invested in creating unified transportation networks for the country as a whole. Not general economic development, but the exploitation of particular, localized resources was the aim of these investments, and as such, they further exacerbated local cultural and physical divisions. While certain areas were the subject of intensive investment and economic development, vast neighboring parts of the same country were left relatively untouched and served as cheap labor reserves. In such areas, not only was there little construction of roads, railroads, or ports, but very little investment in schools, efficient administration, or new economic projects of any sort.

For example, in Brazil:

> Between 1870 and 1900 [railway] lines were opened in nearly every state. . . . British capital was invested in many of the larger private lines. . . . One of the fundamental weaknesses of Brazilian railway development was the lack of any real national integration of the system. . . . A number of different gauges were used, making it impossible to interchange rolling stock, and even today this problem persists. Since most railways were built to bring produce down from the hinterlands to the ports, no railways ever linked the various regions of Brazil with one another.[10]

That is, Brazil's southern coffee area, its Amazon rubber area, and its very poor, virtually subsistence agriculture and sugar-producing northeastern area each operated independently. The lack of interregional transportation has been used to explain a phenomenon that would otherwise defy explanation: namely, that even though the coffee area was short of labor and the northeast was overpopulated and poor, the coffee area imported labor from Europe (mostly from Italy) while underemployed northeasterners remained in their own region.

If the case of Brazil was extreme, this general situation was typical. In Colombia:

> Railway construction divided the country further and made each of its component parts look outward. Since it was cheaper to bring merchandise to Medellín from London than from Bogotá, each commercial region . . . was more or less independent and what it did not produce it brought in from abroad.[11]

Had the governments of Brazil, or Colombia, or of numerous other similar countries been strong and rich enough, they might have built the infrastructures to unite their countries, and they might have used more of the profits from their export sectors to finance general economic development. But their internal divisions and weak state machineries made this impossible, so that the effect was similar to that in colonies where there was not even any intention of effectively integrating and developing the entire country. The contrast with the self-governing, homogeneous, united nation-states of the core, or Japan, points to the critical intervening factor that explains why in some cases being a primary exporter of a few goods worsened regional divisions and hurt further economic development, while in other cases it could be used to promote general economic growth and greater national strength.

All this shows how peripherality was manifested by a whole series of traits which interacted with one another and could then become a continued cause of poverty and dependence. Later in the century, it became the goal of most peripheral societies to break out of this pattern, and the different strategies used to do this make up much of the dramatic variety in global twentieth-century history. Before discussing this, however, it is necessary to show how internal class structures also varied between the several categories of societies, and how these were in part related to position in the world system and to levels of economic development, and so were further causes of the "peripheral syndrome."

Internal Stratification Patterns

Virtually every state in the modern world once had many ethnic groups within its boundaries. Most still do. In nation-states with diversified and developed economies, however, these ethnic groups have invariably been brought into close contact with each other for long periods of time, and this has caused many groups to merge with others and vanish as distinct entities. In the highly developed core societies of the early twentieth century there remained fewer distinct ethnic groups than in the noncore societies. Even in the United States, an immigrant society with many ethnic groups, the Anglo-Saxons were taken as the generally accepted model of proper adaptive behavior, and over time it was the English language and English ways of behaving that formed the core of a more or less unified "American" culture.

Still, ethnic homogeneity was far from perfect, and the existence of competing ethnicities, as well as of competing religions (in practice, where religion and ethnicity were split on identical lines, conflict was worse), was one of the bases of organized domestic political conflict. This was particularly true when an ethnic minority was composed chiefly of individuals in lower, poorer economic classes. Eastern and southern European immigrants in the United States, southern blacks also in the United States, Irish Catholic Celts in the United Kingdom, and Slavs in the Prussian part of Germany were the main examples. In each case, ethnic and religious (cultural) differences coincided with class (economic) distinctions to create a high potential for dissatisfaction. This normally developed when some of the more successful members of the "lower" ethnic group, recognizing that their upward mobility was blocked by the fact that they belonged to a poorly considered ethnic group, turned around to organize their poorer fellows in order to win concessions from the better-established and stronger ethnic, religious, and class groups in the society.[12]

Similarly, there were certain regions in every core society which were richer, and others which were poorer. This produced regionally based ideologies (regional nationalisms) which could become seriously disruptive if they were associated with cultural—that is, ethnic and religious—differences. The most serious such problem in the major core societies at this time was that of the Irish in the United Kingdom. Another example was the strong feeling among southerners in the United States that they were almost part of a distinct nation which should have won its independence during the Civil War but was unfortunately defeated. In Germany, too, in the southern and western regions there were areas in which distinct versions of German were spoken and the people felt a residual Bavarian or Rhinelander sense of local nationalism. This was heightened by the fact that these areas were Catholic whereas the dominant Prussians were Protestants.

In a sense, each core society was like a miniature world system, with its own core and periphery, its dominant and subordinate cultures, and at least some potential for severe conflict based on these divisions. Among the major core countries, cultural divisiveness was strongest in the United Kingdom and weakest in France.

But however grave even the United Kingdom's problems were (they resulted in the eventual separation of an Irish Free State from the U.K.), most peripheral societies faced far greater cultural divisions. In most of them, whether or not they were colonies, the ruling states had not yet achieved cultural legitimacy. That is, various ethnic, religious, and regionally based groups did not recognize the authority of the state even if they had to accept it. The fact that many peripheral societies were economically malintegrated— that is, that certain parts of the society interacted more with core portions of the world than with their own hinterlands—did not help promote loyalty to the state. The cultural malintegration of peripheral elites and masses was but one example of this tendency. Furthermore, in much of the peripheral world, agents of the core powers and other foreign interests deliberately pitted different ethnic, religious, or regional groups against one another. This tactic facilitated the foreign manipulation of peripheral areas. The pattern was most evident in the European colonies in Asia and Africa, and it represents the main difference between cultural divisions in peripheral societies and core areas: in the former, outside power and influence could effectively manipulate differences in order to control local politics. While the strength of core societies made such manipulation virtually impossible within their boundaries, the weakness of peripheral societies made outside manipulation both easy and effective.

For example, while the British could use Muslim-Hindu hostility in India to strengthen colonial rule, India was in no position to use Irish-British hostilities to manipulate British politics. In fact, not even Germany could engage in such manipulation within the United Kingdom, any more than the United Kingdom could split Bavarians from Prussians in order to weaken Germany. And while the European powers (chiefly the United Kingdom and France) had tried to weaken the United States by supporting the South during the Civil War of 1860–1865, the attempt had failed; by 1900, such a policy would have been absurd. Germany's manipulation of German immigrants in the United States during World War I, from 1914 to 1918, proved almost totally ineffective.

Even though peripheral societies were the exact opposite of the culturally well-integrated core societies, and substantial majorities of their populations did not participate in single national cultures that corresponded to the boundaries of existing states, this was considered the normal state of affairs. In most peripheral areas little effort was being made to create strong national cultures that would integrate populations and legitimize existing states.

Semiperipheral societies were on the whole somewhere between the very poorly integrated peripheral societies and the highly integrated core ones. Japan, a notable exception, had essentially no ethnic or religious conflicts within its borders, and virtually all its people shared a strong sense of nationalism. At the other extreme in the semiperiphery, Austria-Hungary suffered from endemic conflict between its two major cultures, the German-Austrians and the Magyars of Hungary. Conflicts also existed among a host of minor ethnic groups—Slovaks, Slovenes, Poles, Czechs, Italians, Croats, Serbs, Romanians, Jews, and Gypsies—both among themselves and with the two major groups. Eventually these conflicts destroyed the Austro-Hungarian state. Russia, with its many minorities, was nevertheless 70 percent Slavic, but White Russians and Ukrainians were not identical to the Great Russians. Italy and Spain, too, had long-standing cultural and political conflicts between regions. Both Russia (late in the decade 1910–1920 and in the early 1920s) and Spain (in the 1930s) were to go through severe civil wars which were partly produced by regional and ethnic conflicts before their national unities were assured. Even today, similar conflicts persist in both countries though at lower levels of intensity.[13]

In short, core societies were substantially integrated cultural units at the start of the twentieth century; most peripheral societies were not; and semiperipheral societies were in the process of becoming so, but with varying degrees of success.

Beyond culturally based stratification, the various types of societies had distinctive class structures, too. These are treated in the three subsections that follow.

Core Societies

The class structure of core societies in the early 1900s was the product of generations of industrialization and the triumph of capitalism over older, more agrarian forms of economic and political organization. Though in Europe titled descendants of the old aristocracies continued to hold prestige, unless they were allied to rich capitalist families by business or marriage ties, or unless they had managed to convert their landed wealth into capital of their own, their position was precarious. On the other hand, those who had made money in industry and commerce were increasingly recognized as the obvious elite, whatever their ancestry. In Germany, France, and the United Kingdom, aristocratic prestige was still valuable as an entrée into the army or some types of civil service positions; but in no core country was it an automatic guarantee of high position. This was even more true in the United States, where the incipient moneyed aristocracy, the great tycoons produced by the late-nine-teenth-century economic boom, could claim no more than one or two generations of money. Though everywhere the supposed ways of the old aristocrats were admired and aped by aspiring rich bourgeois, the material and political base of these aristocracies no longer existed. The illusion of continuity, and the adoption of (largely imaginary) feudal honor codes and virtues in the schools that trained the sons of the rich certainly cast a distinctive aura over this world, one that made arrogant nationalism and worship of military virtues all the more prominent, but which did not for that reflect the preindustrialized social organization it admired.

At the other end of the social scale, the bulk of the lower laboring class was no longer in agriculture but consisted of blue-collar manual laborers and lower-service workers, such as servants who lived largely in cities or towns and worked for the middle and upper classes. Better organized than the peasants of the past because they were better educated and lived in closer proximity to one another, the blue-collar class was seen as the main challenger to the existing order. In the early twentieth century strong unions and working-class socialist parties were just becoming solid competitors for power in the workplace and in the political arena, and to some this seemed to foreshadow the realization of Karl Marx's prophecy that eventually the working class would take power and create an entirely new social order.

In between the small, rich, capitalist elite and the working class, there was a large and diffuse middle class. At the top this consisted of proprietors of middle-sized enterprises, of managerial and professional groups, and of higher and middle civil servants. Then, too, there was a large lower-middle class of lesser white-collar employees, small shop owners, and clerical workers. These often identified with the middle class, though their wages and living conditions placed them in conditions no better than the working classes. But because their self-image as property owners (however small) or as holders of "respectable" bourgeois jobs made them look down on the working class, it was difficult for them to ally themselves with blue-collar workers for political action.

The still-large number of people in agriculture varied from the very rich, large landowners to the middling independent farmers to the many landless agricultural laborers and tenants at the bottom. Those at the top and in the middle could still exercise important political pressures, but they were viewed with much less alarm by the elite than were the urban working class because they did not seem to threaten the very legitimacy of capitalist property.

In terms of actual distribution of income and wealth, the United States in 1910 was the most egalitarian of the core societies, and England the least. In Wales and England 32,000 adults (0.2 percent of the adult population) owned 41 percent of all assets. In the United States, the top 1 percent only owned one-third of all assets. Similarly, in Great Britain the top 5 percent of the population earned 43 percent of all income, and in the United States the top 5 percent only earned 25 percent of all income.[14] This was the approximate range of the elite in core societies, and it is clear that whether in the United States or in Great Britain, a rather small number of people—the controllers of large industries, banks, commercial enterprises, and a few other key sectors of the economy—held a vastly disproportionate share of the wealth, and consequently, of political power as well. But it is important to remember how much larger, and how much more a rational, business-oriented elite this was than were the feudal lords and kings who had been preeminent only a few centuries earlier.

The middle class, however, was also powerful. They voted and held property, they managed many of the enterprises of the rich, and they filled important technical roles in the economy and government. Almost as socially conservative as the elite, and certainly as interested as the elite in maintaining the power and influence of their nations, they nevertheless firmly supported liberal democratic reforms which alone ensured their own political representation and access to higher education and possible advancement for their children.

Finally, the working class, though beginning to organize, was still disproportionately weak. Though they exerted influence by voting in elections or by striking from time to time, they were not yet a match for the upper- and middle-class political organizations.

Table 5-2, compiled from U.S. census data in 1910, shows the approximate distribution of these classes in that year.

The burning issue in the first decade of the twentieth century was the degree to which various classes would support their nation in case of war. Upper- and middle-class investors, managers, and civil servants had an obvious stake in the preservation of their countries' empires and international positions

TABLE 5-2
Class Structure in the United States, 1910[15]

Elite	(Not measured in census; but top 1 percent of population earned 15 percent of all income in 1913 and owned one-third of all assets in 1922)
Middle class	4,220,000 individuals in labor force, 11 percent of labor force
Lower-middle class	3,742,000 individuals in labor force, 10 percent of labor force
Working class	17,797,000 individuals in labor force, 48 percent of labor force
Farm owners and managers	6,163,000 individuals in labor force, 17 percent of labor force
Farm laborers and tenants	5,370,000 individuals in labor force, 14 percent of labor force

(though this was obviously less of an issue in the United States than it was in Europe). But working-class socialists were claiming that their followers had no investments, no power or privilege to maintain, and thus no interest in the increasingly hysterical nationalist competition inflaming the world. Elites feared that if their workers defected, they would find it impossible to mobilize for war, and revolutions might ensue in case of crisis. In the event, this proved to be entirely unfounded. National consciousness in the core was far too advanced to let working-class consciousness and interest get in the way.

Before the frenzied expansionism of the late nineteenth century there had been opposition to foreign expansion in all the core societies, primarily from those who saw no profit in getting involved abroad, but rather, only needless expense. The growing conviction that national survival depended on constant expansion of markets and sources of raw materials and primary goods changed this prospect and reduced the anti-imperialist sentiment. It proved so easy to take over vast domains that the costs did not seem important. As they began to be more apparent—for example, when the United Kingdom became involved in a long war in South Africa, or when Irish opposition to British rule threatened outright civil war—protest revived. But it took the immense cost of World War I to generate enough protest to change the policies of core societies, and later wars to convince majorities in the core that the game was not worth the price.

Peripheral Societies

Peripheral class structures were much more heterogeneous than those of the core. Generalizations about them, therefore, are more suspect. Some were very highly involved in the world system, but others had only recently been absorbed into it and were still lightly touched by commercialization of their economies. Also, traditional class structures and traditions varied from place to place so that, for example, comparing China in 1910 with Nigeria and Brazil is not as easy as comparing the several Western, industrialized core societies with one another. Nevertheless, some common patterns can be discerned precisely because greater or lesser involvement with the world system had created some similarities across the continents, and all peripheral societies shared the element of having within themselves traditions that conflicted with those newly created by outside influence. There were old and new classes, and as often as not these were hostile to one another. The best way to represent this is through a schematic table, such as Table 5-3, which shows an idealized,

TABLE 5-3
Peripheral Class Structure

Elite	Controllers of the land (landowners, authorities with power over the land, and—where they were present—foreign officials and investors)
New upper-middle class	Westernized intellectuals, civil-service and white-collar employees, Western-oriented merchants ("compradors," both foreign and native)
Old upper-middle class	Small landowners, officials of traditional pre-Western bureaucracies, the clergy
New lower-middle class	Clerical and service workers in foreign enterprises or the civil service
Old lower-middle class	Artisans, small, non-Western-oriented local merchants, prosperous peasants
New working class	Blue-collar workers in enclave cities and transportation networks, in the few industries, and in mines; nonagricultural servants in the enclaves
Agriculturalists	Small peasant owners, tenants, plantation or other hired laborers

though not unrealistic, picture of the class structure of a typical peripheral society.

A look at the class structure of one peripheral society, Mexico, which was highly developed and involved in the world system, shows the dramatic difference between core and periphery in population proportions in each class (see Table 5-4). These differences, of course, would seem even greater if a less developed, less export-oriented, and more traditional old agrarian society like China were compared to a core society.

If the upper segment of Mexican society is compared with that of its northern neighbor, the United States, it is striking how much more important landowners, both foreign and native, actually were than in the United States, where control of capital, not land, was the critical factor. In core societies, not only were there few foreigners in commanding positions, but the elites, for all that they were a very small proportion of the population, were relatively larger than in a country like Mexico, and they controlled far less of the total wealth. In general, the importance of a few landowners was typical of most peripheral societies. In colonies, these could be a combination of Europeans and traditional native aristocrats, but the effects were similar no matter which group was involved. In the end, whether the landlords were French planters in Algeria (who owned most of the best lands), United States citizens controlling sugar plantations in Cuba, British rubber planters in Malaya, Indian princes in India, Senegalese marabouts (Islamic priests who controlled the peanut growers) in Senegal, Brazilian coffee planters, Argentinian hacienda owners, or Romanian nobles on whose vast estates poor peasant sharecroppers grew

TABLE 5-4

Class Structure in Mexico, about 1900[16]

Elite	Thirty companies and 8,000 haciendas owned one-third of all the surface of Mexico, and a larger proportion of the useful land
New upper-middle class	(Managerial and professional, private and in civil service) 200,000 individuals and their dependents, 1.5 percent of the population
Rest of the middle classes combined	1,000,000 individuals and their dependents, 8 percent of the population
Working class	2,600,000 individuals and their dependents, 20 percent of the population
Agriculturalists	(Mostly peasants, most of them very poor) 9,100,000 individuals and their dependents, 70 percent of the population

wheat for export, the results were very similar. The more involved the local export economy with the world market, the stronger the position of these controllers of the land, and the more drastically inegalitarian the class structure. Greater involvement with the modern core's capitalist economy, then, created or at least strengthened a small elite and further subjected a large mass of dependent, often only half-free serfs, indentured laborers, or debt-ridden peasants who grew the export crop.[17]

In Mexico, for example, the fact that there had been haciendas since the sixteenth century did not prevent the majority of the land from still being controlled by village communities and small peasants in the early nineteenth century. But the booming export economy and the possibility of huge profits in the late nineteenth century led to the rapid decline of peasant and community control and to the seizure of lands by large landowners and foreign companies. By 1910, Mexican class structure was more unequal than at any time before.[18] Nor was Mexico's situation unique. Throughout much of the periphery in the early twentieth century, peasants were more exploited, less in control of their lands, and more dependent on their masters than they had been in earlier, less commercialized, and therefore less demanding times. This generalization may not hold for the slave plantation areas of the Atlantic in the sixteenth and seventeenth centuries, which were already entirely absorbed into the then-growing capitalist world system, but the observation is reasonable for vast parts of the Asian and African continents which escaped direct involvement with the European system until the late eighteenth and nineteenth centuries.

As the export sector of peripheral economies grew, so did the import of goods manufactured in the core. In order to handle the new exchange there had to be merchants familiar with Western and domestic markets, with the new products, and particularly with the new sources of credit and the peculiarities of the Westerners themselves. In other words, there had to be a class of middlemen to bridge the gap between the core-oriented financial and economic systems of the enclaves and the large mass of illiterate peasants or plantation workers.

In China, at the turn of the century, the members of this new class came largely from coastal cities dominated by European mercantile enterprises; they were known as the comprador capitalists. Hsiao-tung Fei, a distinguished Chinese sociologist, had this to say about them:

> I possess no sufficient data on the family background of those who form the first line of contact with Western traders, but I strongly suspect that those "secondhand foreigners," were, at least for the early period, recruited from the outcasts of the traditional structure, who had lost their positions and sought their fortune by illegal means. Treaty ports [core-dominated coastal cities] are open to them. If they find regular employment in the community, such as servants or interpreters in a foreign concern, they gradually become compradors, . . .

if they fail, they form gangs. . . . They are half-caste in culture, bilingual in speech, individualistic, and agnostic, not only in religion, but in cultural values.[19]

And Barrington Moore, writing about the same group, observed:

By shady methods they could accumulate great fortunes to live life in cultivated ease. On the other hand, many Chinese condemned them as the servants of the foreign devils who were destroying the foundations of Chinese society. From this point onward, much of China's social and diplomatic history becomes a record of Chinese attempts to keep this hybrid society in check and of contrary efforts by stronger powers to use it as an entering wedge for their commercial and political interests.[20]

Culturally alien and hated as this class may have been in China, in many other peripheral societies there were no local people willing or able to take up the role of comprador capitalist. Typically, then, foreigners from other peripheral societies would come in to fill these positions. These were the much-hated, but extremely necessary "pariah capitalists" (literally, outcast or despised merchants and entrepreneurs). The list of such people is long, and the animosity they aroused as retailers, money lenders, tavern keepers, landed estate managers, petty officials in colonial governments, middlemen in control of marketing key export crops, and, later in the century, as professionals and small industrialists has become part of the world lore of ethnic hatred. Class and ethnicity combined to make these foreigners a particularly visible target; they obviously benefited from the pattern of peripheral economies, and they were more accessible to local retaliation than the resident Westerners, who would not stoop to such low jobs. The Chinese in Vietnam, Cambodia, Laos, Malaya, Indonesia, Thailand, and Burma; the Indians and Pakistanis in East Africa and South Africa; the Middle Eastern Christians (Lebanese, Syrians, Armenians) throughout much of the Middle East and even West Africa; the Greeks in the same area as well as in the Balkans; Jews in Poland, Romania, the Baltic countries, the Ukraine, and Hungary; and Chinese and Indians in many Caribbean islands were all pariah capitalists. While a fervent European anti-Semite might have trouble explaining to an Indonesian peasant what it was that he disliked about Jews, he need only say "Chinese" to elicit the same image, the same prejudices, and the same hatreds; for wherever they were present, pariah capitalists served the same necessary but unpopular functions. In East Africa, Indians were first imported by the British to be railway construction workers, but they soon became merchants. And among the Chinese in Jamaica, first imported as plantation workers, a similar change occurred. In Romania the development of the wheat export economy in the middle of the nineteenth century brought thousands of Jews, and it was the growth of the plantation economies in Southeast Asia that attracted most of that area's Chinese.[21]

All over the peripheral (and semiperipheral) world, the pattern repeated itself. The controllers of the land, core investors, and colonial administrators used the pariah and comprador capitalists as a necessary adjunct to their power, only to despise them quite as much as they were hated by local peasants. Later, when a series of anticore, nationalist revolts broke out around the world, the sight of mass reprisals taken against this vulnerable class became common enough for many observers to conclude that this, too, was part of the traditional political pattern in "underdeveloped" countries. But like the rise to power of export-connected controllers of the land, the rise of a comprador-pariah class was only another aspect of the growth of the capitalist world system.

It is quite clear that this type of middle class, important as it may have been in peripheral societies, could not achieve the position attained by the middle class in core societies. Fundamentally alien and deeply entangled in core interests, the comprador-pariah class could not become nearly as politically independent or powerful.

The rest of the modern middle class in peripheral societies was very different. It was composed of partially Westernized native civil servants and white-collar employees. In colonial Africa and Asia a native civil service was trained by the Europeans who did not have enough administrators to run their colonies, particularly at the lower levels. Even importation of "other" (that is, foreign) peripherals was not sufficient, and some locals had to be absorbed into the administration. This meant that they had to be taught Western bureaucratic techniques, and Western forms of organization. In Latin America, where this class was relatively much larger than in Africa, it comprised the bulk of the higher civil service. Eric Wolf has estimated that in Mexico in 1910, three-quarters of the middle class were employed in one way or another by the government.[22] India had a substantial native civil service because the country had been a colony for many decades. In China between 1900 and 1910 those Chinese with Western educations were active in attempts to modernize China and replace its traditional Imperial administration with a regime based on Western models. After the Chinese Revolution of 1911, the Western-educated intellectuals (that is, those with formal Western higher educations) gradually came to dominate the civil service.

In the early twentieth century, such intellectuals and civil servants were still somewhat like the comprador capitalists in that they combined elements of their own and Western cultures, and in general, stood in awe of Western accomplishments. By their thinking, the poverty and dependence of their societies had to be remedied by Westernization. As long as this awe and admiration prevailed, the dominance of core powers was assured. But the administrative middle class was not like the comprador middle class in one important respect: the livelihoods of its members did not depend on the maintenance of core domination. In fact, in colonial societies, the native civil service gradually came to realize that if the core administrators could be expelled, it would become the new elite. Ultimately, as this class learned to synthesize Western and native cultures, and to apply its organizational and intellectual skills to nationalistic purposes, it became the leader of anticore revolts in peripheral societies around the world. In the early twentieth century, most of this nationalism was still in the future.

The modern upper-middle class shaded off imperceptibly into the modern lower-middle class. Those at the bottom of the civil service hierarchy (petty clerks, office boys, soldiers, service workers, interpreters, and even servants of the Europeans) were partially Westernized, but they were not yet much of a self-conscious class. Some could rise to become comprador capitalists, others could get more education and become civil servants or white-collar employees of core-dominated firms. Eventually the modern lower-middle class came to include substantial numbers of individuals, particularly in the enclave cities. As this class grew it became a vital part of the structure that supported core domination. When it became more self-conscious, and also more nationalistic and anticore, the whole colonial and semicolonial system that prevailed in the peripheral world was gravely threatened. Again, however, these were developments yet to come.

The small landowners, officials of decaying but extant traditional empires (for example, the Confucian bureaucracy of China), and the traditional priestly elite (for example, the Indian Brahmins, the malams in Muslim societies, or Catholic priests in Latin America) comprised one part of the old middle class. At the top, this class shaded off into the controllers of the land, and at the bottom, it was only marginally middle class.

On the whole, people in this group were opposed to the domestic influence of core societies from the very start. As foreign influence in their state's affairs grew, as comprador and pariah capitalists gained in wealth, and as economic patterns changed, members of the old upper-middle class lost their power and wealth to representatives of the new interests and to the few big controllers of the land who could adapt to new ways. In many a peripheral society, they became the leaders of the first anticore revolts. For example, it was members of this group, supported by members of the old lower-middle class, that led the great Indian Mutiny of 1857 against the British, the Mahdi anti-British War in the Sudan at the end of the nineteenth century, and the Boxer uprising against Europeans in China in 1900.[23] By and large, however, such revolts were doomed to failure because the old middle class had only traditional, outdated methods and arms to use against the West. The superior organization of the core, or of core-supported elements, their superior armaments, and most of all, their superior economic power made such revolts futile in all but a handful of cases. In peripheral societies, only the new middle class had the skills necessary to organize successful anticore movements.

The old upper-middle class and the old lower-middle class—artisans, small-village merchants, and the more-prosperous-village peasants—had similar interests. Scholarly literature has perhaps overstressed that intrusions of Western goods destroyed artisans in peripheral societies, but the point is still quite obviously true to some extent. The importation of cheap Western goods into a peripheral society disrupted the artisanate and forced a good many traditional merchants to be squeezed out by comprador or pariah capitalists. Furthermore, many a prosperous peasant was destroyed by the growing power of the landlords, by higher taxes, and by the spread of moneylenders—all problems that became more severe as the influence of core economies grew. This destruction was very obvious in Mexico, and it occurred in India, China, much of Eastern Europe, and ultimately, Africa as well.[24]

The experience of India is particularly instructive in this regard because that country was the largest European colony and the oldest large colony in Asia or Africa. India was also the first colony to give birth to a strong, modern anticolonial movement. Gandhi, the leader of this movement through most of the first half of the century, repeatedly stressed artisan interests (thus, the movement's symbol, the spinning wheel). Gandhi's party, the Congress party, was an alliance of Westernized intellectuals, village artisans, and prosperous peasants (joined eventually by members of a growing industrializing business class opposed to British economic domination); it sought to lead the poor peasants in a fight against the British, against native large landowners, and against the princes who ruled many parts of India in collaboration with the British. The ultimate success of this effort—India gained independence in 1947—stands in marked contrast to the failure of the Mutiny of 1857, and was due in large part to the fact that the crucial organizers and ideologues of the independence movement were Western-educated, notably Gandhi and his chief follower, Nehru. Such members of the educated elite, no longer simply aping the British, successfully combined Indian elements with their borrowed Western ideology and organization. The movement's leaders could deal effectively both with the British (organizing strikes, protests, appealing to the appropriate anticolonial segments of the population in Britain, and applying pressure to vital points of the colonial administration), and with the large number of Indian peasants who had to be organized in order to bring down British rule.[25]

They had found the key. To fight domination by a core power, a peripheral society needed more than simple resentment by the old middle class, or even by the mass of peasants. It needed a new group of leaders, individuals dedicated to their country's sovereignty and capable of applying Western ideas and methodology to this end. For the most part, these individuals were to come from the new middle class.

Railroaders, miners, dockers, and laborers in the few industrial enterprises that existed made up the working class of the peripheral society in 1900. In the most highly developed peripheral economies, such as Mexico's, this class was relatively large (though still considerably smaller than its counterparts in core societies); in most African colonies, and in the poorer parts of Latin America and Asia, it was very small. Where this class was large enough, it would eventually become a meaningful political force against foreign domination. The tactics used by working classes in core societies would be applied. Strikes would be organized, railways and port facilities would be disrupted, miners would unite against management, and core investments would therefore be threatened. As in the case of core working-class movements, the first aim would be to raise wages; and later, the working class would combine with other nationalistic, anticore groups to help overthrow foreign domination. But in the first decade of the twentieth century these tactics had not been adopted, and these combinations had not been made. Even in Mexico the working class remained very weak, and throughout the peripheral world it played a small role in shaping events.

Peasants made up a large majority of the population in almost all the peripheral societies of the early twentieth century; the exceptions were the few unusually rich peripheral societies previously mentioned. Though very large, the peasant class of the typical peripheral society was predominantly illiterate, virtually unorganized, and very poor. It was also very heterogeneous with respect to culture. Peasants spoke local languages, and often these were not the main languages of the enclave cities. Their locally oriented religious practices, their ignorance of the outside world, their focus on local and regional rather than national politics, and their poverty made large-scale organization of the peasants virtually impossible.

Even in a country like Mexico, which was relatively well developed, in 1910:

> More than 70 per cent of the population lived in scattered rural communities . . . [and] . . . at least 87 per cent of the population could neither read nor write. The Indians, defined in terms of language, could not participate in the national way of life; some 1,617,994 persons, or about 13 per cent of the population, spoke only an Indian tongue and were thus excluded from markets, jobs, and civil rights.[26]

Though more numerous, Mexico's Spanish-speaking and mixed-language peasants were hardly better off; and in Bolivia, Peru, Ecuador, and Guatemala, Indians excluded from national life comprised considerably larger proportions of the population than in Mexico.[27]

But Latin American peasants were much less divided culturally than the peasants of most of Asia and Africa. There, each state or colony contained many different linguistic groups, and often many nations and tribes that were drastically different from, and could not communicate with, one another. In Nigeria, for example, the seven leading languages (and generally, language defined ethnicity) were Hausa, Yoruba, Ibo, Kanuri, Tiv, Efik, and Edo; but there were dozens of other major languages, and perhaps hundreds of minor ones.[28] India was yet more subdivided. Even in China, the oldest state, there were major linguistic differences between different parts of the country; and while the elite spoke a standardized version of Chinese, most peasants did not. These regional disparities made organization of the peasants very difficult, and they were the main reason that elite direction was necessary before anything approaching mass rural movements could develop.

Peasants were more likely to organize and act as a distinct class where they were in direct and close contact with the export sector. Thus the plantation workers were the first segment of the rural population to organize along class lines. Even so, in the early twentieth century, their organization was weak.

On the whole, peasants in peripheral societies had very definite grievances against the prevailing economic system. As in Mexico, their precapitalist form of organization was based on the solidarity of fellow villagers and their mutual support. But the extended power of the landlords and the incursion of market forces that obliged peasants to produce export crops and pay high taxes destroyed the villagers' solidarity, turned land itself into a marketable commodity, and thus eroded the security of village life. This process was most apparent and most advanced in the more developed peripheral societies—for example, Mexico and Cuba; but even in Africa, colonial powers took strong measures to force peasants out of their old patterns. Cash taxes were imposed, and this made it necessary for peasants to grow cash crops or migrate to cities and plantations in order to earn cash incomes. The French and Belgians in Africa used forced peasant labor in mines and plantations and to build roads, and forced labor was utilized as well in Vietnam's major rice fields and rubber plantations. In Indonesia high taxes forced peasants to grow cash crops and work on plantations. In many parts of Eastern Europe, similar patterns had developed as early as the sixteenth century, when Poland, Hungary, and the Baltic areas were absorbed into the growing capitalist world economy. These patterns continued to prevail in the first decades of the twentieth century; and while legal serfdom had generally been abolished, the big landowners could impose very disadvantageous tenancy contracts on the peasants. In other words, in most of the peripheral world of the early 1900s, coerced peasant labor produced the key export crops.[29]

It cannot be demonstrated that this pattern of coerced labor actually made the peasants any poorer than they had been. But it can be demonstrated that the new demands of the capitalist world system increased the economic insecurity of the peasants by subjecting them to uncertain and fluctuating market conditions, brought them humiliating new forms of subjection, and ultimately uprooted them in vast numbers.[30] While many traditional forms of social organization had been extremely inegalitarian, at the village level, a precapitalist peasant society had at least provided its members with a protective environment. That protection was destroyed by the intrusion of the world system, and one consequence of the displacement was the outbreak of numerous peasant rebellions through the peripheral world. The targets of these rebellions were the comprador and pariah capitalists, the landowners, and of course, the representatives of core powers. But almost everywhere such uprisings failed because the peasantry was not sufficiently coordinated, and because it had only the most rudimentary of weapons.

When the partially Westernized middle class began to organize the peasants and to coordinate their activities, the situation in peripheral societies changed very dramatically. It was at that point that worldwide revolution began to topple the prevailing capitalist world system. The first such event in the twentieth century—that is, the outbreak of the first effectively organized anticore revolt of peasants and members of the new middle class—occurred in Mexico in 1910. However the story of the Mexican Revolution, and the similar revolts that followed it, is best told in later chapters of the book; for this upheaval was only the beginning of a long war that still rages in many portions of the peripheral world.

The Dangerous Middle: Semiperipheral Class Structures and Politics (Russia, Japan, and Austria-Hungary)

The discussion of class structures and politics in peripheral societies has emphasized that various classes in these societies had mutually antagonistic interests, particularly with respect to dealings within the capitalist world system. Specifically, the controllers of the land and certain members of the middle classes were allies of that world system, while other classes were either hostile or at least potentially hostile to it. The discussion has also suggested that as the twentieth century advanced, and as the new civil servants and intellectual middle class became more nationalistic, revolutionary movements broke out, movements which were opposed to core domination and to the capitalist world system.

The key difference between peripheral societies and semiperipheral societies at the start of the twentieth century was that while in the former this revolutionary process was barely beginning, in the latter it was already well under way. Thus, while the class structures of semiperipheral societies were quite similar to those of some peripheral societies (the most highly developed ones), semiperipheral elites were already much more nationalistic than peripheral elites. The semiperipheral middle classes, though still split between the "new" and the "old," were no longer dominated by comprador or pariah capitalists. These individuals were being replaced by a native, modern commercial middle class with a distinct interest in domestic economic independence. The civil service elite, in control of fully independent state structures, was better developed and much stronger than its counterpart in peripheral societies. And the workers, and even the peasants, were also somewhat better organized and, on the whole, more literate than in peripheral societies.

Thus, while the same basic class divisions and grievances existed in all noncore societies, outright violent conflict was more likely in semiperipherals than in peripherals, since in the former the classes were better organized and more conscious of their interests. Moreover, in the semiperipheral society the middle classes and the elite actually controlled powerful state structures, and their nationalistic goals called for strengthening their society's international position vis-à-vis the core. This made the politics of semiperipheral societies particularly unstable. Their governments participated in the expensive and dangerous international power game against other members of the semiperiphery and against the core societies. But national solidarity was weaker through-out the semiperiphery than in core societies, and a semiperipheral government found it relatively much more expensive to maintain internal order and much more difficult to raise the taxes necessary for participation in the international power contest. Consequently, while they did not suffer nearly as much as peripheral societies from direct exploitation and disruption by the core econ-omies, semiperipheral societies were more exposed to internal disorder and to the danger inherent in active participation in the struggle over world resources and markets. This danger was particularly apparent in two of the three main semiperipheral societies, Russia and Austria-Hungary, but less so in the third, Japan.

Russia

The class composition of Russia according to the national census of 1897 shows a pattern very similar to the divisions by class in a fairly developed peripheral society of the same period. Except for the fact that there were relatively more peasants and relatively fewer members of the working class, this breakdown of classes is similar to that which existed in Mexico in 1900 (see Table 5-5).

TABLE 5-5
Russian Class Structure in 1897[31]

Elite and upper-middle class	2 percent of the population and their depen-dents (about half government officials and half consisting of professionals, owners of larger enterprises, and large landowners)
Other middle classes	6 percent of the population and their depen-dents
Working and lower service class	11 percent of the population and their depen-dents
Peasants	78 percent of the population and their depen-dents
Soldiers and police (not counting officers)	1 percent of the population and their depen-dents
In custody, criminals, beggars, prostitutes, etc.	1 percent of the population

Culturally, Russia was divided. The subject European population (Finns, Lithuanians, Estonians, Poles, a large proportion of the 3 million or so Jews, and a number of others) did not accept the legitimacy of Russian rule and remained linguistically and ethnically non-Russian. Ukrainians formed at least 20 percent of the population, and while they were close to the Russians both in terms of language and in terms of perceived ethnic identity, there is some question as to how loyal they were to the Russian state. The Georgians and Armenians in the Caucasus were non-Russians, and from the Crimea to the Pacific there were large numbers of Tartars, Mongols, Turks, and many other non-European, non-Christian populations. In all, the dominant Russians made up only about half the empire's population. Nor were these the sole members of the empire's elite, for they were also culturally divided and contained some regional elites that were only ambiguously loyal to the empire. The elite in the Baltic countries, for example, was neither Russian nor Balt, but German. Even in the two leading cities, St. Petersburg and Moscow, French, English and German fashions and tastes were dominant among the elite and the upper-middle class; and French, not Russian, was the preferred language of the administrative elite.[32]

Russia's economy was, in some respects, typically peripheral. Wheat was the major export, and the economy imported large quantities of manufactured goods. Foreign (chiefly French) capital played a major role in railway construction.

In all these respects, Russian society was distinctly peripheral. Yet, in 1900, Russia was not peripheral within the world system. In terms of international politics, it was at the very center of important power conflicts in Europe and Asia. This was so because, for all its relative backwardness and poverty, the Russian state was immense, relatively united, and in possession of a large and effective army. And because of pressure from the core countries, Russia was in the process of deep change by 1900.

From the 1850s to the 1880s, Russia suffered a series of international reverses that made it clear that a state's effectiveness in international actions depended on a strong industrial economy. The price of economic backwardness was political weakness. Alexander Gerschenkron has observed that "there is little doubt that" in the 1890s:

> military considerations had a good deal to do with the Russian government's conversion to a policy of rapid industrialization. . . . the government turned toward the goal of a drastic increase in the economic potential of the country.[33]

Because its military goals were primary after 1890, the Russian government concentrated on stimulating railway construction, iron and steel production, and a machine industry. The government, rather than society at large, was both the main source of demand for industrial products and the main organizer of industrial production.

But from where could the government draw the funds necessary for importing foreign technology and machinery? It had to rely on increased agricultural exports and higher taxes squeezed out of the peasantry, the overwhelming majority of the population. In order to permit rapid economic growth and to create an environment conducive to foreign investment, social order also had to be maintained—and at the very time that the population was being squeezed harder economically. As Gerschenkron has put it: "Industrialization required political stability, but industrialization, the cost of which was largely defrayed by the peasantry, was itself a threat to stability."[34]

The program worked. From 1890 to 1900, Russian industrial output grew, on the average, by 8 percent a year, a considerably more rapid rate of increase than was shown in the industrial sector of any Western country during the same period (8 percent growth per year means a doubling every 9 years). The structure of the Russian economy was drastically transformed during this decade, but it was also a time of great stress within the society, particularly among the peasants. Gerschenkron points out that in the 1890s Russian agriculture produced less bread grain (the basic peasant food) per capita than it had three decades earlier. This squeeze on the peasantry was translated into growing peasant unrest. Had the Russian state not been relatively strong even at the beginning of the country's industrialization, this process might have collapsed at its very start. As it was, despite all the ethnic and class divisions within Russia in the late nineteenth century, the Imperial army and police maintained order. Still, by the first years of the twentieth century, the degree of unrest had risen dangerously, and it was in the hope of both distracting the population and scoring a major victory that Russia engaged Japan in a war in 1904 over control of Korea and North China. By early 1905 Russia had lost a series of decisive battles. Frustration, loss of confidence in the government, and, most important, years of accumulated grievances (increased by high taxes to pay for the war) combined to provoke a major revolution. That 1905 revolution was crushed.

From 1906 to 1914 major social and economic reforms were carried out to reduce peasant grievances. But the basic transformation of the Russian economy was so well under way that industrial growth continued at a rapid rate, averaging about 6 percent per year during this period. Such continued growth meant, however, that the middle and working classes also grew in number and organization. As long as industrial growth proceeded smoothly, and as long as the state machinery and police remained strong, this change in the class structure did not present much of a problem. But circumstances became different in 1914, when Germany invaded Russia and destroyed its state machinery. Thereupon the suffering of total war combined with the unrest provoked by twenty-five years of rapid change, and in 1917 this combination set off a peasant and working-class revolution. By then the army and police had abandoned the government because of extremely severe war losses, and most members of the middle class or the elite had also lost faith in the government's ability to survive. As a result, this time the disgruntled workers and peasants rather easily overthrew the government.[35]

At least three general conclusions are suggested by this account of Russia's early industrialization. First, semiperipheral societies trying to become core economies but lacking the necessary social and economic structures must have strong state machines. The state must be the primary mover in the process of industrialization. But the process has high costs, at least in the short run. This is particularly true for the peasantry which must bear the burden of providing the necessary surplus for investment. The state will have to repress peasant protest in order to keep consumption down and investment high. If the state is successful in this, and if industrialization advances, the working class will grow as well and present an increasingly greater demand for higher consumption. Since the state's short-term economic goal is to maximize investment while keeping costs down, the demands of a growing working class will also be repressed.

Second, the state's new despotic rule is also not likely to please the middle class—even if it does not suffer directly from the economic strain of state-sponsored industrialization. As the middle class of the industrializing society grows, it will also demand effective political representation (using as its model the Western European middle class). By the start of the twentieth century, the small but growing Russian middle class was demanding political reforms (similar to those achieved earlier by middle classes in Western Europe) that would give it a greater share of power. The slowness of these reforms alienated many members of the class, among them the highly educated, politically dangerous intellectuals who became leaders and organizers of the workers and the peasants.

Third, the very success of the semiperipheral state trying to industrialize creates not only internal dangers but grave external dangers as well. Along with domestic unrest, economic success brings the state into increasingly severe conflict with its neighbors. With large parts of the home population hostile to the government, a military disaster tends to break the coercive power of the state and promote revolution. In other words, an industrializing semiperipheral power is likely to get involved in severe international conflicts, and it must win (despite fragile circumstances) or face drastic consequences at home.

The Russian Revolution of 1917, then, was caused not by economic stagnation but by great economic success followed by military defeat at the hands of more advanced states in the world system.

Japan

Japan, like Russia, was a relatively poor society at the start of the twentieth century; and again like Russia, it was a society well on the way to industrialization. Here, too, the push had been started because of a perceived weakness in the international arena rather than because of any purely domestic economic developments. In the 1860s it seemed that Japan was fated to become another China, a peripheral colonial society dominated by the core states. Japan escaped that fate, mainly because it had the great advantage of being far more unified culturally than any other peripheral society.

In 1868 there was a revolution in Japan. Known as the Meiji Restoration, it was not a "left-wing" uprising but a revolt led by members of the lower nobility. Their aim was to preserve as many traditional Japanese ways as possible, and also to industrialize the economy, create a large and modern armed force, and prevent Japan from becoming subordinate to the Westerners. Because Japan started early enough, before the debilitating effects of peripherality could take hold (until the 1850s Japan had been too isolated from the world system to suffer from peripherality) and because Japan started off with the obvious advantage of being a unified nation-state, the revolutionists of 1868 succeeded brilliantly. Japan never went through a strictly peripheral stage. Rather, it entered the world system as a semiperipheral society.

It is important to note that the Meiji Restoration was neither democratic nor gentle. As in Russia twenty years later, the only source of income for the needed investments was the peasants; and they were drastically taxed. Numerous peasant uprisings occurred, but these were put down. The state became an absolutist, tyrannical instrument of economic and military growth. At first, almost all the key industries were developed by the government rather than by private capitalists. Later, the government gave up many of the enterprises it owned to private capitalists. From the 1880s to 1945, Japan was dominated by a small elite of high government officials, military leaders, and the controllers of the large industrial firms developed and fostered by the government.

In the 1880s, as economic transformation began to give it substantial military strength, Japan began to play with vigor the imperialistic game already in progress among the great powers. It developed a "need" for colonies—for raw materials, for markets, and for growing room—and it began to acquire colonies: first Taiwan, taken from China, then Korea, and eventually various parts of China. Japanese nationalism and involvement in the international competition for territory led Japan to war with Russia in 1904, and quick success in that war marked Japan as a potentially successful challenger to core domination. It was this wish to play the imperialist role in the world system that dominated Japan's drive to further economic progress and military expansion. The general welfare of the population of Japan was not at stake. Quite the contrary, in order to fuel rapid economic growth and great military power the elite kept down wages and consumption for the Japanese masses; and it was not until after 1945 that the standard of living for the average Japanese rose to a level consistent with Japan's great economic progress. Until then, the benefits of industrialization had been applied to the conduct of foreign affairs.[36]

Japan, like Russia, exemplifies three generalizations. First, in semiperipheral societies, the state must be prime mover if peripherality is to be avoided. This means taxing the population, particularly the peasants, to the utmost, in order to obtain investments and maintain social stability during the painful early stages of industrialization. Second, the industrializing semiperipheral state cannot be democratic. Rather, to enforce the necessary policies, it must be absolutist. The true elite in this situation is the government administration (civil and military), not the controllers of private capital. Third, foreign policy is crucial. Japan won all of its colonial expansionist wars until it was defeated by the United States in 1945. By then, Japan had been so transformed by seventy-five years of industrial success that it was no longer in any danger of reverting to peripheral status. Its economic structure was so similar to that of core societies that military disaster could no longer have the impact it had on Russia in 1917.

Austria-Hungary

Austria-Hungary stood in marked contrast to both Japan and Russia. It was certainly richer than either of the two other major semiperipheral societies, and at least in the Austrian half, considerably more democratic. But the Austro-Hungarian state was weak, primarily because power was shared between the Austrian and Hungarian halves of the empire. Every step taken by the state to strengthen itself was met with serious resistance, usually a reflection of the society's great cultural division. In addition, while certain parts of the empire were substantially industrialized, other parts were very rural. And everywhere the army was badly organized and ineffective, especially compared to West European armies.

But while there were complex domestic ethnic and class divisions within the Austro-Hungarian Empire, it was the empire's international position that determined its ultimate fate. Austria-Hungary, like the other semiperipheral states, was deeply involved in the great power game, at least in Eastern Europe. It had its own colonies in Eastern Europe and was expansionist, like other great powers at the start of the twentieth century. Its "need to expand" placed the country in potentially serious conflict with Russia (and, to a lesser extent, Italy) which sought to expand into the same area. But because it was so weak, and so internally divided, the Austro-Hungarian Empire was not a viable competitor in the world system. Rather than succeeding in the early 1900s, as did Japan, Austria-Hungary was destroyed during World War I (a war it had helped to provoke) and vanished from among the world's independent states.[37]

It is important to note that, despite its fate, Austria-Hungary in 1900 was in many ways more developed economically than either Russia or Japan. Its weakness rested not as much in economic backwardness as in the fact that it was not a nation-state; and states that are as internally divided as Austria-Hungary was cannot participate in the twentieth-century competition for world power and hope to succeed. The competition requires too great an effort to allow serious internal division in its winners.

A Note on Democracy

In the early twentieth century three of the four major core societies were political democracies. In these three the large majority of the male adult population had the right to vote, and elections were both relatively free and relatively meaningful in that elected officials had real power. In the fourth core society, Germany, democracy was less well established; but the parliament and party system were strong enough, and becoming stronger at a rapid rate, suggesting that a greater degree of democracy was likely in the near future. In the minor core societies, the same pattern prevailed. Politics were either substantially democratic or at least seemed on the way to becoming democratic.

Among the semiperipheral societies, the pattern was rather different. Parliaments tended to be weaker (in the case of Japan and Russia, very weak) and less representative of the general population.

Among peripheral societies, only the very richest had attained a level of democratic politics. In Chile, Uruguay, and Argentina, the first decade of the century saw considerable progress toward the establishment of democratic parliamentary systems. In direct colonies, of course, foreigners ruled; and even in most independent peripheral societies, stable, parliamentary democracy was virtually absent.

The main reason for this pattern is that democracy developed where there was a strong capitalist middle class. This middle class did not have to be entirely urban; indeed, the landowning rural middle class did very well in pushing for democratic reforms. Urban or rural, most members of the middle class opposed oligarchic rule and authoritarianism, largely because these infringed on their personal liberties. Furthermore, in any society in which a substantial minority of people had property and wealth, that large minority was likely to resist domination by any small elite which would restrict enjoyment of rights over private property. Since most of the middle class tended to be well educated, politically aware, and easily organized, there were, in the most advanced societies, powerful movements for the democratization of national politics. In semiperipheral and peripheral societies (with the exceptions noted above) this was not the case.

It is particularly interesting to look at a part of a core society which had many peripheral characteristics, namely the southern United States, to confirm this point. After the Civil War, the South retained an economic and class structure that was more characteristic of primary exporting peripheral economies than of industrialized core economies. Agriculture remained more important than in the rest of the United States; cultural divisions (based, in this case, on race) were deep; and controllers of the land and foreign (that is, Yankee) investors wielded disproportionate influence on the regional economy and politics. Not surprisingly the South had a weaker middle class than the rest of the United States, and it was by far the least democratic part of the country. Not only a very large proportion of blacks but also many poor whites did not have the right to vote. In many ways, political, economic, and social structures in the South were quite similar to those in the peripheral world, except that the external domination did not come from a foreign core state but from within the United States itself.[38]

But when a peripheral society moves toward semiperipherality, or when a semiperipheral society seriously attempts to attain core status, lack of democracy is not a disadvantage. On the contrary, nondemocratic governments are more likely to keep down consumption (thus freeing funds needed for investment), and they are also more likely to repress discontent powerfully and ruthlessly.

As subsequent chapters will show, the role of democracy became much more complicated as the twentieth century progressed. In part, this was because, as the working classes in industrial societies became stronger, some middle classes became fearful and turned at least partially antidemocratic. Also, dramatic political failure, particularly in the international power game, seriously weakened the legitimacy of certain governments, and several democratic governments collapsed because of international failure. Third, middle classes that grew from the ranks of purely administrative, civil or military service groups tended to be less democratic than middle classes that were composed of private entrepreneurs; this difference is understandable, since the administrative middle classes developed within centralized, bureaucratic systems rather than within economically decentralized systems that promoted individual action and independence.[39]

Pressures for Change

The capitalist world system seemed secure in the early twentieth century, and the core societies appeared to be in firm control of the system. These very successes, however, were creating strong destabilizing pressures.

The first destabilizing element was the intense expansionist rivalry within the core and semiperiphery. Because the world was, in a sense, "filled up" by 1910, further territorial expansion pitted core powers and semiperipheral powers against one another and generally required war. Such expansion may not have been necessary to core states; but the major powers believed that it was, and the consequences of that belief were undeniably real.

The second, severely destabilizing element was that, soon after a peripheral society was brought into the world system, certain natives, notably members of the Western-educated elites, would begin to formulate nationalist, anticore ideologies, and to use their skills in order to organize the classes that had serious grievances against the world system. Since the large majority of the peripheral world consisted of peasants who were oppressed by the expansion of the world system, once organization began to spread into rural areas, the entire structure of world control by a few core societies began to be in doubt. In other words, the more a peripheral area was developed, the more likely it became that some kind of reaction would take place there against the obvious disadvantages of peripherality. In 1910, this response to peripherality was still not a worldwide phenomenon. But the forces that were to make it worldwide were active everywhere, and the very nature of the world economy ensured the continuation and growth of these forces.

Third, by 1910, several semiperipheral societies, notably Russia and Japan, were partially successful in developing economies and state machineries that could challenge the core's domination of the world. The number of participants in the world power game was bound to grow as other societies with plentiful resources and populations made the transition from peripheral to semiperipheral status. Thus, the competition for control of the world system, already very strong in 1910, was certain to grow more acute.

Fourth, class structures within the core were also changing. As the working class became better organized, and as the middle class continued to grow, the balance of political forces changed. The domination of the small capitalist elite began to weaken, a trend that would have a particularly strong effect in times of crisis, when discontent was most likely to surface. In the international crises that developed as the century progressed, the increased organization of the middle and working classes produced certain important changes in the behavior of core powers in the world system.

Fifth, in the early twentieth century, there were many people who were culturally distinct from those who ruled the state in which they lived. As nationalism spread, and as a series of periodic crises shook the entire world, these nonruling peoples developed ethnic, religious, linguistic, or regional nationalisms that challenged the growth and success of their nation-states. This change was to be evident among various cultural minorities in some of the core societies, but it was to be more apparent in noncore societies, where the majority of culturally distinct groups opposed to one another and to the state often constituted a majority of the population.

In the end, the major destabilizing element in the capitalist world system, the element that stood at the heart of the five elements already outlined, involved the very nature of capitalism itself. The rationality of capitalism, its search for constantly increasing profits, and its continuously successful expansion of scientific and technological knowledge had pushed the Western societies into a preeminent position throughout the world. The internal pressures for constant growth that had caused this rise could not stop in 1910. The competition within the core became greater than ever. Growth continued, encouraging ever greater scientific and technological advances, and prompting economic expansion and, thereby, the acceleration of all the destabilizing elements that accompany growth. Not only did growth continue in the core, but as the core's influence spread throughout the periphery, the same elements spread throughout the world. The process was an old one, and in a way, it had been going on since 1500. But the early twentieth century marked an important turning point, because until then the powers in the world system had had continued room for growth into new areas. After 1900, only a few isolated areas remained outside the system; and the growth of any power thus had to involve areas already within the system. Internal growth, spawned by success, was the capitalist world system's major destabilizing element.

Part Two

THE EUROPEAN WORLD SYSTEM IN CRISIS, 1914–1945

CHAPTER 6

The European
Catastrophe

*A*t the beginning of August 1914, war broke out between Germany and Austria-Hungary on one side and Russia, France, and the United Kingdom on the other. The competitive imperialism of the previous forty years had divided most of the world into zones of influence and colonies of the core and semiperiphery. There were few empty peripheral areas left to be seized, and in those, competition for influence was bitter. The Balkans and the slowly collapsing Ottoman Empire were such an area, and Austria-Hungary used the pretext that its heir had been assassinated by young Serbs in Sarajevo to invade Serbia. Such tough and decisive action was meant to strengthen unity in the empire, and show the rebellious minority nationalities that it was dangerous to provoke the government. Germany, eager to demonstrate its resolve and courage in the face of danger, fully backed Austria. On the other side, Russia was Serbia's closest ally and protector and felt obliged to stand by its commitments or gradually see its ambition to take over the Balkans and the Ottoman Empire fade. France, afraid to face the growing strength of Germany alone, sided with the Russians.[1]

The immediate problem was that technological change had gone far beyond the ability of military men to understand its consequences. They felt that with railroads and mass mobilization it would be possible to assemble and hurl into action millions of men within days. This would mean that a country being invaded might have lost before it could defend itself if it delayed its own mobilization by just a few days. But mobilization meant more than putting men in uniform and giving them the guns they had learned to use during their military training as youths. It also involved complex railroad timetables as men and supplies were moved to the front; and the general staffs of Europe had plans for offensives designed to bring lightning victory. Mobilization meant war because the giant machines set in motion had no brakes. To hesitate, it was felt, spelled certain defeat if the enemy had put its own machine into action.

Germany had the most ambitious plan of all, to throw most of its army at France through neutral Belgium, thus surprising the French, rolling around their left flank, and seizing Paris within a few weeks. Then, with France out of the way, Russia could be handled and its western areas absorbed into the German Empire. The British, of course, fully realized that Germany was their most dangerous rival in the competition for world hegemony. The German navy directly threatened England's navy. German industry was growing faster, was more modern, and had made major inroads into British exports. Thus,

Britain was determined to prevent Germany from also gaining military hegemony in Europe, and that meant coming to the aid of the French if necessary. Six days after Austria-Hungary's invasion of Serbia, millions of men were racing toward one another, all of them expecting rapid victory.[2]

But the military men entrusted with the conduct of these operations had planned them in field exercises and staff colleges. Their theories were full of mistakes, particularly in that they had developed modern, technically complex strategies without taking into account the need to alter battlefield tactics. There had been no major European war for over forty years. The Franco-Prussian War of 1870–1871 had been a minor affair compared with the really big wars, the Napoleonic Wars, which had ended a century earlier. Few realized that the invention of rapid-fire machine guns, highly mobile and powerful artillery, and railroads heavily favored the defense, not the offense. Once an army had dug in, it could build railway spurs to its various defensive positions to resupply itself. But an army charging into enemy lines quickly outran the reach of its own rail lines, and bringing offensive reinforcements and supplies was a much slower process.[3]

After a month of mobile warfare on the French-German front, the lines bogged down into desperate trench warfare. For four years, general after general led hundreds of thousands of men on both sides to their deaths in an effort to break through enemy lines, each time at enormous sacrifice. For four years, millions died for no particularly good reason other than the fact that after so much sacrifice, no one could back down. Nor was there any military solution other than to exhaust the enemy faster than yourself, something which only became possible when the enormous, fresh resources and manpower of the United States were thrown in on the Anglo-French side in 1918. (The United States entered the war in 1917, but did not send much direct help for about a year.)

On the Eastern front, however, these years of war were more decisive. Neither Russia nor Austria-Hungary had the industrial or agricultural structure to sustain prolonged, highly costly modern warfare. Supplies shortages destroyed military and civilian morale, and these giant empires crumbled under the weight of war. The Ottoman Empire, Germany's ally, also disintegrated, and the soldiers of the lesser nations of Europe caught in this madness, the Romanians, the Italians, the Serbs, the Bulgarians, died by the millions to enable their leaders to play the game of international politics with the big powers, to defend their honor, and to further dimly perceived, generally erroneous national interests.

The considerable optimism and faith in Western rationality and its ability to promote universal happiness through technological progress was shattered, in some ways for good, as it became obvious that this inane war, too, was the product of Western progress and rationality.

A look at some of the casualty figures (Table 6-1) shows the enormity of what happened, and what is surprising is not that there was so much popular discontent after the war, but rather that there was not more and that so many

TABLE 6-1

Military Deaths as a Proportion of Military-Age Males, 1914–1918[4]

	*Males of Military Age, 1914–1918**	*Military Deaths*	*Percentage of Total (Col.2/Col.1)*
France	7,785,000	1,400,000	18%
Germany	14,341,000	1,800,000	13%
Austria-Hungary	10,415,000	1,290,000	12%
Italy (entered in 1915)	6,969,000	600,000	9%
Bulgaria (on the German side)	878,000	90,000	10%
United States (entered in 1917)	21,610,000	116,000	0.5%

* All those no older than 38 at the start of the war and no older than 42 at the end, and all those at least 18 by the last year of the war.

Europeans continued to accept being ruled by the kinds of governments that had led them into this situation.

In France, out of a total population of about 39 million, almost 16 percent were called up. Of these, almost one in five died, and if captured and wounded are added, there were close to 5 million casualties. This represented 64 percent of the country's total male population of military age during the war.[5] The British Empire lost a million men, Russia something over 2 million, the Ottoman Empire a half million, and the Belgians, Romanians, and Serbians (allies of the Anglo-French) another half million. In all, 9 to 10 million soldiers died, and millions of civilians, particularly in Eastern Europe, died of disease and famine caused by the war.[6] Of the major participating powers, only the United States, which joined the Anglo-French side late in the war, did not suffer large losses. In terms of numbers of soldiers killed as a proportion of the total pool of available men, France's losses were about thirty-six times as great as America's.

It is a measure of the degree of nationalism within the core societies and of the enormous resources they could mobilize and organize, that the war continued so long. There were serious military mutinies in France in 1917, and strikes against the war in Germany. But the war continued until the United States began to contribute enough fresh troops to tip the balance. In 1918, after a last offensive, the German army collapsed, and strikes and mutinies in Germany led to the overthrow of the government. The war ended in November 1918.

An immediate result of the war was the creation in Eastern Europe of a number of newly independent peripheral states carved out of the ruins of the

German, Austrian, and Russian empires. This large belt of small states—Finland, Estonia, Latvia, Lithuania, Poland, Czechoslovakia, Austria, Hungary, and the previously independent Balkan states (Yugoslavia and Romania took large parts of the former Austrian and Russian empires)—created a new peripheral zone that was "up for grabs." Twenty years later, as a recovered Germany launched a new challenge for control of the world system, conflict over this particular area of the world would start the European part of World War II.

In the rest of the world there was little outward political change. Germany's African colonies were divided between France, Britain, and Belgium; Japan and Britain took over the small German possessions in Asia and the Pacific. The Arab portions of the Ottoman Empire were divided between Britain, France, and some Arab states.[7]

The social and economic strains of the war produced more important results than the changes in boundaries. As a reaction against the brutality and waste of the war, the working class and peasants in large portions of peripheral and semiperipheral Europe moved sharply to the left politically and increasingly threatened the old social order. Even in the core societies, the working class made a push for more power; in the immediate postwar years, it seemed as if the entire capitalist world system was on the verge of collapse because of socialist revolutions and increased working-class political activity. But aside from Russia, where the new communist regime managed to hang on to power despite military intervention by the main capitalist countries, the left was defeated everywhere, and the capitalist system survived relatively intact.[8]

The system survived, but it was seriously weakened. The core powers of Europe and the other European participants in the war had gone into debt to finance themselves. Domestically, this produced a serious inflationary problem; and internationally, it put virtually all of the countries in Europe in debt to the United States in one way or another. To pay back their debts and rescue their inflated currencies, and to try to bring the fiscal world system back to its British-backed prewar stability, the winning allies counted on reparations payments that were to be extracted from Germany. But Germany was unable to pay, and in the end, the entire debt structure collapsed.

Britain's attempt to stabilize its currency by forcing balanced budgets in the early 1920s led to severe deflationary pressure and a depression which persisted for almost all of the 1920s. Germany's try at paying its reparations by printing money resulted in wild inflation and the complete collapse of its currency in 1923. The savings of its middle classes were wiped out. The United States, retreating into relative isolation in a vain attempt to return to the past, gave short-term loans abroad, but did not enter either the financial or trading markets of the world in a big enough way to replace the now impotent British. The world capitalist system needed a central banker to stabilize it, extend credit, provide a sound reserve currency, and impose fiscal responsibility on lesser members. This the British had done before 1914, but as Charles

Kindleberger has put it, in the 1920s ". . . the British couldn't and the United States wouldn't."[9]

The new states created from the ruins of Austria-Hungary and pieces chipped off of Russia borrowed money on the international markets to keep their governments and feeble, fragmented economies going. But they were unable to repay their debts, and this further unbalanced the world banking system, undermining the soundness of the lending banks from the major countries.

The worst problem of all was the United States, which had become such an overwhelmingly powerful economy that by 1929 it alone produced 43 percent of all the world's manufactured goods (with only 6 percent of the world's population). The next biggest producer at that time, Germany, only produced 11 percent of the world's manufactured products, and the United Kingdom and France, respectively, produced 9 percent and 7 percent.[10] But the United States was far from being structured like the European great powers because it was so highly self-sufficient. Its huge national product was not heavily involved in international trade, and it provided neither a market for other countries' products nor was it a source for outside buyers, at least not at a level proportionate to its wealth and size. The failure of the European economies to recover fully from the war, and particularly the decline of the British, left international trade underfinanced. Though American investments abroad grew from about $3.5 billion in 1913 to $17 billion in 1929, this was still smaller than British foreign investments, and too little to provide an adequate capital base for the rest of the world. American financial institutions, the American people, and the American government were too short-sighted to see that this might be a problem for them.[11]

In fact, it was. During World War I American agriculture had prospered exporting food to Europe. With the recovery of European agriculture, the farming sector went into a state of depression that persisted throughout the 1920s. American industry grew very rapidly, but productivity outstripped demand, and only by financing more exports could this have been overcome. In other words, the United States was turning into a more conventional core economy, but without knowing it. To prosper, it had to stimulate outside demand for its products.

In 1929, overspeculation on the stock market based on expectations of a continuing boom produced a crash. Many banks, particularly those holding bankrupt farmers' debts, collapsed. American financial institutions that had been involved in the wildly overoptimistic growth of stock prices on the New York stock exchange began to call in their loans to other banks and to foreign debtors, producing a massive liquidity crisis. This might have been overcome had the United States government increased the money supply, but it did nothing. Banks in Central Europe began to fail as their American debts were called in, and the wave of failures spread throughout the capitalist world.[12]

The reaction of the Western governments was to fall back on sound, conventional economics. In times of trouble, balance the budget, be conservative, and wait for the market to right itself. What this did was to further reduce the money supply because falling revenues were matched by greater government restraint. A falling money supply and collapsing banks meant less money for investments, and therefore fewer jobs, and thus fewer buyers of manufactured products. That caused many firms to fail; and they laid off their workers, turning the problem into a vicious, deflationary, downward cycle. Prices fell, but demand did not rise to take up the slack because there was not enough credit available to get the economy moving again.[13]

From 1929 to 1933 the GNP of the United States fell from $104 billion to $56 billion. (Because prices fell, too, real GNP did not fall by quite that much.) Unemployment rose from 3 percent of the labor force to 25 percent. In Germany and the United Kingdom, unemployment rose to 16 percent and 20 percent, respectively. Each country tried to protect its jobs by erecting trade barriers against imports, but this further depressed world trade and exacerbated rather than solved the main problem.[14]

In the peripheral economies, the consequences were as bad or worse. Primary product prices and demand for them fell even faster than the prices of manufactured goods as the core economies lowered their primary imports. From 1926/1930 to 1936/1938 the price of manufactured goods in world trade fell by about 17 percent, but the price of primary products fell by about 27 percent.[15]

This biggest of all "Great Depressions" was a direct result of World War I and the economic mistakes made by government policies after that war, but it probably would not have been so severe if it had not also corresponded to yet another turn in the long-range industrial cycle which, even in normal times, would have been entering the transition from the "third" (steel and chemicals) industrial age to the "fourth." Had the downturn been part of this cyclical change alone, it would not have been as long or harmful, either; but the interaction of both sets of factors combined to create the worst crisis in the history of modern capitalism.

The technological progress of the early twentieth century had paved the way for the start of a truly mass market in expensive consumer goods. The perfection of the internal combustion engine, the discovery of how to use a very widely available, relatively cheap fuel, petroleum, and the improvement in manufacturing techniques created a product that promised to revolutionize social and economic life, the automobile. The First World War temporarily halted this development, and after the war it was only in the United States that the new industrial cycle really established itself. In 1905, the United Kingdom, France, and Germany combined had slightly more registered motor vehicles than the United States. By 1913 the United States had almost three times as many as the three biggest European countries, and in 1921 about ten times as many as all of Europe put together. Though the very small base of European motor-vehicle production allowed it to grow at a faster rate than in the United

States after this, by 1938 United States motor-vehicle registration was still four and a half times bigger than in the three largest European countries, and three and a half times as great as all of Europe's combined.[16]

In the United States it was primarily the innovative production methods of Henry Ford and the realization that workers who were well-paid could purchase more goods that inaugurated the age of high-volume mass consumption. In the 1920s the marketing and production methods of General Motors expanded on Ford's concepts and put the American automobile industry in a dominant position, which it was to maintain for the next half century.

As in past industrial cycles, it was not so much that old types of production collapsed, but that technological dynamism and the greatest returns on investment shifted to new areas. Where the old steel and chemical industries could be harnessed to automobile production, and where the electrical industry could be tied to the new production of consumer electric products, they prospered. But the onset of the Great Depression so lowered demand that the growth of these industries was slowed and they were unable to take up the slack in employment. It took World War II and the enormous expenditure in rearmaments to allow a full economic recovery.

The depth of the economic crisis led many to believe that capitalism was a spent force in the 1930s. Something else, either communism or fascism would replace it. In fact, the United States might have propped up the system in the 1920s, and it retained the ability to do this later. The far-sighted involvement of the United States in the world economy and in the political balance of power after World War II was to save the system and give capitalism a renewed, extended burst of prosperity. That this would happen was not, however, known in the 1930s, and we must now turn to some of the ideological consequences and debates of World War I and the Depression before going to later developments.

The Ideologies of the Twentieth Century

One of the more curious facts about the twentieth century is that the ideologies that have dominated it were creations of the nineteenth and early twentieth centuries, and that by the time the century was a third over, they had become fully elaborated. Despite the immense political and economic changes that were to follow in the next two-thirds of the century, significant new ideologies would not be produced, and if anything, older ones would become increasingly important.

The nineteenth century saw the maturation of nationalism in Western Europe and the beginning of its spread to the rest of the world, a process which continues to this day as it infects the entire globe with increasing intensity. Nationalism has already been discussed (in Chapter 4); and among the prevailing ideological currents in the twentieth century it has been unique. Though unquestionably the strongest of these currents, it has also become so universal that it has ceased to distinguish countries from one another. Only the most backward, culturally malintegrated states of the world do not experience it today; and even among those, it is at least of growing strength among individual regions or ethnic groups within their borders. The growth of school systems sponsored by each state, the improvement in communications that allowed state power to be exercised more effectively in every country, the consequent growth in the size and importance of state bureaucracies, and the fact that these bureaucracies then needed staffing and were able to make decisive differences in deciding who received what economic benefits from state power, all intensified nationalism. Groups that could not get the benefits they felt others were getting questioned the cultural legitimacy of their states. On the other hand, those who did benefit developed strong loyalties to their states, more common ideals, and greater solidarity. So, in colonies and peripheral parts of the world, the fact that it was Frenchmen or Englishmen, not Arabs or Indians who received more of the benefits of the system raised nationalistic feelings against the core. Within core societies, the growing prosperity, school training, and gradual political participation of a majority of the population, also strengthened nationalism.

The great World War to which nationalism led Europe only strengthened it in the long run. To be a member of a weak or losing nation-state was shown to be catastrophic. The Germans, not the French or English, were made to pay reparations, and they subsequently felt that their suffering was the product of their loss, not of the generalized debacle which actually affected all of Europe. The Russian state lost a large portion of its territory simply because it was too weakened by the war to resist. The Turks almost had their state taken away from them. Only the nation-state, in the end, could be trusted to defend its citizens and protect them from foreign exploitation.

If over time almost everyone tends to become nationalistic, this has not been true for any of the other ideologies of the twentieth century. These have divided people, and become an important basis of conflict. Unlike nationalism, none of the other major ideologies has in any sense become "universal," though some of the more important have had more in common with one another than their proponents have generally believed.

These leading ideologies have varied along two basic questions which have been at the heart of all disputes about the nature of politics in this century: How strong a role should the state play in order to maximize the happiness of its subjects? and How possible or even desirable is it to bring about the maximum amount of equality in society? Neither of these questions was particularly important in traditional agrarian societies. Central governments were always trying to retain as much as possible for themselves. Those with power always took more than their fair share, and those without were necessarily much poorer than the few elites who ruled them. Traditional religions sought to explain and justify this condition, and in any case it hardly seemed that it could be changed. With the enormous growth of education, material prosperity, and the growing capacity of governments to carry out deliberate reforms, these questions came to the fore as key issues. Increasing popular participation in elections, universal military conscription, and the forging of stronger cultural ties within nation-states all raised the question of equality in an urgent way. Similarly, for technical reasons—improved communications and vastly improved administrative procedures that came with industrialization—the potential role of governments became much bigger than even the most absolute despots of the past might have imagined. None had ever been able to control the daily lives of all their people in a way that has become possible in the twentieth century.

As far as equality was concerned, there were two opposite poles, and every possible shade of opinion in between. At one extreme were those who believed in radical equality. If some were wealthy and others poor, that was necessarily evil, presumably because, as the nineteenth-century French anarcho-socialist Proudhon claimed, "Property is theft." The poor were only poor because the rich had stolen from them, and to eliminate the property rights of the wealthy would recreate a rough kind of equality. At the other extreme were those who believed that it was natural law to have talented and less talented people, and that in fact, these qualities were hereditary. The rich were not only rightfully rich, but their children deserved to inherit positions of wealth and power because they formed a naturally more talented and deserving section of the population. The poor, on the other hand, were that way because of their own defects, whether of character or simply unfortunate heredity, and to try to bring their level up to that of the natural elite would only cause general social ruin. In the middle of this argument were proponents of various shades of liberalism who believed that though it was, indeed, natural for the talented to enrich themselves, hereditary chance ought not to play an important role in determining position. There should therefore be equality of opportunity, and schooling or advancement ought not be denied anyone because of birth in an unfavored class. But it was unwise to force equality of results as that would take away incentive for hard work, talent, and prudent investment. This middle position, of course, was the one most consistent with the interests of the rising, business middle class of the nineteenth century. The radically egalitarian position was espoused by the poor artisans and working-class followers of the new socialist movements of that time. The radically inegalitarian position was at first primarily the ideology of the old aristocrats and monarchs of Europe trying to stem the rise of the business and professional middle classes, but with time, it also attracted the succeeding generations of rich bourgeois. It was in the nineteenth century, too, that an interesting new version of antiegalitarian ideology was born, the notion that capabilities varied systematically by race, and that there were entire races, even nations, who were naturally favored, while others, for biological reasons, were doomed to be on the bottom of the human pyramid. Fitting very nicely with the emergent world system controlled by a small European core ruling a large, nonwhite periphery of lesser peoples, this ideology could promise a natural and "scientific" principle of life on a global scale.[17]

The opposite poles of the issue of state strength were equally far apart. At one end, there were those who believed that all centralized state authority, of whatever type, was evil. Some claimed that this was because it interfered with the natural propensity of men to get along with each other in small, local groups and to find the best solution to their own local problems. The notion that economies prospered most if left entirely to the hidden hand of the market was consistent with such an antistatist point of view. But so was the anarchist idea that if workers organized their own little production groups and cooperative institutions they could achieve a much greater prosperity than if wealthy capitalists robbed their profits. Rousseau had already argued in the eighteenth century that all government was inherently perverse. But many who were radically antiegalitarian also believed that the natural form of government was for local landholding aristocrats to rule their people as shepherds guide their flocks without state interference. Antistatist positions could be held by those in every part of the spectrum on the issue of equality, from radical egalitarians through liberal businessmen, to profound reactionaries who wished to recreate an idyllic rural, feudal past.

Quite opposite were those for whom the modern state was the ultimate tool of social policy. At one extreme, egalitarian socialists like Lenin felt that only state ownership and control of the entire economy could produce equality, while at the other pole, reactionary nineteenth-century French aristocrats like Bonald and de Maistre favored an authoritarian, centralized state, believing that only an all-powerful, divinely sanctioned hereditary monarch could ensure the natural, highly inegalitarian aristocratic order. There were even those who were not particularly extreme in either direction on the issue of equality who went along with the seventeenth-century English political philosopher, Hobbes, in believing that only a strong, centralized state could maintain order and prevent mass passions and jealousies from tearing society apart. Naturally, in between the extreme statists and antistatists were all shades of opinion maintained by exponents who believed in relatively stronger or weaker state structures but rejected the logic of those who took either position to its extremity.[18]

The issue of equality tended to divide people according to their class, with the richer and more powerful being less in favor of greater equality. Positions on the issue of state power, however, were not so obviously correlated with class. Those in control of, or who were even part of, state bureaucracies—civil servants, high officials, and the like—had a direct class interest in maintaining strong central governments. Local notables, if they felt they could maintain their position without assistance from the center, had the opposite interest. But such interests do not explain who took extreme positions on these issues, or why. Marx, for example, rejected the naïve anarchism of ideologues like Proudhon and called for the seizure of government power by the socialists.

But in the very long run, he agreed that governments were evil and existed only to prop up ruling classes, so that with time socialism would dissolve them and a kind of benign, naturally orderly anarchy would reign.

An important trend in the nineteenth century, however, was that the more nationalistic people became, the more they tended to believe in strong state power, for the obvious reason that assertive nationalism implied a strong army and a nation unified and coordinated to carry out its international role. Anti-state ideologies persisted, but they became less important than statist ones, and most of the disputes along this dimension involved those who favored a moderately strong state and those who tended to believe in an all-powerful one.

Belief in the various positions that existed on these two critical issues became a matter of quasi-religious faith, not often subject to logical argument. Those who believed that it was somehow wrong to have inequality were not likely to be swayed by arguments to the contrary, and those who were certain that all government is evil reached that opinion through an act of faith. Faith, then, is not a matter of tinkering and small adjustments. It is too fundamental and too serious a matter. For those who took strong, particularly extreme positions on one or both of these questions, this could be a powerful spur to political action, and it has been such people, along with the most devoted nationalists, who have provided much of the drama of twentieth-century politics throughout the world.

It is easy to recognize the suitable labels for important ideologies through a kind of graphical representation of the two key ideological axes just described. Such a graph is shown in the accompanying figure.

Communism advocated the use of strong state power—in fact, under Lenin, absolute state power—in order to bring about radical equality. But in practice, as we will see, communist rule under Stalin deemphasized equality for practical reasons, and further reinforced state power.[19]

Anarchism, which in the nineteenth century was often lumped with communism as an ideology, shares the communist desire for creating a radically egalitarian society. Since, however, anarchists believe that this can only be achieved with little or no government, they position at the opposite extreme from the communists on one of their two important principles.[20]

Fascism was the last of the great twentieth-century ideologies to emerge, and it was only at the very end of the nineteenth century that signs of it appeared. It has since had a checkered history, going from great successes in the 1920s and 1930s, to eclipse after World War II, and to a possible revival in the late twentieth century. It too, will be discussed in considerably more detail later. For now, suffice it to say that fascism developed as an answer to the mass appeal of the socialists and communists among those who agreed that liberal capitalist society was corrupt and unfair, but who disagreed about the egalitarian demands of the socialists and communists. For much of its early history, fascism consisted of various movements with different aims, ranging from much more egalitarian to economically very conservative groups. All shared the notion that strong action by the state would solve many of the

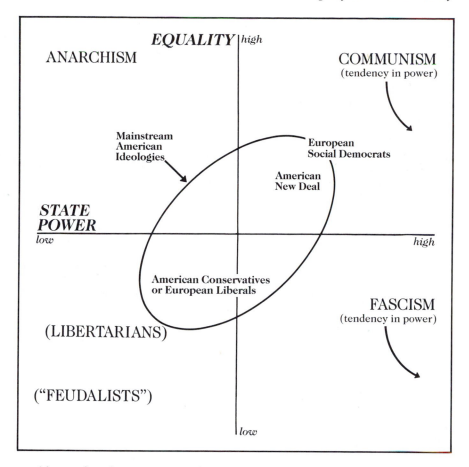

problems of modern society, and with time, the less-egalitarian side prevailed. One of the solutions found by the fascists in order to appeal to large masses of people was extreme nationalism, placing the nation on a pedestal, and claiming that inequality between nations, not within their own, was the natural order. By raising nationalist consciousness they hoped to subordinate internal class disputes. Also, in order to better integrate the various classes of society, they proposed a solution that seemed very different from the radical elimination of distinctions based on property and wealth. They developed the idea of "functional" or vertically-based social organizations, so that all people, high and low, in various sectors of the society would belong to common organizations. Industrial workers and their managers would be organized into industrial "corporations" and act together in their own interest. Class interests, pitting workers against managers and owners, would be eliminated because they were too divisive, and community cooperation within corporate groups would become the rule. For example, teachers and intellectuals at all levels would form their own corporate body, as would rural and agricultural workers ranging from poor peasants to great landowners. So would various categories of professionals, or those involved in heavy industry, and so on. In principle, all people in the society would be integrated into these various corporations, joined together at the top by a coordinating body that would harmonize conflicting interest. The notion of national harmony in one vast corporatist state, where rich and poor, strong and weak would emphasize their shared interests and not their differences, would create a united nation better able to assert itself, and so raise the general level for everyone. In practice, fascism (an alternative name is corporatism) simply favored those with wealth and power, and used corporatist ideology to crush class protest by those less favored.[21]

Politics in the United States, from the very beginning, has tended to develop in a much narrower zone than in Europe or most of the rest of the world. Neither the extremes of the left and right (normally defined to coincide with being more or less egalitarian, with the left being more and the right less) nor any extreme authoritarian tendencies have thrived. In large part this has something to do with the fact that the United States never had a real hereditarily landed aristocracy to promote extremely antiegalitarian ideologies, nor, consequently, any working-class movements obliged to struggle against such notions. A vague, generalized, but on the whole rather mild strain of egalitarianism has always pervaded American ideology along with a feeling that those who worked hard to succeed had a right to enjoy their success. Having almost always believed that there should be rough equality of opportunity, if not of results (except of course, for African slaves and their descendants), America was not conducive, except in the slaveholding South, to radical ideology of any sort. What passes for right and left, ranging from the relatively strong statist, very moderately egalitarian principles of the New Deal Democrats to the mildly antistatist, somewhat less egalitarian principles of the conservative Republicans, would all fit into what used to be called the broad liberal tradition in Europe.[22] (To demonstrate this commonality between what Americans call conservatism and the old-fashioned liberalism of Europe, even today, the kinds of policies advocated by conservative American Republicans are the property of parties which in Europe call themselves "liberal." On the other hand, the left of the American Democratic Party resembles the moderate social democrats of Europe, a pale reflection of what is left of those socialists who did not follow communism.)

The extreme lower-left-hand corner of the ideology graph hardly contains anyone. It was once represented by those retrograde forces in Europe fighting against the emergence of the strong modern state, but such a position is not tenable today. In fact, in Europe, much of the opinion in this area shifted toward fascism as it recognized that radical antiegalitarianism could only maintain itself behind the shield of extreme nationalism. A much milder form of antistatist, antiegalitarian ideology exists in the form of a small movement of people who, in the United States, call themselves "libertarians." In fact, this was a position once held by more Americans, and in some ways approaches the position of Thomas Jefferson, who believed in a weak central state (he originally opposed the Constitution of the United States because it gave too much power to the federal government) and maintained that the best society was one of roughly equal independent farmers who would mind their own business and run their own local affairs. His position was in some ways more egalitarian than that of modern libertarians, who would do nothing at all to decrease inequality; but Jefferson's failure to grapple with the issue of slavery, or of cities and the urban poor, whom he considered dangerous rabble, might have made him a representative of this group. With the increasing power and complexity of the modern state, however, this type of ideology is virtually moot, and in practice, radical antiegalitarianism tends to slip further to the right along the statist axis in the guise of active nationalism and with the excuse that the nation needs a strong and militarily active state in order to protect its freedoms.

Until World War I, there seemed to be a very strong trend in the entire Western world toward the center of both ideological axes. With greater prosperity in the industrialized core, even the socialists were moderating their radically egalitarian demands. The spread of the franchise promised greater democracy, and with the gradual shrinkage of the aristocracy, extremism of the right, too, was on the wane. There were, to be sure, anarchists, communists, and a variety of antiliberal rightists still active, but it might have been thought that the future of politics was going to follow the American pattern. The catastrophe of the war, and the ensuing Depression in the 1930s, dramatically altered this trend and brought the authoritarian ideologies of the left and right, communism and fascism, to the fore.

The Bolshevik Revolution and the Stalinist Solution to Russia's Problems

Of all the consequences of World War I, the first, and in retrospect perhaps the most lasting and important, was the Bolshevik Revolution in Russia. The Russian Revolution began in late February 1917 in the capital of Petrograd (the new name for St. Petersburg, which sounded too German). Strikes demanding food and an end to the war erupted, and the army forces sent to bring the city back under control mutinied. The rule of the absolutist monarchy collapsed almost immediately once it became clear that the army was no longer loyal. There were no longer any major classes to support Tsar Nicholas II, not peasants, workers, bourgeois, or even the huge government bureaucracy which was overwhelmed by the disastrous conduct of the war. The liberal government established to succeed the monarchy, however, continued the war effort in order to preserve Russia's borders and its alliance with the Western European powers. Discontent was not eased, and in late October 1917 the Communist (Bolshevik) Party led by Lenin and Trotsky, launched a second revolution. Petrograd workers, joined by discontented soldiers unwilling to continue the war, took over the government. In November and December similar alliances of workers and soldiers led by the Bolsheviks seized control of the main cities of Russia, including Moscow, the old capital, while in the countryside peasants seized land from landowners, and the old system disintegrated.

Lenin's goal was to bring about Marxist rule in Russia, to create a modern, efficient, egalitarian society based on common rather than private ownership of the means of production. But the Russian state before Lenin had already been heavily involved in industrialization. It had been ruled, even before 1914, by Europe's most despotic autocrat and by its most thorough secret police, and this was the tradition Lenin inherited. Also, the Germans continued to press into Russia, seizing huge portions of its richest farmland and industry in the Baltic, Poland, and the Ukraine. Lenin declared the war over, but to try to keep Russia at war, the Western allies, French, Americans, British, and even Japanese (who were interested in controlling Russia's Pacific Coast) landed in Russia to restore the old government. Combined with a number of antirevolutionary Russian armies, they hemmed in the Bolsheviks who, in 1918–1919, barely controlled the main cities of European Russia and the old Russian heartland. What saved the Bolsheviks was the nationalism of the Russians, who rallied to their government in order to fight the multiple invasion by foreign forces. There was also the continuing resentment of the peasants and the workers, who feared that their newly won rights would be crushed in case of Bolshevik defeat, and the strong anti-Western feeling built up over years among large segments of the Russian population because of the seeming subservience of Russia's economy to European capital and the aping of Western ways among its aristocrats and high bourgeois.[23]

Holding the center, and therefore the best lines of communication against a divided enemy, the Bolshevik army organized by Trotsky gradually built its military force. The Western allies had won the war against Germany by the end of 1918, and the German army was withdrawn. The British, French, and Americans, too, lost interest, and without foreign support or much domestic popularity, the anti-Bolsheviks were pushed out. Though it would take another ten years before the most remote parts of the Russian Empire in Asia were brought under full control, by 1921 the Bolsheviks had basically reestablished Russian unity. The country's new name, the Union of Soviet Socialist Republics, was meant to reflect its socialism and mass democracy (Soviets were councils of workers, peasants, and soldiers organized by the Communist Party to take power). But the system built by Lenin, who only controlled a minority party, necessarily had to rely on the combination of Russian nationalism and the system of police and army controls that had governed Russia before him. The skillful use of these ensured the success of the Bolshevik Revolution.[24]

The war had left the nation devastated, and to restore it to some semblance of economic health, Lenin and the Communist Party allowed a large measure of capitalist enterprise to continue to survive in Russia. The economy was returned to reasonable normalcy and prosperity as the Communists concentrated on eliminating political enemies and strengthening the Party machinery; but they did not yet directly run much of the economy. Lenin died in 1924, and leadership was taken over by Stalin, who had risen to power as a skilled manipulator of the bureaucracy. With his men holding key offices while Lenin's more prestigious and intellectual associates debated Marxist theory, Stalin gained full control by 1928.[25]

Many of the great leaders who had been with Lenin, men like Trotsky, Bukharin, Radek, and Zinoviev, were cosmopolitan intellectuals, some of them brilliant writers and thinkers, who had turned to Marxist socialism as a solution for the inequities, corruption, and poverty of Russia. A substantial portion of the lower cadres of the Party, however, were far less sophisticated, more purely nationalistic, anti-Western, and suspicious of intellectuals who had been exposed to the West. Motivated as much or more by a sense of inferiority, because of Russia's weakness in the world and the fact that their country had lost territory during the war, as by any sense of establishing a more just society, they backed Stalin against his flashier rivals.

Stalin's victory, then, spelled the victory of a Communist party primarily dedicated to building a strong Russia at any cost, and only secondarily to establishing a truly socialist system. But the means available for this were the same as those that had built Russia into a major power in the first place, a strong police state squeezing the peasantry to extract investment, resources, and food for the cities and industries which alone could build a strong military. This had been the technique of the tsars from the time of Peter the Great, and Stalin was able to use the idea of socialism to vastly perfect this type of militarized state control. In 1928, he launched the beginning of a great drive to raise Russia's industrial might to that of the capitalist core. In effect, at that point Russia withdrew from the capitalist world system and chose (or felt forced) to rely on its own enormous resources in order to advance.[26]

Recently, a number of former peripheral societies have tried to accomplish the same program, also by withdrawing from the world system, closing off the outside world in order to stimulate internal development and prevent core control and exploitation of the economy. Developments in the Soviet Union illustrate the possibilities of this approach as well as its limitations and severe negative side effects. The Soviet Union also had two traits that gave it an advantage.

First, it was huge. In 1920 the Soviet Union was the world's largest country in terms of area, and it was inhabited by 134 million people, or about 7 percent of the world's population. The country had immense, largely untapped natural resources, and in this respect was much like the United States.

Second, the Soviet Union did not start its industrialization program from scratch. Poor as it was in 1920, it had the advantage of an intense prewar Russian industrialization (from about 1890 to 1913). It also had a substantial body of trained personnel, fine universities, and a nationalistic civil service. As a result of World War I, the Soviet Union lost many of its most rebellious non-Russian provinces in Europe (Poland, Finland, the Baltic countries, and a part of Romania) while it kept its entire, sparsely populated, Asiatic Empire

(Siberia) and most of the valuable Ukraine. In 1926, 53 percent of the population was Russian, 21 percent was Ukrainian, and 3 percent were other Slavs. Only 23 percent of the population was non-Slavic.[27]

The Soviet Union also had several major disadvantages. First, there was the hostility of the dominant capitalist world system, which feared communist ideology because it might serve as an example for domestic revolution. Second, there had been enormous destruction within the country during the world war and the civil war. Finally, and in some ways most dangerously, there was the fact that the land area of the Soviet Union made it ideally suited for domination by the core or by growing semiperipheral economies. Before World War I, the economy, even while industrializing, had been a major exporter of agricultural products. There were extensive unused resources and huge empty spaces suited for colonization and exploitation. As it happened, the United Kingdom and France were too exhausted to undertake a search for new empires. The United States was not sufficiently interested to mount anything but a few desultory military expeditions, all of them short lived. Japan, though strengthening, was still too weak to undertake to conquer Siberia, especially when easier and more immediately lucrative profits seemed available in China. Germany, which aimed at a colonization of Eastern Europe and large parts of Russia during World War I, was a defeated power, and not until its revival in the 1930s would a threat from this source become severe.

In retrospect, the direction taken by the Soviet Union after 1928 strangely resembles some aspects of Japanese policy in the last quarter of the nineteenth century; and it resembles many aspects of prerevolutionary Russian industrialization as well. First, Soviet industrialization was clearly aimed at strengthening the military position of the state. Heavy industry was emphasized over consumer goods and light industry. The main goal was independence in a hostile world system. Second, the investment for industrialization had to be squeezed out of the peasantry. Third, economic progress was accompanied by strong nationalism and policies aimed at preventing the economy from slipping into peripheral status. That was the whole point of the closure: to prevent the kind of economic and cultural integration into the world system that characterized the relations between weak peripheral societies and strong core ones. As in Japan after 1868, or Russia in the late nineteenth century, foreign investment was allowed only under special circumstances—and then it was tightly controlled by the government. Finally, as in previous semiperipheral efforts at industrialization, the main agent of change was the state rather than the private sector and private capitalist entrepreneurs. These tendencies were even stronger in the Soviet Union than they had been in Russia before 1913 or Japan after the Meiji Restoration. This suggests that while it is important to remember that the Soviet Union claimed to be guided by Marxist ideology, and in certain respects it was, in many other respects its policies after 1928 were more than anything else the product of a nationalistic effort at development in the context of the existing world system.

Based as it was on intense domestic effort, the Soviet Union's developmental effort squeezed the population very hard. In the short run, heavy industry produced no consumer goods; but a growing industrial labor force had to be fed. With few consumer goods to exchange, it was difficult to get rural producers of food to sell their produce; in essence, they received too little in return. Furthermore, the industrial workers themselves could hardly be rewarded with more than the bare necessities. All surplus production had to go to building more industries. In this stage of the process, the very success of industrialization increased social tensions. Workers, both rural and industrial, were being severely deprived for the sake of increased production. The only solution was repression.

Soviet industrialization was very rapid in the 1930s. The Soviet Union went from producing 5 percent of the world's manufactured goods in 1929 to producing 18 percent in 1938. (During that time, the share of the United States, the United Kingdom, and France fell from 59 to 52 percent of the total.) From 1929 to 1940 Soviet industrial production at least tripled.[28]

The dramatic increase in industrial production involved a big shift in the labor force. In 1926, of 85.5 million people in the civilian labor force, 81 percent worked in agriculture. By 1940 the civilian labor force had grown to 97.8 million, of which only 59 percent were in agriculture.[29] This change involved large movements of population from rural to urban areas and important changes in the way of life. At the same time the Soviet school system was vastly expanded, allowing large numbers to be educated. And new public health measures greatly reduced mortality. Although the progress in these areas was part of a long-term transformation occurring throughout the world, and one which had already occurred to a significant extent in industrialized societies, the fact that the Soviet Union made significant advances, even during the hardest periods of its forced industrialization, shows that, judged by these criteria, the developmental program was successful.[30]

However, the forced industrialization of the Soviet Union was extremely costly in terms of human lives and freedoms. In order to ensure needed deliveries of food, the Communist Party of the Soviet Union (C.P.S.U.) collectivized the country's agriculture. In theory, this was done as part of the transformation from capitalism to socialism, but, in effect, it was a way to police the peasantry and squeeze a surplus out of agriculture. The peasants resisted, and some 10 million of them were shot or deported to Siberia.[31] By 1940 nearly 97 percent of all peasants had been forced into collectives, but, as Merle Fainsod has written:

> The collectivization crisis of the early thirties exacted a terrible price
> . . . [it] involved the uprooting and exile of millions of peasants and
> robbed the countryside of its most efficient and enterprising element.
> The slaughter of livestock and draft animals [by the resisting peasants] inflicted a wound on the Soviet economy from which it took

> nearly a decade to recover. The disorganization of work in the new
> collective farms contributed to the disastrous harvest of 1931 and
> 1932. Despite the drastic decline in crop yields, the authorities were
> ruthless in enforcing their demands on the countryside, and near-
> famine conditions prevailed in many rural areas. . . . An unknown
> number of peasants, variously estimated at from one to several mil-
> lion, died of starvation. . . .[32]

As a result, Soviet agricultural production was probably no higher in 1940
than it had been in 1913; and meat production fell considerably from the levels
reached in 1928 before the start of massive collectivization.[33] The average
Russian was thus less well-fed in 1940 than before World War I. This contrasted markedly with the pattern of industrialization in Western Europe and
the United States, where agriculture had improved its productivity as quickly
as, or even more quickly than industry. To this day, Soviet agriculture remains
peculiarly backward, a burden that continues to cause severe imbalances in an
otherwise advanced economy.

It was not only the peasantry which suffered, though as a class it was the
most exploited group in the Soviet Union. The standard of living in the cities
(measured in terms of housing) was no higher in 1938 than it had been in
1913.[34] (This estimate is based on official Soviet statistics, as is the estimate of
agricultural production.) Such lack of movement is to be expected in view of
the rapid growth of cities and the de-emphasis on consumer goods. But the
climate of fear and repression imposed on the population by the secret police
was certainly worse in the 1930s than in prerevolutionary Russia.

The estimated number of people killed, deported, and jailed by the police
during the 1930s (not even counting the legions of peasants) is almost unbelievable. Soviet historian Roy A. Medvedev has estimated that of the top 134
officials of the C.P.S.U. in 1934, 110 had been arrested by 1939, and many, if
not most of them were shot. Possibly up to 90 percent of all local Party
officials suffered the same fate, as did many scientists, artists, military officers,
and thousands upon thousands of civil servants and quite ordinary people.

Medvedev believes that in 1936–1939 4 or 5 million Soviet citizens were
arrested and that at least 500 thousand were shot. He writes:

> In 1937–38 there were days when up to a thousand people were shot
> in Moscow alone. . . . The simple truth must be stated: not one of the
> tyrants and despots of the past persecuted and destroyed so many of
> his compatriots.[35]

Nor did this repression stop in the 1930s; it continued through the 1940s and
early 1950s.

Economist Steven Rosefielde has used Soviet census data to estimate the
total number who died because of Stalin's policies. Excess deaths in
1929–1939 total at least 12.8 million, and in 1939–1949 (not counting any
deaths attributable to World War II), at least 3.5 million died. But these are

the lowest possible estimates, and the actual numbers may have been as high as 14.7 million in the ten years from 1929 to 1939 and 11.6 million from 1939 to 1949. These deaths resulted from murder, starvation, and disease that occurred in forced labor camps, and from the abominable conditions endured during deportations. The near collapse of agriculture produced by collectivization is as much an aspect of this as the mass killings and jailings. Of those who died, as many as 7 to 8 million were children. The Soviet census of 1937 was suppressed because it showed such a huge deficit in expected population, and the published 1939 census probably lied to cover up what had happened. Later, Soviet authorities accounted for the missing population by exaggerating deaths attributable to World War II, but it is reasonable to assume that from 1929 to 1939 the population only increased from about 150 to 156 million. The number who died of unnatural causes as a result of Stalinism in that decade amounted to anywhere from 8 to 10 percent of the total population.

Considering that by the time Stalin died as much as 10 percent of the Soviet population may have been in forced labor camps, and that from 1941 to 1945 an additional 16 million died as a result of World War II (5 to 6 million soldiers, and 10 to 11 million civilians), one begins to realize the almost unbelievable horror of life in the Soviet Union in the twenty-five year span of Stalin's absolute rule from 1928 to 1953. Well over a quarter of the population was directly touched, either by death or imprisonment, and that means, of course, that virtually everyone had many close relatives and friends who were a part of those fantastic statistics.[36]

It is well to remember that a society shaped by such trauma, especially when even more of it was self-inflicted than caused by an enormously bloody war, is likely to be decisively altered for a long time to come. And later, we will see that Russia is not a unique case. At least some other Leninist-Stalinist regimes—China, Cambodia, and perhaps most recently Ethiopia—have had, and in some cases are still having, analogous experiences.

Why this occurred remains hotly debated. Was Stalin mad? (But then, were Mao, Pol Pot, or Colonel Mengistu?) Every modernizing revolution from the time of the French Revolution of 1789 has involved political repression and terror. But the scale of repression in the Soviet Union in the 1930s was so great that most people outside the country could not believe it was happening, and in fact those on the left in Western countries invented elaborate fantasies to explain away the disturbing evidence they heard. Was it perhaps the extraordinarily rapid pace of change in the Soviet Union that provoked such massive terror? Was this seen as the only way to keep the population under control? Did the extreme feeling of vulnerability to the outside reinforce Stalin's zeal? How could officials who were next in line to be shot continue carrying out their orders? Was revolutionary ideology so strongly ingrained? Did nationalism excuse and justify this behavior? In extremely stressful, revolutionary situations, only the most ruthless leaders tend to survive, and they learn to hold on to power by any means. Idealism combined with utter ruthlessness and the means to impose highly authoritarian control on a population create the potential for monstrosities barely imagined by the citizens of more fortunate, less threatened, and more prosperous societies.

The sobering fact is that in a sense, Stalinism in the Soviet Union worked very well. In twenty-five years the U.S.S.R. raised itself from the position of a relatively vulnerable semiperipheral society to the world's second greatest power, an advance even more dramatic than the rise of Japan after 1868. The cost was enormous, but it is conceivable that without it, the Soviet Union would have lost the Second World War and become just another fragmented colonial periphery. No one can say.

Equally sobering is the fact that the gigantic apparatus of repression set up by Stalin remains in place, though it is used much more sparingly than before. Some of the young bureaucrats who served him in his bloodiest times were the old men who ran the U.S.S.R. until the mid-1980s. The next generation of leaders, those now in power, are those trained by Stalin's direct assistants. They are men who went to school and reached adulthood in the 1930s and 1940s as these terrible events were taking place around them. Though it is not possible to predict what turns they will make in policy, it is not difficult to understand that such experiences make individuals cautious and fearful that any rapid change might bring renewed disasters, either from external causes or from an unchained internal repressive machine. Quite the opposite of revolutionaries, these leaders are among the most committed in the world to holding on to their gains without risking innovation because they know the fearful price of disorderly, unforeseen change.

Fascism

Though fascism is often associated with purely reactionary politics, it contains an important revolutionary component. Dissatisfaction with the impersonality and inequities of industrial society, and growing class warfare caused some of Europe's young intellectuals in the early twentieth century to seek solutions outside of conventional socialist ideology. In Italy, early fascist thought derived from an intellectual movement that called itself "futurist." Early fascists were hostile to the entire rational thrust of bourgeois capitalism. They valued spontaneity and enthusiasm, communal solidarity, and they felt that liberal democracy was too slow, too compromising, too tainted by money and greed to bring about necessary reforms. They did not so much emphasize their hostility to any forced redistribution of wealth from the top to the bottom as they more or less ignored the issue. They claimed that once the bourgeoisie's hold on power and the financial power of "foreign" elements were eliminated, a more just society would emerge. "Foreigners" were variously seen as Jews, outside investors, and any who were not part of the majority culture. One of the key intellectual heroes of the early fascists was Georges Sorel, whose *Reflections on*

Violence pronounced the higher morality of symbolic acts of violence against the cynical corruption of parliamentary democracy and capitalism. It is therefore not surprising that he was considered a useful ideologue both by communists and by Mussolini, the first fascist to come to power in Europe in 1922.[37]

In fact, the similarity between fascism and communism is more than coincidental, though each approached its position from a different theoretical stance. The hatred of capitalism and the bourgeoisie was common to both. Both had adherents in core societies, but grew to their greatest strength in the semiperiphery where nationalist grievances against the core and hostility to foreign economic power reached higher levels. Both came to the conclusion that violent revolution was necessary, and both recruited heavily among discontented youth of a variety of classes. Both relied on romantic and noble dreams of perfection that might be reached once the revolution had cleansed away the decadence of the past. Both believed that a self-appointed elite was best suited to represent the "masses," who could not be relied on to know their own best interests, much less plan the tactics of revolution. Both planned to strengthen the power of the state in order to carry out reform. Just as fascist and communist movements shared a centralized, authoritarian party structure, each carried these organizational forms into government when they came to power.[38]

The difference between the two movements was that while communists claimed to represent the interests of the working class and promised radical equality, the fascists were hostile to class-based politics and found forced egalitarianism unnatural. Communists were led to repudiate private property, which Marx had seen as the source of all power and thus of inequality and injustice. Fascists did not attack the basic notion of private property; they accepted inequality and they rejected the need to eliminate class enemies as long as these were not "foreign." Corporatism, the fascist solution for organizing society, was the method to be used for integrating various classes and segments of society into functionally and occupationally based groups that were cooperating and unalienated.

In practice, Communism soon abandoned radical egalitarianism. The Communist Party of the Soviet Union under Stalin became a highly rewarded, all-powerful elite open to those with talent who did not question the Party or its leader. Since communism claimed that classes had been abolished, it organized society along the kinds of functional and occupational lines proposed by fascists. In practice, too, communism abandoned its internationalism for narrow nationalism.[39] Communists in power no more recognized the legitimacy of working-class organization and protest than did the fascists.

Fascism's road to power, however, was quite different from communism's; and, in power, fascists proved to be considerably less revolutionary than the communists, who at least destroyed the old elites before recreating a whole new class structure. Beginning with much less commitment to equality than the communists, the fascists in power were actually antiegalitarian, while communists did work to lessen inequality and promote the more deserving members of the lower classes as quickly as possible into the new elite. In power,

fascists allied themselves to older elites to perpetuate or increase the old in-
equalities. In the fragile economic and political circumstances of post-World
War I Europe, with rising class warfare and the threat of communist revolution on everyone's mind, old elites began to look for ways of mobilizing mass
support against the left. They saw fascism as a way of addressing the problem
without endangering the basis of their own wealth. Fascist movements, on the
other hand, saw cooperation with old upper classes as a way to gain power; and
since they deemphasized class warfare in favor of nationalism, such an alliance
did not seem repulsive.[40]

It was particularly in the semiperiphery and periphery of Europe that fascism struck a responsive note. These economies were the most vulnerable, and
nationalistic grievances were most acute there. Also, much of the elite in these
regions consisted of landowners and descendants of the old aristocracies who
could join with the fascists in contempt for greedy bourgeois businessmen. In
such societies, too, there were still many small landowning peasants attached to
traditional religious beliefs, angered by the damaging intrusion of market
forces into their lives, and providing a residue of good will toward fascist
movements that promised to redress these conditions. Beginning with Italy in
1922 and spreading throughout Southern and Eastern Europe over the decades of the twenties and thirties, fascism took power in almost every noncore
country of Europe, stretching in a great arc from Portugal on the Atlantic to
the Baltic countries in the northeast. Japan, a semiperipheral society with
similar problems and a somewhat analogous class structure, followed the same
pattern. Fascist movements grew in some of the more developed South American countries as well.

European fascist movements after World War I fed on the presence of
unemployed veterans and on the fears of the lower-middle-class shopkeepers,
artisans, and civil servants who saw their savings being eroded by inflation and
their economic standing threatened by the rise of socialist trade unions, and
who were generally disgusted with the older forms of government which had
brought such unparalleled disasters to Europe. Leaders came to the fore who
promised violent, cleansing action to restore national wholeness by destroying
the "foreign" forces held responsible for the corruption of the nation. Mussolini in Italy, Hitler in Germany, and later, Primo de Rivera in Spain, Codreanu
in Romania, and, in the 1940s, Perón in Argentina were the most successful
and charismatic fascist leaders. Fascist movements, stressing as they did innovation, violence, hostility to established rules, and promises of a grand national
unification, relied heavily on leadership by one man meant to embody the
Party and Nation, a kind of superhero who could act as a magnet for the
disaffected. (Of course, with time, communist regimes have also found that in
the absence of other forms of political participation by the population, building a leader to superhuman proportions is a useful tool for ruling; and in
practice there was little difference between the idealization of Mussolini and
Stalin, or the godlike qualities ascribed to Romania's fascist leader Codreanu in

the 1930s and those claimed by Romania's communist boss in the 1970s and 1980s, Ceausescu.)[41]

There were also fascist movements in England, France, and the United States. But they were unable to gain power because, after all, grievances in the core societies, the victors of the First World War and still the dominant economic powers in the world, were more easily managed than they were in the semiperipheral and peripheral edges of Europe. Only in Germany, relegated to a position of political inferiority and humiliation in international politics because of its defeat in 1918, did fascism come to power in what might have been considered a core society. But Germany was not, in 1933, a full-fledged, accepted member of the capitalist core, and its population felt the same sense of persecution by the international order felt by the poorer and weaker countries of Southern and Eastern Europe.

The political history of Germany from 1918 to 1933 is instructive. The first postwar years were chaotic as movements of the right and left fought for control of the fallen empire. Finally, armed bands of veterans enrolled by the right and supported by the bulk of the middle and upper classes brought the communists under control and thwarted the revolution. Then, the democratic form of government mandated by the victorious allies took hold, but from the start it was discredited as a traitor to the German national cause as well as incapacitated by the terrible inflation of 1923. Still, by 1924, the start of a moderate economic recovery stabilized the situation. In December 1924, in the national election, Hitler's fascist party, the Nazis, gained 3 percent of the vote, other far-rightist parties 22 percent, and the Communist Party 9 percent. Parties of the center, including liberals, Christian Democrats, and moderate socialists received 62 percent of the vote. As late as the election of May 1928, these proportions remained roughly similar. But with the onset of the Great Depression, the old grievances combined with new ones. From 1928 to July 1932, the proportion of votes gained by the Nazis went from 3 percent to 37 percent, and the total gained by the far right went from 21 percent to 44 percent. The Communist total rose, too, as some of the working class shifted its allegiance from the moderate socialists. Communist votes went from 11 to 14 percent, and those of moderate socialists fell from 30 to 22 percent (suggesting that the shift tended to move more strongly toward the far right than toward the far left). All of the moderate vote, socialist and liberal, fell from 63 percent in 1928 to 40 percent in 1932.[42]

In 1933 Hitler and his Nazi Party took power, helped by other far-right allies and tacit acceptance by some of the center parties. The opposition socialists and communists were outlawed, anti-Jewish legislation was passed, and the economy was rapidly geared to rearmament (thus solving the unemployment problem). An aggressive foreign policy soon allowed Germany to dominate Eastern Europe, which, by the late 1930s, was being turned into a series of German economic colonies geared to German economic needs. The threat this posed to France and the United Kingdom finally provoked a belated reaction.

Germany had already annexed Austria and Czechoslovakia; when it invaded Poland in 1939, World War II broke out.[43]

Despite the great historical and cultural differences between Germany and Japan, the two societies wound up in rather similar situations in the 1930s. From the very start of Japan's push toward major core status, a primary component of Japanese policy had been its imperialism abroad and heavy industrialization for military purposes at home. Before World War I, Japan had taken pieces of China, conquered Korea, and defeated Russian expansionism in the Far East. After the war, growing prosperity and the influence of the urban middle class liberalized Japanese politics. The Depression reversed this process of liberalization. Japan had become dependent on its export trade to finance the import of vital raw materials, and the Depression in the capitalist world system resulted in steep tariff walls raised by the core powers to protect their economies. (The United States, the United Kingdom, and France all followed very protectionist policies after 1929.) Edwin Reischauer, America's foremost expert on Japan, has observed:

> The businessman's program of continued economic expansion and prosperity through a growing export trade was suddenly revealed to be dangerously dependent on the good will and tolerance of foreign powers. Huge political units like Russia, the United States, and the British Empire could ride the storm of world depression, for they had their own sources of supply for most raw materials and their own consuming markets. But a smaller unit like Japan, which depended on other lands for much of its raw materials, and on China, India, and the Occident for a vital part of its consuming market, seemed entirely at the mercy of the tariff policies of other nations.[44]

The Japanese military and the large corporations which dominated the economy combined in the late 1920s to return Japan to authoritarian nationalism at home and vigorous expansionist imperialism abroad, much as the same forces combined in Germany to install a fascist regime. Between 1929 and 1938, the only major industrial powers that increased their share of world manufacturing output were Germany and Japan (along with the Soviet Union). German and Japanese fascist policies certainly seemed to pay off in terms of expanding the national share of world trade. In short, while the Depression clearly weakened the capitalist core, the fascist societies of the semiperiphery that were the main challengers of the core societies grew stronger.

In 1932 Japan officially annexed the northern Chinese province of Manchuria. The military effectively took over the Japanese government. It gradually strengthened its position, and in 1937 launched a full-scale invasion of China. In 1941, in order to take over the rich oil, rubber, and other mineral and agricultural riches of Southeast Asia (then controlled by the British, French, Dutch, and Americans), the Japanese tried to destroy the only military force capable of resisting them, the American Pacific fleet stationed at Pearl Harbor.

By this act, Japan signaled its full entry into the core of the capitalist world system as a challenger of the old core.[45]

A list of political and economic events in Germany and Japan in the 1930s barely indicates the magnitude of the social changes that accompanied these events. Strict antilabor laws, hysterical xenophobia, militarization of every aspect of civilian life, extreme police repression, and the glorification of war turned these two societies into fiercely imperial machines. At a more mundane level, change was equally dramatic. In the capitalist core, the 1920s and 1930s saw an improvement in the status of women (who had gained the right to vote in Britain and Germany in 1918, and in the United States in 1920), an improvement in the lives of the working classes, and a great outpouring of literary and artistic work. The same trends prevailed in Germany and Japan in the 1920s. In the 1930s they were reversed. German and Japanese women were supposed to go back to their homes and breed new soldiers for the empire; literature and the arts were censored and suppressed; working-class wages were frozen; and democratic practices eliminated.[46]

The Marxist-Leninist interpretation of fascism was that it was the final stage of imperialistic capitalism. According to Lenin's theory of imperialism, once the world was filled up and no new colonies were available, the capitalist powers would wage a life and death struggle against one another for survival. To the communists in the 1930s it seemed that this was exactly what the hypernationalism and expansive militarism of Nazi Germany, Fascist Italy, and Imperial Japan were about. Where the theory was wrong was in the assumption that this phenomenon was purely the result of machinations by the big capitalists trying to preserve their position against the rise of working-class socialist movements. It is correct that in many cases these major capitalists joined in with the fascists, seeing them as a solution to both national problems and to the threat from the left. But fascist movements were widely popular and often fit the demands of large portions of the population better than did the positions of the communists whose class appeal was more restricted, and whose frequent manipulation by the Communist Party of the Soviet Union made their nationalism suspect.[47]

There were two broad forms of fascism in power. Both were shaped by compromises between the established, old elites and the rising fascist movements, and so in all cases fascism in power was far less innovative and revolutionary than it had been in its earlier days. But in highly industrial, big powers like Germany and Japan, the sentimental ideology about a return to a more idyllic, rural, and traditional life was abandoned in favor of more rapid industrialization in order to build stronger war machines. Industrial fascism, in practice, behaved exactly as the Leninist theory predicted, even if its internal dynamic was different.

But in more backward countries, and in smaller ones, fascism could take on a more rural, traditionally authoritarian, and less aggressive role. In Spain and Portugal, with time, fascism became far less harsh and dangerous than in Germany. Much of the almost amusing bombast of Mussolini (not so amusing, of course, for the Libyans and Ethiopians killed by his soldiers in a vain attempt to create a great Roman Empire) was the result of this, the inability of fascism in an agrarian setting to carry out its dynamic, grandiose dreams. So, in such cases, fascism turned into more of a conservative than a revolutionary force.

But in Germany, in particular, the fact that Nazism was considered a movement of the far right should not conceal the fact that by enormously strengthening state power, galvanizing the population, and totally crushing working-class union movements, it revolutionized society. It is therefore perhaps not so much of a coincidence that after World War II the most dynamic economy in Europe became West Germany's, and the most dynamic in the world that of Japan. In a sense, the structural transformations of fascism in these countries were as important as the different ones brought about by communism where it triumphed.[48]

The New Deal Alternative to Fascism

In the United States and the United Kingdom of the 1930s, fascism was never a serious threat. In France, which was economically weaker and politically less stable, the decade was marked by the electoral triumph of the left rather than the right, even though a number of fascist movements did develop. In none of the core societies was frustrated nationalism nearly as strong as in Germany or Japan. The Depression consequently produced a rather different reaction in these societies.

The main example of the moderate democratic reformism that prevailed in core societies was the American government's New Deal. Franklin Roosevelt and the Democratic Party won overwhelming electoral control of the United States in 1932, and there followed a dramatic series of federal reforms designed to alleviate the Depression. Banking, corporation law, and the stock exchange were reformed. Social security and numerous public welfare schemes went into effect. The rights of labor unions to strike and bargain collectively were strongly affirmed by law. Although these acts did not end the Depression, they made the government both popular and stable; and extremist challenges from both the far right and the left were easily pushed aside.

The New Deal did not end capitalism or bring about economic and social equality between classes (this was not Roosevelt's intent); but it did lessen inequality a bit, and more importantly, it created the impression of greater equality. Income distribution figures for the United States during this period show the small but significant extent of the redistribution (see Table 6-2). The index of inequality decreased steadily from 1929 to 1944, and was then to remain pretty much unchanged into the 1960s.

Another aspect of the New Deal was that it marked the first time in the United States that the federal government became a major force in the peace-

TABLE 6-2
**Percentage Distribution of Family Personal Income
in the United States, 1929–1941**[49]

Consumer Units		1929	1935–1936	1941	Percentage of Change 1929–1941
Lowest	20%	3.5%	4.1%	4.1%	+17%
Second	20%	9.0%	9.2%	9.5%	+ 6%
Third	20%	13.8%	14.1%	15.3%	+11%
Fourth	20%	19.3%	20.9%	22.3%	+16%
Top	20%	54.4%	51.7%	48.8%	−10%
Top	5%	30.0%	26.5%	24.0%	−20%

time economy. This does not signify that the government ended private enterprise (though right-wing criticism of the New Deal has often declared so), or that the government took over a significant portion of the means of production; but, rather, that it became a major spender in the economy as well as an increasingly important regulator of private enterprise. The growth of government spending is indicated in Table 6-3, which lists the percentages of the GNP spent by the federal government in the years between 1900 and 1941.

Just as the political right has criticized the New Deal for being too socialist (a criticism with no basis if socialism is to mean government seizure of the key means of production; that is, of key businesses), the left has criticized it for not being socialist enough. Since the reformers wanted to save the capitalist system by defusing discontent and shoring up a shaky financial system, the New

TABLE 6-3
GNP and Government Spending[50]

	GNP (in billions of dollars)	Federal Government Spending (in billions of dollars)	Spending as Percentage of GNP
1900	17	0.5	2.9%
1910	31	0.7	2.3%
1920	89	6.4 (remnant of wartime spending)	7.2%
1929	104	3.3	3.2%
1933	56	4.6	8.2%
1937	91	7.8	8.6%
1941	126	13.3 (start of wartime spending)	10.6%

Deal was actually quite successful—even if it did not end the Depression.

But the New Deal cannot be analyzed in purely local—that is, national—terms, because similar measures were taken in other core societies as well and because these measures were all responses to changes that had occurred in industrialized societies quite independently of their political ideology. These effects of industrialization can be summarized in six main points.

1. Industrialization had shifted the distribution of population. Ever larger proportions of the population lived in cities rather than in small towns or villages. In such small settlements, in times of economic depression, people relied on help from relatives and neighbors, and tried to survive by simply growing more of their own food. The residents of large cities were usually somewhat more cut off from their relatives, particularly if they had moved to the city quite recently, and neighbors were not as likely to help each other. More importantly, city people were firmly in the cash economy and could not, like peasants, get by on local production. The city dweller without a job was helpless. The Depression of the 1930s finally brought home the point that some kinds of social insurance were absolutely necessary.[51]

2. Increasing competition in the world system required much greater government participation and protection. Governments had always participated in helping certain sectors of the economy; but as the world system grew tighter, such government help became more important. This was particularly true in the semiperipheral economies, which probably explains why their governments took over more of their national economies than governments did in core societies. But even in the core, the electorate finally accepted the idea that the government had to play a major role in the economy.

3. The rise of working-class, egalitarian ideologies, and the dangerous example of the Soviet Union set the ideological tone during the interwar period. Capitalist elites rejected and feared socialism, but there was little doubt that the challenge had to be met one way or another. The fascist response, of course, was one possibility. The only other possible response (except for socialism itself) was to give in to certain working-class demands, and to create somewhat greater equality and government action simply to save the system.

4. The spread of egalitarian ideals was particularly important because continued economic growth for a long period of time had accustomed populations in core societies, for the first time in world history, to a continually rising standard of living. Since rising standards of living had become normal, falling standards were even more threatening during the Great Depression than they had been in previous economic depressions.

5. World communications and domestic communications in each core society were far more developed in the 1930s than ever before. Radio, movies, the spread of literacy, improvements in railroads and automobiles, as well as the concentration of people into cities made core populations more aware of what was going on nationally and internationally than they ever had been in the

TABLE 6-4
**Decrease or Increase in Income Shares of Top 5
Percent of Consuming Units, 1920s to 1930s**[52]

United Kingdom (1929–1938)	− 6%
United States (1929–1941)	−20%
Sweden (1930–1935)	− 7%
Denmark (1925–1939)	− 6%
Germany (1928–1936)	+15%

past. The spread of egalitarian ideals was more rapid, and the awareness of falling standards of living was more thorough.

6. Finally, the main capitalist economies had experienced a great concentration of businesses. A few giant corporations had acquired a disproportionate amount of power, and the electorate demanded that governments step in as regulators. Business had become so concentrated that the private interests of the corporation could set economic policy, and free-market forces were becoming less important. By 1929 the largest 100 manufacturing corporations in the United States, for example, owned 40 percent of all assets in manufacturing.[53] The onset of the Depression convinced the middle classes that some form of government participation in economic decisions was obligatory.

Placed in a world context, then, events in the United States were neither unique nor based purely on the vagaries of Roosevelt's actions.[54] Other core societies experienced similar, moderate declines of gross inequality because of reforms like the New Deal. Among the advanced industrial societies, only Germany had a different pattern during the 1930s (see Table 6-4). There, the degree of concentration of wealth at the top increased rather than decreased. This, of course, reflects the fascist "solution" to the Depression.

There had already been a noticeable decrease in economic inequality in industrial societies during and immediately after World War I; social insurance, recognition of unions, and government participation in the economy were not entirely inventions of the thirties. The New Deal and similar reforms merely accelerated existing trends and certified transformations that had been occurring for many decades.

The Second World War and the Postwar Arrangement

By the late 1930s the capitalist world system seemed to be approaching collapse. Measures on the order of the New Deal had maintained political stability in the core, but the Depression was not yet over. From Germany, Italy, and Japan fascism was expanding. By 1939 large parts of China had been seized by the Japanese; Italy had conquered Ethiopia and incorporated Albania; and Germany had annexed Austria and Czechoslovakia. In a bitter civil war in Spain (1936–1939), Germany and Italy had given decisive help to the fascists and the Spanish left had been defeated. By the end of that war, it was no longer a matter of a struggle between democracy and fascism because the democratic countries of Europe had abandoned the Spanish left entirely to Soviet help. The Spanish Civil War had turned into a symbolic conflict waged between what seemed to be the only two forces contending for the future of the world, fascism and communism. The success stories of the 1930s seemed to be the most cruel, ruthless, totalitarian regimes of the world, not the timid, mildly reformist, floundering core democracies.

In fact, if instead of looking at the world situation as a contest between the left and the right we see it as the rise of the semiperiphery against the core, a different pattern emerges. Germany, Italy, Japan, and the Soviet Union all had this in common: they wished to overthrow the existing international order controlled by the old liberal core, and they had used their nationalistic, strong state ideologies to harness their populations for just such an effort.

As the world moved toward war, it finally struck the leaders of these countries that they had a common goal in mind and could, at least in the short run, collaborate to bring down the old core. On August 23, 1939, the Soviet Union and Germany signed a nonaggression pact in which they agreed to divide Eastern Europe and keep out of each other's way.[55] Germany, Italy, and Japan already had treaty obligations to one another, so that all of a sudden a gigantic bloc, the "totalitarian semiperiphery," was united against the old core.

One week after the Stalin-Hitler pact, Germany invaded Poland, and the British and French declared war. To have failed to act would have meant surrender of Europe to Hitler and Stalin, and probably the fatal weakening of the French and British positions in Asia to Japanese conquest as well. (Although this is what happened in any case.)

George Kennan, historian and diplomat, has pointed out a fact which, even today, is little appreciated:

> Before the war began, the overwhelming portion of the world's armed strength in land forces and air forces had accumulated in the hands of three political entities—Nazi Germany, Soviet Russia, and Imperial Japan. All these entities were deeply and dangerously hostile to the Western democracies. As things stood in the late thirties, if these three powers were to combine their efforts and stick together in a military enterprise, the remaining Western nations plainly had no hope of defeating them on the land mass of Europe and Asia, with the armaments at hand or even those in prospect. In Europe and Asia, Western democracy had become militarily outclassed. The world balance of power had turned decisively against it.[56]

By mid-1941, Germany, its junior partner Italy, and several East European satellite allies had conquered all of Europe except for the U.S.S.R., the United Kingdom and the neutral countries of Sweden, Switzerland, Portugal, and Spain (an unofficial German ally). France had been overrun in a few weeks in the spring of 1940 because it had tried to fight the defensive kind of war that might have been suitable in 1914. The perfection of tanks and airpower, however, and the possibility of transporting supplies on roads with large numbers of trucks had given the offense an advantage again, and the German army had been built on these new premises. Only the fact that England was an island, and was increasingly supplied by the United States, kept it free.

At that point the world was saved by the logic of German imperialism. Because of a perceived need to gain the vast spaces of Russia and its resources, Hitler turned his attention to his recent ally. Nazi race theories, too, played an important role, as Germanic peoples were assumed to be superior to the Russian Slavs whose fate it would be to become slave laborers for the new masters of Europe. In June 1941 Germany invaded Russia, and by the end of that year it had seized a large part of that country.[57]

On December 7, 1941, Japan struck the American fleet in Pearl Harbor, and with the Americans temporarily incapacitated it launched an invasion of Southeast Asia to seize the petroleum, rubber, and other resources it needed. Dutch, British, and French colonies there fell under its control, as did the American colony of the Philippines. By mid-1942 Japan, too, had added immense new territories to its empire, which now included Manchuria, most of the rich coastal plains of China, Korea, Indochina, Burma, Thailand (formally a Japanese ally), as well as the Philippines, Indonesia (the Dutch East Indies), most of New Guinea, and most of the islands of the South Pacific. On its western border, it threatened India, on its south, Australia, and in the far northeastern reaches of its domain it seized a few Alaskan islands.

As the Germans and Japanese conquered Europe and East Asia, the full consequences of the years of racist nationalist ideology manifested themselves. In Europe the Nazis began a systematic campaign of extermination of Jews and Gypsies, and the "inferior" Slavs were consigned to servitude. In Poland this meant that the intellectuals and leaders were slated for extermination while the bulk of the population was to be slowly worked to death; and in occupied parts of Russia the plan was the same. France, Belgium, the Netherlands, Norway, and Denmark, though assigned a higher place in Nazi race theories were squeezed dry to feed Germany and supply its industries with resources and forced labor. People from all of occupied Europe were enslaved and removed to Germany to replace German labor drafted into the armed forces. This was imperialism followed to its ultimate, logical conclusion. What the core societies had been practicing in the periphery for the previous century was but a foretaste of what such policies meant taken to their extremes. German cultural arrogance and military power were attempting nothing short of the peripheralization of all the rest of Europe. Such policies naturally provoked resistance in the occupied countries, particularly in Eastern Europe which was so harshly treated. In the horrible repression that followed and the series of civil wars it let loose, millions were killed. Added to the systematic slaughter of certain peoples and military deaths, at least 30 million Europeans died from 1939 to 1945 (see Table 6-5). Of this number some 5 to 6 million were Jews, out of a total of 9 million Jews in Europe at the start of the war.[58]

The Japanese were only marginally more lenient occupiers. In China they plundered, raped, enslaved, and killed immense numbers. It is difficult to know how many died as a consequence of these acts, to say nothing of the famines that resulted from the war and the general chaos of that period. In other occupied countries, too, like Indonesia and the Philippines, the Japanese established a reputation for brutality worse than that of the European colonizers; and resistance movements sprang up against them.[59] At least 25 million or more Asians died during this war, so that the total number of deaths from the Second World War reached over 55 million.[60]

In the end, the manpower reserves of the Soviet Union and the industrial might of the United States stopped the Germans and the Japanese. By the end of 1942 both the Germans and Japanese had suffered decisive defeats, and were being outproduced by their enemies. The United States alone, for example, was able to produce almost 50 percent more airplanes during the war than Germany and Japan put together, and more than three times as many tanks as Germany. When this was added to the considerable industrial might of the Soviet Union and the United Kingdom, it was evident by early 1943 that the fascist powers had lost.[61] Yet it took two more long years, and in the case of Japan the use of two atomic bombs, to get them to surrender; and during that time much of the worst carnage of the war took place.

The end of the war, and the complete victory of the Americans, British, and Russians, brought some important political changes. The Germans and Japanese lost their empires, and Germany was split into western and eastern parts. The Soviets took over Germany's Eastern European empire, and have ruled it ever since. The Europeans and Americans reclaimed their empires from the Japanese, but the period of Japanese occupation had stirred strong resistance movements, which proceeded to try to gain their independence. China achieved full independence, but plunged into civil war between communists and anticommunists.

The boundary changes in Eastern Europe entailed large-scale human migrations, putting a finishing touch to the territory disruption of the war. Some 14 million Germans left Eastern Europe for Germany, and some 7 million Slavs were moved into areas evacuated by the Germans. In Asia, millions of Japanese returned to Japan, and huge internal migrations took place in China as people tried to return home or to flee from the competing forces in the civil war. In terms of immediate social disruption, the effects of the war were felt until the early 1950s, and at least until that time most of Europe and Asia remained impoverished and highly dependent on American aid and capital for economic reconstruction.[62]

The end of the war marked the end of the great twentieth-century conflict

TABLE 6-5   167
Deaths During World War II[63]

Country	Population in 1939 (in millions)	Military Deaths	Civilian Deaths	Deaths as Percentage of Total 1939 Population
Western Europe	113.6	610,000	692,000	1.1%
United Kingdom†	47.8	326,000	62,000	0.8%
France*†	41.7	250,000	350,000	1.4%
Belgium & Luxembourg*	8.7	16,000	77,000	1.1%
Netherlands*	8.7	12,000	198,000	2.4%
				less than
Denmark*	3.8	400	1,000	0.1%
Norway*‡	2.9	6,300	3,900	0.4%
Occupied Eastern Europe	72.8	570,000	5,975,000	9.0%
Poland*†‡	34.8	100,000	4,220,000	12.4%
Czechoslovakia*†	15.3	150,000	215,000	2.4%
Yugoslavia*‡	15.5	300,000	1,400,000	11.0%
Greece*	7.2	20,000	140,000	2.2%
German Allies in Europe	159.3	4,492,000	1,436,000	3.7%
Germany†	69.7	3,500,000	700,000	6.0%
Austria†	6.7	230,000	104,000	5.0%
Italy	43.8	330,000	80,000	0.9%
Finland	3.7	82,000	2,000	2.3%
Hungary†	9.2	140,000	280,000	4.6%
Bulgaria	6.3	10,000	10,000	0.3%
Romania†	19.9	200,000	260,000	2.3%
Others				
United States†	131.4	460,000	—	0.3%
Japan	72.5	1,200,000	300,000	2.1%
			about	
Soviet Union*†‡	156.0	5,000,000	11,000,000	10.3%
	about		about	
China	450.0	3,800,000	18,000,000	4.9%

* Countries occupied or partially occupied by Germans.
† Countries where, in 1938, there were many Jews. The United States contained 4.8 million, the Soviet Union 3 million, Poland 3 million, Romania 850,000, Hungary 400,000, Czechoslovakia 360,000, the United Kingdom 300,000, France 300,000, Germany 200,000 and Austria 200,000. Of the five to six million killed, about half were Polish Jews.
‡ Countries occupied or partially occupied by Germans and having strong resistance movements. All the occupied countries mounted some kind of resistance. China had a very strong Communist guerrilla movement against the Japanese.

over control of the capitalist world system. The United States had won and was the primary core power. France and Britain, which kept their overseas empires (in any event, for a few years), were nevertheless economically ruined. The German and Japanese challenges had failed. Western Europe (and soon, Japan) took on roles formerly filled only by the minor core powers, such as Belgium or the Netherlands; that is, they became subsidiary members of the core, profiting from the world system, but neither controlling nor maintaining it. After 1945 the capitalist world system held together, but primarily because the United States took over most of the costs of maintaining that system. The willingness of the United States to take on this imperial burden contrasted with the aftermath of World War I. The result within the capitalist system was a prolonged period of success and economic expansion rather than financial and economic chaos. The political and economic hegemony of the United States prevented the emergence of any challenge within the core.[64]

The other major development of this postwar period was the emergence, for the first time, of a dynamic, industrial, powerful, yet fundamentally anticapitalist society. (Although one might argue, with good reason, that Germany and Japan in the 1930s were just as strongly anticapitalist, these societies being very strongly dominated by authoritarian state structures.) The Soviet Union had existed since late in 1917, but not until World War II did it emerge as a great world power. After the war, the Soviet Union, in effect, created its own "socialist" world system by taking over Eastern Europe and East Germany. This presented a serious challenge to the world system now dominated by the United States.

For some years, it seemed that the two world systems would quickly come to war. That they did not can be attributed to three main factors. First, neither side needed conquests in the other's domain. Both the Soviet Union and the United States were absorbing vast new areas and burdens and creating imperial structures to rule their new empires. Second, both sides were war-weary, particularly the Soviet Union. Public opinion in the United States was also not ready for a new war, and in Western Europe there was enough sympathy for communist ideas and for the Soviet Union that an aroused United States would have had to fight such a war pretty much alone. Third, and possibly most important, by 1950, when both sides seemed ready to take up war again, they both had nuclear fission weapons, and after 1954, fusion weapons. War would then have meant an unacceptable scale of destruction.

CHAPTER *7*

Revolutions in the Periphery, 1910–1950

*T*he roots of instability in peripheral societies, touched upon in Chapter 5, will be more systematically discussed in this chapter. Three trends of the early twentieth century will form the basis of this discussion: first, the increasing commercialization of agriculture, which created a set of problems that made the entire economic and political structure in the periphery unstable; second, rapid population growth and pressures for economic change created by contact with the West; and third, the appearance of a new, highly nationalistic elite that could channel the mass discontent created by the development of peripheral economies.

The review of these topics will be followed by a close look at Mexico and China, two examples of the revolutionary process in peripheral societies. This process, which began in the early part of the century, has spread and created a large number of new societies hostile to core domination. This has created a challenge which continues to trouble the world order.

Commercialization of Agriculture and Its Consequences

Commercialization of agriculture in peripheral societies turned former village-based landholding arrangements into money-based private-property systems. Powerful controllers of the land (usually, but not always, direct landowners) appropriated the profits of commercial agriculture, which was in turn based on exports to the world economy. The relative security of old village social arrangements was destroyed and replaced by more demanding and less secure market pressures. This process actually began long before the twentieth century, but in the years that preceded World War I, the change accelerated and absorbed large portions of the peripheral world that had not yet been fully transformed.

One typical example, Mexico, has already been mentioned. Egyptian economic integration into the world system exhibits a similar pattern—rapid growth in the production of cash crops and in foreign trade. In the first half of the nineteenth century Egypt became an important cotton exporter. From 1848/1852 to 1908/1912 the amount of cotton (by weight) exported yearly increased about nineteen times, and by World War I cotton made up about 87 percent of all Egyptian exports.[1] As it happens, in Egypt (as in Mexico) there had been large landed estates long before the nineteenth-century growth of modern capitalist market forces. But the system of land tenure was totally overhauled in the first half of the 1800s. New landholding patterns emphasized private rather than communal property and initiated schemes for irrigation and development that were designed to increase cotton production. By 1896, 44 percent of Egypt's cultivated land was owned by 12,000 landlords (no more than 2 percent of all owners). The huge majority of peasants held increasingly fragmented small plots, and therefore had to lease land from landowners in order to ensure survival. After World War I the spectacular growth of cotton production ceased, and production grew slowly until about 1950. But the basic landholding pattern remained unchanged. In 1952, 0.1 percent of all Egyptian landowners held 20 percent of the cultivated land; the top 6 percent held 65 percent; and the millions of peasants shared the rest.[2]

Inequality in landholding does not necessarily produce unrest. But combined with other aspects of peripheral economies, it is an important destabilizing force. In Egypt those other aspects were rapid population increase, great poverty, stagnation of economic opportunities and relative neglect of all aspects of the economy that were not related to cotton production, and finally, a large degree of foreign control over the Egyptian political system and economy. From 1895/1899 to 1945/1949, the per capita GNP in Egypt declined from a meager $440 per year to $390 (measured in 1985 U.S. dollars),[3] while the economy of the core capitalist societies and the successful semiperipheral societies made great advances. (Population growth will be examined below.) After World War I, some industry developed, but slowly, and only in those areas where the supply of local cheap labor made it economical to substitute domestic production for imports. By 1937, 70 percent of the working population was still involved in agriculture, and by 1950 that proportion had only fallen to 60 percent,[4] a figure that seems quite high when compared with the proportion of the population in agriculture in core societies even at the start of the twentieth century, and very high when compared with the figures for core societies in the middle of the century.

To make the ordinary person's poverty seem worse, there was the example of the few very rich landowners. More bothersome were the Europeans who gave orders to the Egyptian government and lived in what appeared to be splendid luxury as their own economies were constantly growing.

Much the same story can be told about India, where in the nineteenth century, British colonial policy systematically favored the landowners and the growth of commercial agriculture. Barrington Moore has observed:

> In addition to law and order, the British introduced into Indian society in the nineteenth century railroads and a substantial amount of irrigation. The most important prerequisites for commercial agriculture and industrial growth would seem to have been present. Yet what growth there was turned out to be abortive and sickly. Why? A decisive part of the answer, I think, is that *pax Britannica* simply enabled the landlord and now also the moneylender to pocket the economic surplus generated in the countryside. . . .

Moore adds:

> To lay all the blame on British shoulders is obviously absurd. There is
> much evidence . . . to demonstrate that this blight was inherent in
> India's own social structure and traditions. Two centuries of British
> occupation merely allowed it to spread and root more deeply through-
> out Indian society.[5]

The transformation to a commercial agricultural system was probably less
thorough in India than in many other colonial societies, and India's middle
peasant class survived the experience without being expropriated by landowners. Yet, from the 1890s to the 1940s, the production of food crops in India
declined by 7 percent (while population rose by almost 40 percent) and commercial crop production (mainly of cotton, jute, tea, peanuts, and sugarcane)
grew by 85 percent.[6] Furthermore, British colonial policy leaned on the very
rich Indian landowners for support; and the lavish style of life of this small
segment of the population contrasted sharply with the stagnating, or possibly
even declining, standard of living of the average peasant. From the 1880s to
the early 1900s India's per capita GNP declined by about 5 percent, and by
the middle 1950s, it had risen only slightly, to $260 (in 1985 U.S. dollars) per
year (compared with $200 in the 1880s).[7] As in Egypt, industrial growth was
not great enough to absorb very much of the poor rural work force. And the
privileges, powers, and arrogance of the British colonial population could
hardly fail to arouse discontent.

India and Egypt were not unique. China, Vietnam, Indonesia, and other
societies went through similar experiences—growth of a commercial agricultural sector, concentration of landownership, Western domination, economic
stagnation or decline for the bulk of the peasant population, and ultimately,
extreme resentment against the domestic and foreign elite that profited from
this situation.[8]

Here one should not lose sight of an important point: while the activities of
the imperialist powers may invite the conclusion that the main force leading to
subjection of peripheral masses was willful and carefully planned colonialism,
and while willfulness was a factor in some measure, total responsibility for that
subjection cannot be assigned so easily. The impersonal power of the market,
combined with the military and political power of the capitalist core, generally
acted as the main agent of peripheral change. This can be seen by examining
the case of Turkey, which never became a European colony.

The declining Ottoman Empire began to reform itself as early as the late
eighteenth century. The obvious approach to reform was to imitate the West,
since the West seemed to be getting stronger while the Turks were becoming
weaker. In the nineteenth century the empire's landholding laws were reformed, and private property was assured by the state. At the same time,
Western demand for agricultural goods was growing. As Bernard Lewis has
written:

The commercial and financial developments of the time, including the expansion of Turkish agricultural exports, brought a flow of steady money, and created a class of persons with sufficient cash to bid for leases, buy estates, and lend money on land. The new laws gave them legal powers to enforce contracts of debt and sale; the new police protected them from the hazards which formerly attended such enforcements.[9]

Why was there a "new police"? In order to strengthen the state, the Turkish government had created a modern police and military apparatus based on the Western model. This innovation was essential in order to collect taxes and build a structure that might resist foreign military intervention. The very attempt to strengthen the state created the possibility of extending commercial agriculture. But the Turks did not take the next step, heavy taxation of agriculture in order to yield a surplus that might be invested in industry. Rather, the partial modernization of the Turkish administrative system helped duplicate the kind of condition that typified colonial societies. A new landowning class came into existence. Lewis observes:

> In the Balkan provinces this gave rise to bitter social struggles. . . . In western and central Anatolia it produced the familiar figures of the Aga, the rich peasant or landlord, dominating and often owning the village, and of his still more powerful protector, the merchant landowner residing in the town. The position of the peasant was much worsened by these changes.[10]

Economic opportunities for Western Europeans were created by these changes, and European finance, through loans, railway construction, and investment in agriculture, penetrated Turkey. By 1914 Europeans owned the railways, tramways, key port operations, electricity, gas, and water utilities in the cities, and most of the country's few operating mines and factories. Native handicrafts were ruined by European imports, and a new comprador class came into being, serving as the agents of the Europeans.[11]

The Turkish experience was particularly tragic because a large portion of the compradors were "pariah capitalists." Greeks and Armenian Christians were especially prominent in this class, and while they had always been present in the Ottoman Empire, in the nineteenth century their situation became precarious. For one thing, they were the agents of foreign penetration. Second, the Turks were trying to revive their state by creating a sense of nationalism, and in return, the Greeks and Armenians, who felt no sense of shared nationalism with the Turks, were becoming nationalistic in their own right. The Turkish state was deeply split on cultural as well as economic grounds, and this produced a series of bloody massacres and wars between the Turks and various Christian populations in the Ottoman Empire. There were many Turkish massacres of Christians, which culminated during World War I in the killing of over one million Armenians. To the West, this was only one more example of barbarism, for which the Turks were supposedly well known. But like many of the tragedies that have afflicted the modern world, it was nothing of the sort. In the early 1800s the Armenians were considered among the most loyal minorities in the Ottoman Empire, and far from being persecuted, they were allowed their own laws and institutions. It was the economic and political changes of the nineteenth century that changed all this.[12] Rising nationalism, the attempt to create a strong nation-state, the intensification of a cultural division of labor based on growing commerce, and finally, the outbreak of World War I and the violent xenophobia it bred everywhere produced this tragedy. Paradoxically, it was the very progress of the world system that created the conditions for supposedly "traditional" barbarism. The Middle East, knocked about by progress and foreign intervention, has remained a fertile ground for nationalistic hatreds to this day. With the experiences of World Wars I and II, and with the other slaughter that has accompanied modern social change, today's Westerners can perhaps understand such events somewhat better than the smug Europeans of the early twentieth century.

Population Problems and the Need for Economic Change

A second, critical problem in the peripheral world in the first half of the twentieth century was rapid population growth. Alluded to in the preceding section, it now requires a more detailed examination.

In Western Europe in the eighteenth and nineteenth centuries the introduction of at least minimal scientific health care and control of epidemics, the extension of cropland in response to market forces, and the improvement of transportation (thus allowing either the shipment of food to areas of temporary shortage or outmigration from famine areas) caused death rates to fall. In the nineteenth and twentieth centuries these beneficial effects of the world economy spread to peripheral societies.

In largely rural societies, birth rates had always been high. Faced with high infant mortality, peasants gave birth to many children in order to assure themselves of at least a few adolescents. The motivation is clear enough. Children provided essential agricultural labor, labor especially required by the extended cultivation of relatively high labor-demanding cash crops. Children were also the only existing form of old-age insurance. As death rates fell, these concerns did not change. Individual peasants were probably not aware of the rapid decline in mortality, and in any case, the need for old-age insurance and extra labor did not diminish. It probably increased. A pattern of population growth is evident when one examines the demographic history of several peripheral societies. (See Table 7-1.)

The rapid rate of increase was not much greater than that in the industrial core during the nineteenth century. From 1800 to 1900, for example, the population of England, Wales, and Scotland went from 10.5 million to 37

TABLE 7-1
Peripheral Populations, 1800–1950[13]

	1800	1850	1900	1950	Percentage Increase 1800–1950
India (including Pakistan and Bangladesh)	125	255*	285	437	+250%
Indonesia	8.5	16	38	76.5	+800%
Indochina	about 7	8	16	29.8	+325%
Egypt	about 2.5	6.8†	9.7‡	19§	+660%
Mexico	6.5	7¶	13.6	25.4	+290%

* for 1871   ‡ for 1897   ¶ for 1840
† for 1882   § for 1947

million, a 252 percent increase. From 1800 to 1950, the British population increased about 365 percent. Because of immigration, as well as high birth rates and low death rates, the population of the United States grew from 5.3 million in 1800 to 151.7 million in 1950, an increase of 2,760 percent.[14] The United States may not be a good basis of comparison because so much unsettled land was available there; but European populations also grew very rapidly in the 1800s, and in some relatively crowded countries, like the Netherlands, the rates of population growth from 1800 to 1950 were about the same as those in some of the overcrowded peripheral societies. However, the industrialized societies easily absorbed their growing labor force through industry. As the economy progressed, and as the population migrated from rural to urban areas, the incentives for having many children changed, and birth rates began to fall. By the mid-twentieth century population growth rates in highly industrialized societies had slowed, and now their populations are almost stable. This contrasts sharply with the trend in peasant societies of the periphery. There, as death rates continued to fall in the twentieth century, birth rates remained high, and the rate of population growth increased. The population problem in peripheral societies has been directly related to a lack of industrialization. After almost two centuries of rapid population growth, contemporary industrial societies are not overpopulated; they are also no longer experiencing rapid increases in population.

In societies composed largely of peasants, overpopulation is severely felt in the form of an agricultural land shortage. The scarcity of arable land lowers the standard of living among the peasants and creates a strong migratory pressure—some farmers simply have to leave the land for the city. But if the cities do not afford these migrants real employment opportunities, a floating, unemployed or underemployed population is created; meanwhile the rural villages remain economically overcrowded. This process explains the stagnation of per capita GNP in such societies as Egypt and India during this century, as well as the volatile nature of urban masses in the peripheral world. The only possible solutions are rapid industrialization, which creates a new demand for labor, and provision of new land for the growing rural population.

The Solution of Industrialization

Unfortunately, the more advanced the technological level of the world system, the more difficult it is to find a solution to the population problem through industrialization. In the early period of industrialization, when manufacturing was growing rapidly in the Western core societies, the state of technology was not advanced, and new factories required large new labor forces. Increasingly, however, mechanization and progress have diminished the labor demand of new industry. Industry is generally now capital or machine intensive, and it takes huge new investments to create significant increases in the demand for labor.

India is an excellent example of this problem because, while it is still struggling to become industrial, in some ways it actually began to industrialize in the late nineteenth century. Its abundance of cheap labor and cotton and jute, as well as the large demand for textiles within the large Indian population, meant that some form of import substitution (in this case, the manufacturing of domestic textiles to replace British imports) was more or less inevitable despite the antiindustrial policies that Britain set down for its colonies. Modern textile mills developed in India in the 1880s, and by 1914 the country had the world's fourth largest textile industry. Jute mills, and eventually a small iron and coal industry (to service India's railroads), were developed. But by 1911 only 1.1 percent of the labor force was employed in modern industry, while about 9 percent of the labor force was still employed in traditional handicraft activity. Industrial output grew much more rapidly than industrial employment. Throughout the next decades the same pattern persisted, and even by 1951 only 11 percent of India's labor force was employed in manufacturing, mining, or construction (including traditional handicrafts). Industrial growth had hardly absorbed the surplus rural population, since by 1951 the same total percentage of the labor force was involved in industry and crafts as in 1911.[15] The inability of Indian industrialization to provide adequate employment has continued into the second half of the century. Although it was able to develop a sophisticated nuclear industry in the early 1970s, and a considerable steel industry along with its large textile industry, India still cannot employ its growing population. Large portions of the peasantry remain very poor and underemployed.

The Indian situation shows the effects of peripherality, but these are somewhat more subtle than the discussion has indicated. Peripheral status does not mean that industrial growth is entirely prevented (at least, it need not in the twentieth century), but that it may be slowed down at a critical juncture and tends to be too specialized to be of much assistance when a serious peasant-population problem begins to develop. Why does this incapacity happen? In India, inadequate industrialization resulted from the joint influences of the social structure, which was dominated by the controllers of the land and of the colonial state. Along with maintaining a colonial class structure, the British also prevented the imposition of protective tariffs which would have helped Indian industry compete against the more advanced British industries. As it was, import substitution could occur in the few areas in which India's comparative advantage was overwhelming (like textiles), but not over the broad range of industrial areas that are necessary to a balanced economy. Again, it was a case of overspecialization rather than absolute lack of development. There was slow industrial growth instead of rapid and broadly based growth. By the time India escaped from British colonial rule in 1947, it was, in a sense, very late for an easy solution. By then the country's overpopulation problem was quite severe, and world technology still more advanced and capital intensive than in the early 1900s.

Land Reform as a Solution

Another possible solution to peripheral overpopulation is the acceptance of agricultural reforms that give more land to the peasants. As with industrialization, this solution has temporal limitations. The longer the reforms are delayed, the harder they are to carry out successfully.

One possible reform is the development of new land—by extending irrigation, draining land, or clearing previously forested areas. However, the development of new land is expensive, and another problem of these poor economies is their lack of capital. This insufficiency keeps down both their rate of technological progress in agriculture and their development of new land.

Another possible reform is the confiscation and division of large estates for redistribution to the peasants. Done early enough, or in a society in which there are good credit facilities for peasants (to allow them to purchase the machines and fertilizer needed to cultivate their land efficiently), land reform can boost agricultural production and reduce agricultural problems. In a poor society, without adequate credit facilities, without enough industry to absorb the growing population, and where the land is already seriously overcrowded, land reform has only marginal effects. Peasants may gain title to the land they are cultivating, but they do not gain access to new land as such. By breaking up large estates, some land reforms have actually eliminated an area's only source of capital for a mechanization of agriculture (the big landowners), and have thus caused regression rather than progress. (A good example is Romania, where there was a land reform in the 1920s, and where average crop yields returned to pre–World War I levels only in the late 1950s and early 1960s.) In Egypt when land-reform laws were finally passed in the 1950s, there was little positive effect. The population was already too large, and the land was already as intensively cultivated as possible, given the poverty and inability of the peasants to use modern machinery.[16]

A further disadvantage of land reform is that it almost always entails a bitter political fight against the controllers of the land. This fight must be undertaken if a society is to remedy the root problems of its peripherality, but if the land-controlling elite is supported by a core power (as it was in colonial India, Indochina, and Egypt), the struggle is particularly difficult and costly.

Despite the uncertain nature of land reform, the pressure for such action is strong. The peasants want more land in order to survive, and big landowners, particularly if they are foreigners or foreign supported, are a natural target for discontent.

It is not likely that many peasants in peripheral societies of the twentieth century have formulated all their land problems in such explicit terms. But it is no exaggeration to say that peasants have felt the consequences of these problems—subjugation to landowners or their agents, land shortage and poverty, and disintegration of traditional forms of social protection. Certainly it is clear that the Westernized intellectuals in peripheral societies have grasped the nature of these problems. For that reason, when organizing people for anticore revolts, they have almost invariably centered their economic programs on the twin promises of land reform and industrialization.

Nationalist Intellectuals: Civilian and Military

Peasant discontent, economic hardships, and subjection to foreign rule, direct or indirect—all were important sources of instability and revolution in the periphery. But discontent was not translated into revolution easily or quickly. The opposition to change was strong, both because the entrenched elites opposed it, and because the world system—that is, the interests of the core powers—resisted. To overcome that resistance took considerable organization. As described previously, the early revolts against the economic and political transformations imposed by the core invariably failed, except in the unusual case of Japan. Starting in the twentieth century, this pattern of failure was slowly reversed as a new group of leaders emerged to challenge the preeminence of the core and its local allies. This group consisted of intellectuals, both civilian and military.

The new intellectuals in peripheral societies were "all persons with an advanced modern education"[17]—the word modern should probably be replaced here by Western. This category must be distinguished from the "traditional intellectuals," the bearers of traditional learning and religion, for it has not been the fact of being "learned" that has made the modern intellectuals a powerful revolutionary force. Rather, it has been their understanding of Western ideology and Western organizational techniques that has made them so important.

In the early stages of contact between the periphery and the modern world system, those peripheral citizens who acquired a Western education tended to be admirers, and even servile imitators, of the West. As such, they supported the extension of core influence. But with time, disillusion inevitably set in. First, there was the increasingly evident fact that Western influence was clearly intended to dominate peripheral societies for the advantage of the core, not of the local populations. Second, and this was particularly important in the direct colonies of the West, "natives," even if they had an advanced Western education, were still treated as inferiors. The dawning realization of permanent inferiority in the world system, both for themselves and for their societies, pushed the intellectuals into opposition. Finally, there was the circumstance that in peripheral societies, what native elites there were tended to be the major controllers of the land and traditional aristocrats who collaborated with the core, but who did not accept Westernized native intellectuals as members of the local elite. A revolt against the core also meant a revolt against the collaborationist controllers of the land, and *vice versa*.

The prime ideological aim of the intellectuals was to "catch up" with the core. Whether one speaks of the "conservative" Japanese elite after 1868, the "radical" Chinese Communist leadership in the mid-twentieth century, or the military dictatorship of Kemal Ataturk in Turkey in the 1920s and 1930s, all the leaders of strongly nationalist movements in peripheral societies (and in semiperipheral ones as well) have been obsessed with this need to catch up, to raise their own societies to a higher level in the world system so that they would no longer suffer the economic and emotional consequences of being subjected peripherals. In that sense, all nationalistic movements in the periphery have been "revolutionary," for their aim has been to change the world system. The success of revolutionary movements led by modern intellectuals has been the result of their decision to "catch up" by adapting Western techniques and ideas. It is in this respect that the new intellectuals differed greatly from the original anticore movements, which simply tried to keep the core out in order to preserve traditional societies.

An ideological commitment to modernizing revolutionary change is not, however, the same thing as actual power. In order to carry out their programs, the intellectuals needed to seize control, which meant ousting domestic and core elites. Here, one should distinguish between states that were legally independent (even if their economies were heavily influenced by the world system and dominated by core interests) and those that were direct colonies.

Formally independent peripheral states in the twentieth century have all had armies in which the officer corps was heavily influenced by Western ideas and technology. As Harry Benda has observed:

> Westernization—thinking and acting in western, rather than traditionally indigenous ways—can extend to types of social activity that in the west have not, as a rule, formed part of intellectual activity as such. The most common, and historically the most significant, representative of this category is the new military group, the "Young Turks" so to speak, of the non-western world. Nor is this at all surprising, since one of the prime contacts between west and non-west during the past century-and-a-half has been military in nature. As a result, the desire to attain equality with the west has often found expression in terms of military equality, and officers were often the first social group to receive western training.

Further:

> Wherever . . . the impact of the west did not lead to outright political domination . . . there the officer has almost invariably emerged as the modern political non-western leader. Since he as a rule possesses a monopoly of physical power, he can fairly easily grasp control in a society where he represents the most powerful—even if numerically weak—social group with a vested interest in modernization and change.[18]

The career of Kemal Ataturk, a member of the "Young Turks" who sought to modernize the Ottoman Empire at the end of the nineteenth century and in the first decade of the twentieth, is a perfect example of this kind of Westernizing, nation-building officer. After the defeat of the Ottomans and the disintegration of the empire in 1918, it seemed that Turkey would be divided among the European powers. Ataturk, a successful World War I general, retreated into the interior, organized a powerful army, and drove the foreigners out (primarily the Greek army, which was being encouraged to invade Turkey by Great Britain). Ataturk himself was an almost fanatical Westernizer who felt that Turkey's only hope was to adopt a Western way of life. He abolished Islam as the state religion, prohibited the wearing of traditional clothes, changed the Turkish alphabet from Arabic to Latin script, reformed the language, and established a Western legal system. In the process, he created modern Turkey.[19]

Chiang Kai-shek, first a follower and then a leader of the revolutionary movement that overthrew the Chinese Empire (1911), replaced it with a more modern republic. He also derived his power from his military command and influence with the modernized segment of the officer corps. Like Ataturk, it was his ambition to create a modern China, independent of Western and Japanese control. That he failed, while Ataturk succeeded, does not negate the example, for in the 1920s and early 1930s, his failure was not a foregone conclusion.[20]

Gamal Nasser, a colonel in the Egyptian army, carried out a revolution in 1952 similar to Ataturk's revolution.

The movements led by Ataturk, Chiang Kai-shek, and Nasser all had this in common: they were based on control of the military, and sought to impose modernizing change from above. They did not require long periods of organization among the masses, particularly among the peasants.

In colonial societies, however, there were no armies, at least not native ones, since the occupying colonial power had its own local army. While many of the soldiers, and even noncommissioned officers in colonial armies were natives, the officers were Europeans. But local intellectuals, particularly those who had attended Western universities, were almost inevitably drawn into revolutionary activity. For one thing, they could not find employment commensurate with their education. Top positions were monopolized by colonizers, and the overspecialized, relatively-stagnant colonial economies afforded few opportunities. Intellectuals could become school teachers or clerks in the colonial governments or European commercial enterprises, scarcely the sort of thing to satisfy their ambitions. Those who became inspired by the revolutionary cause found themselves in need of an army. In order to carry out a revolution, they would have to organize the masses, their only source of enough force to counteract the military superiority of the colonizers.

The wave of decolonization that occurred in the 1960s has created an impression that the British and French generally gave up their colonies peacefully; but when one's perspective includes the first half of the twentieth century and the 1950s, this is seen to be a false impression. Early nationalist movements were repressed, usually with much bloodshed, and it was only after the main colonies had forcefully ejected the West that the core gave up most of what remained in order to avoid an endless series of colonial wars. In such colonies as India, Indochina, Indonesia, and Algeria, Europeans were ejected by force, not withdrawn in kindness. This meant long organizational campaigns, and particularly the mobilization of the peasants into revolutionary armies capable of wearing out and defeating the West. Success went to those intellectual leaders who combined Western knowledge with extensive efforts in their own rural hinterlands.

Although their tactics and policies were quite different, Gandhi and Ho Chi Minh were the colonial world's most successful intellectual organizers of the masses before 1950.

Gandhi was trained as a lawyer in England, and in 1914, after practicing law in South Africa and being horrified by the naked racial injustices in that society, he returned to India to organize a revolution. Combining British ideas with an extraordinary ability to promote pride in Indian culture (by using Indian languages rather than English, by dressing like an Indian, not like an Englishman), he organized a host of strikes, protest movements, and ostensibly passive actions designed to paralyze the colonial government. After years of activity, the climax came during World War II when in 1942–1943 the "Quit India" movement led to violence, and the British realized that the only way to maintain their control was through constant repressive war. For this they did not have the strength, and shortly after the war, in 1947, India became independent. What made Gandhi's movement so effective was the threat of mass violence, and particularly, the actual violence of 1942–1943. Gandhi's organization had spread so thoroughly across India that the threat of even greater violence impressed the British.[21]

The revolutionary career of Ho Chi Minh was also a combination of Western training, nationalism, and extraordinary organizational effort. Educated in Vietnam in a school that offered what the Franco-American journalist Bernard Fall has called a "blend of all that was best in French education with a solid anchoring in Vietnamese culture," he traveled widely in Europe, America, and Asia, and became a communist in France in 1920 because of the anti-imperialist platform of the new French Communist Party.[22] There followed long years of undercover organizational work, and in the early 1940s, while French Indochina was occupied by the Japanese, he formed a guerrilla army, relying on support from discontented peasants. After World War II, rejecting the "British" solution to colonial unrest, the French launched a war of reconquest to reverse the Vietnamese Revolution. In 1954 the Vietnamese Communist army destroyed a French army and Ho became the leader of an independent North Vietnam.[23]

In both India and Vietnam the main nationalist leaders were intellectuals. Nehru, Gandhi's chief disciple, also received a British education, as did hundreds of the organizers of the Indian independence movement. General Giap, Ho's main military leader, and Pham Van Dong, long the Prime Minister of North Vietnam, attended the same school as Ho. In both the Indian and Vietnamese cases, the struggle of the intellectuals would have come to naught without support from the countryside. As a result of that support, when the nationalist parties came to power, they had far deeper roots within the society than did the military regimes of Turkey, Egypt, or Chiang Kai-shek's China, which built their support from the top down instead of from the bottom up. Because India gained its independence more through the threat of violence than through a protracted war, however, India's independent regime did not develop as thorough an organization, particularly in the countryside, as did the Vietnamese Communist Party. This ultimately made an important difference in the degree of social change in the two countries; the Vietnamese were able to carry out a much more rapid and total social and economic transformation than the Indians.

This last point reflects a basic one. Although the motivation for nationalist anticore revolts has been quite similar throughout the peripheral world, and although the successful leadership has tended to come from the ranks of Westernized intellectuals, the particular circumstances of the struggle, and the different types of organizations that characterized the revolutionary movements have resulted in disparate rates of social change.

The Class Basis of Revolutions—Two Examples

Knowing that peasant unrest, slow industrialization, an overspecialized economy, and discontented intellectuals constitute basic causal forces in the revolutions of peripheral societies does not really explain the varied development of these revolutions. There have been hundreds, if not thousands, of revolutionary movements in the peripheral world during the past century, and while most have failed, there have been major variations even among the successful ones. A look at two major cases between 1910 and 1950 may begin to explain why some peripheral revolutions have produced more radical outcomes than others.

Mexico, 1910–1950

In the decades preceding the outbreak of revolution in 1910, Mexico underwent rapid, peripheral economic development (that is, development oriented to the export of primary products). By 1910 land had become concentrated in a very few hands (1 percent of the population owned 85 percent of the land, and 95 percent of the peasants had no land.[24] The revolution broke out unexpectedly, rather than being planned. A strong peasant component emerged, led primarily by the peasant leader Zapata, but though this movement was somewhat inspired by what Eric Wolf calls "disaffected intellectuals with urban ties," it remained too local and insufficiently organized to take over the country.[25] The way was thus left open to more moderate middle-class forces which gained control of the revolution. The revolution as such was a failure, and the civil war, which lasted into the early 1920s, involved the deaths of a million or more people. In all these years, no revolutionary organization developed that was capable of seizing the state and carrying out a radical social and economic transformation.[26] Nevertheless, the revolution accomplished several important objectives. First, it created a much more integrated national culture in which Indian and peasant rights were at least accorded legitimacy, and in which efforts were made to create a nation-state rather than continue with the culturally malintegrated state in existence before 1910. Second, and partly as a result of the first change, the revolution created an embryonic state machine dedicated, at least in principle, to the goals of economic improvement and active government participation in that process. While little was actually done before the 1930s, the institutional basis of revolutionary change was established in the preceding decades.

In 1934, Lázaro Cárdenas, a military general, became president of Mexico. Using the state machinery created by the revolution, he carried out a massive land reform, took over many foreign-owned interests (particularly oil companies), and had the government invest large sums in economic development.[27] It was under Cárdenas (who was president until 1940) that the revolution really took place, a quarter of a century after the outbreak of civil war.

But even under Cárdenas, and especially under the presidents who followed him in power, change has been only *somewhat* radical, and Mexico has neither experienced the kind of overwhelming change that occurred in Russia nor has it ever left the world system. Since, in fact, the kind of total revolution experienced by the Soviet Union has been the exception rather than the rule, the reasons for frequent moderation such as this must be considered.

First, the largest of the revolutionary armies were composed of peasants (Zapata at his strongest had 70,000 men, while the moderate army that ultimately won the civil war had only 26,000). But such revolutionary armies tend to fall apart rather easily unless they are tightly organized and led by intellectuals with a coherent economic and social plan. Zapata and the cowboy revolutionary leader, Pancho Villa (who mobilized some 40,000 men), lacked the necessary sophistication. Their followers, essentially rural anarchists, had no program beyond immediate land reform.[28]

Second, even if unsuccessful in the short run, peasant violence frightens moderates, who try to temper the process of change. The threat of renewed violence remains real, but latent, and encourages moderates to carry out partial reforms to head off greater turmoil.

Third, revolutionary change requires a strong state. But by the time the real social and economic revolution began in Mexico in the 1930s, a new class structure had developed. Primarily, the new state had created a bureaucratic machine which, while concerned with social and economic progress, was conservative in wishing to preserve its own privileges and position. It was the government bureaucracy, acting as a distinct class, that carried out Mexico's reforms and moderated the extent of change. Had a peasant-intellectual alliance won the revolution in the period 1910–1920, Mexico would have experienced much more rapid and extreme change.

Fourth, the kind of partial revolution experienced by Mexico was hardly a failure for being moderate. Mexico emerged in the 1940s as an industrializing, progressive society. Even while it continued to permit foreign investment, it did not fall back into the extreme overspecialization and dependence from which it had suffered before 1910. The revolution moved Mexico into the ranks of the semiperiphery. In many ways, this was similar to the results of other "revolutions from above," namely those of Turkey and Egypt.

The extent of the change brought by the Mexican Revolution can be seen by looking at Table 7-2 and its national statistics for several years between 1910 and 1950.

Though Mexico's revolution was limited, it was certainly the first Latin

TABLE 7-2
Social and Economic Changes in Mexico, 1910–1950[29]

	1910	*1921*	*1930*	*1940*	*1950*
Illiterate population	77%	71%	67%	58%	43%
Change by decade*		−8%	−6%	−13%	−26%
Poor population (according to Wilkie's poverty index)	57%	53%	50%	46%	39%
Change by decade*		−7%	−6%	−8%	−15%
Growth by decade* of per capita GNP		3.3%	12.0%	23.2%	43.3%
Manufacturing index (1910 = 100) by value	100	123	242	466	1,066 (for 1945)
Change by decade*		23%	96%	93%	129% (for half decade)

* Year indicates end of decade.

American revolution to achieve any success. Was the rate of change in Mexico after 1910 faster than in the rest of Latin America? Unfortunately, this question cannot be answered without also having statistics on other countries, and for most cases, these are not available. Yet it is at least suggestive that by the late 1960s, Mexico, the second most populous society in Latin America, had a per capita GNP that was exceeded only by those of Argentina (which was almost three times as rich as Mexico in 1910 but less than twice as rich in 1970) and Venezuela (which has a much smaller population and immense oil resources). (Other exceptions are not meaningful because they relate to small societies with highly unusual attributes.) What makes Mexico's progress striking is that at the start of the century, a number of other Latin American societies were no poorer than Mexico and several were richer. Of the Latin American societies with large numbers of Indians (who have always been at the bottom of the social scale), Mexico has made the most progress by far.[30] Finally, Mexico's political life since the late 1930s has been unusually stable, and compared with other major Latin American societies, it has been relatively free of violence. This is the case even though Mexico is not a democracy, but rather a fairly mild one-party dictatorship where the ruling party allows elections but always wins.

China, 1910–1950

The revolt that overthrew the Chinese Empire in 1911 had been brewing for a long time. In the middle of the nineteenth century, a largely peasant uprising, the Taiping Rebellion, almost succeeded in overthrowing the reigning dynasty. By 1900 the old regime was in a state of virtual collapse. Foreigners controlled the main ports, dramatic changes had occurred in the coastal economy, and the outdated institutions of China could no longer cope with either foreign intervention or domestic discontent. But the 1911 change did not produce a revolutionary government. Rather, the country fell into many pieces, each province governed by this or that general, governor, or warlord. By the early 1920s, a nationalist government had been established under Sun Yat-sen, but it was not until his party, the Kuomintang, built up an army under Chiang Kai-shek that the central government gained a real measure of power over much, if hardly all, of China.

From the very start, however, the Kuomintang was based on urban, largely middle-class support, on the army, and on an alliance with the landed gentry in rural areas. The Kuomintang was nationalistic. It was led by men familiar with Western ideas, imbued with a sense of humiliation because of China's subjection, and at least among its urban supporters, eager to strengthen China through industrialization and legal reform. The alliance with controllers of the land (either gentry or local warlords) was more tactical than ideological. Yet because of the support he received from the gentry, Chiang (who became the leader of the Kuomintang after Sun Yat-sen) never pushed a program of rural reform. Because the overwhelming majority of China's population consisted of poor peasants, the Kuomintang never received the support of the majority of the population. Chalmers Johnson has noted:

> The National Movement . . . that began with Sun Yat-sen and developed among the students and educators in Peking after May 4, 1919, was not a mass movement; it was confined almost entirely to the socially mobilized but unassimilated intelligentsia and to the small middle classes that grew up in the treaty ports.[31]

The Chinese masses were more or less indifferent to the Kuomintang, which based its efforts to control the countryside on "opportunistic alliances among military leaders" and sheer military force rather than mass organization and support.[32] In that sense, the Kuomintang was "a head without a body" (just as, in a sense, Zapata's movement in Mexico was a body without a head).

Had China isolated itself from a hostile world, this nonsupport might not have made a decisive difference. In 1927 Chiang succeeded in crushing the Communist Party which had based its support on the urban working class. The working class was too small to mount a revolution, and what was left of the Communist movement barely escaped extermination. This failure of the Communists provoked a drastic shift in strategy, and in the 1930s, under Mao

Zedong, the Communists began to organize the peasants.[33] Still, the Kuomintang succeeded in extending its control over most of China until the Japanese invasion of 1937. It was then that the failure of mass support for Chiang did prove decisive.

Because the basically conservative Chiang regime had not modernized China sufficiently by 1937, the Japanese quickly conquered most of the coastal cities, thus eliminating the only progressive base of Kuomintang support, the small but growing class of urban industrialists. The gentry and the warlords were left, and the Kuomintang, feebly resisting from the interior, became yet another corrupt, landlord-controlled regime. The Communists, on the other hand, stepped into the rural vacuum and organized an effective anti-Japanese effort among the peasants, particularly in northern China. A decade of patient organization, of promoting rural security, and of uniting the peasants against the Japanese yielded impressive results. Johnson observes:

> The devastation and exploitation that accompanied the Japanese invasion produced a radical change in the political attitude of the northern Chinese. The peasants of north China gave very strong support to Communist organizational initiatives during the war, and the largest number of Communist guerrilla bases was located in the rural areas of the north.[34]

By 1945 when the Japanese were defeated by the United States in the Pacific War and were forced to evacuate China, Chiang had no mass support, only a loose alliance of local controllers of the land, and the financial and material aid of the United States. This proved to be insufficient against the Communist mass organization, which finally took complete control in 1949.

Because of the nature of the revolutionary struggle in China, the Communist Party came to power as a radical movement deeply committed to massive land reform, industrialization, and the creation of a strong Chinese nation-state. Backed by its grass-roots organization, it set out to accomplish these tasks, and within a decade had transformed Chinese society and made China a major world power.

Interestingly, several aspects of the Chinese Revolution strengthen the theory that a successful revolution in a peripheral society requires a combination of Westernized intellectual leadership and mass peasant support. Comparing the revolutionary program of the Communist Party with the conservative, antiland-reform program of the Kuomintang, one might suppose that the social origins of the Communist and Kuomintang leadership were quite different. In fact, this was not the case, since both were led by similar types of people. The main difference was in their organizational strategies and political programs. Because China turned so deeply inward after the Communist Revolution, and severed so many of its ties with the world system (as did the Soviet Union after 1928), one might suppose that the leadership of the Communist movement was more "native" than that of the Kuomintang. Again, this was

TABLE 7-3
**Education of Chinese Revolutionary Elites,
1920s–1940s** [35]

	Kuomintang Executive Committee	*Communist Politburo*
No higher education	2 (1%)	2 (7%)
Chinese higher education only	123 (47%)	2 (7%)
Foreign education	136 (52%)	25 (86%)
Total known	261 (100%)	29 (100%)
Unknown	26 —	13 —

not the case, and if anything, the Communist leaders had been more exposed to Western ideas than the leaders of the Kuomintang. While Chiang's ideology stressed old-fashioned Confucian loyalty, the Communists stressed their version of Western Marxism.[36] Although in both parties a majority of the elite had foreign educational experience, the Communists had a larger proportion of members with such experience (see Tables 7-3 and 7-4).

The leaders of the two movements, then, did not differ much in their social origins. The Communists, to be sure, had more lower-class representation in their leadership, but like the Kuomintang, the overwhelming majority of their leaders came from the upper and middle classes. Like other successful mass

TABLE 7-4
**Class Background of Chinese Revolutionary Elites
(Determined by Father's Occupation)** [37]

	Kuomintang Executive Committee 1929, 1926, 1924	*Communist Executive Committee, 1945*
Wealthy landlord, traditional scholar-official	34%	33%
Wealthy merchant and other upper class	15%	7%
Small landlord, merchant, wealthy peasant, or other middle class	45%	37%
Other peasant	6%	17%
Worker	0%	7%

revolutionary movements in peripheral societies, the Chinese Communists were led by intellectuals from the upper strata of society, but succeeded in combining their ideological and organizational talents with the resentments and needs of the peasantry. What effects this had on China after 1950 will be discussed in a later chapter.

Conclusion: The New Semiperiphery

This brief summary of revolution in peripheral societies in the first half of the twentieth century allows certain general conclusions.

First, while the causes of the revolutionary situation throughout peripheral areas tended to be the same, the nature of the various revolutions that took place varied considerably. The major basis of difference was the degree to which various classes were mobilized in the struggle. The more strongly the mass of peasants were organized, the more radical the outcome was likely to be.

Second, while the intellectuals who led the major revolutions had many programs in common (strengthening the state, encouraging economic diversification and growth, asserting national independence against the world system), there were major differences of opinion about how to carry out these reforms. The Chinese Communist Party had a vastly different program than the Kuomintang, just as the various factions in the Mexican Revolution had different programs. But it was perhaps not so much ideological differences but the source of support of the various revolutionary movements that produced different outcomes. Leaders have certainly been important, but their sources of support have been more important. The conservative basis of the Kuomintang was far more responsible for Chiang Kai-shek's failures than any personal shortcomings he might have had.

The relative influences of support and leadership are illustrated as well by India's nationalist movement. Rarely, if ever, has any new state had as dedicated, intelligent, and humane a set of leaders as India in 1947. Yet, because the independence movement was heavily based on support from prosperous (rather than poor) peasants in the countryside and on the urban commercial and industrial middle class, the radical components of the movement were submerged, and independent India did not carry out a policy of revolutionary social and economic change. Consequently, many of India's colonial problems have remained, and the pace of economic growth has been slow.[38] This slowness has perpetuated the poverty, divisiveness, and terrible social inequality which characterized preindependence India.

Third, the major common outcome of every peripheral revolutionary movement has been the creation of a new kind of elite. Control of the state machinery has been crucial in determining the rapidity of change. The key question about peripheral revolutions is, what social groups take control, and how solidly do they establish their power? The more solidly the state controls its population (that is, the better and more thorough its organizational base), the more likely it is that revolutionary policies will be carried out effectively.

This last conclusion provides a direct link to Chapter 5 on the nature of change in semiperipheral societies. In effect, successful anticore revolts in peripheral societies created a new set of semiperipheral societies. By 1950, China, Mexico, India, and Turkey were all semiperipheral. By 1955, Egypt and North Vietnam had also achieved this status. All were striving to change. All had powerful governments that were the main agents of change. Semiperipheral societies in the 1950s faced many of the same problems and tensions as semiperipheral societies at the start of the twentieth century. Not the least of these problems was the continuing supremacy and hostility of the capitalist core.

Part Three

TOWARD THE NEXT CENTURY— CONTEMPORARY SOCIAL CHANGE

CHAPTER *8*

Social Change and International Relations in the Second Half of the Twentieth Century

A t the end of World War II the industrial economies of most of Europe and of Japan were in shambles. Of the countries at the core of the capitalist world only one, the United States, was in good condition. In the late 1940s it produced more than 60 percent of the world's total manufactured output.[1] The only other capitalist country with any real claim to international power was the United Kingdom, with its still enormous, but now collapsing overseas empire, a weak economy, and a strong desire to concentrate on internal reform rather than global politics. In 1945, the British elected a socialist government to carry out these policies, and in 1947, they handed India its independence.

The only potential rival of the United States was the Soviet Union. Though it, too, was huge and one of the winners of the war, it was much less developed, much poorer, and still technologically quite backward. Moreover, it had neither any sizable fleet nor any atomic weapons; and though it had an enormous army, it was much closer to exhaustion than was the United States. It was able to assume a dominant role in the demoralized, ruined countries of Eastern Europe that it had occupied while pushing toward Germany during the last year of the war. The only way to dislodge it would have been to continue the war after 1945 with an invasion of Eastern Europe by the United States, and this was in no one's immediate interest in the West. But elsewhere, the Soviet Union's power was limited by America's presence.[2]

The challenge to the United States was to reanimate the economies of Western Europe and Japan so that their desperate populations would not turn to communism out of free choice, and to make sure that its own economy did not sink back into the Great Depression that had only been ended by the rearmament that had come with the war. The challenge, in other words, was to prevent the ruin and chaos that had followed World War I, and that in this case promised to be more severe.

Pax Americana

These twin goals were accomplished by a series of coordinated economic and political moves which were outstandingly enlightened and successful. In July 1944 at Bretton Woods, the United Nations monetary and financial conference took place to create a sound basis for the revival of the world economy after the end of the war. The proceedings were of course dominated by the United States, with considerable British input. The International Monetary Fund was established and empowered to provide emergency money for economic stabilization. The currencies of the countries of the world would be fixed with respect to the United States dollar, and American currency would become a reserve currency convertible into gold at $35 per ounce. The old gold standard, backed by the most powerful economy in the world, had been effectively reestablished.[3]

This did not, however, solve the problem of revitalizing the capitalist world. The United States could produce enough to export huge amounts of goods, but how would the rest of the world pay if they could not produce exports to balance their imports from America? And how could they produce such exports without making investments in their industrial plants? The solution was the Marshall Plan, announced in 1947 and first put into effect in 1948. Under that plan, the United States granted substantial aid and credits to Europe, thus providing both money for investments and the wherewithal to purchase American goods.

There were American and European domestic forces opposed to the goal of the United States to create a largely open, free-trading world economy. In Europe, on the left, there were the socialists and communists for whom centralized state control promised greater economic and social justice, but for whom it was necessary to impose strict control of foreign exchanges, travel, and trade in order to be able to carry out their policies. On the right were the forces which Fred Block has called the "national capitalists," for whom nationalist closure of their economies promised a safer economic environment free from international, and particularly American, competition. Whether on the left or right, those desiring more controls threatened to recreate the world of the 1930s and resume the drift toward either fascism or communism. But the fear of communism, and the power of Americans, persuaded Europe's "national capitalists" (whose French incarnation, Charles de Gaulle, would later return to power and try but fail to create a kind of closed Europe equally hostile to both American free trade and communism) to accept the American solution.[4]

In the United States, the old tradition of isolationism that had dominated policy after World War I was still represented by the conservative Republican leader, Senator Taft. It was defeated because the more enlightened representatives of large business saw the expansion of foreign trade and investment as a way to avoid a new depression that would be followed by America's version of increased state control and "national capitalism." Confident that they could compete in an open world, and eager to expand, these forces joined President Roosevelt, and in 1945 Truman, to back outward-looking policies. Their task was facilitated, too, by the outbreak of the Cold War, a kind of hostile near-war with no actual battles in Central Europe, but with skirmishes in more peripheral areas between the Soviet Union and the United States.[5]

Because the U.S.S.R. saw every American move as another step toward encirclement and eventual elimination of communism, and the United States saw every Soviet move as the expression of a desire to conquer the world for Marxism-Leninism, their mutual hostility intensified. This made American policy easier to carry out. Both domestic opposition in the United States and European (eventually, too, Japanese) nationalism could reconcile themselves to this policy as being necessary for survival. The final event that made the Roosevelt-Truman policy successful was the outbreak of war in Korea in 1950.

That war began as an essentially domestic civil war between communist revolutionaries and nationalist conservatives vying for power. The United States came to the aid of the conservatives in South Korea to crush leftist rebellion; and North Korea, armed by the U.S.S.R., invaded the South to save the revolution. Interpreted by the West as a deliberate move by the Soviet Union to expand communist rule, this invasion was resisted by the United States. American victories then brought in China, newly conquered by its own communist revolutionaries. Nothing served the interests of either the Americans or the Soviets better, as this largely inconclusive, stalemated war solidified the Soviet-Chinese alliance and made it possible for the United States to become firmly internationalist and push its vision of a united, free-trading, dollar-dependent capitalist core.[6]

In 1949 the North Atlantic Treaty Organization (NATO) was established. In 1955 West Germany joined it, and the American consolidation of Western Europe was essentially complete.[7]

From 1945 to 1955 the United States gave or loaned some $38 billion to other countries. Seventy-five percent of this amount was for Western Europe and Japan, and almost 5 percent for South Korea and Taiwan, the nationalist remnant of China still controlled by America's anti-communist ally, Chiang Kai-chek (see Tables 8-1 and 8-2 on foreign aid).

If anything, American aid in the 1945–1955 period worked too well. Not only did it secure the old core from communism and bring back its prosperity, but it provided an outlet for American economic activity that generated a boom of unparalleled proportions. The effects of this prosperity completed the transformation of most of the core into fully industrialized, high-consumption societies. The fourth industrial revolution, the spread of automobiles and electrical appliances to the majority of the population, had not yet occurred in Europe before the war. But in the 1950s and 1960s, it did; and in the 1960s and 1970s, Japan was also included. Industrial efficiency improved throughout the core, so that eventually the dominant role of the United States came to be threatened by its own allies.[8]

Another consequence of the success of this period was that an illusion was created that foreign aid combined with American investment and firm anti-communism could turn troubled, poor countries into rich, firmly capitalist and pro-American ones. Indeed, this proved possible in the old core and Japan, societies with already highly skilled labor forces, well-developed industrial traditions, strong native capitalist bourgeoisies and well-integrated national cultures. But outside the old core, it was a different story.

By the mid-to late 1950s, it seemed that the struggle to expand the capitalist world economy dominated by the United States, to make foreign investment safe, and to prevent the spread of communism, was shifting to another front. The core was safe, but not the periphery. In the immediate postwar years, the United States had promoted the liberation of Europe's colonies in order to open their economies and take them out of the narrow imperial networks into which they had been forced. But as it became obvious that it was precisely in this area, in the colonial periphery of Asia and Africa, that anticapitalist, procommunist ideology had the most fertile ground for growth, the United States changed its position.

As the Europeans lost their empires, the United States found itself as the main protector of the capitalist system in the former colonial, poor parts of the world, the so-called "Third World." (This name, established at a conference of newly independent African and Asian countries at Bandung, Indonesia, in 1955 was meant to accentuate the differences between these countries and the "First," or capitalist world, and the "Second," or developed communist world of the Soviet Union and Eastern Europe.) Various attempts were made, particularly during the years of John Kennedy's presidency (1961–1963) to extend the idea of the Marshall Plan to these countries, to make them safe for capitalism, and to win them to the side of the Americans in the struggle against communism.[9]

But the program did not work. For one thing, the American electorate and Congress would no longer support the kind of massive aid given to Europe in the late 1940s and early 1950s. Second, many of the Third World countries were distinctly anticapitalist and analyzed the causes of their poverty by pointing to their past dependency on the capitalist core. Third, the challenge of revolutionary nationalism came to be identified by the United States as part of the communist drive to conquer the world; and more often than not, the Americans found themselves on the opposite side, defending conservative forces identified as antinationalist in their own countries. More than anywhere else, this came to be the case in Vietnam, which, from 1964 on, absorbed an increasing portion of American energies overseas.

An examination of the quantity and distribution of American foreign aid (Tables 8-1 and 8-2) reveals the pattern. From 1945 to 1955, aid was concentrated in the old core and in a few direct military allies of the United States. From 1956 to 1975, it was more evenly distributed, with Latin America, Africa, and Asia receiving much more than before. Neutral India became the single biggest recipient of American aid, though by the late 1960s, it was South Vietnam that was the key to American policy in the Third World. The absolute amount (in constant dollars—that is, taking into account inflation) of American aid, however, was lower in this period than in the 1945–1955 period, and as a proportion of the growing American GNP, it was lower. Finally, after the fall of South Vietnam to the communists, American aid shrank further, but became much more concentrated. The direct allies of the United States, Egypt and Israel, now became the chief recipients of aid. (In terms of

TABLE 8-1
Geographic Distribution of Foreign Aid (nonmilitary) Given by the United States, 1945–1982[10]

	1945–1955		1956–1975		1976–1982	
	In millions of dollars	*Percent distribution*	*In millions of dollars*	*Percent distribution*	*In millions of dollars*	*Percent distribution*
Western Europe	24,770	65.1	−811	—	206	0.4
Among which:						
United Kingdom		(18.1)		—		—
France		(14.4)		—		—
West Germany		(10.3)		—		—
Eastern Europe	1,097	2.9	727	1.1	1,015	2.1
Near East	2,761	7.3	15,810	24.1	24,163	49.3
Among which:						
Greece		(3.5)		(0.8)		(0.6)
Turkey		(1.0)		(3.7)		(4.5)
Pakistan		(0.5)		(6.8)		(1.5)
Egypt		(0.1)		(1.9)		(14.6)
Israel		(1.0)		(4.0)		(22.8)

Africa	143	0.4	5,454	8.3	5,923	12.1
South Asia, Far East, and Pacific	7,156	18.8	27,620	42.1	7,436	15.2
Among which:						
Japan		(6.6)		—		—
South Korea		(3.6)		(6.9)		(4.4)
Republic of China–Taiwan		(1.2)		(2.1)		(2.1)
Philippines		(2.2)		(1.2)		(1.3)
South Vietnam		(0.6)		(9.8)		—
India		(0.1)		(13.1)		(1.7)
Americas	1,151	3.0	10,836	16.5	4,056	8.3
International	976	2.6	5,236	8.0	6,186	12.6
Total	38,054	100.0	65,683	100.0	48,985	100.0

TABLE 8-2
Characteristics of Foreign Aid (nonmilitary)
Given by the United States, 1945–1982[11]

	1945–1955	*1956–1975*	*1976–1982*
Per year during period (in millions of dollars)	3,459	3,284	6,998
Per year during period (in millions of constant 1985 dollars)	15,185	11,001	10,173
Per capita yearly amount (amount divided by U.S. population) in constant 1985 dollars	100	57	45
As percent of U.S. GNP	1.2	0.5	0.3
Percent given to U.S. allies in Western Europe (including Greece) and to Japan	75.2	—	1.0
Percent given to America's key strategic allies and clients outside the core: South Korea, Taiwan, Turkey, Pakistan, Egypt (since 1976), South Vietnam (until 1975), and Israel	7.9	34.5	49.9

total aid, by the 1980s Israel received close to one-quarter of American non-military aid, and one-third of all its military aid, while Egypt's proportions, respectively, were one-eighth and one-sixth.) The share not going to direct allies and loyal clients of the United States fell correspondingly, reflecting a kind of distaste for general Third World problems and resignation about the possibility of transforming most of the Third World into a loyal bastion of capitalism and pro-Americanism.

American Foreign Investment and Economic Performance

American investments abroad, which grew enormously after 1950, also reflect the relative importance of various parts of the world and the increasing concentration on other core, rather than peripheral, areas. In this sense, the predictions of the Leninist theory of imperialism, however much they have been accepted by a good many leaders and intellectuals in the Third World and by Marxist analysts in the West, are not really confirmed. Rather than becoming increasingly important to the United States and the rest of the core, the Third World has become somewhat less important, except for some very select, specific countries and regions. On the other hand, it is quite obvious that foreign investment as a whole has not only grown enormously for the United States, but that investment, and foreign trade in general, have become a much more vital part of the American economy than they were before World War II.

An examination of American foreign investments and profits (Table 8-3) shows this pattern at work. Even between 1972 and 1982, the shift can be seen very plainly.

United States foreign investment, which was worth $7.5 billion in 1929, and only $7 billion in 1940, had reached $14.7 billion in 1950, $34.3 billion in 1960, $94 billion in 1972, and $221.3 billion in 1982. Of these amounts, an increasing proportion has been placed in other core capitalist economies. By 1982, well under 25 percent was in the Third World (taking into account the fact that within the Other category are included American ships under flags of convenience not actually consisting of any real investment in the countries where they are officially registered).

There was a time when profits from investment in primary exports from peripheral societies contributed a large portion of the profits of American companies abroad. As late as 1972, the Middle East petroleum investments and those in other resource-extraction enterprises in other non-core societies contributed well over half of all American foreign profits. But by 1982, even this had changed and investments in the core, primarily in manufacturing and services, were yielding more profits than those in primary extraction outside the core (see Table 8-4).

It is worth noting, however, that foreign profits have become a major component of American corporate business profits. In 1929, they amounted to

TABLE 8-3
United States Foreign Investment by Area, Percentages[12]

	1929	1940	1950	1960	1972	1982
Canada	27	30	30	35	27	20
Western Europe	18	20	15	21	33	45
Oceania		(with Other)		3	5	4
Japan		(with Other)		1	2	3
Latin America	47	40	39	26	18	15
Middle East		(with Other)		4	2	1
Other	9	10	16	10	13	13

TABLE 8-4
American Foreign Corporate Profits, Percent Distribution by Area[13]

	1972	*1982*
Canada	12	13
Western Europe	23	40
Oceania	3	2
Japan	2	3
Latin America	12	12
Middle East	31	5
Other	17	24
Total	$8 billion	$22.9 billion

only 1.9 percent of such profits. By 1940, they made up 3.1 percent. Over the next four decades, the percentage increased steadily to 3.4 percent (1950), 6 percent (1960), 9.1 percent (1972), and 13.1 percent (1982). This source of profits, then, has become an important part of the American economy. In that sense, the United States in the last part of the twentieth century has become much like the classic hegemonic core economy of the nineteenth century, the United Kingdom.[14]

Over time, the United States has become more "British" in another way, too. As the United States spent a large amount of its time, capital, and energy on foreign investment, on defending the capitalist world against revolution, and on general fiscal and military policing of the world, less-burdened economies of the smaller core powers were better able to concentrate on pure economic growth. As they recovered, they began to surpass the United States in productivity and economic dynamism, and the United States began to lose the competitive advantage it had had in world markets. It moved from having a favorable balance of trade (exports exceeded imports) throughout the 1940s, 1950s, and 1960s to becoming a chronically deficitary economy in the late 1970s and 1980s. Combined with foreign aid and with continuing outflows in military spending abroad, this caused the United States to gradually slip into a net negative position in its overall balance of current accounts (more money going out than coming in). But as in the case of the United Kingdom, which also had growing trade deficits in the late nineteenth century, "invisible" earnings somewhat made up for these. ("Invisible" earnings are not based on direct trade but on flows of money from foreign investments and payments for certain services.)

Table 8-5 shows how important earnings from foreign investments have become as the United States struggles in the 1980s to restrain its ballooning deficit in international transactions. (If this is allowed to continue too long, it

TABLE 8-5
**Yearly Average Balance of Current Accounts
(in billions of dollars)[15]**

	Merchandise ("Visible" Trade)	Investment Income	Total (Including all Other "Invisibles")
1946–1950	5.8*	1.2	3.1
1951–1955	2.5	2.3	0.2
1956–1960	4.1	3.2	2.0
1961–1965	5.4	4.6	˙4.8
1966–1970	2.3	5.7	1.8
1971–1975	−0.9	11.2	4.0
1976–1980	−25.5	23.1	−5.3
1981–1984	−63.1	28.1(1981–83)	−33.2

* No sign = surplus; −sign = deficit.

could cause a major international fiscal crisis. The United States dollar simply cannot rise and fall like currencies of smaller economies because it has remained, to this day, the crucial reserve currency on which most international trade and settling of accounts is based.)

As in the case of the British in the late nineteenth century, the Americans in the late twentieth have seen their capacity to make rapid improvements in their productivity eroded, a problem which accounts for at least a good portion of the growing deficit in the trade balance. From 1970 to 1975, U.S. manufacturing productivity rose at an annual rate of 3.4 percent, while those of France, Germany, and Japan, rose at 4.6 percent, 5.4 percent, and 6.8 percent, respectively, per year. From 1975 to 1980 America's manufacturing productivity rose at an anemic yearly rate of 1.7 percent, while France's rose at 5.1 percent a year, Germany's at 4.3 percent a year, Japan's at 8 percent a year, and even the United Kingdom's at 2.7 percent a year. And the improvement in American productivity, which averaged well above 2 percent, and usually over 3 percent a year in the 1950s and 1960s, now consistently averages below 2 percent a year.[16]

None of this means that the United States is now a second-rate economic power. It is still overwhelmingly dominant, though not as much as before. It remains the key economy of the capitalist world, and therefore, of the globe. Its power is still unmatched in other respects, too. But as in the case of the British in the nineteenth century, it has been unable to prevent serious economic rivals from growing, and it has paid a steep price to maintain its political hegemony over recalcitrant peripheral areas it has not always been able to control. Despite many political differences between the nineteenth and twentieth centuries, then, the British Empire and the American "Empire" have evolved in somewhat similar ways.

This raises three questions. Why has the United States had such problems in the periphery? To what extent has its policy there been rational? Finally, is

TABLE 8-6
Economic Growth in the "Three" Worlds[17]

	Gross Domestic Product Per Capita, in 1985 U.S. Dollars		Percent Change (Averages for Groups of Countries Weighted by 1965 Populations)
	1950	*1980*	
Western Europe			
France	4,308	13,024	+202
West Germany	3,594	13,408	+273
Italy	2,775	9,040	+226
Sweden	6,146	13,219	+115
Switzerland	5,916	12,636	+114
United Kingdom	5,257	10,033	+ 91
Greece	1,790	7,648	+327
Average Western Europe			+220
Australia	7,079	12,067	+ 70
Canada	6,872	14,529	+111
United States	8,931	15,573	+ 74
Japan	1,578	11,183	+609
Average "First" World (Old core + Japan)			+231
Eastern Europe			
East Germany	2,886	10,787	+274
Czechoslovakia	4,255	9,571	+125
Poland	2,956	6,843	+131
Hungary	3,009	7,529	+150
Romania	1,457	5,394	+270
Yugoslavia	1,500	6,470	+331
Average Eastern Europe			+212
Soviet Union	2,677	7,689	+187
Average "Second" World (European communist countries)			+195

the relationship between the United States and its core capitalist allies likely to change because of the shift in patterns of productivity? But before any of these questions can be dealt with, it is necessary to establish the basic facts about economic growth in the period after World War II. It is on this that all of the controversy and conflict in the world ultimately rests. Table 8-6 shows rates of growth for key countries from 1950 to 1980.

TABLE 8-6   Economic Growth in the "Three" Worlds *(continued)*

	Gross Domestic Product Per Capita, in 1985 U.S. Dollars		*Percent Change (Averages for Groups of Countries Weighted by 1965 Populations)*
	1950	*1980*	
Latin America			
Mexico	2,073	5,027	+143
Argentina	3,742	6,164	+ 65
Brazil	1,474	4,159	+182
Chile	2,843	4,643	+ 63
Colombia	1,880	3,726	+ 98
Peru	1,839	3,530	+ 92
Venezuela	3,531	7,112	+101
Average Latin America			*+138*
Asia			
India	647	969	+ 50
Philippines	907	1,970	+117
Taiwan	993	4,764	+380
Thailand	893	2,280	+155
Pakistan	798	1,285	+ 61
Turkey	1,355	3,994	+195
Average Asia (not including China or Japan)			*+ 73*
Africa			
Egypt	993	2,295	+131
Nigeria	1,067	2,995	+181
Ethiopia	433	657	+ 52
Zaire	413	577	+ 40
Ghana	1,899 (for 1954)	1,381	− 27
Average Africa			*+124*
Average "Third" World (Old periphery, not including China)			*+ 92*
China	585	2,213	+278

The World Economy, 1950–1980

Table 8-6 is based on the latest and best estimates of economic growth over the last three decades, but it requires further explanation.

The selection of countries makes it seem that Africa has grown more quickly than it really has, because Nigeria is such a populous country and happens to have had a major oil-exporting boom in the 1970s. Egypt, too, is a highly populated country, Africa's second largest, but it is not representative of the very poor black African countries south of the Sahara. Among these, Ethiopia, Zaire, and Ghana are more typical, and most of them rank as among the poorest but also the most slowly growing, or even, in many cases, declining economies of the world.

The contrary case may be made for India. Because it is so large, it brings down average Asian statistics. At the same time, India itself is not quite as poor as it seems. Economist Morris D. Morris has calculated a "physical quality of life index" for the countries of the world, based on comparison of literacy rates, infant mortality, and life expectancy at age one. Utilizing these criteria, the data presented in Table 8-7 emerge (for the early 1970s). All of the core countries have indexes of between 93 and 97. The European communist countries have ratings in the low 90s, except Yugoslavia, which was rated at 84 in 1968. The distinctions between industrialized countries on this index are small. Though the differences in GDP or GNP reflect very real differences in standards of living, all industrial countries have high "p.q.l.i." scores.[18] But in real physical terms, average Indians are better off than average Nigerians

TABLE 8-7
Physical Quality of Life Index for Selected Countries (Early 1970s)[19]

Mexico	71
Argentina	85
Brazil	66
Chile	77
India	43
Philippines	72
Taiwan	87
Thailand	70
Pakistan	38
Turkey	55
Egypt	43
Nigeria	25
Ethiopia	15
Zaire	32
Ghana	35

even though their per capita GDP is lower; and, in fact, most Asians are considerably better off than most Africans. Latin Americans score even better on this index, but this is reflected by differences in GDP per capita as well.

Looking at economic growth rates among industrialized core countries, some well-known, but still interesting conclusions emerge. Though still very rich, the United States has had a very slow economic growth rate in the second half of the twentieth century compared with other core economies. So has every other English-speaking country! As it happens, none suffered any substantial damage during World War II, and this may account, in part, for their slow growth. Sweden and Switzerland have also been relatively slow, though rich, growers since World War II, and they also escaped damage. It may be that societies not shaken by catastrophic experience have been less willing to innovate, that their various interest groups have been less willing to compromise, and that the very absence of a need to rebuild physical plants has deterred economic vigor.

But these differences within broad groups of nations cannot conceal two basic facts. The gap in wealth between the old rich core (now joined by Japan) and the old periphery (some of which is now clearly semiperipheral) has grown substantially since the end of World War II. The average core economy has grown by 231 percent in product per capita between 1950 and 1980, while the average Third World economy has only grown by 92 percent. The enormous gap in wealth that existed in 1950 was bigger in 1980, and shows no sign at all of being reduced.

Communist countries in Europe have not quite kept up with average growth in Western Europe or in the capitalist core as a whole, but they have not fallen much further behind either. Their performance seems unspectacular by Western standards, but excellent by Third World standards.

With Latin America currently mired in a serious debt crisis and seemingly chronic inflation, with Africa suffering increasingly frequent droughts and famines, and with the highly populated parts of South Asia experiencing economic stagnation, the prospects for the rest of the century appear to indicate that, if anything, the gap between rich and poor will grow even faster.

Only East Asia—including Taiwan, South Korea, Singapore, Hong Kong, Malaysia, and even (though the statistics are less than fully reliable) China itself—is experiencing the kind of spectacular growth that might reduce the gap between itself and the old core. If China is still so poor that it will take many more decades of rapid growth to accomplish this, the same is no longer true for these other countries. But East Asia seems to be an exception in the Third World.

In light of these facts, it is possible to return to the questions posed above: Why has the United States had so much trouble dealing with the peripheral world? To what extent has its position been rational? Only after these two topics have been dealt with will it be useful to go on to the third question: What will happen to the relationship between the United States and the rest of the core as patterns of productivity and economic growth change?

The Revolt of the Periphery

The basic theoretical issue is the extent to which core prosperity depends on the exploitation of a periphery, and the degree to which it is necessary for capitalism to intensify its extraction of a surplus from abroad in order to maintain the standard of living of its own working and middle classes. Lenin answered this question in 1916 by saying that indeed it was essential for such exploitation to occur, and in fact, it was so vital that the major capitalist powers would be forced into wars of increasing severity with one another over the acquisition of colonial peripheries to exploit. Without this, they would collapse. More recent Marxist theorists, such as Paul Baran or Andre Gunder Frank, have repeated the assertion and amplified it.[20]

But looking at the world before 1914 and at the reasons for economic growth suggests that the frenetic imperialism of that era, and consequently the entire prelude to World War I, was caused more by massive error on the part of statesmen and military planners than by any inherent need for colonies. It was in the research laboratories of Europe and America that economic growth was spawned from the late nineteeth century on, not in the tea plantations of Ceylon or the gold mines of South Africa.

In the years after World War I, the fascist nations of Italy, Germany, and Japan, and in minor ways some of the smaller fascist states, too, accepted the Leninist theory (though of course they were violently anticommunist) that colonies were important for economic growth and national prosperity. That is what led to the Second World War. The fact that the defeated fascist powers, stripped of their colonies, ruined by the war, and politically humiliated have done extremely well since the end of the war, that Germany and Japan have been the world's two most spectacular economic success stories, should demonstrate once and for all that internal social structures are a more important determinant of economic growth than is the possession of external empires.

But since 1945, the main core powers, and increasingly since 1960 the United States, have behaved as if they also believed in the Leninist theory of imperialism. The United States has poured enormous efforts into keeping control of what it considers important parts of the peripheral Third World. Why, if not to protect its interests in these areas has the United States supported counterrevolutions meant to contain anticore, anticapitalist, nationalist movements? The best-known examples have been China (1946–1949), Greece (1946–1949), the Philippines (1948–1952), Iran (1952), Guatemala (1954), Indonesia (1958–1960), Cuba (1959–1961), Laos (1959–1975), Vietnam (1956–1975, although American involvement in the form of aid to the French started even before 1956), Cambodia (1970–1975), the Dominican Republic (1965), Chile (1971–1973), El Salvador and Nicaragua (1979 to the present), Angola (1974–1975), and Grenada (1982).[21] Why has the United States supported such a long string of largely unpopular, repressive, but pro-Western dictatorships in Central America, South America, the Caribbean, and Asia? And why, furthermore, has an increasing proportion of aid gone to friendly regimes in the Middle East, where so much of the world's oil reserves lie? (The fact that Israel is not Arab but acts as America's closest ally and maintainer of order in this area does not negate that argument. Egypt, though less reliable, is Arab and serves the same function.)

The other side of the same question is: Why has it been the case, time after time, that nationalist, anticapitalist, anti-Western revolutionary elements have arisen to demand that their societies be removed from the world capitalist system, and that they be allowed to develop on their own? Why have they believed that the core, specifically the United States, has been the greatest impediment to their development?

If Lenin's theory, which certainly seems to fit events, is not correct, what accounts for the uncomfortable facts?

One argument must be disposed of immediately. It might be thought that the primary concern of the United States is for strategic bases against the Soviet Union, to be held in case of war. The felt need for such bases definitely plays a role in military thinking, both among Americans and Soviets, so that both powers are eager to gain bases for themselves and deny bases to their enemy. But with time, the actual need for such bases has declined if their object is to be used against the other great power. If, in the late 1940s and early 1950s, heavy bombers needed forward airfields to reach other continents, and if ships needed fueling and repair bases, the need for such facilities in an age of nuclear submarines and intercontinental ballistic missiles is much smaller. Even the need for forward radar and radio listening posts diminishes each year with the increasing sophistication of satellite electronic spying devices. If strategic bases were primarily at issue, the United States and the Soviet Union would now be less involved than ever in the Third World.

The United States has a very different reason for fearing the spread of leftist regimes in the periphery and semiperiphery. Such leftist regimes apply the principle of greater equality (which is the defining characteristic of the left in domestic politics) on a global scale and accept the Marxist-Leninist notion that by exploiting peripheries the capitalist core has become unfairly rich. Since poverty is explained by subjection to the core, the remedy is partial or complete withdrawal from the world capitalist system. Leftist revolutionary regimes in the Third World recognize the many disadvantages of peripherality (as these have been spelled out in the previous chapters) and believe that the only way to escape them is through some form of closure followed by a long period of internal effort to catch up to rich societies. Only in this way can successful economic diversification, industrialization, national unity, and the base for ultimate internal equality be laid. A rightist regime, on the other hand, does not accept the notion of inevitable inequality between societies in a capitalist world. It therefore accepts keeping the economy it rules within that system. There are obvious benefits: continuing investment from the core, aid, technical advice, a ready market for primary goods, and a source of manufactured goods that can be imported from core economies. As the capitalist core remains far richer and more technologically advanced than the communist countries, being tied to it seems a better bargain for those who do not have a Marxist-Leninist view of the causes of underdevelopment.

The policy of the United States has systematically pushed to keep peripheral economies and societies open to the capitalist world system, both by promising benefits to those that remain open (aid) and threatening or actually carrying out punishment against those that do not (either economic sanctions or military intervention—covert, and sometimes, overt). While this is close to saying that American policy seeks to protect cheap natural resources and American investments in the periphery, it is not quite the same thing. Venezuela remains an open economy although it has expropriated local oil companies controlled by citizens of the United States. Saudi Arabia is in the same position. They therefore continue to receive support and aid from the United States and they remain "allies." In short, if the "imperialism" theory holds at all, it does so now in a rather more subtle way than in the early part of the century. Direct ownership and control of colonial areas are no longer particularly important. Openness, however, is crucial. Even communist states, if they reenter the capitalist world system, or make serious moves toward re-entry, become acceptable. Yugoslavia, and today much of Eastern Europe, are no longer seen as potential threats to the capitalist world system; the communist Eastern European economies have become trading partners with core economies, even while they remain formally the enemy.

This does not resolve the argument about whether or not the core really needs to keep large parts of the world "open" and within the world capitalist economic network. But there is little doubt that the United States and most of the rest of the core have behaved as if that were the case.

Seen in that light, the jockeying for position between the United States and the Soviet Union in various corners of the world takes on added significance. A society closed to the capitalist world system becomes a loss to that system; an open society remains a potentially profitable asset. In time, if enough peripheral societies are closed, the capitalist world system will shrink, and, according to the theory that both the United States and the Soviet Union seem to believe, this shrinkage will reduce prosperity in the core. Whether or not the theory is correct becomes secondary, at least in the short run, if the main international players behave as if it were correct. But keeping the periphery "open" has become costly.

As both nationalism and awareness of the immense, growing discrepancy between standards of living in the First and Third Worlds have grown, the pressure for some sort of leftist solution, and therefore of at least partial closure, has grown. The failure of the Soviet Union or its allies to catch up to the capitalist core, and the increasingly obvious difficulties socialist economies have had in managing their economic problems have slightly dampened this tendency, but that is not really what is at issue. Rather, it is the international distribution of economic and political power, not a kind of cost-benefit comparison between the Soviet Union's and the United States' internal means of running their affairs that is at stake. When this feeling has been successfully tapped by revolutionary organizers, as in Vietnam or Cuba or Nicaragua, it has become a fearsome force against which the United States has been unable to stand except with naked military might. Even that does not work unless the enemy is either poorly organized (as leftists were in Central America in the 1950s) or very small (as in Grenada). Against determined resistance in Vietnam, the United States found (as did the French before them), that the cost of winning exceeded the American population's willingness to fight. After all, for the American population what was at stake was not an immediate interest but a kind of long-term notion that perhaps capitalism might ultimately fail if enough "Vietnams" occurred. What was at stake for Vietnam was, in the eyes of its leaders and much of its population, something much graver—national survival. It is not that the United States could not, in some absolute sense win such a war. Against Nicaragua, for example, it certainly could. But the cost would vastly exceed any possible short-term gain.

Nor is communism itself the main issue. America's worst defeat in the world since the Vietnam War has been at the hands of Muslim nationalists in Iran, who are as anticommunist as they are anti-American. Yet, the Iranians, too, have a vision of a strong, united Iran, free of the evil and exploitative presence of the Western core, and primarily of the United States. Iran, then, is as much a danger to the preservation of an open periphery as is Vietnam; and at least in the Muslim World, it worries the United States more than do the communists.[22]

For the Soviet Union, which strongly believes in Lenin's *Imperialism*, the issue is as critical. It is obvious by now that the Soviet Union will never catch up to the West in its standard of living and in technological sophistication. Centralized bureaucratic control of an economy can work to bring it up to a high degree of military power and enable it to produce the necessary industrial structures that allow a big power to maintain its strength. But beyond that, the weight of overbureaucratization crushes innovation (as it did in the great agrarian empires of the past). Therefore, the only long-run hope of success in the world competition between capitalism and socialism for the Soviet Union is to have the capitalist core ruined by an increasing number of defections in the periphery. If the Leninist theory is correct, neither a great world war nor greater economic efficiency on the part of the Soviets is necessary to bring down the United States.

Both sides, then, accept the same theoretical world view that is based on outdated nineteenth-century economic reasoning. Both sides will wage long and costly struggles, either to keep as many areas of the world open to capitalist investment, or, for the others, to keep them closed. The irony, of course, is that in trying to keep their Eastern European dependencies as closed as possible, the Soviets have aroused intense nationalist hostilities against themselves. They have also failed to keep the doors of Eastern Europe tightly sealed, as country after country has turned to the West for investments, loans, markets, and technologies. In trying to bring Afghanistan within their orbit, the Soviets have created a whole new area where nationalism can be legitimately anticommunist without becoming a stooge of American capitalist interests. In countries controlled by the Soviets, nationalists trying to develop their economies no longer believe in Lenin's world view.

To what extent then, is American fear of closures in the Third World justified? American investments in the periphery are of declining importance, but this is not true of world trade patterns.

Table 8-8 shows the destination of exports from various groups of countries. It is clear how little change there has been over time in the basic pattern, even though the total volume of world trade has vastly increased (from 1965 to 1983 it increased in dollar value about tenfold, or more than threefold in constant, noninflated dollars).

Throughout the 1960s, 1970s, and 1980s, about two-thirds of world trade has originated in the old core or Japan, and about two-thirds of that, or between 40 and 45 percent of all world trade has been between core economies. In 1965, 68 percent of all the world's exports originated in the core, and in 1983 that number had fallen only slightly to 63 percent. In 1965, only 14 percent of all of the world's exports originated from non-OPEC (Organization of Petroleum Exporting Countries) Third World economies; and by 1983 that proportion had only risen to 16 percent. Only OPEC significantly increased its share, going from 5 percent of all world export to 9 percent from 1965 to 1983 (and reaching a high of 14 percent in 1980, when petroleum prices hit their peak). The proportion of exports from communist countries, including China, has remained roughly constant at 11 percent of total world exports during this period.[23]

American export and import patterns have also shown relatively little change in their distribution except for a significant rise in the importance of trade with OPEC as petroleum prices rose, and a decline in OPEC's role since 1980. A significant part of the shift since 1980, however, has been in the form of higher imports of petroleum from non-OPEC, primarily Mexican sources.

TABLE 8-8
Exports of Industrial Market Economies (Core Countries), 1960–1981, by Destination[24]

	1960	*1981*
To other core economies	67%	65%
To rich OPEC (Organization of Petroleum Exporting Countries)	less than 1%	4%
To Eastern Europe and U.S.S.R.	3%	3%
To the Third World (minus rich OPEC)	30%	28%

Still, close to two-thirds of all American exports have continued to go to other core economies, and about 60 percent of imports to come from the same sources.[25]

To say that 28 percent of all core exports went to the non-OPEC Third World in 1981, and that in 1983, 28 percent of all American exports did the same, while 31 percent of its imports came from these areas, is not to say that this trade is insignificant. If OPEC, which is, after all, the most critical part of the peripheral world as far as the industrial capitalist core is concerned, is added to these figures, the periphery now regularly accounts for a third of the core's trade. The loss of the trade, both as a market for exports and as a source of primary goods, and increasingly of certain cheap industrial goods, would be no small matter.

What the combined information about core investment and trading patterns indicates is that over time direct investment by the core in the periphery has decreased in importance, but trade with the periphery remains as important as ever; and though it is less than trade between core economies themselves, it is large enough so that it would be a major blow to the world capitalist system if it were seriously reduced.

In a very real sense, then, the concern of the United States with keeping world trade as open as possible is entirely reasonable. If the entire peripheral and semiperipheral world managed to restrict its role in world trade as much as have the large communist economies of the Soviet Union and China, this would certainly reduce the standard of living of the core and plunge capitalist economies into crisis. This does not mean, however, that the foreign policy of the United States, its attempt to prevent any revolution in the periphery or semiperiphery which might threaten closure of an economy, is justified by practical considerations.

Tracing the evolution of political relations between core societies and the old peripheral world since the end of World War II shows that these relations have gone through three stages; and with each shift, the core has put up stiff resistance to change, but has been obliged to accommodate itself. And at each stage, it has turned out that neither the prosperity nor enormous material advantage of the core has been seriously threatened. Each time, then, resistance has proved to be costly, useless, and in the light of subsequent events, unreasonable. These stages began with the period of "old" colonialism; that is, the attempt by the Europeans to keep their empires, which finally ended in a long series of bloody anticolonial wars. Second was the period of "neocolonialism," the attempt by the core powers to maintain their hegemony by directly owning key resources in the periphery, even while recognizing the formal political independence of the countries in which they operated. Though far from over, this stage has been yielding to a new stage ever since the assertion of OPEC power in 1974. This third stage, which is only emerging in the 1980s, might be called the "neocapitalist" stage, in which core countries will discover that their great strength lies in their economic efficiency, technological prowess, and financial reserves, not in their ability to impose political control and to try to force market distortions through sheer exercise of power. These three stages will now be described briefly.

The End of Old Colonialism

In 1947, India, Europe's largest colony, became independent and split into two hostile states, India and Pakistan (which itself later split into Pakistan and Bangladesh). Burma, another part of the British Indian Empire, also became a separate state. The reasons for this independence, the rise of the nationalist movement, the long struggle against the British, and Gandhi's ultimate triumph have already been discussed. Faced with the virtual certainty of a long, hopeless war against their rule, the British gave up before that war broke out. The fact that after 1945 the British Labour Party came to power accelerated India's independence. The British working class, eager to push domestic reform and to recover from the hardship of World War II, and in any case, ideologically opposed to colonialism, was hardly likely to launch a war to keep India British. But even without this change in British public opinion, India would have gained its independence.

France and the Netherlands, facing similar situations in their Asian empires in Indochina and Indonesia, resisted and both became involved in debilitating wars which they could not win. When the costs of maintaining colonies so far exceeded possible gains that the French and Dutch populations refused to fight any longer, the wars ended. A colony is profitable only if it does not require immense economic cost to keep it. Since the conditions that lead to colonial revolts cannot be eliminated in a colonial situation, the colonized people will keep on fighting even if they lose their first attempt at liberation. The number of discontented intellectuals, of poor peasants, and of humiliated natives cannot, in the long run, decrease. It can only increase until balanced, rapid economic growth is achieved and until the natives themselves gain power. The old controllers of the land and the comprador middle class, as well as their allies from the core, the colonial rulers, cannot, in the long run, survive against skillfully led mass revolts.

At first, the United States favored decolonization. In a sense, colonialism involved partial closure of the colonies to the trade, investment, and influence of any core economy except the metropole. Liberated colonies became open to wider—that is, American—influence and investment. As the United Kingdom, France, and the Netherlands were gradually forced to abandon all their colonies, American influence, investment, and trade became freer to move in. As late as 1956, when the United Kingdom and France made a brief, rather desperate, last attempt to retain their empires by invading Egypt, the United States strongly opposed this move. After all, this last effort was directed at the Middle East, where American oil companies already had things their own way. At that time, it seemed that the United States could gain from both ends. It could avoid the stigma of old-fashioned imperialism by opposing European military rule, and it could gain the benefits of economic imperialism by investing and trading with the newly liberated colonies.[26]

The short war against Egypt in 1956 ended the British Empire, even though it took a few more years for the remainder of the African and Asian segments to gain full independence. Not only were the British facing determined opposition to their rule from the people in their colonies as well as from their main ally in the core, the United States, but even within Britain a large portion of the population was unwilling to fight colonial wars that seemed likely to hurt rather than help the British economy.

France held on a few more years, but its surrender in Algeria ended its empire in 1962. Again, the cost of maintaining colonies had far exceeded the possible benefits. First, the war in Indochina had milked France, and in the late 1950s, war in Algeria did the same. It was not that France could not afford to fight the Algerian war, or even that it was militarily defeated. Rather, the high cost of arms, the drain on manpower (drafted for military service in Algeria), and the consequent political turmoil proved unacceptable. Nor was there any chance that control could be maintained while lowering these costs, since every military defeat suffered by the Algerians merely put off the end without eliminating the root causes of revolution. By the time it gave up Algeria, France had already given up most of its African empire to head off more wars.

In 1960, Belgium, panicked by the thought that it, too, would be drawn into a war in its Congo colony, withdrew.[27]

Portugal, Western Europe's poorest country, and with Spain the only undemocratic one until the 1970s, continued to fight to keep its colonies. If the strain was too much for the British and French, it was that much worse for smaller, weaker, and poorer Portugal. But because Portugal had not pressed as much in educating its colonies, and because it had not developed its colonial economies as much as the British and French had, revolts in the Portuguese African colonies took longer to consolidate. Eventually, however, revolutions broke out throughout Portuguese Africa, and after a series of long, debilitating wars, Portugal cracked in 1974. The Portuguese people and army revolted against their government, instituted democratic reforms, and in 1975, gave their colonies independence.[28]

Rhodesia, a white-ruled British colony with a substantial number of white settlers, tried to hold out on its own rather than give political power to the majority Africans. But it, too, was unable to win the long guerrilla war this entailed, and after a ten-year struggle, in 1980, the whites surrendered power to the black majority.[29]

The only remnant of the old colonialism in Africa, in a rather strange form, persists in South Africa, where 4 million whites controlling a rich economy and enormous resources still rule a basically black country.

In Asia, except for Hong Kong—which will persist as a British colony until 1997 because that suits Chinese interests—there is no more European colonialism. (Macau, a tiny coastal enclave, remains formally Portuguese, but again, only because this suits China, which actually runs it.) In Latin America, with a few minor exceptions, the same is true. The old colonialism, still very much alive in 1945, was dead thirty years later.

Few could have foreseen the rapid demise of European colonialism in 1930, or even in 1945, and yet tensions provoked by the development of colonies could have produced no other result. The seeming paradox is that economic development of colonies does not reduce the probability of revolt; it increases it. Economic development uproots peasants from their land, it throws agriculture into an uncertain, fluctuating world market, it tends to concentrate land ownership in the hands of a relatively small number of people, it brings to the fore an alien merchant middle class, and it trains potential leaders of rebellion. Economic development instills modern nationalism, teaches Western organizational skills, provides an explicitly anticolonial, largely Marxist-Leninist revolutionary doctrine (taught, ironically, in European and American universities), and it concentrates the colonials in cities where they can be organized more effectively. The greater the efforts to develop a colonial economy, the sooner the anticolonial revolution. This, no doubt, explains why Portugal, the poorest European imperial power, which did the very least to develop its colonies, did not face a successful revolutionary movement until a full ten to fifteen years after the French and British.

The revolt of the European colonies was certainly more than a purely economic movement. It was also a major cultural phenomenon, one that continues, and one that provides much of the ideological base of those forces pushing for rapid social change in the peripheral world.

No people like to be told that they are inferior. In the heyday of early twentieth-century imperialism the Europeans explicitly put forward racist explanations for their domination. Whites were said to be inherently superior to blacks, browns, reds, or yellows, and Christianity was said to be morally superior to other religions. The colonial world was overwhelmingly nonwhite, and outside of Latin America (which was, by and large, only indirectly colonized) overwhelmingly non-Christian. The crusading fervor of Gandhi in India, Sukarno in Indonesia, or Nasser in Egypt, along with many other leaders of anticore revolutionary movements, expressed more than the discontent of uprooted peasants, poor urban migrants, underpaid workers, or hostile intellectuals. It also expressed pride in local cultures and hatred of the supposedly superior Europeans. In fact, peripheral revolutions began to be successful only when their leaders began to reject the assumed superiority of European ways. Peripheral revolutions, therefore, contained a strongly symbolic aspect as well as being expressions of economic discontent. Since the creation of united national cultures is necessary for the creation of strong nation-states, and strong nation-states are necessary in order to reorder the economies of the former colonial areas, this symbolic content of revolution has been a necessary ingredient of peripheral revolutions.

When peripheral intellectuals realized that no matter how Westernized they might become, Europeans would never accept them as equals, the inevitable seeds of successful revolution were planted. Again, it was not a matter of insufficient education in the colonies. The more colonial natives were brought to Europe to study, the more likely their revolution. The British, who educated more natives of their colonies than the French, particularly in India, were first to face this problem. The French were next. The Belgians and Portuguese, who educated very few Africans in European universities, were faced by revolution even later.

The reactive cultural component of peripheral revolutions is best seen in the intractable issue of Israel. Arab nationalism in the Middle East had been active since the early twentieth century. The French and British were driven out of the area after World War II, but in one part of the Arab world, Palestine, European Jews (joined by Jewish refugees from Muslim countries) established an independent European state in 1947–1948. In doing this, they uprooted about 600,000 Palestinian Arabs. Many populations have been driven into exile by political events, both in the twentieth century and before. But in this case, the entire Arab world reacted, not simply the Palestinians. Why was this so? Largely because symbolically the Jewish state became a Western (even if non-Christian) enclave in the Arab world. The continuing bitter hostility of the Arabs toward Israel can be explained neither by economic reasons nor by any direct interests of Arab societies. The Arab Palestinians have a direct interest in seeing the Jewish state eliminated, but it is relatively clear that Syria, Israel's most determined enemy, has little to gain by establishing an Arab Palestinian state. Iraq, Saudi Arabia, Libya, Algeria, Morocco, Sudan, and Kuwait (much less distant Mauritania), have nothing to gain at all, except pride. Israel has become, by proxy, the West, the symbol of technological arrogance, material success, and in a strange way, a symbol of the imperialism of the past. Whether Jewish Israel wishes to symbolize all this is another question. (Clearly it wishes it did not have to bear the resultant burden.) The irony is that a non-Christian, previously persecuted minority in Europe has come to stand for the sins of the Europeans and of Western cultural arrogance. Since Israel has come to symbolize the legacy of the West, it will remain under attack until Arab resentment of the West disappears. The United States, the United Kingdom, and France may try to disavow their legacy, but resentment can end only when Arab countries become as rich and powerful as the old core. And while a few oil-producing Arab societies have become rich, they constitute a small minority of the Arab world.[30]

Israel has become the key emotional issue on which most peripheral societies have been able to express their hatred of the West, and the Arab cause receives overwhelming support in most of the periphery and former periphery. This should awaken the old core to the fact that there is far more at stake than the fate of the Arab Palestinians. The world is not outraged by equal, or greater, injustice elsewhere because the Palestinian issue has become the symbolic focus of the entire peripheral world's hostility to the capitalist world system. Even if Israel were to vanish, this hostility would remain, and other symbolic issues would come to the fore.

This was demonstrated by the revolution in Iran in 1978–1979, when America's most important Middle Eastern ally, the Shah, was overthrown by an alliance of almost all of his people who resented America's presence and the rapid Westernization of the Iranian elite. As a result, the most socially conservative, fundamentalist Islamic, and anti-Western forces took control, and attempted to eliminate Western influence. The violently anti-American, anti-Israeli, and anti-European manifestations of this revolutionary government show how they are associated with one another and how the West is seen as a deeply anti-Islamic, foreign intrusion. Only if the West were entirely excluded from the Middle East would the Iranian religious government be satisfied. That may mean Israel, of course, but it also means the United States, France, England, and any other Europeans (including, in this case, Russians) who might have designs on the Middle East.[31]

But this hostility to the West is no longer part of the first stage of anti-colonialism. There are no more formal colonies in the Middle East, unless one counts the Israeli-occupied territories of Gaza and the West Bank of the Jordan, so the hostility of the radical fundamentalist Muslims, originally aroused during the old colonial era, now expresses itself against newer forms of core domination.

Neocolonialism

As the old type of colonialism was crumbling under the pressure of armed revolts combined with the West's distaste for expensive, long, and ultimately fruitless colonial wars, a new type of colonialism emerged. Investment and indirect political control through manipulation behind the scenes became a more important way for the core to dominate the periphery. The chief instrument for this type of manipulation in the 1960s and 1970s was the multinational corporation, generally based in one of the major core countries, though some were based in lesser core countries such as the Netherlands or Switzerland. Using their huge financial assets and technological superiority, these firms, backed by their governments, became adept at bribing and subverting peripheral governments and, if necessary, mobilizing their home governments in order to get their way in the periphery. They won substantial profits for their efforts, often at rates that exceeded what they could make from their investments at home or in core countries.

Chief among these multinational firms were the giant oil corporations. In 1970, 1971, and 1972, for example, American oil companies operating outside the core had annual profits (as a percentage of their investments) amounting to 26 percent, 31.5 percent, and 34.4 percent. These compared with profits amounting to only 5.1 percent, 5.3 percent, and 5.1 percent in those years by American corporations operating in the core. Returns on mining investments were also high in these years, though not as high as with petroleum, and generally American overseas investments gained rates of profit about three times as high in the peripheral world as in the core. In the early 1970s, average investment by American companies outside the core earned profits of almost 16 percent per year. By comparison, within the United States itself during these years, industrial corporate profits averaged 11 percent of equity.[32] (Part of this disproportion was an accounting trick. Multinational corporations shifted profits to low-tax countries. But a lot of the discrepancy in profit rates was real, as demonstrated by the fact that the really high rates of return were in mineral and petroleum extraction, not manufacturing.)

In the mid-1970s the fifty largest multinational corporations controlled something close to one-third of all investments and up to 15 percent of all industrial production in the world capitalist system (excluding communist countries). This excludes the very substantial financial power of core multinational banks, insurance companies, and other nonindustrial corporations, which probably had an even greater degree of control in their respective spheres than did the large industrial corporations. Of these fifty, twenty-three were American, six were British (though two of these were jointly British-Dutch), five were Japanese, seven were West German, three were French, two were Italian, one was Swiss, one was purely Dutch, and only two, both government-owned oil companies, were based outside the core. Of the forty-eight in the core, fifteen were oil companies, and that included six of the largest ten corporations. The others were automobile corporations (ten), electronics or electrical firms (seven), chemical producers (seven), steel (five), or general consumer goods manufacturers (four).[33]

At the time there were serious fears about the power of these corporations. The governments of small and economically backward countries would be unable to resist their depredations. By distorting market forces—that is, by keeping the price of raw materials artificially low, by charging too much for their manufactured exports, and by concentrating research and development in their home bases—these corporations were ensuring the continued backwardness of the periphery and preventing the emergence of future competitors.

Also, as some of these corporations moved into manufacturing in the periphery, it was said that their exploitation of cheap labor would create an immense class of exploited proletariat in the slums of the Third World, but not give Third World countries the compensating advantages of developing strong research capacities, a secure and entrepreneurial middle class, and the improved welfare systems that eventually come with industrialization. This trend would weaken labor movements in the core itself, and so give the large corporations, who could threaten to cause unemployment at home if they did not gain their political aims, that much more power.

Finally, by keeping the world system open, they also encouraged labor flows from peripheral societies into the core, so that more cheap labor found its way into Europe from the Mediterranean region and Africa; into the United States from Mexico and Latin America; and into England from the West Indies,

India, and Pakistan. Moreover, the best-educated, skilled professionals and scientists from poor countries were being sucked into the core where they also contributed to lower costs by providing relatively cheap, highly skilled labor.

Fed by a growing stream of giant profits, it seemed, the multinationals, able to control both their home governments with their increasing political clout and the weak periphery, were going to dominate the whole world.[34]

But by the mid-1980s, this worry was shown to have been excessive. Expropriated by Middle Eastern and other Third World governments, the great oil companies seemed a lot weaker than they had been a decade earlier. The giant American automobile companies had proven unable to compete with the smaller but more innovative Japanese firms. Big steel corporations throughout the core were losing vast amounts of money. Exposed in numerous scandals, and no longer able to freely manipulate either their home governments or those of most Third World countries, the great multinational corporations were evidently not nearly as strong as they had seemed to be. Robert Gilpin's analysis in the early 1970s has proved correct. Without the backing of a strong state, no corporation has the political strength to manipulate markets to its will, except in the most poorly integrated, backward, weak countries. With the growth of nationalism and state power throughout the world, the number of such countries available for manipulation has steadily decreased.[35]

Neocolonialism was always more than merely multinational corporations spreading their tentacles into the periphery. It also meant a continued, substantial degree of core military and political pressure applied in the periphery in order to protect and control markets. But as the costs of applying such pressures have risen, neocolonial empires, too, have been disintegrating. The French, who maintained considerable power in their former African possessions for decades after granting them formal independence, have begun to balk at the high costs of continual intervention. The Americans, unwilling to fight damaging counterrevolutionary wars, have seen their position threatened even in some of the tiny Central American states. They have been ignominiously expelled from Iran, as well as Indochina.

The relative decline of American investments in the noncore economies of the world, and the declining rate of profit extracted from these areas shows that the recent trend is more than superficial. The most important, and in many ways the most revealing development in the 1970s and 1980s has been the so-called "oil" crisis of 1973–1981. The development and resolution of this crisis point the way toward the next stage of core involvement outside the core, though it remains far from certain whether the political leadership of the United States has understood the meaning of this crisis.

In 1970, OPEC oil was selling at an average price of $2.53 per barrel. In real terms, adjusted for inflation, this was less than the price of oil in 1940. Between 1970 and 1973, largely as a result of political pressure from Colonel Qaddafi, who had led an anti-Western revolution in oil-producing Libya, the price rose to $3.65 per barrel, still only about 80 percent of the price of oil in 1950 in real dollars. The main reason for this low price, despite the enormous increase in demand for oil since World War II, was that the major oil companies controlled the product entirely and could force OPEC countries to keep their prices below those paid American producers.

Then, using the threat of an oil embargo against the United States during the October 1973 Arab-Israeli war, OPEC (led by the great friend of America, the Shah of Iran, who was himself friendly to Israel), managed to raise the price of oil sharply to almost $12 per barrel. Within a few years, the major oil companies had control removed from their hands. The dramatic increase in the price of the world's most important fuel provoked a unique economic situation. Increased cost produced inflation, but the sudden, large amounts of money going to OPEC depressed demand for products within the industrial countries, so that these two phenomena were combined in something that came to be called "stagflation" (stagnation and inflation). Economists were unable to explain this, because in a self-contained economy, on which their models were based, inflation stimulates demand, and stagnation depresses prices. But of course, core economies were far from self-contained.

During the rest of the 1970s, core economies adjusted to the change in prices, and learned to recycle OPEC money through their own banks. Stagflation gradually eased. The price stabilized at 1974 levels and in real terms declined slightly. But if it had not been for the bitter Vietnam experience, it is very likely that the pressure of these events would have led the United States, perhaps with French and British help, to invade at least one of the major Middle Eastern oil producers to avert the expected catastrophe.

In January 1979 the Shah of Iran was overthrown. In the panic about a possible closure of Iran to the West, OPEC succeeded in raising prices once again. By late 1980, an OPEC barrel was worth about $41, but the price then fell and stabilized at $34 in 1981. There followed a new round of stagflation. This time, the rise in price was not justified by market conditions, as the big oil companies had not been keeping the price artificially depressed. In response to the sharply higher costs, the capitalist world reduced its consumption, and much new production (some of it planned since the early 1970s) came on line.

Again, if it had not been for the recent experience in Vietnam, it is quite likely that military action against Iran would have been taken, using as a pretext the seizure of American hostages by Muslim fundamentalists in 1980. But all the Americans dared to try was a weak, poorly planned response.

Yet, because of conservation and new sources of oil from the North Sea, Alaska, and Mexico, OPEC prices did not hold. By 1985, in the midst of renewed economic expansion, which should have provoked increasing prices and consumption, the price of OPEC oil had fallen to between $26 and $27. Adjusted for inflation, this was just about what the price had been in 1974, right after the first, justified rise in prices.

For OPEC, the 1979–1980 price rises resulted in a sharp drop in earnings. From a high of almost 32 million barrels of oil produced per day, by 1985, with the world having a surplus of petroleum, OPEC production was down to just above 17 million barrels per day, and even the richest OPEC members

were suffering fiscal problems. The highly populated, much poorer oil exporters, particularly Nigeria, were in serious trouble as a result of this shift.[36]

It is fortunate that the major capitalist powers, especially the United States,
felt powerless to use their military and political power to alter OPEC behavior. Rather, by letting core economies and the world petroleum market adjust
to events, what had briefly seemed like a major crisis (in 1980 there were
panicked articles about the "decline of the West") was resolved.[37]

A "Neocapitalist" Stage?

In the world economy of the late twentieth century, no major resource exporter can do without core markets. No major economy, not even the long-
isolated Chinese economy, can hope to progress quickly if it shuts itself off
from core technology, science, and finance. To let those revolutionaries who
want to close off their economies go ahead, and to rely on the power of the
market to convince most peripheral and semiperipheral governments that
some degree of integration with the world capitalist system is wise, would be
the most rational avenue. It would also correspond with the original spirit of
rational capitalism and avoid the problems caused by the mistaken belief that
imperial expansion and the carving of the world into colonial spheres is the
only solution to the core's economic problems.

Yet, it is not certain that this "neocapitalist" solution will be followed or
that a transition to this stage of core-periphery relations will go smoothly.
Another alternative, much more alarming, exists. Robert Gilpin has labeled it
"mercantilism" (though "neomercantilism," to distinguish it from the seventeenth and eighteenth-century version, would be better).[38]

Neomercantilism, advocated by some powerful manufacturing and labor
interests in the United States and other core societies, would erect a series of
trade barriers around each economy to protect it against foreign competition.
Though primarily a response to intracore competition, it would have severe
implications in the periphery, because it would mean that the various powerful
core societies would seek to carve out their own neocolonial zones of influence
to protect markets and sources of raw material. Neomercantilism would set off
a new race for empire in the periphery, much as a similar sentiment turned the
late nineteeth-century world toward an irrational competition for colonies.

The biggest participant, and in many ways the country that would have the
most to gain in the short term if it followed such a policy, would be the United
States. With its still enormous military and economic resources, it could follow
the example of the British in the late nineteenth century and wrap itself into
an empire to ward off increasing competition from more dynamic core competitors.

It is a fortunate irony that in the mid-1980s the Republicans who stand for
military aggression abroad also stand for free trade, while the Democrats, who
have strong protectionist tendencies, are more passive on foreign policy mat-

ters, and more willing to learn the lesson of Vietnam. What there is to fear is that both foreign military adventurism and economic protectionism will come together in the future and create a serious possibility of neomercantilism.

It is evident, then, that the entire future of core-periphery relations depends heavily on intracore relations, and on the future of economic competition between the world's most dynamic economies. If these can be handled fairly smoothly, then the Leninist theory will have been proved wrong. Core-periphery relations will move into a new "neocapitalist" stage. But the other possibility remains, that this will not happen, and that in the end, the Leninist theory of imperialism will be shown to have been correct, even if its execution depends on mistaken perceptions.

This does not answer the question of why poor economies have not been catching up to the core economies. If dependency is not the answer (and I have been suggesting it is not, without yet discussing the issue directly), what is? What has been answered is the question of what American and other core behavior toward the periphery and semiperiphery should be. There exists ample evidence to suggest that, left to their own devices, few nationalist revolutionaries will really persist in trying to close off their economies. By the mid-1980s, not only the countries of Eastern Europe and China, but the radical regimes of Angola and Mozambique, and even bitterly anti-Western Iran, were all trying to maximize their trade with the West. Only under the threat of direct American or other core intervention—that is, only in the situation of having to fight anticolonial wars—will many revolutionaries be willing to push their societies into extreme isolation. Why this is so, and what its consequences are, will be explored in a later chapter.

Right now, it is necessary to turn back to the third question asked above: What will happen to the relationship between the United States and the rest of the core as patterns of productivity and economic growth change?

The Fifth Industrial Revolution and American Hegemony

Each time technological and scientific changes bring about major shifts in production and a new industrial cycle begins, there are cries of despair from those who prefer the status quo, and cries of hope from the left. Each sees the old primary industries in trouble, and so foresees the end of capitalism and of the world order which it has built. And each time, there are losers, but also winners. The best-established workers in the dominant old industries, those who have had time to organize themselves and who have a sense of superior achievement as well as relatively high wages, suddenly become the most threatened as upstart industries with as yet unorganized, less-militant labor forces come to the fore. Not only workers, but the owners and managers of the old, established industries complain most loudly, and the regions in which they are located suffer most. New areas draw in the new industries because they have space and lack the restrictive practices of the better-established old industrial centers.

The first industrial revolution of the late eighteenth century was itself a similar process as old artisanal centers were bypassed and eventually ruined. The end of the first, textile, cycle created an atmosphere of crisis in England in the 1820s and 1830s and on the European continent into the 1840s. The end of the second, iron and railroad, cycle brought what then seemed like a "great depression" to the capitalist world in the 1870s and 1880s. The shift from the third cycle—in which organic chemistry and then electrical machinery were in the forefront of change, and where for the first time the essence of change came directly from scientific research—to the fourth industrial cycle of the automobile and mass-consumer production began in the 1920s and 1930s. Accompanied by the massive dislocation of the First World War, it produced the biggest "Great Depression" of all in the 1930s. The fourth industrial age only picked up again after the Second World War. Automobiles, combined with the development of the petrochemical industry, revolutionized life throughout the world, but particularly in the core economies, which experienced an extraordinary growth of prosperity from the early 1950s to the early 1970s.

Then, once again, the key source of energy fueling this particular cycle began to become more expensive. Along with rising oil prices there also came rapidly increasing competition from newer industrial centers able to adopt and improve on the now routinized technology and production methods that dominated the "fourth" industrial revolution. And again, scientific progress, ever more intimately connected to industrial production, began a new cycle in which the world now finds itself, the age of electronics, computers, and advanced biotechnology. Quite foreseeably, too, this has given rise to the same cries of ruin and complaints of social dislocation, justified from the point of view of those most deeply affected, but largely wrong from that of the capitalist world system as a whole.

It should be very clear by now that a shift in cycles does not mean that old industries are entirely eliminated. Textiles are still made today though largely with petrochemically produced synthetics, even in the most advanced economies. Steel adapted very nicely to the age of the automobile, and in fact prospered and grew, though it ceased to be a technologically leading sector. Similarly, in the next industrial age, automobiles will not disappear, nor will steel production or textile production. But automobiles will join older products in no longer being a sector of leading growth and dynamism, and those countries and regions which predominate in this sector will not necessarily be dominant industrial areas, at least not if they rely too heavily on that particular sector of industry. Employment in old sectors of industry will gradually decline, and the most exciting manufacturing developments will occur in the newer areas.[39]

At the same time as a shift to a new industrial cycle, the 1970s and 1980s have seen the continuation of a trend begun earlier, in the fourth industrial age. Demand for all sorts of services has grown. In the nineteenth century, there was a large service sector composed of servants to the upper and growing middle classes. With rising wages, and the immense growth of the middle class, this part of the service sector declined as fewer people became available for that kind of low-paid, low-status work. But starting in the 1950s and 1960s and growing quickly in the 1970s, a new type of relatively poorly paid service sector came to replace it. Composed disproportionately of women entering the labor force in industrial countries, this sector, ranging from health care workers to teachers to restaurant personnel to secretarial-clerical employees became the most rapidly growing labor sector in the economy. Governments and private businesses alike have vastly increased their demand for such services.

Knowing about these two concurrent phenomena, the growth of a large service sector and the decline of the traditionally central industries of the fourth industrial period, explains much about what has happened to the world capitalist economy and to the position of the United States in the 1970s and 1980s.

The service sector is labor intensive and cannot increase productivity as quickly as can manufacturing, which is able to become increasingly machine and capital intensive. In other words, while manufacturing can count on technology to improve its productivity, many service sectors are different. If secretarial and clerical workers can increase their productivity with computers and word processors, teachers, nurses, and waitresses cannot. The United States, as the world's leading economy, and the one in which women have entered the labor force in the greatest numbers since the 1960s, has therefore also had a low rate of increase in its productivity. It is likely that other industrial countries will eventually go through similar phases.[40]

But at the same time, the fact that the United States was the leader in the fourth industrial age has meant that its old industries were particularly prosperous, powerful, and well organized. This has enabled both labor, organized into strong unions, and management, highly committed to older styles of running their enterprises, to hold out against change. New industries, or those in countries such as Japan and Germany where industry and society had been much more disrupted by World War II and the ensuing poverty, have not had to suffer from such innate conservatism. Resistance to change in the old industries, of course, merely repeats old, past patterns of trying to stop one industrial cycle from being replaced by the next. Locally, or even within entire societies, this may work, but all this does is allow new industrial centers to emerge. This explains why the English-speaking, very rich countries of the world—relatively shielded from the damages of war in this century, accustomed to being the strongest and richest countries, and having the most traditional styles of business management combined with very strong unions in their old industries—have been that part of the industrial world with the slowest rate of economic growth since the 1950s.[41]

It was not possible for England to shield itself from changes in industrial productivity in other countries in the late nineteenth century, or for any country to escape the trauma of the 1930s. Today, far more than ever before, the capitalist world is interdependent. Financial and trade flows, facilitated by the progress in communications, are far beyond the power of any single government to control. If shielding an economy from the consequences of industrial cycles was difficult 100 years ago, today it is totally impossible without trying to break the interconnections that hold the world capitalist system together. A powerful economy like that of the United States has lost the power to protect itself from the consequences of change, even in the short run, unless it is willing to use its immense political power to totally alter the rules of the game, and end the world capitalist system.

Therefore, the changes in patterns of productivity and the emergence of a "fifth" industrial revolution have important international implications, and understanding the interaction between economic change and global political relations can help us obtain a glimpse of the several alternative roads that lie ahead. Again, this is nothing new. One of the key characteristics of the world capitalist system, since its earliest days, has been the connection between internal and external events, and the importance of economic rivalry between the main actors in the capitalist world. But now, as never before, this connection needs to be emphasized because there are still too many people who refuse to accept its implications. At each major change in the past there have been powerful forces which have tried to resist change and protect their own societies and economies from its consequences. Only by misunderstanding the underlying causes of economic progress have such forces justified their policies. The results have included the mad imperialist scramble of the late nineteenth century, and thus World War I, and the intensification of the Great Depression of the 1930s, and thus the rise of fascism and World War II. A new misunderstanding could be even more catastrophic.

The fact that a transformation was under way in the 1970s and 1980s can be charted with a few statistics about changes in the economy of the United States. Between 1950 and 1980 the proportionate contribution of agriculture to the gross national product of the United States declined by 60 percent, that

TABLE 8-9
Percent of the Labor Force Producing Goods or Services (United States)[42]

	Goods	Services (Including Government)
1950	41	59
1960	38	62
1970	33	67
1980	28	72

of manufacturing of goods by 19 percent, and the proportion contributed by the service sector grew by 18 percent.[43]

Changes in labor force composition have been even more dramatic. Leaving aside agriculture, which now occupies less than 2½ percent of the labor force, the division between goods producers and service producers since 1950 has been as shown in Table 8-9.

The industries that were the backbone of America's past industrial strength have declined. This can be seen with steel and particularly automobile production, which have not only shifted to lower production levels but have been increasingly unable to meet foreign competition from lower-priced, more efficiently produced products (see Table 8-10).

Even within the United States major regional shifts are occurring. In 1963, 32.4 percent of all manufacturing employment was in the northeast. By 1981, only 25.3 percent of a generally smaller manufacturing labor force was in the northeast. In 1963, 32.4 percent of all manufacturing employment was in the north central part of the United States (the Middle West). By 1981, that had fallen to 29.3 percent. On the other hand, the South increased its share from

TABLE 8-10

Average Yearly Production of Automobiles (in millions) and of Steel (in millions of tons), and the Growing Role of Imports, as a Percent of Total Sales in the United States[44]

	Automobile Production	Percent of Sales from Imports	Steel Production	Percent of Sales from Imports
1930–1934	1.9		28.6	
1935–1939	3.2		46.6	
1940–1944*	3.7		82.8	
1945–1949†	3.7		79.6	
1950–1954	5.6		99.0	
1955–1959	5.9		104.7	1960 = 4.7
1960–1964	6.9	1965 = 6.1	106.4	1965 = 10.3
1965–1969	8.5	1970 = 15.3	133.0	1970 = 13.8
1970–1974	8.2	1975 = 18.6	136.3	1975 = 13.5
1975–1979	8.4	1980 = 22.1	128.6	1980 = 16.3
1980–1984‡	6.5	1982 = 27.8	102.4	1982 = 21.8

* Automobile production virtually ceased during the war years 1942–1945. This yearly average is only for 1940–1941 for automobiles, but 1940–1944 for steel.
† This yearly average is only for 1946–1949 for automobiles, but 1945–1949 for steel.
‡ This yearly average is for 1980–1984 for automobiles, but only for 1980–1982 for steel.

22.9 percent to 29.8 percent, and the West from 12.3 percent to 15.6 percent during the same eighteen-year period.[45]

In the 1960s, the United States was the unrivaled top producer of automobiles and steel in the world. In the 1980s, Japan produces as much steel and as many automobiles as the United States, and it is quite likely that by the 1990s it will produce more. (The Soviet Union now produces about 50 percent more steel than the United States, but that is a symptom of its industrial backwardness, not of strength. More will be said about this in the chapter on communist societies.)[46]

Does this mean that the United States is finished as the major industrial power of the world? Not at all.

In many high-technology sectors, the United States has preserved its dominance: office machines and computers; artificial resins and plastic materials; scientific and controlling instruments; jet airplanes, both civilian and military; and medicinal and pharmaceutical products. Japan continues to lag conspicuously behind the United States in these areas. In total high-technology exports, the United States still leads, followed closely by West Germany, but far ahead of Japan. The United States also continues to lead in providing increasingly important world financial and insurance services, which are ever more dependent on the revolution in communications that originated within the United States itself.[47]

The United States still enjoys unmatched strength in the application of high technology to primary production. Its agricultural sector, though small in terms of its labor force, remains its largest single source of exports, and is certainly the most productive in the world because of the application of ever more sophisticated technological inputs. It is now on its way to being computerized. It is quite likely that by the end of the century the United States will be well along the shift in agriculture from overreliance on chemical fertilizers and pesticides to greater control of production and pest control through genetic manipulations. The combination of agriculture and biotechnology, in which the United States also leads the world, is almost certain to expand America's advantage in this sector.[48]

There are, however, a number of reasons for Americans to worry. One is the seeming decline in the proportion of the GNP devoted to research and development and to the production of holders of advanced degrees in some of the most important scientific fields. In the 1960s, the Soviet Union and the United States had higher proportions of their GNPs devoted to research than any other countries, and of course, with its much larger GNP, the United States committed far more to research than did the Soviet Union. Though the United States still leads the world in research spending, the proportion of its GNP devoted to this task has fallen, while Japan has almost caught up, West Germany is ahead, and the Soviet Union is far ahead. In 1982 the United States granted fewer Ph.D. degrees in the sciences than it did in 1970. The decline was particularly evident in the physical sciences, in engineering, and in mathematics. (The only scientific field to have kept pace with general population growth in granting Ph.D. degrees has been psychology.) From 1966 to 1982, the number of American college students majoring in mathematics decreased, and the number in physical sciences increased so slightly that as a proportion of all students the rate fell from 3.8 percent to 2.4 percent. In other words, the rest of the industrial world, but particularly Japan and West Germany, as well as the Soviet Union, are making strong efforts to catch up to the United States in those critical areas that determine future economic success; and the United States is lagging in its growth in precisely those areas. That, much more than the decline of the steel or automobile industries, is something to worry about, because continued dominance in high-technology fields in the twenty-first century will depend on research and the production of scientists in the 1980s and 1990s.[49]

The second reason for Americans to worry about international economic trends is that these may produce an extremely harmful political reaction. Because not many understand, even today, what the real basis of economic growth is, namely strength in higher education and scientific research, not in the defense of old industries, there is a possibility that the United States will retreat into a kind of neomercantilistic shell. But protection of increasingly obsolescent industries would eventually have to be accompanied by a general scramble among industrialized countries to carve out protected markets. World trade would decline, but the pressure to redivide the old periphery into favored economic zones would be strong. With less dynamism in the world economy, poor economies would have even less chance to grow, and revolutionary pressures for withdrawal from the world system would increase. So, what might begin as protectionism and neomercantilism at home would, in the long run, certainly lead to a series of new colonial wars and intense rivalries among industrial nations. With the Soviet Union acting as the protector of peripheral and semiperipheral revolutionary movements, the stage would be set for a series of major international crises.

Which direction the world's leading economic power, the United States, will take, cannot be predicted. Neither alternative is inevitable.

In the early and mid-1980s, the government of the United States, though ostensibly committed to free trade and an open world economy, has taken a number of alarming steps which suggest that it may actually be pushing in the opposite direction. The United States has run up large budget deficits to finance a major rearmament program. This program cannot possibly yield decisive military superiority over the Soviet Union in nuclear weaponry, because even an inferior nuclear force retains the ability to destroy any enemy and the world with it. But this military construction program seems designed to force the Soviets into expending greater resources on their own armaments, and thus weaken their ability and resolve to support revolutionary movements in the periphery. This might then be translated into an American push to contain anti-capitalist revolutionary movements.

But to pay for its deficits, the United States has simply used its enormous economic power to borrow money abroad by keeping interest rates high. As foreign funds have poured into the United States, the demand for the American dollar has increased, thus greatly raising its value. While this has made it ever easier for Americans to buy foreign goods, it has damaged American export industries and raised the pressures for domestic protective tariffs.[50]

High interest rates, furthermore, have produced what is called the "Third World debt problem." That is not a problem of excessively large absolute debts (mostly the obligations of several large Latin American economies), but of high interest rates which have made it difficult to service these debts. So, to meet onerous interest payments, several important peripheral and semi-peripheral economies have had to depress their standards of living, and this has increased resentment against the United States.[51]

In short, in the 1980s the United States has set out on a policy track that leads to eventual neomercantilist pressures at home, to growing dissatisfaction with the open capitalist economy in the periphery and semiperiphery, and to increasing militarization of the American economy. Combined with a tendency to neglect education, and to forget that the success of modern economies is based on the maintenance of free markets on a global, not a narrow domestic scale, this augurs very poorly for the future. But again, there is nothing inevitable about such a policy, and for at least the next decade, it is quite reversible.

In any case, the era of American hegemony in the capitalist world system is far from over. For better or for worse, there is no country in the system that will have the power to determine its course as much as the United States at any time in the remainder of the twentieth century or well into the twenty-first.

CHAPTER 9

Social Structures in the Late Twentieth Century

*T*hrough all the changes that have occurred in the twentieth century, it remains as true at its end as at its beginning that there is a high correlation between internal patterns of social stratification and the position of a society in the world system. It also remains an important fact that there is a core which dominates the system, a periphery which consists of weak and dependent societies, and a semiperiphery of countries weaker and poorer than the core, but relatively independent and making major strides toward developing their economies. The biggest difference is that now there are also communist societies that might be considered to exist outside the capitalist system.

The capitalist core, led by the United States, also includes Western Europe, Japan, Canada, Australia, and New Zealand. Together, in the mid-1980s, these countries have just under 16 percent of the world's population, but produce between 55 and 60 percent of the gross world product and consume some 54 percent of all the world's energy. They thoroughly dominate the forefront of scientific and technological developments. Their political control over the world may be less than it was, but except for a rather limited challenge to their economic and scientific supremacy from the Soviet Union, they are as far ahead of the rest of the world in those two domains as ever.

The European communist countries—that is, the Soviet Union and its Eastern European allies, dependencies, and imitators—are also highly industrialized, though they remain poorer than the core. They contain some 9 percent of the world's population, produce between 22 and 25 percent of the gross world product, and consume about 25 percent of its energy.

The rest of the world, the periphery and semiperiphery of the world capitalist system, contains about 75 percent of the global population, although it produces no more than 20 percent of the entire gross world product and consumes about the same proportion of all the world's energy. But this is a category that is much more diversified than either the core or the European communist world.[1] It includes a number of small oil-exporting countries that control significant financial resources despite their lack of either military or other economic power. Saudi Arabia is the most important of these. This category also includes some countries that remain poor but that have such strong state structures and large populations that they are major political actors on the world scene. Far from being the colonial or semicolonial peripheries that they were in the past, these countries wield considerable regional if not global power. China and India are the most important; but Indonesia,

Pakistan, and Brazil are in this group, and in some ways, though it is much weaker, so is Nigeria. There are lesser, but still independent and strong medium-sized states, such as Turkey, Iran, Algeria, Mexico, Argentina, Egypt, and a number of others. There are some countries in the old periphery, such as Taiwan, South Korea, Singapore, Hong Kong, and Brazil, that have experienced spectacular industrialization in recent decades, and whose economic power has become an important factor in world affairs. There are garrison states whose internal cohesion, great military power, and fierce independence place them well outside the classical "periphery." North Korea, Vietnam, Iraq, Cuba, South Africa, Israel, and Syria are in this group, though most of them have little else in common with one another. Some are communist, some are capitalist, but none of them operates within the world system in a conventionally subordinate role, though none are economically or politically part of the core except, perhaps, Israel. Finally, there are some truly peripheral societies in the old sense of that word. Most of the sub-Saharan African countries, the smaller countries of Central and South America and the Caribbean (except, in 1985, Nicaragua), and some of the South and Southeast Asian countries, as well as the tiny island states of the Indian and Pacific oceans remain poor, weak, and dependent on a few primary exports. Some, like Afghanistan, Tahiti, Laos, or Lesotho, are virtually old-fashioned colonies of another power. Others have less fictional, but nevertheless fragile independence. But taken all together, such pure, old-fashioned peripheral parts of the world now make up a small and diminishing proportion of those countries broadly lumped into the "Third World."

In discussing the social structure of these types of societies, some important examples will be examined, but it will not be possible to explore the full diversity which exists, particularly within the peripheral and semiperipheral categories. (Communist societies will be discussed in the next chapter in much greater detail.)

Class and Politics in the Core

Theorists who view the capitalist world system as strictly stratified see a core (upper class) dominating and exploiting a periphery (lower class). Immanuel Wallerstein goes so far as to explain the role of the semiperiphery by claiming it is a kind of middle class acting as a buffer between the ruling minority, the core, and the exploited majority in the periphery. It does some of the regional policing of the system for the core, provides a safe home for investments in sectors for which labor has become too expensive in the core, and it deflects the revolutionary anger of the periphery by making it seem that economic development really is possible.[2] Those who agree with this view explain internal stratification along analogous lines. In any society, or at least any capitalist society, there is a small upper class which derives most of the advantages of the system, an exploited, fragmented lower class, and a middle class to act as a buffer. Internal class structure and the global division of power are tied together by the fact that the upper classes of the core, acting through their allies and servants outside the core, rule the entire system. Thus, it is not just the United States, but a small elite of Americans who dominate the system. The fact that they have to maintain relatively high wages to satisfy their middle and lower classes only reflects the greater degree of education and awareness in the core. To do otherwise would court disaster. But, by analogy, the growing awareness of the situation in the old periphery risks the same end, revolution against the entire system.

Just as there is serious doubt that the capitalist world system really does rest on the exploitation of an impoverished periphery, or that political independence in the periphery necessarily brings economic development and greater prosperity, so is there a debate about how correct the strict class model of capitalist society really is. Those who believe that capitalist, and particularly American society works this way are called "power elite theorists," and their view fits very nicely with the Leninist interpretations of the world system as a whole.[3] Are they right?

Though it is impossible to give a definitive answer, a good start can be made by looking at income distribution and its patterns of change over the last half-century or so. (We will look primarily at the United States.) In the United States, the period of the New Deal saw a clear trend toward some redistribution of income toward greater equality. The trend slowed, but continued in the 1950s and 1960s. But since about 1970, the trend has slowly been reversed, though it has not come close to returning to the level of inequality which existed in 1929 (see Table 9-1).

Income distribution is not the same thing as distribution of economic power, which is better reflected by ownership of key resources and investments; but income distribution does reflect some important facts about how power is exercised in a society. It is obvious that between 1929 and 1950 the dominant economic elite lost a considerable share of its income, which it was forced to yield to the lower and middle classes. In the prosperous times of the 1950s and 1960s, though all sections of the population grew wealthier, the poor and middle classes continued to get increasing shares of the national income. In the 1970s and 1980s, that trend has been reversed. The top 40 percent of society have increased their share of national income from 64.7 percent of the total to 67 percent, and the bottom 60 percent have had their share reduced from 35.2 percent to 33 percent. These differences are fairly small, but by showing the reversal of what had been a forty-year-old trend, they suggest that decisive economic power has definitely not shifted out of the hands of the top categories of the population, but rather has been somewhat more broadly distributed to the upper middle class. The reduced commitment to equality shows, if anything, a renewed confidence on the part of the economic elite that they will no longer be forced to erode their share of national income in order to maintain their dominant position.

TABLE 9–1
Percentage of National Income Received by Families, 1929–1982 (United States)[4]

	1929	1950	Percent Change 1929–1950	1970	Percent Change 1950–1970	1982	Percent Change 1970–1982
Lowest fifth	3.5	4.5	+29	5.4	+20	4.7	−13
Second fifth	9.0	11.9	+32	12.2	+ 3	11.2	− 8
Third fifth	13.8	17.4	+26	17.6	+ 1	17.1	− 3
Fourth fifth	19.3	23.6	+22	23.8	+ 1	24.3	+ 2
Top fifth	54.4	42.7	−22	40.9	− 4	42.7	+ 4
Top 5 percent	30.0	17.3	−44	15.6	−10	16.0	+ 3

This trend is confirmed by recent shifts in the number of people officially defined as poor by the American government. From 1959 to 1973, the proportion of such people fell by half, from 22.4 percent to 11.1 percent. It remained roughly level for the rest of the 1970s, reaching 11.7 percent in 1979. From 1979 to 1983, it rose precipitously to 15.2 percent, a relative increase of 30 percent in just four years.[5] Observers tend to believe that this trend is continuing in the mid-1980s, and that both legal and ideological shifts in the United States now point toward increasing inequality, away from the redistributive mentality of the New Deal and the reform mentality that prevailed through the 1960s.

The United States is not unique. Though the poorest fifth of its population receives a lower share of total national income than in any other industrialized, rich capitalist economy except Canada, its distribution statistics at other levels are quite comparable to those in Western Europe and Japan. But there is certainly a drift away from extending welfare benefits and greater redistribution of income throughout the entire capitalist core in the 1980s. Whether governments call themselves conservative, as in the United Kingdom, or "socialist" (that is, social democratic) as in France, similar policies are now being pursued. Though they will not remove the basic reforms of the New Deal and post-World War II eras, they will reverse egalitarian trends and keep the majority of wealth and economic power firmly in the hands of the upper-middle and upper classes. Evidence from Great Britain, for example, shows increasing inequality of income in the late 1970s and early 1980s.[6]

Economic power is much more concentrated than income. In the 1960s and early 1970s, one-half of 1 percent of all persons in the United States owned between 50 and 55 percent of all corporate stock, and somewhere between one-third and one-half of all bonds. (Figures for 1976, the latest currently available, suggest that in the mid-1970s stock and bond ownership became less concentrated, but even then, about 40 percent of all stock was held by one-half of 1 percent of all persons. Whether this trend toward slightly greater equality holds, or is being reversed in the 1980s, remains to be seen.) As with income distribution, comparative figures from the 1920s until the 1970s indicate that the economic elite lost some of its control over total wealth in the United States during the 1930s and 1940s, but that since about 1950 there has been no important change.[7]

Looking at ownership of capital gets closer to the heart of economic power, but it is not yet as good a measure of who controls the economy as seeing who sits on the various corporate boards and in important managerial positions in America.

There is little question that a relatively small number of large corporations have a predominant role in that economy. In 1929, the largest 100 corporations in manufacturing in America owned 40 percent of all American manufacturing assets. In 1970, the largest 102 corporations in manufacturing owned 49 percent of all such assets. In 1980, the top one-tenth of 1 percent of all corporations, some 2,900 firms, owned 70 percent of all assets of American corporations. Ownership was particularly concentrated in finance, where 0.3 percent of all corporations owned 77 percent of all assets; in transportation and utilities, where 0.2 percent of all corporations owned 89 percent of all assets; and in mining, where 0.2 percent of all corporations owned 64 percent of all assets.[8]

The power elite theorists, then, are not wrong when they claim that economic power in the United States is highly concentrated. The top managers, lawyers, and financiers who run the large corporations form a small elite of people who are either directly members of the upper class, or its highly rewarded servants. What G. William Domhoff said in 1967 remains as true today as ever:

> Our findings on all corporate boards can be summarized as follows: Interlocking directorates show beyond question that there is a national corporate economy that is run by the same group of several thousand men.[9]

Not only is corporate ownership narrow, but those who run these giant firms tend to belong to several boards, and the overlap means that power is even more concentrated than ownership. As a matter of fact, all of this information underemphasizes concentration, because even among the top firms there is great concentration. Among the top 500 corporations, for example, the top 100 in 1982 had 69 percent of all sales, 67 percent of all assets, 70 percent of all after-tax profits, and they employed 58 percent of all employees.[10]

If there is no question that economic power is concentrated, as it is in the world system as a whole, does this mean that political power is equally concentrated, and that in some sense this kind of economic concentration is nefarious? World system theorists like Immanuel Wallerstein and Andre Gunder Frank, or power elite theorists like C. Wright Mills or G. William Domhoff believe that the unequivocal answer is, yes.

But within a rich capitalist society like the United States the answer has to be much more cautious. The middle class has grown to include almost 30 percent of the working population (see Table 9-2). If the lower middle class shades into the working class (in fact, in many families, some individuals work as blue-collar employees and others as clerical or other lower-middle-class ones) and can hardly be called "middle class" in any real sense, this is not true of the professional and technical, managerial, and administrative workers who make up the real middle class. Highly educated and prosperous, politically active, and well aware of their interests, they are the dominant sector of the electorate, not only in the United States, but in other core capitalist democracies as well. The consumer movement of the 1960s and 1970s, the antiwelfare, antitax movement of the late 1970s and the 1980s, and conservationism have come from this group. It has been this group's turn away from New Deal liberalism to fiscal conservatism that has pushed governments throughout the core toward the right. The group may not hold economic power, but it is capable of vetoing political behavior it dislikes, and of preventing the holders

TABLE 9–2
**Changes in Class Distribution in the United States,
1910–1980**[11]

	1910	1950	1982	Percent Change 1910–1982
Middle class	11	17	29	+164
Lower middle class	10	19	25	+150
Working class	48	52	44	− 8
Agriculturalists	31	11	3	−90

of great economic power from monopolizing too great a share of income. It is a particularly important group in restraining the United States from renewed colonial wars, if only because this would cut into its available income and threaten its sons with a new military draft. If its economic interests and material comforts are put in doubt, it can be a dangerous class because it is so large and well organized.

All through the middle years of the twentieth century it seemed as if the working class, increasingly unionized, would also become an equal partner in governing the democratic capitalist societies. There was even talk of a new form of "corporatism," an alliance between government bureaucracies, unions, and economic managers to run affairs. As Charles Maier has pointed out, however, this sort of alliance reached its high point where social democrats were most powerful, and had little to do with the fascist type of corporatism of the prewar years.[12] But in the 1970s and particularly the 1980s, throughout most of the core unions have declined. In the United States the proportion of unionized workers fell from 33 percent of the nonagricultural employed labor force in 1955 to below 24 percent in the late 1970s. In France and Italy, as well as elsewhere in Europe where they had been strong, communist political parties and unions have lost membership and influence. In Great Britain a conservative government and electorate have drastically weakened the leftist labor union movement. Connected as this is with the switch away from old industries, this suggests that in the future it will not be the organized working class, but the still rising, technocratic and professional middle class that will be the main counterweight to the small elites who still dominate economic life in the capitalist world.[13]

There is every indication that within capitalist societies something analogous to developments in the world system as a whole is going on. The old economic elites have maintained their elite position. But this position rests less and less on the exploitation of a poor working class. Instead, the truly poor, like the bulk of the periphery, are becoming ever more redundant, and even the larger working class is becoming less important. But politically, both within rich capitalist countries and within the world system as a whole, it is necessary to share political power with a significant and still growing middle class.

The analogy should not be stretched too far. But the parallels are suggestive, and demonstrate that in an ever more sophisticated technological environment the basic Marxist-Leninist assumptions about the importance and eventual rise to power of the exploited masses, both in the periphery and within capitalist countries, will turn out to be wrong. At the same time, it remains perfectly true that in the world system and within individual capitalist societies a rather small minority benefits disproportionately. It can hardly get its way all the time, and has limits placed on its power, but there is no indication that it will vanish or be superceded by the broad middle class that can check its power, share some benefits, but not become a new ruling class.

The analogy between the world system as a whole and the internal working of individual capitalist societies breaks down, however, if class structure is analyzed more deeply. There is another powerful class that is neither the automatic servant of the dominant capitalist elite nor purely the representative of an electorate dominated by the middle class, though it has been accused of being the former, and likes to pretend that it is the latter. That is the government and the large bureaucracy that has grown within it. Governments have been central to social structures since the development of the earliest states. Kings, emperors, princes, and their retainers—or later, their bureaucracies— were always a distinct interest group, fighting with local notables, with controllers of the land, with villagers, with towns, and with religious authorities to assert their power and maximize the collection of revenues. Just as the study of how the multisided class struggle in Europe in the Middle Ages and the early modern period is necessary in order to understand the uniquely progressive outcome that occurred, so it is important to understand the role of governments in modern societies. The state remains a powerful engine for collecting economic surpluses and directing them to favored classes, or using them for foreign affairs. This in turn has a primary role in economic development and social change. The increasing democratization of governments in the capitalist core has meant that they have become more responsive to the wishes of the middle classes, and even to the working classes, but it has hardly ended the semi-independent role governments can play, or the fact that government bureaucracies are, after all is said and done, primarily interested in preserving their own position and privileges above all else.

In 1913 in the United States, local, state, and federal governments spent about 8.1 percent of the total gross national product. During World War I, this proportion went up sharply, but fell back after the war. During the Great Depression, however, the proportion rose to 20.5 percent in 1940. Another sharp rise during World War II was temporary, but during the 1950s and 1960s, partly in response to the creation of a large, permanent military, and partly in order to provide the ever-increasing number of social services demanded by the electorate, the proportion went back up. By 1975 some 34.5

percent of GNP was being spent by governments, and 19 percent of the total nonagricultural civilian labor force worked for government. By 1982, despite strong campaigns against "big government" waged by many federal, state, and local political administrations, the percentage of GNP spent by all levels of government was 35 percent, but the percentage of the labor force employed by various governments had fallen back to 17.6 percent of the total.[14]

Among core capitalist countries, the United States devotes an exceptionally low proportion of its GNP to government spending. In most European countries, well over 50 percent goes to the government (including government-owned businesses).

Such statistics have little meaning alone. What matters is not that a rather large portion of the population works directly for the government, but that governments dispose of enormous power. If presidents and prime ministers in capitalist democracies are genuinely elected, bureaucracies are never run on democratic principles. (Of course, neither are large corporations, which are as highly bureaucratized as any government department.) Top officials of bureaucracies are appointed. If they succeed in mastering the intricacies of how their organizations work, and if they do not directly threaten the interests of the permanent members of their bureaucracy, they can wield power for good or evil in ways electorates are unable to control. Fighting for tax revenues and for power within bureaucratic structures, then, becomes more of a determinant of policy than anything else.

In a sense, the class structure and division of power within modern capitalist societies reproduce something of the structure of the *Ständestaat*. The top economic elites, at most one-half of 1 percent of the population, and probably considerably less than that, are a kind of upper class akin to the old landed nobilities. With their wealth largely secured through inheritance,[15] they are primarily concerned with preserving their status and privileges against the demands of the majority. But against them they have that portion of the working class which is organized and demands greater benefits, and a growing middle class which must be placated and rewarded in order to stabilize the system. Above this struggle is the government, somewhat independent of all these forces, but fought over by all of them, and in a position to swing key disputes in favor of one side or the other. Now, it is no longer the towns and a small middle class that are the key balancing group in a struggle between kings, nobles, and the church, but the state itself which holds the balance of power.

One element, however, has not changed. Just as in the past it was the towns and the middle class that were the root of rational, progressive economic dynamism, so does it remain the technocratic, highly educated, professional and intellectual segments of the middle class that perform this role today. Neither the inheritors of large fortunes nor the top lawyers, accountants, and business bureaucrats who run most big corporations can be counted on to provide the new ideas and products on which continued economic growth relies. Nor, for that matter, are large, inherently conservative government bureaucracies suited to this task. It is, rather, lower-ranking personnel in private business, or in research institutes and universities, who are the source of modern rationality. Insofar as they are given the freedom to be independent, and the material rewards necessary to keep them at their work, society as a whole benefits. But if they are crushed by overly powerful bureaucracies, either governmental or business, if they no longer have the facilities necessary to think, carry out research, and innovate, then society will stagnate.

In a sense, then, the danger to the future remains what it has always been. The survival of an innovative, rational class depends on a continued balance of class forces that prevents either the powerful economic elites or the huge state bureaucracies from gaining absolute power. If the balance fails, continued progress is put at risk.

An interesting example of the dangers of excessive state power and of the irrationality of bureaucratic inertia is the story of America's involvement in the Vietnam War.

During World War II, a large armed force was drafted into service in the United States. Most of that army was quickly disbanded after the end of the war, and by 1947 the American military had shrunk to about one and one-half million men, where it remained until the start of the Korean War in 1950. From that time until the end of the Vietnam War, American military personnel included between 2.5 and 3.6 million. (Since the Vietnam War, the armed forces of the United States have shrunk to 2.1 million.) Civilian employees of military agencies during all these years have numbered about 1 million. As the military and related institutions have become a major part of the government and of the society as a whole, the high-level civilian employees of the defense establishment, plus the career officers in the military, have turned into an immense bureaucratic interest group, regardless of how well or how poorly they have accomplished their primary goal. Furthermore, that bureaucracy controls enormous amounts of money—through most of the 1950s and 1960s, over half of the federal budget. (Recently, military expenditures have been 30 percent of federal expenditures.) This money was used not only to pay soldiers and employees of the military but also to purchase vast amounts of equipment, to fund research, and to procure some of the most expensive and complicated machines produced by the economy. The private companies and the research institutes, both privately and publicly owned, that participate in these expenditures have become, in effect, adjuncts to the military bureaucracy, or at least interested parties in promoting the bureaucratic health of the military.[16]

The claim has been made that the corporate interests that have made large profits from military contracts are strong supporters of an active American role in the world system that ensures continuing high military spending. It has also been pointed out that the personal and financial ties between many high military officers, civilian employees of the military, and the main military contractors are close enough to suggest that there exists a "military-industrial complex" inexorably pushing for continuous foreign involvement in order to boost military spending. Some go so far as to claim that this complex is the main source of international tensions and war, and that it has become the dominant elite of the entire capitalist world system. The extreme Leninist variant of the position claims, of course, that without all this military spending the United States and subsequently the entire world capitalist economy would go bankrupt and break down through revolution.

It is quite true that the large defense contractors include many of the largest American corporations and that some large companies rely almost exclusively on military work for their business. There is no doubt that this combination of entrenched bureaucratic and corporate interest is one of the main forces active in making foreign policy.

So powerful is this combination of interests that disputes within the various branches of the military-industrial complex (air force versus navy versus army, as well as the competition between various corporate contractors) have an effect on certain policies. The sociologist and China specialist Franz Schurman (*The Logic of World Power*) has persuasively argued that internal conflicts within the armed forces, and between the State Department, the presidency, and the armed forces played a predominant role in getting the United States involved in Vietnam in the 1950s and early 1960s. His argument is complex, and to summarize it does it an injustice. But the heart of the argument proposes that the basic reason for the first massive American intervention in Vietnam, planned in 1964 and executed in 1965, was the effect of bureaucratic pressures within the American government. Fights were going on between the civilian wing of the Pentagon, the branches of the armed forces, the CIA, and the State Department, and all sides were appealing to their supporters in the population at large in an effort to extend their influence. When a crisis arose over the imminent collapse of South Vietnam, a series of bureaucratic compromises were worked out that gave each of the participants a partial victory. The escalation was not something done by an "imperial presidency" but the result of confusion and presidential weakness on the part of Lyndon Johnson after John Kennedy's murder in 1963.

The compromises produced a massive but poorly planned, poorly coordinated effort designed to minimize the government's internal rivalries. When the war began to be costly, public opinion, which is never properly informed about foreign events until a major crisis occurs, turned against the war, and the United States was forced out of Vietnam because it could not win there quickly and cheaply.[17]

The corporate interests allied with the military, the nation's ideologically committed anticommunists (a fairly small if vocal and influential group), and widespread acceptance of a Leninist view of the world in the bureaucratic and corporate elite all played major roles in getting the United States involved in Vietnam in the first place. (It is not that this elite likes socialism, but that it agrees that American interests demand maintenance of American power throughout the periphery.) But the decisive input, the actual planning, and the subsequent course of events were determined by the existence of a large, permanent, internally bickering military bureaucracy, and by the President's failure to control his bureaucracy. The war was therefore pursued far beyond the point of strict rationality. Profit motives, the potential for direct economic gain, were secondary from the start of this adventure and became irrelevant by 1965. Fundamentally, the top decision makers were obliged to rely on the information given them by their various bureaucratic services, which invariably falsified their information in ways consistent with their bureaucratic interests. The President and his top aids received biased information and became the arbitrators between the various bureaucratic interests within the nation's military and foreign policy establishments rather than independent decision makers acting on the basis of accurate information or perception of the situation.

To be sure, pure bureaucratic infighting can never explain everything. The question remains: Why were such high and powerful military bureaucracies created in the first place? What economic interests were served by their creation? What purposes were they supposed to fulfill—that is, before bureaucratic imperatives took over and displaced the original goals of the institution? These questions cannot be answered fully, but preceding paragraphs have already suggested a major part of the reply: namely, that after 1945 American policy makers, corporate interests, and much of the general population accepted a basically Leninist view of the world system, and therefore feared any communist victories in the periphery; such victories would remove parts of the system from capitalist influence and put them to work helping the Soviet Union and China. This fear led to the creation of a large, permanent military bureaucracy. But after the main question, why, is answered, the fact remains that once a large bureaucracy is established, it acts in part to advance its own interests, regardless of the original goals for which it was created. Much of what happened in Vietnam and much of what has happened in all American foreign policy in recent decades can be explained by this peculiar but universal tendency of bureaucratic organizations toward self-promotion.

In the end it was only the massive protests of the most enlightened parts of the middle class, and of their children, that put an end to this unnecessary and wasteful war. Had the bureaucracy, particularly the military, been stronger, the war might have gone on much longer. As it was, the accumulated weight of nationalism and bureaucratic inertia on the part of the Americans made it last a good seven years after it had become obvious that the only way to defeat the Vietnamese was to obliterate them entirely, a task that could only have been accomplished through the use of atomic weapons. As this risked the escalation of the war into a general world war, and probably the complete alienation of America's allies in Europe, such a step was never seriously considered.

But it is not only military bureaucracies that behave in nonrational ways. Large civilian programs, too, acquire an inertia and conservatism which distorts the original goals toward more self-serving, narrowly bureaucratic ones.

In all modern societies this is a major problem, and one which can only be controlled by maintaining powerful political forces outside the government which can act as a check.

Japan: The Corporatist Model of the Future?

The European core societies are quite similar to the United States in many respects. In most of them the working class is better organized and plays a more important political role through social democratic parties, or in the case of Italy, the Communist Party. Social spending is higher than in the United States, and societies tend to be somewhat more egalitarian, particularly in northern Europe. Military spending is lower. In large measure these differences are due to the primary political and military role played by the United States in the world system, a role which requires a different appropriation of funds and energies.

A good case can be made, however, that Japan is rather differently organized, and that the Japanese pattern is not simply a minor variation of the general core capitalist pattern. And despite its historical and cultural uniqueness, it is at least possible that Japan is more a harbinger of the future than is the United States or Western Europe.

Murakami Yasusuke has argued that the high degree of group spirit and cohesion found in Japanese bureaucracies and businesses is a legacy of centuries of *ie* organization (loosely translated as household, but in fact, implying a combination of joint contractual and kinship solidarities). Thus, in a Japanese organization, loyalty to the institution, or vertical solidarity, is much more important than divisions between the top, middle, and bottom of the hierarchy. In most large Western firms and organizations, a wide gulf separates these various strata, which more or less correspond to class divisions within the society. Western societies, then, remain largely horizontally rather than vertically divided. This makes it much harder to coordinate efforts within an organization and tends to emphasize conflict rather than consensus. Of course, this conflictual, class-based tradition in the West was the origin of the entire Western political and social pattern which eventually produced parliamentary democracies and fostered capitalist rationality. In the United States, furthermore, such conflict is not only a tradition, but remains the basis of the legal system as well as the political and economic one. Murakami, then, is quite right to point to a fundamental difference between Japanese and Western civilizations. It is hardly a simple matter of somewhat distinct organizational forms, and it would be foolhardy to suppose that Western societies, especially the United States, might be able to make a few changes in order to emulate the extraordinary success of the Japanese economy in the second half of the twentieth century.[18]

And yet, as Japanese economic growth continues at a more rapid pace than economic growth in any other country of the world, it seems evident that by the end of the century Japan will have the highest per capita GNP of any industrial country. The United States will continue to have a larger GNP because its population is more than twice that of Japan, but Japan's total GNP will be the second highest in the world, ahead of even the Soviet Union, despite the latter's much larger population. Were it not for protectionist measures limiting Japanese exports of electronic goods, automobiles, and steel to Europe and the United States, it is entirely possible that Japan could simply destroy these basic industries in the West by outproducing and outpricing them, and by producing products of higher quality. It is therefore important to see what part of the Japanese pattern can be transposed to other societies.

The consensual, highly cooperative nature of Japanese society and government based on vertical organizations is combined with a mixture of competitive free-market capitalism and central government planning and direction of the economy. Within strict guidelines meant to enhance Japan's competitive position in the world economy, Japanese firms compete fiercely with one another for domestic market position. Nevertheless, when a critical business organization is threatened by failure, major efforts can be made to save it. Banks, the government, the employees, and the unions can work together extraordinarily smoothly.[19]

Big Japanese companies guarantee lifetime employment. Their unions are actually company unions which combine white- and blue-collar workers, and their goal is growth of market share rather than short-term profits. This allows these companies to automate freely. Unions are not afraid that technological progress will put their members out of work. Thus, companies can plan far ahead. And in case of need, they can demand extreme sacrifices of time and money from their employees. Japan is thus well adapted to keep abreast of new industrial cycles.[20]

The situation should not be idealized. A substantial portion of the Japanese labor force works in smaller companies that cannot provide lifetime employment for adequate benefits. By subcontracting work to these smaller firms, the large ones are able to take the pressure off themselves in times of slow economic growth. Instead of firing their own employees, the large firms cut their orders to their dependent small firms, whose employees are then left out on their own. But even with this taken into account, unemployment in Japan remains very low. The large firms that dominate the economy are able to plan ahead and adapt to changing conditions more quickly than can big American firms. And underlying the seemingly sharp status differences that characterize Japanese social interaction are fewer differences between the rich and the poor, and a relatively much larger truly middle class than in either the United States or most European societies.[21]

As the Japanese state has the primary goal of economic growth, the parts of the government bureaucracy devoted to this aim, primarily the famous Ministry of International Trade and Industry (MITI), are staffed by the most capable university graduates and benefit from enormous prestige and authority. This arrangement stands in marked contrast to the United States, where government bureaucrats, even as they have become ever more necessary to coordinate and manage the complex modern economy of the country, are generally dismissed as time-servers, and accorded neither the status nor authority to be first-class technocrats.[22]

Underpinning the entire Japanese order is the fact that since the destruction of World War II, Japanese society has been remarkably egalitarian. According to World Bank data, only one Western country, the Netherlands, provides a greater share of national income to its poorest 20 percent or 40 percent of the population.[23] The Netherlands, however, does this through welfare schemes and very high government involvement in nonproductive, redistributive schemes. In Japan, on the contrary, the government takes a lesser role in redistributive schemes and in direct administration of social welfare than in Western industrial countries. Instead, the relatively high degree of egalitarianism is the function of a salary structure much less skewed than in the West. Compared with Japanese executives, American executives are grossly overpaid. But compared with American workers, Japanese workers get a greater share of profits and a greater sense of participation by receiving periodic bonuses.[24] Japan, then, much more than the United States, and perhaps even more than some of the small, social democratic welfare states of Scandinavia, has become a mass middle-class society in which the old class conflicts, status differences, and political disharmony of classical Western industrial societies have become things of the past.[25]

That this combination of organizational traits produces good results cannot be doubted. The question is, How unique is it, and is any of it applicable to the West? Compared with the United States, Japan is a culturally homogeneous, better educated, more disciplined society, and in some sense, it was that way even before it industrialized.

But there is a strong parallel in the prewar fascism of both Europe and Japan. The notion of a vertically organized society, coordinated at the top by a more or less impartial authority, with everyone cooperating for the sake of the national good, is at the essence of fascist corporatist ideology. (It is also central to contemporary communist ideology, but that is a topic which will be discussed in the next chapter.) In its pre-World War II European incarnation, fascist corporatism made two fundamental errors. First, it forgot that the original ideology of corporatism called for much more than the defense of propertied elites. It called for at least some measure of egalitarianism so that vertical organizations were to become legitimate vehicles for all classes of society. If private property and some market principles were to be preserved, this did not mean that inequality was supposed to increase and that the working classes were simply to be repressed. Second, in both Europe and Japan, corporatism was accompanied by intense militarization and expansionist policies. But such policies led to marked overcentralization and economic distortion that were not conducive to healthy, long-term economic growth. They also led to war, which made no rational sense unless it could be won quickly and painlessly. In a world occupied by powerful nonfascist states, this was improbable at best. Militarization and war, combined with corporatism, produced totalitarian societies which also dampened new thoughts and so blocked the emergence of those new ideas which would have been necessary to continue economic growth.

Japan after World War II, however, was able to avoid these mistakes. Militarization and any kind of foreign adventure were ruled out by the American military presence. The Americans also created a constitution designed to prevent a return to totalitarian methods. But they did not destroy the efficient bureaucratic tradition of Japan, and by allowing Japan to reindustrialize and compete on favorable terms in the world market, the American victory over Japan in 1945, and the ensuing American occupation, prepared the way for what has been called the "welfare corporatism" of today. (Chalmers Johnson's phrase, the "developmental state," is just as apt.)[26]

There are other analogous models. At least some American corporations have tried to create this kind of all-encompassing, self-contained vertical structure in which group loyalty and a high degree of consensus govern. IBM is such a corporation, and at least internally, it operates a Japanese-style organization. But on the whole, the United States does not resemble Japan. In the United States, the poor are too poor, and though relatively powerless, remain a reservoir of bitterness that can disequilibrate society. Giant American corporations do not do enough to protect their employees, and they maintain overly adversarial relations between management and labor. Government officials are not sufficiently respected, and the bureaucracy has no united goal. The recent deemphasis on university funding and research is exactly the opposite of trends in Japan. Finally, there is not much effective economic planning.

It is quite likely that as the twentieth century comes to an end, some Americans and Western Europeans, impressed by Japan's success, will revive corporatist ideology, and propose it as a solution to their own problems. If corporatism is interpreted as a move toward the elimination of class conflict and the reduction of differences in income between classes, and if it is taken to mean that freedom of thought, a relatively free internal market, and a continued emphasis on peaceful economic growth are its essence, such a form of corporatism can have beneficial effects. If, on the other hand, it falls back toward the xenophobic, imperialistic, neomercantilism that prevailed among fascist regimes in the 1930s, the almost certain revival of corporatist ideology will have consequences quite the opposite of those it has had in Japan.

The Newly Industrializing Semiperiphery

Achieving balanced industrialization, strengthening the nation-state, raising the skills of the population, and generally disciplining a society in order to accomplish this quickly are not easy tasks. Western societies underwent long periods of mass poverty, human displacement, popular resistance to change, and violent internal and international wars in the process of modernizing. But at least they spread out these changes over centuries, and the major Western societies were never under great pressure to catch up to more advanced societies. They were in the forefront of the advances going on themselves. Today, however, there is a sense of urgency about change that gives no society the luxury of planning in terms of centuries, or of passively accepting an inferior and backward role.

On the other hand, in some ways the process of modernization should be easier today because technology is more advanced and can be imported quickly. Indeed, this partly accounts for the fact that most of the countries in the old periphery have made significant economic progress since 1950, even if their rates of growth have not been as high as those of core or communist countries. India's per capita GDP growth rate from 1950 to 1980, for example, averaged 1.4 percent per year, a rate as fast as France's growth from 1870 to 1913, faster than the United Kingdom's during that period, and only 0.3 percent less than Germany's at that time. Average Third World economic growth, as measured by per capita GDP change between 1950 and 1980, has been about 2.2 percent per year. This is as high as average American per capita GNP growth from 1870 to 1913, and at that time America had the fastest-growing economy in the world. Average growth in Latin America from 1950 to 1980, and in many Asian countries—such as Turkey, Thailand, Indonesia, the Philippines, Malaysia, Taiwan, South Korea, and even in most North African countries, including Egypt—has been significantly above this rate.[27] It is only because many of the leaders, intellectuals, and, increasingly, ordinary people in the old periphery have come to expect that they might actually catch up to the old core in fairly short order that these results have been so disappointing. By historical standards, comparing the Third World of the late twentieth century with the old core at any previous time, average economic growth in the poor parts of the world has been nothing short of astounding.

But success is always measured in contemporary comparative terms, not in abstract historical ones. By those standards, the scientific-technological advantage of the old core remains as formidable as ever. If some newly industrialized countries like Brazil, Taiwan, or South Korea are now beginning to enter into the world of high-technology manufacturing, most of the Third World remains far from being able to develop the most modern industries, and instead, must rely for its industrialization on obsolete technologies in fading industries such as textiles.

There are two basic, fundamentally opposite theories of economic development that compete in the world. One calls for an open strategy, the other for a closed one. To remain open means to allow, even to encourage, exchanges of capital, goods, and technology between the developing economies and the capitalist world system. A closed strategy demands the exact opposite. The former is based on the notion that there are more advantages to be gained by being a part of the system than by attempting autarky. The latter theory is based on the Leninist vision of the world which sees exchanges between the core and periphery as being fundamentally harmful to the periphery, deepening dependency and backwardness rather than stimulating growth. There is very little room for compromise between these two approaches. In general, communist countries have followed the closed approach, though several Eastern European countries have deviated from it, and since the late 1970s, so has China. India, on the other hand, though not communist, has developed in a startlingly autarkic way, trying to be as self-sufficient as possible. So has Burma. The issue, then, is not simply one between capitalism and communism.

The basic disadvantages to remaining open are said to be as follows:

my reaction

✗ 1.   Borrowing technology may be useful, but it always needs to be adapted to local conditions, particularly to the fact that poor countries are labor rich but capital poor. Simply taking Western advanced technology produces poor results.

✗ 2.   Remaining open leads local elites to want expensive, difficult-to-make manufactured products which can only be imported from the core. These range from luxury consumer goods, fine cars, communications facilities, and a host of seemingly trivial food and personal clothing items to extremely expensive military hardware demanded by the professional officer corps of the Third World. (In this respect, importing such hardware from the Soviet Union is no more beneficial than importing it from the West.) This causes a significant drain on capital resources which get wasted on foreign purchases instead of contributing to development.

✗ 3.   Foreign multinational corporations simply take profits out of the Third World; they have no interest in real development. Since they want local markets and extraction of local primary products or cheaply produced low-technology goods, their investments worsen backwardness instead of relieving it. Most foreign aid has the same effects.

✗ 4.   Finally, remaining open distorts local cultures. It corrupts the masses by making them want Western styles of life. These they cannot afford, so they become discontented with their governments and increasingly unwilling to suffer the necessary hardships to develop their own economies.

More than economic arguments, this last point appeals to the intellectuals of the old periphery because of their sense of injured pride. The traditional cultures they valued seem to be purer and less degenerate than the contemporary Western ones which peddle sex and unbridled consumerism at the expense of serious religiosity and national solidarity. The outrage of Iranian religious leaders, or Vietnamese communists, or Latin American intellectuals when they confront the seeming laxity and sheer wastefulness of advanced industrial societies is quite understandable. It is, in fact, shared by a good many Westerners themselves, particularly those on the far right who would like to return to "purer," "cleaner," old ways, and by those on the left who believe that no one has a right to behave like this as long as there remains so much inequality and misery in the world.

None of these entirely reasonable opponents of Western cultural materialism and consumerism likes to remember that the entire basis of modern industrial progress is the drive and ability of Westerners (and now Japanese, too) to use their personal freedoms to gain increasing personal comfort and variety in their lives, to escape the drudgery suffered by most humans during the dismal centuries in which they lived as peasants in agrarian societies. Subordinating individuals to the needs of the state, to religious ideals developed in the agrarian past, or to utopian visions of a distant future recreates the conditions under which peasants lived in the past, and promises, where successful, to stifle progress just as surely as did the great agrarian civilizations of that past. The main argument for remaining open is simply that this is the only way for societies without adequate educational and scientific establishments to build up their knowledge and to hope to be able to compete effectively in the still-advancing world system. While recognizing that technology and capital imports can be dangerous if controlled by foreigners, states that follow an open strategy need not accept rule by outsiders. Rather, a number of them, the most successful semiperipheral societies, have learned how to control core investors and technologies to their own benefit, and have thus managed significant economic progress. Also, remaining open, while it raises the possibility of corruption and contamination of local cultures, nevertheless eases other kinds of pressures. Importing some luxuries means that they can be disseminated fairly broadly. If automobiles and fancy houses are not yet enjoyed by many in poor countries, television, enhanced public transportation, widespread electrification, and improved standards of health through the import of foreign medical technologies are available, and can increasingly be produced domestically.

One of the more important ironies of the late twentieth century is that communist societies, by using Western technologies and combining them with a relatively high commitment to equality, have managed to spread the benefits of these technologies more widely than have open societies, which have not stressed egalitarianism. So, they have reached fairly high levels of public service, and this has been an argument used against the open, capitalist, semiperipheral societies which have made economic progress but not improved their highly inegalitarian social structures.

It has remained as true in the late twentieth century as it was in the mid- and early parts of the century that semiperipheral societies are subjected to disruptive conflicting forces. To meet their people's expectations, they must industrialize, but in the face of competition from more advanced core economies, they are also under pressure to keep wages relatively low. That is one of their few comparative advantages. They are often obliged to forge national unity in conditions where a long history of religious, ethnic, and class divisions makes this difficult. Rising expectations that are not met cause outbursts of discontent, frightening potential investors, domestic and foreign. These pressures tend to push semiperipheral societies toward nondemocratic forms of government. Also, in most of them there is no democratic tradition because class structures were never characterized by a rough balance of power. Until the recent past, in most of them, a small landowning elite ran everything. What small bourgeois class existed was an almost alien comprador merchant class. The rise of industrial and commercial bourgeois middle classes is recent, and in most cases, though these classes demand some form of democracy for themselves, they have been frightened of the revolutionary, egalitarian pressures that have come from growing urban working classes or from discontented peasants. The solution, in most cases, has been to revert to military rule, freeze the political process, and concentrate on economic development to the detriment of political freedom. But this, too, creates increasing pressures for change when economic development enlarges the size of the middle and working classes and leads them to demand that some power and a more just, rational legal order be established to safeguard their newly won prosperity.

The three major, highly successful semiperipheral societies that experienced the most rapid industrialization in the 1960s and 1970s, Taiwan, South Korea, and Brazil, were all ruled by military dictatorships during most of these years. (The successful city-states of Singapore and Hong Kong are best left out of these generalizations; they are too small and in situations too unique to permit much interesting generalization.) Indonesia, the world's fifth most populous country, and one which has experienced a moderately successful industrialization and development program, has also been a military dictatorship since 1965. Nigeria, black Africa's most important state, has been a military dictatorship for most of the time since 1966, though it has gone through several periods of relative democracy. Turkey, a fairly well-developed, semiperipheral society, has alternated between periods of democracy tending toward political chaos and military rule. There is only one major semiperipheral society that has been unambiguously democratic throughout the latter half of the twentieth century (except for a few short years of partial dictatorship under emergency rule in the mid-1970s), and that is India. Though all of the open semiperipheral societies have had democratic movements, only in India have these been strong enough to ensure long periods of democratic stability.

Of course, military or other types of dictatorship do not characterize only the successful new semiperiphery. Such governments prevail throughout the old periphery, though they range from highly ineffective, corrupt, weak tyrannies to relatively efficient organizations able to unify and develop their societies.

To understand the paradoxes associated with the new semiperiphery, it is useful to look at a particularly well-studied and important case, that of Brazil.

Brazil and Latin American Development

Brazil began its industrialization in the 1930s, partly in response to the Great Depression which caused the price of its chief export crop, coffee, to fall more rapidly than the cost of industrial imports from the core. Under the leadership of an army-supported dictator, Getulio Vargas, Brazil's federal government gained ascendancy over the previously strong provincial governments, and import substitution industrialization was fostered. After World War II, the process of industrialization continued; but with the growth of a significant and relatively well-organized working class in the major cities of Brazil, leftist and populist pressures for a more equal distribution of income, and for some sort of closure against outside economic control, particularly from North America, grew. In response to this, in 1964, the army took power and instituted a new dictatorship.[28]

The policy of the military regime, which ruled from 1964 until 1985, was to base Brazilian development on a tripartite alliance: the state machinery, run by the military and its technocratic advisers; large domestic capitalists and banks; and large multinational firms, mostly from the United States, but some from Western Europe and Japan. Brazil's capitalists had not been strong enough to control the political process without military aid, and multinational capital was neither particularly interested in, nor able to create a strongly industrialized, united Brazilian economy. The army, then, provided the missing muscle and drive, not only by keeping political order but also by obliging foreign capital to contribute to Brazil's development and by directly running some large state-owned enterprises on its own.[29]

It is interesting to compare Brazil with Argentina, where a somewhat similar political process occurred, but with different results. There, during the 1940s and early 1950s, Juan Perón, originally from the army, came to rely on working-class urban support, and in order to maintain it, he allowed wages and social benefits to rise too steeply too early. He also favored a highly nationalistic form of populism, similar to European fascism, and so rejected collaboration with foreign capital. Argentina began the twentieth century much richer than any other Latin American country, and by the middle of the century, Perón thought he could sustain this kind of relatively egalitarian, nationalistic development policy. In fact, it failed, and plunged Argentina into a long period of economic stagnation and political turmoil from which it has not yet recovered. It became impossible to control the labor unions, or to raise sufficient investment funds for development. Local industry operated inefficiently behind protectionist trade policies, and so failed to push the economy ahead.[30]

In 1950 Argentina's gross domestic product per capita was 2.98 times as large as Brazil's. In 1964, it was 2.28 times greater. But by 1981, it was only 1.43 times larger.[31] By the end of the century, it is likely that Brazil's per capita GDP will be larger than Argentina's.

Brazil may also be compared with the other major Latin American country, Mexico. Though it took a long time after its revolution to work out a stable alliance between the army, the government, local capitalists, and foreign, mostly United States', interests, Mexico eventually moved to such an arrangement in the 1940s. By that time, thirty years after the start of its revolution, it had evolved a workable, nationalistic, but still open strategy of development. As the P.R.I. (Institutional Revolutionary Party) consolidated its rule over many decades, however, it also became increasingly corrupt and less dynamic, so that Mexico's development came to be seriously impeded. In systems like those that prevail in the semiperiphery, the role of government bureaucracies, both civilian and military, is so important that they must maintain a high level of efficiency, and relative honesty, to push forward their development programs. This becomes difficult to do as the years go by and various sectors of the bureaucracy simply become vehicles for personal enrichment. Only truly democratic governments, with free elections and periodic changes in ruling personnel, can keep such organizations clean for a long time. This is precisely what Mexico lacks. Therefore, despite its relatively good level of economic growth, it has not done as well as it should have. Unlike Brazil, Mexico is oil rich, and it should have been able to capitalize on this, instead of wasting its assets during the years of the oil boom in the 1970s.[32]

In 1950, Mexico's per capita GDP was 65 percent higher than Brazil's. In 1970 it was 62 percent higher. But by 1981, it was only 38 percent higher.[33] Again, by the end of the century, it is highly likely that Brazil will be ahead of Mexico. In fact, by 2000, it is probable that Brazil will have gone from being one of the poorer Latin American countries to being the richest except for Venezuela, which is far too dependent on its large oil reserves and relatively small population.

This does not mean that military rule ensures development. It has not in Argentina, where it has only produced continuing political instability. Nor has it succeeded in Chile, where local industry was too weak to sustain competition from foreign products which entered the country during the very open policy of the military regime which took power in 1973. Without the strict control over foreign investment and trade exercised by Brazil, Chile simply perpetuated its dependent condition under its open development strategy. It remained overwhelmingly dependent on one export product, copper, and when the price of that product fell, this spelled economic catastrophe. Nor has the excessively heavy-handed repression of Chile's military regime allowed Chile's most educated and enterprising individuals to benefit their society. Instead, Chile under military rule has remained a brutal part of the periphery.[34]

But even successful development, as in the case of Brazil, does not remove certain critical problems. The one most evident in Brazil, and in other Latin American countries, is extreme inequality, which ultimately threatens political stability and, if too extreme, economic development. By keeping a large portion of the population very poor, great inequality restricts the potential market for manufactured goods and services, and so dampens economic growth. Table 9-3, which shows income distribution in Brazil, demonstrates the problem.

Comparing this income distribution with that of the United States is very revealing. Brazil in 1980 was less egalitarian than the United States was in 1929, before its New Deal reforms; but in 1960, Brazil was slightly more egalitarian than the United States was in 1929. The entire trend of change in Brazil is going in the wrong direction, and far from becoming socially more like a core society, it is creating a vast and increasingly marginal lower class that is not being integrated into the modern economy. Under such circum-

TABLE 9–3
Income Distribution in Brazil, 1960–1980[35]

	1960	*1980*	*Percent Change*
Poorest 20 percent	3.9%	2.8%	−28
Poorest 50 percent	17.4%	12.6%	−28
Richest 10 percent	39.6%	50.9%	+28
Richest 5 percent	28.3%	37.9%	+34
Richest 1 percent	11.9%	16.9%	+42

stances it is easy to see why leftist critics of the military-technocratic government belittle its substantial economic achievements.

Nor is Brazil unique. The same trend of increasing inequality exists in Mexico, too, as shown in Table 9-4.

Mexico's poor have become relatively poorer during a long period of economic growth, and its rich relatively richer. Insofar as the Brazilian and Mexican tables can be compared (the categories are the same for the bottom 20 percent and top 10 percent, and the top 5 percent, Mexico's income distribution in 1975 was almost identical to Brazil's in 1980. In both cases, the poor have very little of the national wealth.

A 1958 survey suggested that in that year Brazil's middle and upper classes, as these are defined in modern industrial or industrializing societies, amounted to no more than 11 percent of the total population. This roughly corresponds to the relative size of the middle class in the United States in 1910. But judging from income statistics, the size of that class has not grown significantly

TABLE 9–4
Income Distribution in Mexico, 1950–1975[36]

	1950	*1975*	*Percent Change*
Bottom 20 percent	6.1%	2.6%	−58
Second 20 percent	8.2%	5.4%	−34
Third 20 percent	10.3%	9.7%	−6
Fourth 20 percent	15.6%	16.2%	+4
Top 20 percent	59.8%	66.1%	+11
Top 10 percent	49.0%	51.1%	+3
Top 5 percent	40.2%	35.9%	−11

in Brazil since then, as the top 10 percent of the population now earns slightly over half of all income. (In the United States in 1980, the top quarter of the population earns half the income, and about 30 percent of the population are middle class.) The small middle class in Brazil has become much richer, but it has not absorbed significant sectors of those who were not previously middle class. Mexico's income distribution statistics, and the trend of increasing inequality, suggest that the same analysis is applicable there.[37]

Is this the necessary price of open development? Peter Evans, the best American analyst of contemporary social and economic change in Brazil, suggests that it is; and he calls development in the new semiperiphery "dependent development." By remaining tied to the world capitalist system and dependent on it for capital, trade, and modern technology, Evans claims, such seemingly successful semiperipheral societies have been unable to solve the problem of internal inequality. The alliance among bureaucratic, local business and multinational elites leaves the large majority of the population out of political power, and so unable to force a redistribution of income.[38]

In a real sense, not only politically, but economically as well, the only long-range solution to the problems of such successful semiperipheral societies as Mexico and Brazil is increased democratization that would force better distribution of income, substantial growth of the middle class, and ultimately much greater political stability than exists today.

South Korea and Taiwan

That a high degree of inequality is not only not necessary, but actually harmful for economic development, is demonstrated by Taiwan and South Korea. In 1976, South Korea's income distribution was as shown in Table 9-5. This is not a highly egalitarian income distribution, but it is much more so than either Brazil's or Mexico's. In fact, it is quite similar to income distribution in the United States.

Taiwan is also considerably more egalitarian than the new semiperipheral

TABLE 9-5
1976 Income Distribution in South Korea[39]

Bottom	20 percent	5.7 percent
Second	20 percent	11.2 percent
Third	20 percent	15.4 percent
Fourth	20 percent	22.4 percent
Top	20 percent	45.3 percent
Top	10 percent	27.5 percent

countries of Latin America. The reasons for this are largely historical. In both Taiwan and South Korea it was evident to the authorities that in order to prevent communist revolution in the 1940s, land reform was essential. In Taiwan, the defeated Nationalists were trying to salvage what they could after being expelled from the rest of China. In South Korea, the Americans were trying to prevent the South from rejoining a communist North. Effective land reform laid the basis for a relatively egalitarian social structure and pacified the peasantry, which could then be used as a source of labor for the growing industries. It also became possible to squeeze the peasants in order to keep agricultural prices low, because they were relatively contented and willing to continue working hard on their own property.[40] In Latin America such effective land reforms have not yet occurred, even in Mexico, where land reform was less thorough.

There are many other differences, too. Korea and Taiwan are relatively small, culturally homogeneous societies. Both received large amounts of American foreign aid to help begin their industrialization. In both, the old, pre-World War II elites were Japanese colonizers, and it was politically painless to expropriate them. Japan was a particularly efficient colonial power in building good education and transportation systems. Nevertheless, these cases do demonstrate that it is possible to progress while remaining open and without increasing inequality. Both these countries have actually experienced much faster economic growth than even Brazil. But like Brazil and Mexico, both could now profit from increasing democratization which would ensure continued bureaucratic and political efficiency as well as freedom for the growing middle class on which further progress will depend.

If the success of a few semiperipheral societies suggests that an open strategy can work, if coordinated by a firmly nationalistic, strong government, this does not explain why in so many cases there has been too little economic progress. That can best be done by reviewing some of the main problems of the remaining periphery, and of those large but still very poor semiperipheral societies that have not made as much progress as they might wish.

Overpopulation, Poverty, and the Angry Periphery

No discussion of peripheral societies or of world poverty in the late twentieth century can ignore the problem of overpopulation. The basic causes of this problem have already been discussed in Chapter 7. Essentially, with modern health measures and communications facilities that can bring emergency food relief to areas struck by famine, death rates throughout the world have fallen. But in the poorest countries it remains advantageous for individual families, if not for the society as a whole, to have many children. Children can aid families with their labor, and do so from an early age. They are also the only source of social insurance against old age. And in any case, the means of birth control are not as readily available as they are in richer countries.

In richer countries, on the other hand, it has become less advantageous to have many children. Children cost a lot of money, have to be educated for very long periods of time, and then move away, so that they are not necessarily a source of support for parents in later life. Nor is their help necessary, as there are various forms of social insurance to help the old. Once people moved off farms, and work was separated from home life, children became more of a cost than a benefit. The people of rich countries may still want children, but not for economic reasons, and they therefore limit births. It is, of course, much easier to do this in a modern, rich society than in a poor one.

The nature of the problem can be unambiguously represented by basic demographic statistics (see Table 9-6).

There is little question that progress has occurred. Despite a continuing drop in death rates, birth rates have fallen even faster, and the total rate of increase is not growing as it was in the first half of the twentieth century. There is good reason to be somewhat optimistic about the future. One reason the death rate in poor countries is almost as low as in rich ones is that in poor societies a much larger proportion of the population is young. Young people die less than older ones, so that the comparative absolute death rates conceal the fact that at any given age an individual in a rich country is less likely to die. Nevertheless, the absolute birth and death rates determine how large will be the excess of births over deaths. It is likely that in time the average age in poor countries will begin to rise. As birth rates fall and as the population ages,

TABLE 9-6
Birth Rates, Death Rates, and Population Growth in the World, 1960–1981[41]

	Birth Rates Per 1,000 Inhabitants Per Year		Death Rates Per 1,000 Inhabitants Per Year		Rates of Increase, as Percent Per Year	
	1960	*1981*	*1960*	*1981*	*1960*	*1981*
Core societies of Europe, North America, and Japan	20	14	10	9	1.0	0.5
Communist European countries	23	18	8	11	1.5	0.7
The rest of the world	43	32	21	12	2.2	2.0

death rates will stabilize, and the rate of increase of population will fall fairly rapidly.

But this global picture hides important differences between various societies of the old periphery. In Table 9-7 these are divided into countries that have made significant progress in controlling their rate of population increase, countries that have made moderate progress, and a set of countries that have made no progress at all.

In general, it has been African countries, most (but not all) Islamic countries, and the poorest countries of Latin America (but not the ones with substantial economic growth) that have had the least success in curbing population growth. On the other hand, the countries of East Asia and some of those of southern and southeastern Asia have been more successful.

Much of the difference has to do with the differential treatment of women in these various societies. Where women are more easily allowed to enter the labor market and circulate freely, there is a more pronounced tendency for birth rates to fall fairly quickly in response to increased job opportunities.

TABLE 9–7
Birth Rates, Death Rates, and Population Growth in Selected Countries, 1960–1981[42]

	Birth Rates Per 1,000 Inhabitants Per Year		Death Rates Per 1,000 Inhabitants Per Year		Rates of Increase, as Percent Per Year	
	1960	*1981*	*1960*	*1981*	*1960*	*1981*
Successful:						
China	39	21	24	8	1.5	1.3
Taiwan	40	23	7	5	3.3	1.8
South Korea	43	24	13	7	3.0	1.7
Moderately Successful:						
India	44	35	22	13	2.2	2.2
Egypt	44	36	19	12	2.5	2.4
Indonesia	46	35	22	13	2.4	2.2
Brazil	43	30	13	8	3.0	2.2
Mexico	45	36	12	7	3.3	2.9
Unsuccessful:						
Nigeria	52	50	25	17	2.7	3.3
Zaire	48	46	27	20	2.1	2.6
Pakistan	51	46	24	16	2.7	3.0
Iran	46	43	17	11	2.9	3.2

Where women are more tied to traditional roles, or secluded, as in much of the Islamic world, or in parts of Latin America, the reverse is true. Of course, in large parts of Africa, where women are relatively free to engage in their own, nonhousehold economic activities, there are simply too few opportunities to do so, and birth rates still have not fallen.

Aside from regional cultural patterns, it is fairly clear that increasing economic opportunities and rapid economic growth lead to falling population growth. It is also abundantly clear that certain governments can impose the kind of discipline on their populations that will make birth rates fall. This is what has happened in China, which has conducted the most successful birth limitation program in the world, though often by use of rather brutal force. But using much less force, Taiwan and South Korea have had equal success, and even Brazil, with very little government participation, and a strong Latin Catholic tradition, has responded to its economic growth with a significant fall in its birth rate.

Even in the most successful cases, however, rapid population growth has probably kept average per capita GNP growth lower than it would otherwise have been. In the less successful cases, there is little doubt that this has been the case. The problem has become a vicious circle. Lack of economic opportunities keeps birth rates high, and these, in turn, prevent rapid economic growth as new mouths consume whatever economic growth occurs, leaving little or nothing for new investments or for improvements in the standard of living.

Unlike the West, which experienced rapid population growth at a time when it needed the extra labor, this is no longer the case in the Third World. The problem is compounded by overly rapid urbanization in most of the peripheral and semiperipheral countries of the world.

Urbanization is a normal part of industrialization, but in overcrowded, poor societies, pressure on the land has pushed people into cities that have not experienced rapid enough industrial growth to absorb them. A number of gigantic, slum filled, desperately crowded cities have grown in the Third World: Kinshasa (Zaire), Lagos (Nigeria), Cairo (Egypt), Mexico City, Rio de Janeiro and São Paulo (Brazil), Jakarta (Indonesia), Bangkok (Thailand), Calcutta, Bombay, and Delhi (India) are only the most notorious examples. Table 9-8, which depicts the rate of urbanization in the world, shows what has happened.

The large cities in poor countries are a volatile mixture of rich and poor with fairly small middle classes in between them. The poor can be quickly mobilized for riots and political demonstrations which can endanger governments. In conditions of slow industrialization, which does not absorb the growing masses of urban poor, such cities are a growing threat, not only to political stability but to economic progress itself. In order to keep the urban masses quiet, most Third World governments subsidize food products and try to keep agricultural prices as low as possible. The rural peasantry is much less easily mobilized, and is thus considered more easily exploitable. Governments, more-

TABLE 9–8
**Percent of Population That Was Urban,
1960–1981**[43]

	1960	*1981*	*Percent Change*
Core societies	68	78	+ 15
European communist societies	48	62	+ 29
China	18	21	+ 17
South Korea	28	56	+100
India	18	24	+ 33
Egypt	38	44	+ 16
Indonesia	15	21	+ 40
Brazil	46	68	+ 48
Mexico	51	67	+ 31
Nigeria	13	21	+ 62
Zaire	16	36	+125
Pakistan	22	29	+ 32
Iran	34	51	+ 50

over, tend to be run by the small urban middle and upper classes, and these naturally understand urban problems better than rural ones. But keeping agricultural prices depressed has proved to be a major disincentive for agricultural improvements and investments by the peasants. So, one major result of urban overcrowding has been agricultural stagnation in countries that must still rely on their agriculture as a major base of their economies. This problem has been particularly acute in Africa, and is largely responsible for the now endemic famine conditions in much of that continent.[44]

Armed with this information, it becomes easy to see why in the remaining countries of the periphery, and in most semiperipheral ones as well, there is an enormous amount of resentment. It is quite understandable that the rich core, the former colonial powers, and those who still seem to lord it over the world system should be blamed for much that goes wrong.

But it should be equally clear that the causes of continuing poverty are now largely internal ones. A combination of overly rapid population growth, lack of political cohesion and discipline, and the absence of a large enough base of educated skilled workers and middle classes makes economic development difficult at best. Only in exceptional cases can these problems be overcome quickly enough to defuse discontent. That requires strong and honest governments able to attract domestic and foreign investments, but able to channel them through realistic government planning. It requires that the middle classes and business entrepreneurs be given enough leeway to expand their economic activities. It demands a growing effort on behalf of education—not merely mass primary education that teaches basic literacy, but secondary and university education as well—to train large numbers of highly skilled individuals.

The work necessary to carry out such programs is generally not glamorous, and in the past it has not appealed to the great charismatic leaders who dominated many formerly peripheral societies. The Nassers, Sukarnos, Nkrumahs, and their lesser imitators who ruled the newly emergent Third World in the 1950s and 1960s turned their countries toward foreign adventures and dreams of a vengeful crusade against the old core. They failed, and left ruined economies in their wake. Egypt and Indonesia have been rescued from the follies of Nasser and Sukarno, but Ghana has never recovered from Nkrumah.[45]

Fortunately for most of the Third World, the realization of these mistakes in the past has brought somewhat more realism today, except in the Middle East, where Khomeini, Sadam Hussein, Assad, and Qadaffi keep the old illusions alive. But the temptation to return to such a style of leadership will remain strong, particularly where economic growth is not rapid enough.

The dream of world revolution, of the periphery turning the tables on the core, and obtaining its goals by changing the distribution of power in the world will remain appealing, but elusive. Its fundamental intellectual premises are false, and just as it would be foolhardy for the core to try to contain all of the revolutions which will inevitably occur in the future in the Third World, so would it be equally in vain for future revolutionary leaders to believe that the secret of economic development somehow lies in the destruction of the capitalist core.

CHAPTER 10

Leninist Regimes

*T*he most important difference in the international political balance of power between the early and the late twentieth century is that today a third of the world's population is ruled by governments that are explicitly not capitalist. They offer a model of social and economic organization that is not the same as that in the leading core powers and that claims to be the prelude to a revolutionary and much improved world system. At least two of the communist powers are large and strong enough to pose serious potential threats to the long-term survival of the world capitalist system.

Before proceeding, it might be appropriate to relabel these regimes. They are not, by their own account, "communist," but only on the road to communism, which will be reached at some unspecified, increasingly vague future. On the other hand, to call them socialist confuses them with the rather benign, and now barely Marxist social democratic parties that exist in the core. A suitable term is simply "Leninist." It was Lenin who first worked out a system of rule by communist revolutionaries after they had taken power. The Soviet Union, though it certainly does not rule a united communist world system, has remained the primary source of institutional ideas for all communists, and these continue to be highly influenced by Lenin's ideological blueprint and Stalin's concretization of Lenin's ideas. It was not Marx, but Lenin, who thought up the details of a party elite that would rule a country dictatorially for an indefinite period of time while it consolidated its power and prepared to spread the revolution elsewhere. It was Lenin's successor, Stalin, who turned this elite into a self-perpetuating bureaucratic machine.[1]

A list (Table 10-1) of those countries that are formally Leninist, and firmly enough dominated by communist parties so that they are almost certain to remain that way for the rest of the twentieth century, and probably much longer, shows the spread of Leninist regimes since the original Bolshevik Revolution in 1917.

There are some countries that might be said to have Leninist regimes ruling them: South Yemen and Ethiopia, for example. Angola, Mozambique, and Nicaragua are also ruled by regimes that claim, in some respects, to be Leninist. But in none of these cases is the future viability of the regime, or even its long-range commitment to this type of rule, certain. There are other regimes throughout the world that have, at one time or another, also called themselves socialist, and that are run as tight, one-party dictatorships. Syria, Iraq, the Congo, Libya, Somalia, Burma, Benin, Guinea, and Guinea-Bissau might be put on this list. Some are now allies of the United States (such as Somalia).

TABLE 10–1
Leninist Societies[2]

Country	Date of Leninist Regime	Process by Which Leninist Regime Took Power	Population in 1985 (in Millions)
Soviet Union	1917	Revolution	277
Mongolia	1924	Revolution with Soviet aid	1.9
Yugoslavia	1945	Revolution	23
Albania	1945	Revolution with Yugoslav aid	3.0
Poland			37
German Democratic Republic		Occupation by Soviet army after World War II	17
Czechoslovakia	1945–1948		16
Hungary			11
Romania			23
Bulgaria			9.0
Democratic People's Republic of Korea	1945	Occupation by Soviet army	20
China	1949	Revolution	1,092
Vietnam	1954, 1975	Revolution, South Vietnam joined to communist North Vietnam through revolution and Northern invasion in 1975	59
Cuba	1959	Revolution	10
Laos	1975	Revolution with Vietnamese aid	3.8
Kampuchea	1975, 1979	Revolution with Vietnamese aid, then a new regime installed by Vietnamese invasion in 1979	6.2
Afghanistan	1979	Soviet invasion	12

Total population 1985 (33 percent of world total) = 1,621 million

Others have never come close to having entirely state-run economies and are more socialist in name than in practice, and yet others may one day turn into genuinely Leninist societies. But in 1985, it would be stretching the definition of Leninism to include any of them on a definitive list of Leninist regimes.

Drawing in large measure on the work of Kenneth Jowitt, it is possible to outline the characteristics of a Leninist regime as follows:

1.   The ruling Communist Party of the state claims an absolute monopoly of political power.

2.   The key sectors of the economy—that is, all major branches of industry, services, and agriculture—are controlled by the state. They are either directly run by the state and the Party, or at least subject to strict guidelines from the Party and the state's planning apparatus.

3.   There is a formal commitment to producing a highly advanced, highly egalitarian society. Though the degree of real commitment to these goals varies from case to case, and in fact, the two of them often conflict, no Leninist regime has entirely abandoned them.

4.   The regime justifies its existence by an appeal to the laws of Marxist-Leninist historical development, and to the claim that by following them it can improve the material and spiritual condition of its population far faster and more effectively than through capitalist economic organization.

5.   Because the Party is presumed to be the ultimate interpreter of Marxist-Leninist scientific truth, its decisions are not subject to doubt. The Party feels justified in using almost any degree of force deemed necessary and efficient in order to carry out its decisions and maintain itself in power. In practice, this generally turns into a dictatorship run by a very small number of party leaders, often dominated by one man. But even under the broadest interpretation, it is only an elite within the Party, which is itself an elite within the society, that ever plays an effective, legitimate political role.

6.   Because all aspects of social life are related to one another, and to the political-economic imperatives set by the development plan of the Party, societies living under Leninist regimes have far more aspects of their daily lives regulated by the state than in typical capitalist-democratic regimes.[3]

Having spelled out these details, it is crucial to emphasize two points. One is that simply by virtue of having common ideological bases, Leninist regimes do not combine to create anything close to a unified "world socialist system." China and the Soviet Union are not even formally allies; and Vietnam, North Korea, Yugoslavia, Cuba, and Albania are fully independent states that are in no way satellites or dependencies of any other state. On the other hand, Mongolia, Afghanistan, and Czechoslovakia are politically entirely dominated by the Soviet Union. Laos and Kampuchea are ruled by the Vietnamese. Poland, East Germany, and Bulgaria have only marginally more independence than Czechoslovakia. Hungary has a bit more, and Romania yet more. But in these cases, independence is tenuous, and in Eastern Europe, individual countries gain or lose small bits of independence from the Soviet Union without, in the long run, really escaping one key fact: The Soviet Union would intervene immediately and massively to prevent any of them from overthrowing their Leninist regimes.

The second, and in some ways much more interesting, point is that within these constraints, there exists much diversity between various Leninist regimes, even in those parts of Eastern Europe dominated by the Soviet Union. Furthermore, Leninist societies are no more unchanging, fixed entities than are capitalist ones. Within particular countries, over time, there have been important organizational and social changes, and these will continue to occur. There has been some experimentation in increasing efficiency and attempting to carry out various goals. Therefore, comparisons can be made and insights can be gained into the operation and possible future of Leninist societies.

Types of Leninist Regimes

Leninist regimes vary along five key dimensions: degree of commitment to equality; degree of commitment to rapid, heavy industrialization over light consumer industries and improvements in the general standard of living; degree of centralization of the economy; degree of repression of the population; and the extent to which foreign ideas, contact with foreigners, and travel abroad are allowed.

Given that all Leninist societies are somewhat committed to equality, there remains substantial variation between the radical leveling attempted by the Khmer Rouge in Kampuchea from 1975 to 1979 and that by Eastern Europe or the Soviet Union, where inequality is almost as great as in capitalist Western societies.

All Leninist regimes seek to modernize and industrialize their societies. But whereas some, such as the Soviet Union under Stalin, pushed producer goods, military production, and gigantic heavy industrial projects, others, such as Hungary in the 1970s and 1980s, have emphasized agriculture, light industry, and consumer goods to a far greater extent. The first policy produces very rapid growth in gross national product or gross domestic product (though these are measured somewhat differently in Leninist economies), but not in the real standard of living. The second emphasis produces much more consistent growth in the real standard of living, but less spectacular GNP growth.

Economies may be more or less centralized. Of course, all Leninist regimes have central planning and control to a greater degree than capitalist democracies, but there is substantial variation. Contemporary Romania, for example, is highly centralized. Its neighbor, Yugoslavia, is highly decentralized on the basis of regions; and another neighbor, Hungary, gives individual firms or agricultural cooperatives much more leeway. China moved from centralization to relative decentralization during the late 1970s and the early 1980s. In some Leninist societies, almost all the land, and almost all enterprises, even very small service ones, are state owned. In others, for example Poland, most of the land remains owned by individual peasant families. In some Leninist societies, many small firms, restaurants, and shops are privately owned and operated.

No Leninist society lacks a substantial repressive apparatus. But whereas in some cases these have engaged in exceedingly bloody massacres to terrorize their populations into total submission (Stalin's Soviet Union, Kampuchea under the Khmer Rouge), others are much more relaxed, either by design or because they are too weak to risk such measures. Poland in the mid-1980s, for example, is far less repressive than most Leninist regimes, though this seems more a case of state and Party weakness than of real tolerance. On the other hand, Hungary does allow considerable freedom of expression to its citizens. Yugoslavia has done the same in the past, though it is now somewhat more restrictive. Albania, North Korea, and Vietnam allow very little freedom of writing, reading, speech, or personal movement.

Finally, whereas some Leninist societies, such as Yugoslavia or Hungary, allow foreign individuals, books, and other cultural materials relatively free entry, and permit their own citizens to travel fairly easily, other Leninist regimes are very closed. Albania may be the most closed society in the world. North Korea is hardly better. Kampuchea under the Khmer Rouge, Stalin's Soviet Union, and Mao's China were almost as closed as these extreme cases.

Of course, on most of these five dimensions the majority of Leninist societies are not at any of the extremes, though some are. Nevertheless, a typology of Leninist regimes can be made (see Table 10-2).

These categories require more explanation. For one thing, to label them using the names of individual leaders who originated them is merely a way of sidestepping such misleading labels as "right wing," "left wing," "orthodox," "deviationist," "revisionist," and others which have proliferated in debates among Marxist-Leninists. On the other hand, using names of leaders creates other problems. For example, on close inspection, it turns out that for all his rhetoric of favoring the peasant over industry and of promoting equality over heavy industrialization, Mao oversaw the precise opposite, perhaps against his will. The economic results in China under Mao's rule were closer to those achieved by Stalin than those achieved by the most perfect Maoist of all, Pol Pot of Kampuchea. But Mao's stated plan, and probably his intention as well, was to emphasize radical equality over all other aspects of economic planning, and as he will long be remembered for his writings and ideological stance, it seems suitable to use his name as a label.[4]

Similarly, Tito ruled over an important experiment in economic decentralization, opening Yugoslavia to the West and allowing his citizens more personal freedom. In the long run, it may turn out that with some important modifications in Tito's plan, Janos Kadar of Hungary will have achieved these goals for his society more effectively than Tito, whose experiment is now in a

TABLE 10–2
Five Dimensions of Leninist Societies

Regime type	Commitment to Equality	Commitment to Heavy Industrialization	Centralization	Repression	Openness to Outside World
Stalinist*	Low	High	High	High	Low
Maoist†	High	Low	High	High	Low
Titoist‡	Low	Low	Low	Low	High
Liberalized Stalinist§	Low to medium	Medium	Medium	Medium	Medium

* Important examples of Stalinist regimes: U.S.S.R., 1930s, 1940s, 1950s. All of Eastern Europe except Yugoslavia, late 1940s, early 1950s; Romania, 1970s, 1980s; North Korea 1950s to 1980s.
† Important examples of Maoist regimes: China from the mid-1960s to the mid 1970s; Kampuchea 1975–1979; possibly Albania in the 1960s, 1970s, and 1980s.
‡ Important examples of Titoist regimes: Yugoslavia from the late 1950s to the 1980s; Hungary 1960s, 1970s, 1980s; possibly China from the late 1970s to the 1980s; Czechoslovakia from the mid-1960s until 1968; Poland in the late 1970s.
§ Important examples of liberalized Stalinist regimes: U.S.S.R. from late 1950s to 1980s; most of Eastern Europe over the same period; Cuba 1960s, 1970s, 1980s.

state of near collapse. But Tito emphasized his own role as leader and ideological innovator, while Kadar has not.[5]

There is no question that Stalinism is a suitable name for the type of policy pursued under his rule. Nor is there any question that an almost undiluted form of Stalinism exists today in Romania and North Korea, along with the near deification of the leader, crushing of all open debate, and at least in the case of Romania, deliberate lowering of the population's standard of living in order to carry out the grandiose industrialization plans of the leader.

The residual category, "liberalized Stalinism," is necessarily somewhat vague and conceals within itself a wide range of regimes. Most of the European Leninist regimes fit into this category. They are less repressive, less closed, less single-mindedly determined to pursue heavy industrialization than they were in the past. But they are still far from being as open, as committed to some decentralization of control, or as concerned with the real standards of living of their populations as Hungary, or as Yugoslavia in the prime years of Tito's rule. It therefore seems wiser to create this category than to try to fit these regimes artificially into the purer types. It is probably true, however, that even in these types of regimes, ideological debates among the top Party people keep in mind the possible benefits and dangers of each of the pure types, and knowledge of these types guides much long-range planning.

It should be emphasized that some Leninist regimes are not sufficiently consolidated to have decided in which direction they will move. Afghanistan is of course still in the middle of an intense war which basically pits the Soviet army against the local population. It is quite possible that in the future Afghanistan will simply become a part of the Soviet Union. Vietnam is also unsettled. It remains at war in Kampuchea against rebels seeking to oust it from that country. In the south, particularly Saigon (now Ho Chi Minh City), the system remains far more open and loose than in the north. But whether Vietnam will eventually follow a Stalinist, a Maoist, or a somewhat liberalized Stalinist path remains unclear. (A Titoist path seems unlikely.) Even after a quarter century of Fidel Castro, it is far from clear in which direction Cuba will go.

But for all its oversimplification, the typology is of use. It points to the fact that on these important dimensions, variation is not random. It is not possible to have a very strong ideological program, either a push toward heavy industrialization or to radical equality, and avoid very severe repression and closure to the outside. In either case, demands made on the population to alter its ways and to make extreme sacrifices are too high to allow much freedom of movement or thought. Only a Titoist or liberalized Stalinist system can allow some relaxation.

On the other hand, what "Titoism" really stands for is the introduction of some market forces into the economy. This increases economic efficiency, but can only work if the Party bureaucracy loses some of its regulatory power. Also, individuals must be given more freedom to inform themselves and to test their ideas, otherwise the market cannot operate. So a greater degree of economic liberalization necessitates greater personal freedom. This is not optional: the two go together. "Titoism" also necessitates greater contact with the more advanced Western economies which are a source of capital and technology. This, in turn, means that there has to be more contact with Westerners and with Western ideas. One of the severe problems of the limited liberalization in the Soviet Union has been that the Party has been unwilling to give up any of its control, to allow citizens significantly more freedom, or to increase contacts with the West. Therefore, even though the terror of the Stalin years no longer exists in so obvious a form, the economic benefits of liberalization have not gone very far. Economic reform without social and political reform will not have much impact.[6]

The same applies for the contrast between the "Maoist" and "Stalinist" paths of development. To emphasize radical equality means to devaluate technical expertise and education as well as managerial skills. When Stalin began his program for rapid heavy industrialization in Russia in the 1930s, he also reintroduced wage differentials, opened higher schooling to the most skilled, rather than to the children of the previously disadvantaged, and protected his technocrats with important material privileges. When Mao tried to equalize Chinese society, he did the opposite, and paid the price of increasing incompetence and mismanagement. When Pol Pot's Kampuchea set out to produce the most drastically egalitarian society in the world, it systematically exterminated those with higher education and skills. It thus deliberately set itself back in the quest for modernization and economic growth.[7]

In other words, for a Party elite to choose one or another of these paths means making very difficult choices about the entire future of their societies. For these reasons, in times of bureaucratic indecision, or weak leadership, as in the case of the Soviet Union in the late Brezhnev, Andropov, and Chernenko years, it was much easier to drift along in the "liberalized Stalinist" path than to head in any of the other, more decisive directions which involved making too many changes.

One last point is important. Degree of openness to the outside, Western world is a critical variable. By being willing to reintegrate themselves into the capitalist world economy, Titoists fundamentally accept the capitalist order, and give up their revolutionary aspirations. Only the Stalinist or Maoist types of regimes are still genuinely revolutionary. A liberalized Soviet Union may engage in great power competition, but not in truly revolutionary activity if it decides to take a liberal, Titoist path to economic reform. It is perhaps for this reason that it finds such a path distasteful and ideologically repugnant, even if many of its top elite believe that it would be practical. The direction chosen by the various major Leninist regimes, then, can have impact on the stability and security of the world capitalist system. Domestic and international consequences flow from any important policy choice, and cannot be separated.

Contemporary Soviet Society

Because the Soviet Union is such a large and important country, and the main rival of the United States as well as a major challenge to the existence of the world capitalist system, there is a tendency to either exaggerate or denigrate the extent of social change that has occurred there in recent decades. A few comparative numbers about these changes may set what happened in better perspective.

One of the most meaningful, yet easy to interpret statistics about well-being in a country is its infant mortality rate (deaths of newborn children between birth and first birthday as a proportion of all live births). In 1911, 232 of every 1,000 infants died per year in Russia (almost one-quarter), a rate that was almost the highest in Europe. (Romania was probably as high, and Albania, for which no statistics are available, might have been even higher.)[8] By 1925, the Russian infant mortality rate was down to 198 per 1,000 per year. By 1960 it was 33 per 1,000. But it began to rise after reaching a low of 22.9 per 1,000 in 1971, and now the Soviet Union no longer publishes the rate. Specialists have estimated that it was about 39 or 40 per 1,000 per year in 1979.[9] This means that today the Soviet Union has by far the highest infant mortality rate of any country in Europe except Albania (which has also stopped releasing such figures).[10] No other industrialized country has ever experienced a consistent, sharp rise in its infant mortality figures. The comparative statistics shown in Table 10–3 reveal an interesting pattern.

Compared with the Third World, then, the Soviet Union has done well in this key area of promoting national well-being. Compared with advanced capitalist countries, to which it was quite similar in the 1960s, it has done poorly. Recently, even poor countries like Spain and South Korea have done better.

In terms of sheer economic growth, the record of the Soviet Union is also mixed (see Table 8–6 in Chapter 8). Between 1950 and 1980, its rate of economic growth was higher than that of the United States, though below more dynamic capitalist economies such as West Germany and Japan. But compared with most of the Third World, the Soviet Union has also done well.[11]

The problem is that the rate of economic growth in the Soviet Union has visibly slowed in recent years, and there is no indication that this will change. In the 1950s gross national product grew in the Soviet Union by an average of 5.7 percent per year. In the 1960s, the average growth fell to 5.1 percent per year. In the 1970s, it fell to 3.4 percent. In the 1980s, it is running at no more than 2 percent per year, which translates into a per capita growth of no more than 1 percent a year.[12]

Given the current low rate of economic growth in the Soviet Union, there is no prospect that it will catch up to any of the capitalist industrialized countries in its standard of living any time soon. After years of operating an overcentralized, highly bureaucratized economy geared to military production and the growth of heavy industry, the Soviet Union finds it difficult to change. It is inflexible, and it is increasingly ill-adapted to the shift going on in the capitalist world to a "fifth" industrial era. In a sense, the Leninist-Stalinist model worked very well to propel the Soviet Union into the "third" industrial era dominated by steel and chemicals, less well in making it keep up with the

TABLE 10–3
Infant Mortality (Deaths Per Thousand Per Year)[13]

	1920	*1960*	*1980*
Soviet Union	198 (1925)	33	about 40
United States	86	26	12
Japan	166	30	7
Spain	114	50	10
South Korea	?	78	33
Mexico	?	91	54
Brazil	?	118	75
India	?	165	121
China	?	165	71

"fourth" industrial era of the automobile and mass consumption, and it will work even less well in the new age of electronics, information, and biotechnology. Nor is this entirely surprising, as the original Marxist-Leninist vision of the world was a nineteenth and early twentieth century one. Frozen into institutional rigidity by a very powerful bureaucracy eager to protect its power and privilege, working through long-range planning based on outdated concepts, and unwilling to allow the kind of individual initiative and play of market forces which might reinstitute greater economic rationality, the Soviet Union is condemned to a kind of ponderous backwardness for a long time. Though it can, by immense effort, keep itself militarily powerful enough to threaten the destruction of the world, it can no longer threaten to weaken capitalism by presenting a better social and economic model.

The fact that its infant mortality is rising, however, bespeaks more serious problems than this alone. In the past, and in most Leninist regimes even today, the government was at least able to distribute basic social services and provide schooling more effectively than the developing capitalist economies which were less committed to social equality. Why the Soviet Union may be losing this ability is an important question that can be considered after a short examination of its pattern of stratification.

Formal distribution of income may be somewhat more egalitarian in the Soviet Union than it is in Western countries. At least this is the case in Eastern Europe, though not by very much, and the Soviet Union is probably somewhat less egalitarian than other Leninist European societies.[14] But this moderate egalitarianism in income distribution can hardly mask the existence of a very strongly marked class structure with great disparities between the elite, the middle class, the working class, and the remaining peasants.

At the top of the social and political hierarchy are the Party bosses and top managers. They live in special districts, have access to summer homes, travel, special stores, special health care facilities, the top schools for their children, and freedom from the daily inconveniences of the lines, crowds, and poor housing that is the lot of ordinary Soviets. In this respect they are fully as privileged compared with the majority of their society as are the capitalist elites in the West.

Below them, but sharing many of their privileges, are the top ranks of what the Soviets call the "intelligentsia," the educated specialists in various fields. This group includes artists, writers, the better professors, scientists, top doctors, engineers, and other professionals. This class shades off into lower-white-collar employees who have fewer privileges.

Further below this are those who perform working-class or clerical functions. These two groups cannot really be separated because so many of the lowest white-collar positions are actually held by women who are relegated to low-paying, low-prestige jobs that place them below working-class males. In many service occupations, the top positions are held by men whereas the lower ones are held by women.

Finally, at the lowest rung of society, are the peasants. Those who work for large, relatively modern state farms, run like rural factories, are on the whole better off than collective-farm peasants. The latter are the descendants of the old peasant class. Their lands have been expropriated and are now run by the state, but in return for working on the collective, they are allowed to cultivate small private plots. They suffer from the lowest standard of living in the Soviet Union, though there is significant variation from area to area. Rural schools are the poorest, and it is difficult for peasant children to aspire to higher positions. As more migrate off the farms, however, they enter the ranks of the urban working class which somewhat improves their standard of living and the opportunities of their own children.[15]

This class structure is not, after all, so different from the one found in the West. But as might be expected, because the Soviet Union is still more backward than the advanced capitalist economies, it has a relatively smaller middle class and a higher proportion of its labor force in agriculture (see Table 10–4). In some ways there is a startling similarity between Soviet stratification patterns and those in the United States forty years earlier. Taking into account the fact that in the West there existed more of a distinct lower-white-collar or lower-middle class than in the Soviet Union, and that many of those in all the categories were independently self-employed, the likeness in the two sets of figures remains real. At similar levels of development one can expect various societies, even if they have vastly different political systems and historical traditions, to bear considerable similarity to one another.

The expansion of the Soviet economy in past decades opened opportunities for considerable social mobility. But the slow growth of the present restricts such opportunities. Combined with the spread of secondary education, this has meant that growing numbers of young people have their aspirations frustrated. In the early 1950s over half of secondary school graduates could move into higher education and be promised membership in the middle class, but by the 1980s, only one in seven could do this.[16]

TABLE 10–4
Class Structure: Soviet Union and United States[17]

	Soviet Union in 1970	*United States in 1930*
Elite and middle classes	16%	14%
Lower white collar	{ 65%	15%
Working class		49%
Agriculture	20%	21%

The reduced chances for upward mobility have been exacerbated by and a further cause of, what Gail Lapidus calls the "crystalization of a new social hierarchy." This process began under Stalin, but is now a firmly fixed part of the Soviet social structure. The elite and upper ranks of the middle class use their power and privilege to give their children better educations and access to the system. Increasingly, the top ranks recruit members of their own class to succeed them, so that a semihereditary class structure is forming. Even in the1970s it seemed that the Soviet elite and upper-middle classes were better able to pass on their advantages to their children, because of the crucial importance of schooling, than their professional, white collar, and managerial equivalents in the West.[18] Today that tendency is yet more pronounced.

What seems to have happened was that under Stalin the class deemed crucial for development was given a secure position of power and privilege. After Stalin, some attempt was made to return to more egalitarian principles. This, among other factors, led to the Party bureaucracy's dislike of then Soviet leader Nikita Khrushchev, who was overthrown in 1964. Since then, the combination of conservative Party rule and slower economic growth has frozen the inequality of Stalin's past and made it far more secure. For the upper-middle class and elite groups, there is no longer even the fear of the purges that existed under Stalin.[19]

In the Soviet Union, as in other Leninist regimes, one of the beneficial remnants of the old Marxist-Leninist idealism is that job security for the working class is high. But though socially beneficial, of course, this makes it that much more difficult to force greater efficiency from the system. Now that security is also high at the top, the incentive for change is small.

The final element needed to understand the situation is the realization that the real standard of living of the average Soviet individual is quite a bit lower than GNP or GDP figures indicate. Though per capita Soviet GDP is about half that of the United States, it takes 2.9 times more working hours for an average Russian urban dweller to purchase the daily necessities of life than it does an average urban American. It takes eleven times as many working hours to purchase a color television in the Soviet Union as in the United States, and also eleven times as many days of work to purchase a car. Only housing is cheaper in the Soviet Union than in the United States, but much of it remains very crowded and poor.[20]

Such a system produces a high degree of corruption and frustration. This is probably the main reason for rising alcoholism which, among other effects, has caused a steep rise in middle-aged male mortality.

It is now possible to see how all this is related to rising infant mortality. The low priority on consumer goods has meant that few good birth control devices or medications are available in the Soviet Union. But urbanization and overcrowding along with the near universal participation of women in the active labor force have reduced the desire for children, just as in the West. The result is that abortions, often performed under less than ideal circumstances, are the most common form of birth control. Damage done through repeated abortions can lead to problems later when live births do occur. Also, as almost all women work, those with children must leave them in state-run day care centers. These are generally understaffed and poorly run, like most services, thus increasing the incidence of disease. Finally, women too, suffer the effects of rising alcoholism. Combined with what seems to be a poorly organized health care service that receives a low priority from the state, the results translate into more infant deaths.[21]

It would be a grave error to believe that all these signs of social and economic crisis in the Soviet Union foreshadow any imminent change or great weakness in the government. On the contrary, it is precisely because repression is so effective, and the elite so protected by an elaborate array of police, military, and secret police defenses, that it is so loyal and so unshakable. From its very strength comes the weakness of the system, its resistance to change. The possibility of any kind of upheaval seems very remote.[22]

The strengths and weaknesses of the Soviet Union are as evident in its foreign relations as in its domestic organization. By concentrating great energies on military research and development, it can more or less keep up in the arms race with the United States. This means that there will not be any serious intervention from abroad either in the Soviet Union or in its Eastern European empire, which it treats as a military border zone with which to shield itself from the West. There is no imaginable development, in this century, or well into the twenty-first, that seems capable of altering this situation.

To a remarkable degree, the Leninist-Stalinist regime of the Soviet Union has succeeded in reproducing the kind of giant, anachronistic imperial structure which used to characterize the ancient and medieval agrarian civilizations of Europe and Asia. By the rigid application of a quasi-religious ideology, with Marx as its distant god and Lenin as its prophet, by monopolizing all intellectual activity, and encasing its increasingly hereditary elite in a protective shell, it has managed to secure this imperial structure from outside influence.[23] The price, of course, is stagnation. But unlike the Spanish Habsburgs of the seventeenth century, or the Chinese Ming dynasty of the sixteenth, the Soviet elite allows just enough contact with the West, and enough domestic intellectual vigor, to keep itself scientifically abreast of the latest developments and able to use them for necessary military technology. For a long time, then, it will avoid the fate of those past agrarian empires, even as it will continue to resemble them in many ways.

The Crooked Chinese Path

China's modern history has taken a different path from the Soviet Union's. The civil war in which the Chinese Communists came to power was much longer than the one in Russia. It began in the late 1920s and only ended in 1949. The Chinese Communists were obliged to build secure bases in the rural hinterlands of China, and could not, as did the Russian Bolsheviks, take command by their control of a few urban centers.[24] China was also much more backward in 1949 than Russia had been in 1917. It was poorer, had a smaller modern scientific and technological base, and was less industrialized than Russia had been at the time of its revolution.

The first years of Leninist rule, under the leadership of the Communist Party's Mao Zedong, allowed the country to return to a level of prosperity it had known before the long series of civil and foreign wars which had afflicted it for most of the twentieth century, particularly in the 1930s and 1940s. Though accompanied by the expropriation of landlords and land reform as well as by major investments in heavy industrialization, communist rule until 1956 continued to rely on market mechanisms to allocate resources and determine prices in its most important economic sector, agriculture. In 1956, and then much more intensively during the years of the "Great Leap Forward" from 1958 to 1960, the Chinese Communist Party attempted to revolutionize agriculture and Chinese society as a whole. Market mechanisms were abandoned in favor of direct production planning. Peasants were forced into communes. The purpose was to launch a massive industrialization drive and turn China into the Party's vision of a true, egalitarian, advanced, nonmarket socialist society. The effort proved a disaster. Average per capita food grain consumption fell by 20 percent from 1957 to 1960, and did not return to the levels of 1956 and 1957 until 1979!

In a country that was poor to begin with, largely rural (84 percent of the labor force was in agriculture in 1952, and still 73 percent in 1979), and reliant on staple grain crops for its nourishment, this shortfall was translated into widespread distress and famine. By 1957, average food consumption had only returned to what it had been in the early 1930s, before the Japanese invasion. Various studies now estimate that somewhere between 16 and 28 million people died as a direct result of the Great Leap Forward's effects on agricultural production after 1957.[25]

Mao made much of his "peasant" strategy for developing China, and for creating a true socialist society, more egalitarian and less urban than that of the Soviet Union.[26] In fact, however, the policies of the 1950s and 1960s produced a result somewhat similar to that which had occurred in the Soviet Union in the 1930s. The peasants suffered and starved, and a large, relatively inefficient heavy industrial sector was built by taking produce from the peasants to feed the cities and factories. In return, the peasants were forced into collective arrangements that simply made it easier for the government and Party to control them. From 1957 to the 1960s, rural per capita food consumption fell by 24 percent, but urban food consumption fell by only 2 percent, so that by 1960 the cities were much better fed than the countryside. From 1953 to 1957, heavy industrial investment was almost six times as great as investment in agriculture, and almost eight times as large as investment in light industry. From 1957 to 1965, heavy industrial investment was four and one-half times greater than investment in agriculture, and almost eleven times greater than in the light industry that might have made the consumer goods with which peasants could have been paid, but were not.[27]

In the early 1960s, Mao was obliged to back away from his Great Leap Forward policies, but this seemed to him to push China further in the direction of Soviet bureaucratization. The Party officials, and especially those who had expertise in running economic affairs, seemed to him to garner excessive rewards. To overcome this and push China back toward radical egalitarianism, he launched the "Great Proletarian Cultural Revolution" in 1966. This was meant to produce equality by making all of China's regions self-sufficient, eliminating market mechanisms, persecuting intellectuals and experts of all types, turning schools into political training institutions rather than educational ones, and promoting individuals, whether into university or managerial positions, on the basis of correct (that is, proletarian or peasant) social origin and loyalty to Maoism. To carry this out, Mao unleashed militant youths, the "Red Guards," throughout the country, urging them to travel and overthrow staid old bureaucratic ways.[28]

This policy created chaos in many parts of China, but particularly in key urban centers, in schools, and in the Party.[29] Rural areas seem to have fared relatively better than during the Great Leap Forward, and though in some areas there was fighting between various factions that amounted to near civil war, the death rate from this long exercise in Maoist social policy was not as high as during the Great Leap Forward. From 1965 to 1976, per capita food grain consumption remained even, at a rate 10 percent below the high of 1956–1957. On the other hand, the standard of living of the mass of peasants, already very low, stagnated during this period, and the cities, now politically more volatile, received extra benefits. Also, for all the talk about peasants, between 1960 and 1975, investment for heavy industry remained almost five times higher than for agriculture and eleven times higher than for light industry.[30]

The spreading disorder unleashed by the Cultural Revolution persuaded Mao to try to bring the youthful Red Guards under control. Workers were used in some areas to do this. In others, the army was called upon to reestablish order. A power struggle between the army, under Lin Biao, and the remaining Party apparatus, under Zhou Enlai, erupted under the guise of continuing the Cultural Revolution. But in fact both groups wanted to demobilize the Red Guards, and the young enthusiasts who had done so much to try to create a completely egalitarian, unbureaucratic, socialist society were disbanded and sent out to rusticate in remote rural areas.[31]

By the time of Mao's death in 1976, the issue of the future direction of China was still far from settled. A radical segment of the Party, led by Mao's favorites (the "Gang of Four," which included his wife), was, however, outmaneuvered, and ultimately, Zhou Enlai's successor among the moderate, more practical Party elements, Deng Xiaoping, came to power.

The results of Mao's long rule were far from what socialism had originally promised. A Communist Party report in 1978 said that 100 million peasants, about 10 percent of the population, did not have enough to eat. Other communist sources doubled that estimate to 200 million peasants living in a state of "semistarvation." In many of the poorest regions the rural standard of living in the late 1970s was lower than in the 1950s, and even than in the late 1930s. Far from being an accident, this was the result of misguided government policies. While industrial production, and thus gross domestic product, rose sharply, China, as Nicholas Lardy has written,". . . is probably the only country in modern times to combine, over twenty years, a doubling of real per capita national income and constant or even slightly declining average food consumption." The benefits of economic growth were very unevenly distributed. Despite the supposed egalitarian thrust of the Cultural Revolution, the income of state employees rose substantially while that of the peasants stagnated. In general, through growing subsidies, the standard of living of the cities also increased, so that the gap between the cities and the countryside grew.[32]

For all the ideological innovations of the Maoist period, then, the result was that in the end the Party was still in control, the peasants had been used to further industrialization, and the country was faced with severe economic problems.

Since 1978, under Deng Xiaoping, China has attempted to reform itself by reintroducing market regulation at many levels. The most important changes have been in agriculture, which has made very substantial progress. Now China is trying to introduce the kind of partially market-driven, partially centralized socialist planning policy that Hungary has successfully begun in Eastern Europe. This means, of course, that inequality is not only accepted, but encouraged up to a point. Experts, intellectuals, and economic entrepreneurs must be rewarded along with successful peasants who now have substantial control over the land they work. It means, too, that China must be more open to the West, to sending students abroad, to trading more, and to inviting foreign investment. All these things have happened, often against the wishes of the more entrenched Party bureaucrats who fear losing their power and privileges.[33]

During the 1960s and 1970s, Maoist China became an enemy of the Soviet Union. One of the chief reasons for this was that Mao offered a more radical, antibureaucratic, egalitarian model of Leninism. Now that this period is over, however, China has swung in the other direction, and offers a more decentralized, open "Titoist" model. Whether this will make the Soviets more or less fearful is an open question.

If China should succeed in continuing on this more open path, and experiencing significant, broadly based economic development, the Soviet model will be more fully discredited than before. If, on the other hand, some of the conservative Party elements in China have their way, China will slip back into a conventional Stalinist, overcentralized stagnant pattern, and this would no doubt reassure the Soviet Union.

Reforms, Orthodoxy, and Nationalism: Socialism or Fascism?

The Soviet Union and China are by far the most important Leninist regimes simply because they are so big and powerful. But the diversity among Leninist regimes cannot be grasped simply by looking at these two most significant cases. Looking at lesser cases increases our understanding of Leninism's potential for change.

The first Leninist regime to deviate from Stalinism was Tito's Yugoslavia in 1948. Forced to face Stalin's attempt to seize control of their country, the Yugoslavs defected from the Soviet Bloc. Because Tito had led native communists in a protracted guerrilla war against the Germans and Italians during World War II, he was able to get away with this. He had his army and people with him, and the Soviets had never been able to gain the kind of control they had in the regimes that had been established as a result of their direct military occupation. But faced with the need to strengthen its own local support, and to justify its Marxism while in opposition to the center of Marxist-Leninist orthodoxy, Tito's Communist Party evolved what it thought would be a unique and truly socialist solution. This came to be what is called "workers' self-management." Under this system each enterprise was to be regulated by a kind of consensual association of workers and managers, and was to enjoy a substantial measure of autonomy.[34]

Workers' self-management became one of the great hopes of socialist idealists in much of the world. It promised a more humane and rational version of egalitarian socialism than Stalinism. Indeed, by the late 1950s and 1960s, Yugoslavia seemed to offer its citizens more freedom and a more rapidly rising standard of living than other Leninist societies. But, in fact, partial decentralization raised expectations and inflationary pressures. Without real market mechanisms deciding prices or allocating investment, economic efficiency did not increase fast enough to accommodate those pressures.[35] The main benefit of Yugoslavia's relative openness was that it allowed millions of Yugoslavs to emigrate to Western Europe as workers, and to remit substantial sums of hard currency back home. Also, Yugoslavia was able to enjoy significant tourist revenues from Western visitors. But as the Western European economies became labor surplus ones in the 1970s, Yugoslavia's peripheral role in the European economy became a serious problem. Labor could no longer be exported, and Yugoslav industrial goods fared poorly as exports. Furthermore, Yugoslavia's relative decentralization played into the hands of its ethnic and linguistic tensions. Local Party elites, rather than economic firms, seized the initiative and weakened central control. But as the basic levers of investment decision and ultimate control remained in bureaucratic and political hands, the stimulating effects of market mechanisms were blunted.

Since Tito's death in 1980, the contradictions of his system have become more obvious. It is difficult to maintain Leninist Party control and to encourage decentralization at the same time. In conditions of extreme ethnic polarization, such a combination becomes particularly dangerous as it splinters the ruling Leninist Party without allowing more autonomy to economically dynamic forces. Decisions come to be taken on the basis of regional alliances that have little to do with economically rational considerations.[36] This is one important reason why Leninist regimes with large ethnic minorities, particulary the Soviet Union, are unlikely to risk a Titoist type of decentralization.

The Hungarians have been able to carry out a policy of economic decentralization more effectively than the Yugoslavs. Hungary is an ethnically and socially homogeneous, small country. Since its anticommunist uprising was crushed by Soviet troops in 1956, the Party has been in unquestioned control. Faced by the certainty of Soviet intervention in case of too great a swing away from Leninism, but under the guidance of exceptionally far-sighted leaders willing to engage in limited experimentation, Hungary has done better than other Eastern European societies in legitimizing its Leninism, in providing its citizens with a considerable degree of freedom, and in improving its real standard of living. The key, as Tamas Bauer, a Hungarian economist has pointed out, is not so much that a real free market has been established, but rather that the centrally determined economic plan has ceased to be as elaborate or compulsory as in other centrally planned economies. Therefore, considerations of efficiency somewhat akin to market profitability can be used, and corrective actions can be taken more easily than in the economies of most other Leninist regimes.[37]

This policy has been particularly beneficial in Hungarian agriculture, which is collectivized, but in which individual farms are allowed to make their own decisions and profit from good performance. Combined with significant investment in agriculture, this has made Hungary a major agricultural exporter, it has reduced the urban-rural differences in standard of living and provided a sounder base for Hungary's industrial economy.[38]

The main worry in Hungary is that the Party remains politically all powerful and that continued reform depends on the tolerance of the Soviet Union. But within its limited scope, the Hungarian reforms can serve as an interesting model of how to introduce quasi-capitalist market mechanisms into a Leninist regime.

Very different from Hungary is its neighbor Romania. There, the beginings of reform in the late 1960s were stopped by the regime. Centralized Party control combined with Stalinist heavy industrialization policies were maintained, and Romania's real standard of living ceased to progress. In the 1980s, it has turned into a typically brutal, inefficient, Stalinist regime. Because the government's legitimacy is low, it has tried to stimulate loyalty by increasingly strident nationalism and official worship of the ruler, Ceausescu. Romania claims record economic growth, and yet food lines, fuel shortages, and increasing repression are its lot.[39]

At yet another extreme was the Khmer Rouge regime in Kampuchea (Cambodia) from 1975 to 1979. Rather than Stalinist industrialization, its goal was the elimination of urban life and the promotion of radical, entirely self-sufficient, rural equality. An exaggerated version of Maoist theory, it was carried out much more effectively than Maoism in China. Rough estimates are that between 1 and 2 million people were killed or died of forced labor, hardship, and famine during these years, out of a total Cambodian population of 8 million.[40]

Faced by such extreme differences in behavior, without mentioning the more confusing cases of partial liberalization, such as in Poland, which produced a collapsing regime that had to be rescued by a military coup, it becomes difficult to specify the essence of Leninism. There is as much variation, even within Eastern Europe, as in the Third World, and in many respects more than in the purely Western capitalist core societies.

Nevertheless, aside from the formal similarities outlined at the beginning of this chapter, there are some points in common. The attempt to create a new type of society, free of the defects of capitalism, produced one of two types of outcomes: Stalinism or Maoism. The former is ineffective in eliminating inequality but produces industrialization at substantial cost to its population. The latter needs equally strong applications of force and seems to produce such enormous economic inefficiencies that economic development is actually retarded. The only solution is to allow decentralization and greater liberty, but this means abandoning the original claims of Leninism, and ultimately risking the return of capitalism. Since Leninist parties cannot envision such outcomes, except under very special, protected circumstances, as in Hungary, no really satisfactory path to reform has been found thus far.

But what, then, holds Leninist regimes together, other than brute force? One of the major sources of legitimacy in the Soviet Union, China, Vietnam, Romania, Yugoslavia, Albania, Cuba, Kampuchea, North Korea, and even in Hungary, has been nationalism. National independence, cultural integrity, and ethnic solidarity have turned into the most powerful sources of regime support in many of the Leninist societies. In Yugoslavia, fear of outsiders will be the only force capable of overcoming internal ethnic tensions. In the Soviet Union, old-fashioned Russian chauvinism gives the regime support from the dominant ethnic group without which it would be seriously weakened. Vietnamese militarism would be impossible without the national pride it engenders. Hungarians are proud that they, of all Eastern Europeans, have been able to carry out liberal reforms, and this combined with fear of new Soviet intervention, gives the regime extra legitimacy. On the other hand, where nationalist sentiment perceives the regime as antinational, as in Poland, Afghanistan, or in today's Vietnamese-occupied Kampuchea, there is no possibility of political stabilization. Even East Germany must try to create a sense of nationalism to solidify the regime. Brute force, effective in the short run, is too costly in the long run, and as Stalin, Mao, Ceausescu of Romania, and Enver Hoxha of Albania discovered, state-fostered xenophobia is one of the best tools for controlling a nation.[41]

The other common aspect of Leninist regimes is that they all emphasize vertical rather than horizontal social organization. Though social equality remains an elusive dream, societies are organized along functional, vertical lines according to the corporatist model. Any sign of class-based solidarity, as in the union movement in Poland, is totally anathema to Leninist regimes. Whereas vertical organizations can be coordinated at the top by a single elite Party, horizontal, competing groups can only express their interests in political conflict. In capitalist democracies, such conflict is resolved through elections and parliamentary politics. But that, of course, denies the elite of the bureaucracy a monopoly of power. If the Japanese style of consensual, corporatist democracy might not seem so dangerous to a Leninist Party, the kind of politics that exist in Western democracies would eliminate the leading role of the Party.

In well-established Leninist societies, vertical organizations under the power of the Party have spread throughout all levels, and are more than a mere paper formality. In schools, factories, on farms, in hospitals, everywhere there exists a set of institutions within which people carry out their lives. They work, vacation, obtain housing, health care, privileges, and to a certain extent even social support from them. These institutions are coordinated with each other, and actually provide the only fully legitimate expression of political sentiment.[42]

If corporatism and aggressive nationalism are combined, one might ask, what differentiates Leninist from fascist regimes, except for a residual commitment to equality? The answer, of course, is that historically the Leninist regimes have been much more successful at creating vertically organized, institutionally united societies. In practice, fascist regimes tended to protect old elites and renounce their original reformist goals. Leninist regimes, however, have been genuinely revolutionary in this respect. Their societies are quite unlike the Western capitalist societies that still dominate the world system. Nor is there any indication that the Soviet Union has any intention of becoming more Western in that respect. Whether or not "Titoist" reforms lead any major Leninist society away from corporatism cannot yet be known. Until now, however, it is possible to say that in that substantial part of the world that is ruled by Leninist regimes it has been the corporatist rather than the original Marxist vision of social organization that has proved to be the most important revolutionary organizing force in the twentieth century.

Leninism in the World System

We can now answer the question: Where do Leninist regimes fit into the world capitalist system, if at all? Associated with this question is another one: What are the prospects for the spread of Leninism?

The diversity of regimes that might be called Leninist precludes a single answer. It is quite evident that China and Yugoslavia might be considered fairly typical semiperipheral societies. They are industrializing, but remain much less developed than the core. Yet, they participate in the world system.

Their social and economic organizations are not typically capitalist, but they are now sufficiently oriented to the world market to which they are obliged to export in order to pay for capital and technology imports so that their Leninism does not make them entirely anticapitalist.

Isolates like North Korea and Albania are not in the world system though they engage in some limited trading with the outside world. But they are not, either, part of any world socialist system, and it is perfectly clear that in the future, if they wish to develop modern technologies, they will have to reenter the world the way China has.

Most of the other Leninist societies, including the Soviet Union and the countries of Eastern Europe, engage in substantial trade with the rest of the world. Yet, they are part of another system, a virtual Soviet empire, with close enonomic, political, and cultural ties. Even Hungary, for all its outward orientation in matters of trade and economic reform, is part of this system, and is far from being a fully independent entity. The question, then, is whether or not the Soviet Union is a kind of new Leninist "core" with its own dependent "peripheries," or whether perhaps, as it claims, the Soviet Union's relations with its loyal allies, including not only Eastern Europe but also Cuba, Mongolia, and Vietnam, are the model for a new type of egalitarian world socialist order.

All the evidence indicates that neither assertion is correct. The Soviet Union certainly does not exploit its lesser clients and allies in a typically colonial way. It is not, on the whole, techologically superior to the more advanced Eastern European economies of East Germany, Czechoslovakia, Poland, or Hungary. But even in its relations with less-developed parts of its system, it does not primarily seek to extract raw materials or dump industrial goods. It does some of each, but its primary relationship with the less-developed parts of its empire is one of giving aid, large amounts of it in the cases of Cuba and Vietnam, in return for military alliances. In Eastern Europe, too, it subsidizes the economies of its clients largely by selling them raw materials at below world market prices in order to keep relative internal peace, and thus a firm allegiance to the military-political aims of the Soviet Union. On the other hand it has not achieved the kind of regional specialization and cooperation which would create a really unified socialist international economy.[43]

There are two distinct parts of the Soviet-led system. Cuba and Vietnam are fully independent, fiercely nationalistic countries with large international ambitions that could not possibly be satisfied if they acted alone. Dominated by strongly ideological leaderships, their ambitions fit with those of the Soviet Union, which seeks to weaken the world capitalist system. The other part of the Soviet international system is its true empire, Eastern Europe and Mongolia (and presumably, eventually Afghanistan). These countries are not free agents, but remain politically subservient to the Soviet Union. Only Romania has a somewhat intermediary position, in some respects like Cuba or Vietnam (it has its own, highly ambitious international political aims), but in others still dependent on the Soviet Union.

Aid to the distant militants of the Soviet international system, Cuba and Vietnam, is extremely costly. Both countries have inefficient economies because of their ideological rigor, and both have depressed the standard of living of their societies to sustain the military posture that their leaders' international goals demand. Cuba is a major military force in Africa, and Vietnam occupies Laos and Kampuchea. (Vietnam spends some 30 percent of its GNP on its military.)[44]

Cuba in the early 1980s received some $3 billion worth of aid a year from the Soviet Union, amounting to close to one-quarter of its entire GNP.[45] Vietnam probably received some $2 billion a year, equal to something on the order of 20 percent of its GNP.[46] (This is analogous to what the United States does for its own favorite ally, Israel.) Together, these two countries alone probably cost the Soviet Union 0.5 percent of its entire GNP, or a proportion greater than the entire foreign aid burden that the United States has taken upon itself.

It is easy to see why the Soviet Union is careful about taking on new commitments of the Cuban or Vietnamese type. It is quite correct that these two countries contribute significantly to Soviet strength by providing firm allies and distant bases they would otherwise lack, and especially by creating foci of potential anticapitalist activity in Latin America and Southeast Asia. But the power of the Soviets to maintain such allies in the face of the inevitably disastrous economic results brought about by ideologically committed Leninists, is limited by the Soviet Union's own economic weakness.

The Eastern European empire of the Soviet Union is a different matter. Under Stalin, it was a profitable undertaking. It provided industrial goods for the Soviet Union, it was a source of sheer plunder, and it gave the Soviets strategic protection against possible Western attacks. The costs were lower than the gains. But since Stalin, the situation has changed. The immediate postwar chaos that allowed the Soviets to install Leninist regimes with relative ease has been replaced by stability. The promises of the Eastern European regimes to their people have been somewhat met, and have raised expectations for even greater material progress. The repression that characterized the Stalinist years has eased, but what seemed acceptable in the days right after World War II now strikes many as intolerable. Local nationalist sentiment now views the Soviets as the main enemy. In this situation, the relative economic stagnation of Leninist economies, and their inability to provide the desired levels of consumer goods exacerbates the problem. To meet this problem, the Soviet Union encouraged the Eastern European countries to borrow capital and technology from the West and to trade more with the West during the 1970s. This, they felt, would relieve the Soviet Union of subsidizing Eastern Europe and yet maintain some loyalty to the Leninist regimes the Soviets feel they must have to protect their imperial domination. The results were not what the Soviets had expected. Capital infusion into overcentralized, inefficient economies simply produced temporary booms. But investments did not yield products that could be marketed with any ease on the world capitalist market, so it became difficult for the Eastern European countries to pay back their loans. For the Soviets, who pay for their Western imports with raw material exports, the problem could be solved. For resource-poor Eastern Europe, it was more difficult, so the Soviets had to assume many of the debts of their European dependents in order to maintain the credit-worthiness of the entire system. The Soviets also had to subsidize Eastern Europe in other ways, through favorable trade deals, direct loans and grants, and by selling raw materials, especially oil, at below world market prices. Overall, by the early 1980s, this was costing the Soviet Union some $21 billion a year.[47] This amounted to roughly 2 percent of its GNP.

The Soviet Union, then, is neither at the core of a "socialist world system," akin to the capitalist world system, nor has it created a new international system that might foster rapid economic growth. It has succeeded in creating a veritable empire, and has so bound most Eastern European countries to itself that they can hardly be said to have autonomous institutions or even armies.[48] But it pays for whatever strategic benefits it garners, not only by directly subsidizing its colonies and allies, but also by having to maintain an enormous military machine, a large part of which is devoted entirely to keeping Eastern Europe and now Afghanistan under control. The Soviet military budget is something on the order of between 12 percent and 15 percent of its total GNP. (The United States spends about 7 to 8 percent of its GNP for its military.)[49] There is little question that all these costs seriously depress the Soviet living standard and economic growth.[50]

Does this mean that the Soviet Union is not a threat to the world capitalist system, and that Leninism is no longer a viable, dynamic ideology? An awareness of the severe limitations on the Soviet empire also reveals its strengths, and its potential threat. Rather than maintaining itself by the strength of its economic system, it keeps itself strong by controlling its own population and its imperial holdings and allies at tremendous economic cost. In so doing, it prevents or slows innovation and progress, insists on considerable ideological orthodoxy, and stifles the kind of flexibility which would allow it and its dependencies to escape their dilemmas. Its empire neither contributes to its economic strength by being a source of profitable trade nor by being part of a growing market system that might allow all of its members to expand their GNPs. But when all that is said, it does not eliminate the fact that the Soviets operate a formidable military machine, and that they remain willing to pay huge costs to keep their power intact and thus to continue to challenge the world capitalist system. Their own resource base is so great that they can continue to do these things.

The Soviet system has in effect generated a self-perpetuating bureaucracy whose entire legitimacy and measure of success is increasingly based on its international power and prestige. To admit to itself, or to the Soviet people, that Leninism is not the wave of the future, and that it cannot, without very thorough reform, achieve its internal goals, would be to question the quasi-religious foundation of almost seventy years of history. Such an admission, of course, would decisively shake the power base of the bureaucracy, both civilian and military, which rules the Soviet Union. As this bureaucracy, unlike Western bureaucracies, has a monopoly of power and does not tolerate the growth of rival power centers, there is no likelihood that this would happen. Its internal weakness makes it all the more necessary for the Soviet Union to maintain its international position and improve it.

Nor is there any chance that in a world of nuclear weapons anyone could seriously threaten Soviet hegemony in its own empire. The Soviets do not have to match American technological prowess to be able to destroy America in case of war. They only need to have such a large array of nuclear weapons that some would be guaranteed to hit the United States under any conceivable conditions, and this they have. Therefore, the United States would never risk challenging fundamental Soviet interests, anymore than the Soviets have ever been willing to engage the United States in its critical areas of interest. The outcome would be too unpredictable and dangerous.

In the past, the giant, inefficient empires that kept much of the world stagnant for so long eventually collapsed because the costs of maintaining themselves against outside invasion and internal revolts became too great to bear. This is unlikely to happen to the Soviet system. Modern technology makes both defense and internal repression easier, and the Soviet's resource base, however inefficiently used, is large enough to pay for them.

But if the Soviet system seems secure for the foreseeable future, and potentially highly dangerous if provoked too far, the dynamism of Leninist ideology is another matter. The evident failure of orthodox Leninism to produce anything but sheer military power makes it less appealing than it was when it could promise rapid economic growth with relative social equality. For those nationalists fighting for national independence and trying to promote rudimentary economic and social progress, Leninism continues to have considerable appeal. In Nicaragua, Ethiopia, and Angola—all beset by domestic dissension and dangerous outside enemies—the Stalinist model promises solutions. If the Soviet Union or Cuba can also provide aid, such regimes may well become loyal Soviet allies running very orthodox Leninist-Stalinist societies. There may be other, future cases that will take the same direction, particularly in Africa. But it should be noted that now the model only appeals to the very poorest, most frustrated parts of the periphery. No longer is Leninism nearly as appealing to semiperipheral societies as it was earlier in the twentieth century.

As for the appeal of Maoism, it retains some popularity among intellectuals in the Third World, and among some in the capitalist core. It may even, under some special circumstances, come to power. It will then produce economic and social catastrophes, but it is very unlikely to produce allies of the Soviet Union, which is as much a target of Maoist hatred as the capitalist West. In sum, then, Leninist regimes have to be taken into account as major actors in international politics. But they lack the dynamism that might make them a long-term threat to the future of the world capitalist system. They will remain as a peculiar kind of semiperiphery, neither entirely in the world capitalist system nor entirely isolated from it. Like nuclear weapons, they will not go away. But they will not fundamentally alter the future direction of social change for the rest of the world, either, unless there happens to be a great global war. There will be more societies that will become Leninist in the future, but not many, and probably not many significant ones. Whatever conversions there will be will be balanced by some defections away from Leninism, so that the balance of forces between the capitalist world system and the Leninist societies will remain roughly at its present point for a long time to come.

Only if the major actors in the capitalist world retreat into a kind of neo-mercantilistic position and begin to fight among themselves, would the Soviet Union, its empire and allies, have much chance of significantly increasing their power. But if this happens, it will not be because of the inherent strength of Leninism. It will be, as Lenin himself originally saw when he predicted the ultimate fall of the world capitalist system, because of rivalries generated by capitalist competition.[51]

CONCLUSIONS

CHAPTER *11*

Eras and Cycles: Patterns of Social Change

*T*here is no single theoretical model capable of encompassing all forms of societies, just as there is none that can account for all the types of social change that have occurred. To say that it is necessary to look at class structures, at global as well as local types of interaction, at geography, at science and technology, and at law is merely to offer a list of important aspects of social structure. This is not particularly helpful in trying to uncover the patterns that might govern change.

The key to a sensible theoretical approach to the study of social change is the recognition that there exist long periods of history in which the essential forces at work remain quite similar. Within such eras it is possible to construct a model that takes into account these forces, because roughly similar cycles of events occur repeatedly. These cycles can be compared with one another, and some common causes of change can be uncovered. But repetitive cycles are limited to specific eras. Within any single era, cyclical changes are not actually unvarying; and over time, enough permanent changes accumulate to make the general model invalid. Eventually, eras end, to be replaced by new ones, with different sets of cycles and new mainsprings of change. To understand new eras, new models are necessary.[1]

Chapter 2 of this book is about social change in a now dead era, the era of advanced, preindustrial agrarian societies. Because of their fairly advanced technology (for their time, that is) the great civilizations of Europe, the Near East, and Asia were able to support dense populations, powerful states, and highly literate, elaborate cultures. But because populations in that era grew more quickly than technology advanced, societies tended to experience recurrent crises of overpopulation, malnutrition, disease, and social chaos. Nor could they escape the destiny imposed on them by their geographical limitations. Proximity to nomads, dependence on fragile irrigation systems, and endemic diseases combined with population cycles to magnify the periodic catastrophes.

Western Europe, however, was able to escape these limitations because of several fortuitous geographical circumstances. It was relatively immune from nomadic incursions after the tenth century, it was not dependent on irrigation, and it was far less subject to tropical endemic parasites than were the other great centers of civilization. But this was not all. Its unique class structure allowed independent towns to gain more independence than in other parts of the world, and this fostered a systematically rational approach to law, science, and religion. It also produced a type of government more favorable to the growth of trade and technology than in the classical empires of the East. Western Europe was therefore propelled out of the era of advanced agrarian societies into a new stage of history.

Most of this book—the part following a description of the transition into the new era, Chapter 3—is about the modern era, the era of industrial societies. This era differs fundamentally from the previous one because technology and science advance much more rapidly than population growth. In the modern era it has become possible, for the first time in human history, to have a prolonged, sustained rise in the average standard of well-being of the population. Societies have been less limited by their geographical circumstances than in previous eras. The old cycles of overpopulation and recurrent disaster have ended. But new cycles have taken their place, and much of this book has been an attempt to describe these cycles and show how they affect social change.

The key element in the cycles that dominate the modern era, as might be expected, is technological change. Each industrial cycle has witnessed an early stage in which new technologies are applied to production, great profits are made, and new firms developed; but then markets become saturated, overinvestment in now aging economic sectors produces more failures, and a crisis sets in. Each time, however, the accompanying unemployment, political anguish, and social disruption of a declining industrial period have only been the prelude to the development of new processes, much more advanced technologies, and the start of a new cycle of dynamic expansion.

Not only the economies, but also the politics of the industrial era are fundamentally different from those of the preceding, agrarian era. Whereas in the previous era politics consisted mostly of various elites competing with one another for control over the key resource, taxable peasants, from which they all lived, in the modern era whole populations have become more active participants in political competition. Modern states, whether or not they are democratic, claim a much higher degree of loyalty from their subjects than do agrarian states. They are also much more concerned with the general welfare of their subjects, not only to maintain political legitimacy, but also to sustain economic production, which is the base of all political power. While rivalry between states may seem like a mere repetition of the endless wars of the past, in the modern era international conflict has actually been more intimately linked to economic and social change than in the past. The economy of the modern era has increasingly been a global one, and the swings of the various industrial stages have both provoked and been intensified by their international ramifications.

The first industrial cycle, the age of the textile industrial revolution, lasted from the 1780s to the 1820s. The fact that it took more than a decade for the next cycle to develop and restabilize the industrialized economies had much to do with the unstable political atmosphere of Europe in the 1830s, and particularly in the 1840s. The second cycle, that of iron and railroads, lasted into the early 1870s. The transition to the next stage, that of steel and the growth of the chemical industry, was sufficiently painful to provoke intense imperialistic rivalries among the advanced Western powers. This led directly to the international tension that produced World War I. That war, in turn, made the transition to the fourth industrial age of automobiles and high mass consumption particulary difficult. Instead of the relatively smooth transition that might have taken place in the 1920s and 1930s, there was the Great Depression of the 1930s and the Second World War. The fourth cycle, then, only began to benefit the large majority of people in the industrial countries after 1950. The great tragedies of the twentieth century can only be explained as the unfortunate conjunction of normal cyclical changes combined with bitter international conflicts that have stemmed from them. The question, of course, is whether or not the present cyclical change that began in the late 1970s will produce a renewed series of traumatic events.

The expansion of the West in the modern era was the result of its technological and scientific dominance. But in the twentieth century, one of the main themes of global social change has been the revolt of the periphery against the Western core. Some analysts, for example, Immanuel Wallerstein, have seen in this movement the seeds of a transformation from the present era to the next one, the era of a world socialist system. It was about 140 years ago that Karl Marx noted that the class conflicts of any particular era foreshadow the nature of the next era. The emergence of towns and the bourgeoisie as an independent force in the Middle Ages set the stage for the capitalist, or modern industrial era. Marx felt that the rise of the proletariat, an organized working class in the present era, would eventually produce the next, socialist era. Wallerstein has elevated this prediction to an international level, trying to show that the modern era rests on the growing intensification of exploitation in the periphery, and that eventually revolutionary forces in the periphery will alter the system.[2]

There is little doubt that in the future the growing power of the new semiperiphery will have some potential to disequilibrate the present world system. On the other hand, there is little evidence that the modern era has run its course. As the world moves into the fifth industrial stage, the same patterns of sectoral decay in the old leading industries, and the rise of new firms, new regions of technological dynamism, international tensions, and pressures on governments to help smooth the transition are being repeated. The model that has been used to describe these changes seems as operative today as ever. This means that the main source of political instability remains, as it has long been, within the advanced part of the world, not the periphery.

It might seem that the rise of a large communist, or better, Leninist, set of countries has changed the pattern of the modern era so fundamentally that the old model no longer applies. In fact, this is not the case. Technological dynamism does not come from Leninist societies, the most powerful of which in some ways more closely resembles a classical agrarian empire than a modern society. Only insofar as Leninist societies manage to escape the Stalinist type of regime that still exists in the Soviet Union, however modified it may be, will they be able to join the core of the modern world system.

This is not to suggest that there has been no important change since the onset of the modern, industrial era. On the contrary, along with changes in technology and science, which have been immense, there have been ideological transformations which point to a future that may be quite different.

In the nineteenth century, the main ideological dispute was between bourgeois liberalism and the remnants of older, preindustrial world views. But by the end of the century, and certainly by the early twentieth, this had changed. Three ideological currents competed with one another: liberalism (now a more conservative, established force), socialism, and corporatism. All three have operated within the framework of growing nationalism. By the late twentieth century it is beginning to seem that socialism is a spent force, but that corporatism, under one guise or another, is likely to dominate the next century. With continuing waves of industrial progress and decline, and the ever-growing pressure on governments to act in order to assuage the ills produced by these cycles, corporatist solidarity will increasingly appear as a satisfactory solution. If this happens, a whole new set of political constraints will be produced to block further progress and change. To some extent, this has already happened in the Soviet Union and some other Leninist societies, which explains why they have taken on a strangely old-fashioned, preindustrial aspect.

But predicting the future is impossible. In Japan, the evolution of a benign corporatism has certainly helped the entire society make very rapid progress. In large measure, this is because the aim of the entire political and social system is to make Japan highly competitive in the international marketplace. Could such a form of corporatism exist in a country with its own, fully independent foreign policy and stake in the international power game? Or is it merely possible, as in the case of Japan, when a country has been forced to abdicate a major role in international politics by a powerful patron such as the United States? Can such unusual circumstances ever be maintained, much less repeated?

A key question for the future is whether or not technological and scientific progress can continue if the long-term strengthening of the state and of nationalism also continue. Originally fostered by free-thinking, rational intellectuals and businessmen in the towns, such progress is increasingly subject to state-sponsored intervention and manipulation. Will modern states overturn the old law that the more powerful the state, the less likely it is to foster innovation? That is really what is important about the possible emergence of a corporatist solution to social and economic problems. It is conceivable that in the fairly distant future such an outcome would end the present era and lead to a more stagnant new era. But that is too far away to be able to say what such a new era might look like.

Prediction is all the more impossible because increasing technological prowess has made it possible for global disaster to occur on an unprecedented scale. Nuclear war, or massive alteration of the environment through some kind of ecological change is always possible, and seems to most people to be of far greater concern than the rather abstract notions of future change outlined here. Even without such cataclysms, however, it remains the case that political leaders do not fully understand the basic causes of social change and progress, and therefore they tend to take narrowly short-term views of both economic change and international competition. That makes some sort of catastrophic outcome far more likely than if a greater understanding of social change were available.

The paradox is that competition between states, economic and political rivalry, and international tension are the best guarantees of continuing progress. Thus, just as the emergence of the modern, rational era came from a long series of unresolved class conflicts within Western societies, so is the continuation of this era dependent on permanent international conflict. The very tension which presents the greatest threat to our survival assures that if we survive at all, some states, in order to compete better, will be obliged to encourage intellectual freedom and progress.

In conclusion, then, it is obligatory to study social change as a global phenomenon. Not only are all societies linked in an obvious way, but it is by their very interaction that one of the main driving forces of the modern era continues to operate. The original social setting of the late Middle Ages which caused Western progress in the first place has long ceased to exist. Only the modern world system's configuration reproduces an analogous, conflict-ridden setting. For the near future, certainly well into the next century, there is little likelihood that this will be changed very drastically. Instead, we can expect that the present, fifth industrial cycle will gain ground, transform economies and societies, make life ever more materially comfortable, and then come to some sort of end in a half-century or so. Then, a new crisis will come; and a sixth, as yet quite unknowable, industrial cycle will begin. As long as the present world system can walk the thin line between state-imposed stagnation and intense international rivalry, the modern era will continue. When the world steps over that line, in one direction or the other, into global war or into a uniform kind of corporatism, then, and only then, will a new era dawn. What its shape will be is as difficult for us to tell as it would have been for a thirteenth-century individual to predict the twentieth century.

NOTES

Chapter 1

1. This is Immanuel Wallerstein's view of the world. It is explained in his *The Modern World-System: Capitalist Agriculture and the Origins of the European World-Economy in the Sixteenth Century* and in *The Modern World-System II: Mercantilism and the Consolidation of the European World-Economy.* For a discussion of the strengths and limitations of this world view see Chirot and Hall, "World-System Theory," pp. 81–106.

Chapter 2

1. McEvedy and Jones, *World Population History,* pp. 41–72, 133–53, 166–73, 182–85, 219–29.
2. E. Jones, *European Miracle,* pp. 8–9, 21–44.
3. Ibid., pp. 48–51.
4. McEvedy and Jones, *World Population History,* pp. 227–30.
5. E. Jones, *European Miracle,* p. 150; Ashtor, *History of the Near East,* p. 254.
6. Thrupp, "Medieval Industry," in Cipolla, *Fontana Economic History,* Vol. 1, p. 226.
7. A. Wright, *Sui Dynasty,* pp. 177–81; E. Jones, *European Miracle,* pp. 210–12.
8. E. Jones, *European Miracle,* pp. 104–109.
9. Bloch, *Feudal Society,* pp. 3–56.
10. Poggi, *Development of the Modern State,* pp. 36–42.
11. M. Weber, *Economy and Society,* pp. 1351–52.
12. Bloch, *Feudal Society,* p. 352.
13. Anderson, *Passages from Antiquity to Feudalism,* p. 150.
14. Ibid., pp. 135–37.
15. Bloch, *Feudal Society,* pp. 428–29.
16. Barraclough, *Medieval Papacy,* pp. 52–117.
17. Poggi, *Development of the Modern State,* p. 48; M. Weber, *Economy and Society,* p. 1086.
18. Ullman, *Short History of the Papacy,* pp. 213–74.
19. Stephenson and Marcham, *English Constitutional History,* pp. 115–26.
20. Ibid., pp. 150–61.
21. Myers, *Parliaments and Estates,* pp. 59–95.
22. Poggi, *Development of the Modern State,* pp. 42–59.
23. Eberhard, *History of China,* pp. 78–79; Ortei, "Economic Life of the Empire," in Cook et al., *Cambridge Ancient History,* Vol. 12, p. 248.
24. Schluchter, *Rise of Western Rationalism,* pp. 101–102.
25. Ostrogorsky, *Byzantine State,* pp. 69–70, 213–14.
26. Derrett, "Entwicklung des indischen Rechts," in Schluchter, *Max Webers Studie,* pp. 178–201.
27. M. Weber, *Economy and Society,* pp. 814, 832.
28. Ibid., p. 812.
29. Ostrogorsky, *Byzantine State,* pp. 416, 496, and more generally, pp. 311–509.
30. Ronan and Needham, *Shorter Science and Civilization,* p. 84.
31. Hodgson, *Venture of Islam,* Vol. 2, pp. 329–68; Brooke, *Twelfth Century Renaissance,* pp. 35–37.

32. Schluchter, *Rise of Western Rationalism,* pp. 162–65.
33. Cohn, *Pursuit of the Millennium.*
34. M. Weber, *Economy and Society,* p. 468.
35. Ibid., p. 472.
36. Ibid., p. 476.
37. Ibid., pp. 482–83.
38. Elvin, "Chinese Cities," in Abrams and Wrigley, *Towns in Societies,* pp. 85–87.
39. M. Weber, *Protestant Ethic and Capitalism.*

Chapter 3
 1. McNeill, *Plagues and People,* pp. 203–205; Wolf, *People Without History,* Pt. 2.
 2. Boxer, *Dutch Seaborne Empire,* p. 236.
 3. Cipolla, *Guns, Sails and Empires.*
 4. McEvedy and Jones, *World Population History,* p. 171.
 5. Ibid. For more details, see Ho, *Population of China.*
 6. Levenson, *European Expansion,* pp. 11–22.
 7. Cipolla, *Guns, Sails and Empires,* pp. 106–109.
 8. Braudel, *The Mediterranean and the Mediterranean World,* Vol. 1, pp. 154–58; Wallerstein, *Modern World-System I,* pp. 43–44.
 9. Payne, *Spain and Portugal,* pp. 205–23.
10. Ibid., pp. 126–30.
11. Chaunu, *Conquête et exploitation,* pp. 245–76.
12. From J. H. Parry, *The Establishment of the European Hegemony, 1415–1715,* cited in Levenson, *European Expansion,* pp. 24–25.
13. Bovill, *Caravans of the Sahara.*
14. Godinho, "Création et dynamisme économique," pp. 32–36.
15. Boxer, *Portuguese Expansion.*
16. Hamilton, "American Treasure," pp. 338–57; Chaunu, *Conquête et exploitation,* pp. 300–310.
17. Payne, *Spain and Portugal,* pp. 232–38.
18. De Vries, *Economy of Europe,* pp. 27–38.
19. Elliott, *Old World and New,* p. 73.
20. Boxer, *Portuguese Expansion,* pp. 53–54.
21. Wolf, *People Without History,* pp. 150–52, 159–63.
22. Hobsbawm, "Crisis of the Seventeenth Century," in Aston, *Crisis in Europe,* pp. 5–62; De Vries, *Economy of Europe,* pp. 16–21.
23. Wilson, *Dutch Republic,* pp. 206–29.
24. De Vries, *Economy of Europe,* p. 117.
25. Ibid., p. 120.
26. Wilson, *Dutch Republic,* pp. 42–58.
27. Davis, "English Foreign Trade," pp. 150–66.
28. Deane, *First Industrial Revolution,* p. 56; E. B. Schumpeter, *English Trade Statistics,* pp. 17–18.
29. E. B. Schumpeter, *English Trade Statistics,* pp. 11–12, 17–18; Barnes, *History of the Corn Laws,* p. 10.
30. Hobsbawm, *Age of Revolution,* pp. 51–55.
31. Crouzet, "Croissances comparées," p. 262.
32. Thomson, *Plantation Societies,* pp. 43–49, 115–17, 213–63; Genovese, *World the Slaveholders Made.*
33. Curtin, *Atlantic Slave Trade;* Wolf, *People Without History,* pp. 196–231.
34. Wolf, *People Without History,* pp. 192–94.
35. Hobsbawm, *Industry and Empire,* pp. 48–49.
36. Kula, *Théorie économique;* Blum, "Rise of Serfdom in Eastern Europe," pp. 807–36; Maddalena, "Rural Europe," in Cipolla, *Fontana Economic History,* Vol. 2, p. 300.

37. Wallerstein, *Modern World-System I,* pp. 97–99.
38. McNeill, *Plagues and People,* pp. 6–7.
39. Eberhard, *History of China,* pp. 280–96.
40. Parker, *Spain and the Netherlands,* pp. 17–43.
41. Tilly, *Sociology Meets History,* p. 114.
42. Ibid., pp. 115–17; Sée, *L'Évolution commerciale,* pp. 107–11; Hecksher, *Mercantilism,* Vol. 1, pp. 82–84.
43. Tilly, *Sociology Meets History,* pp. 118–20.
44. Wedgewood, *Thirty Years War.*
45. Braun, "Taxation," in Tilly, *Formation of National States,* p. 271; Anderson, *Absolutist State,* pp. 265, 338–42.
46. Anderson, *Absolutist State,* pp. 123–25, 135.
47. Moore, *Dictatorship and Democracy,* pp. 3–39; Poggi, *Development of the Modern State,* p. 58.
48. Braun, "Taxation," in Tilly, *Formation of National States,* pp. 282–98.
49. Beard and Beard, *Rise of American Civilization,* pp. 189–296.
50. Rudé, "Bread Riots in Paris," in Kaplow, *French Revolution,* pp. 191–210; Moore, *Dictatorship and Democracy,* pp. 40–110; Cobban, *Social Interpretation of the French Revolution;* Lefebvre, *Coming of the French Revolution.*
51. Lefebvre, *The Great Fear.*
52. Tocqueville, *Old Regime and the French Revolution,* pp. 157–211.
53. G. Wright, *France in Modern Times,* pp. 66–106.
54. Hampshire, *Age of Reason,* p. 32.
55. Bronowski, *Common Sense of Science,* p. 30.
56. Ibid., p. 56.
57. Elvin, *Chinese Past,* pp. 179–99.
58. Ibid., p. 180.
59. Ibid., p. 194.
60. Merton, "Science and Economy," in Merton, *Social Theory and Structure,* pp. 150–61.
61. Elvin, *Chinese Past,* pp. 215–25.
62. Ibid., p. 180.
63. Hodgson, *Venture of Islam,* Vol. 2, p. 473.
64. Ibid., Vol. 3, pp. 121–22.
65. Merton, "Puritanism," in Merton, *Social Theory and Structure,* p. 333.
66. Ibid., pp. 329–37.
67. Cohen, *Birth of a New Physics,* pp. 137, 165.
68. Merton, "Puritanism," in Merton, *Social Theory and Structure,* p. 334.
69. Huizinga, *Dutch Civilization,* pp. 58–59.
70. Singer, "Religion and Science," in Needham, *Science, Religion and Reality,* pp. 136–42.
71. Elliott, *Imperial Spain,* pp. 217, 223, 363–64.
72. Merton, *Science, Technology and Society.*
73. Kuhn, *Essential Tension,* p. 59.
74. Ibid., pp. 52–65.
75. Ibid., p. 142.
76. Bronowski, *Common Sense of Science,* p. 55.
77. Berlin, *Age of Enlightenment;* Letwin, *Origins of Scientific Economics,* pp. 207–28.
78. Kiernan, "Revolution," in Burke, *Cambridge Modern History,* Vol. 13, pp. 224–25.
79. Hobsbawm, *Age of Revolution,* pp. 22–43, 277–85.

Chapter 4

1. Kuznets, *Growth of Nations,* p. 24. Phyllis Deane, in *The First Industrial Revolution,* p. 6, estimates that England's per capita GNP at this time was about 50% higher. Part of the difference is that her estimates are based on the overvalued British pound of the 1950s. But her estimates of growth rates during the eighteenth century are also higher;

she states that English GNP/capita grew almost 2½ times from 1700 to 1800. Kuznets's estimates are based on more thorough and recent research.

2. Deane, *First Industrial Revolution*, p. 10.
3. Kuznets, *Growth of Nations*, pp. 13, 24.
4. World Bank, *Development Report 1983*, pp. 148–49.
5. Kuznets, *Growth of Nations*, pp. 27, 31.
6. Landes, *Unbound Prometheus*, p. 65.
7. Mitchell, *European Historical Statistics*, pp. 251–52.
8. Mitchell, "Statistical Appendix," in Cipolla, *Fontana Economic History*, Vol. 4, p. 747; Deane, "Great Britain," in Cipolla, *Fontana Economic History*, Vol. 4, pp. 221–22; Pollard, "Discipline in the Industrial Revolution," pp. 266–71.
9. Hobsbawm, *Industry and Empire*, p. 64.
10. Ibid., pp. 76–77.
11. Deane, *First Industrial Revolution*, p. 233; J. Schumpeter, *Business Cycles*, Vol. 1, pp. 224–25.
12. Hobsbawm, *Industry and Empire*, p. 94.
13. Ibid., p. 110.
14. Sweezy, *Theory of Capitalist Development.*
15. Hobsbawm, *Industry and Empire*, pp. 109–11.
16. Mitchell, *European Historical Statistics*, pp. 216, 316.
17. Bureau of the Census, *Historical Statistics (to 1970)*, p. 731; Rostow, *World Economy*, p. 152; Mitchell, *European Historical Statistics*, pp. 215–18.
18. Rostow, *World Economy*, p. 155; Mitchell, *European Historical Statistics*, pp. 315–18; Briggs, "Technology and Development," p. 59.
19. Kuznets, *Growth of Nations*, pp. 11–14, 24.
20. Mitchell, *European Historical Statistics*, pp. 12–14.
21. Kuznets, *Growth of Nations*, pp. 250–51.
22. Rostow, *World Economy*, pp. 70–71. Rostow uses Michael G. Mulhall's estimates of 1892 from his *The Dictionary of Statistics.*
23. Woodruff, "Emergence of an International Economy," in Cipolla, *Fontana Economic History*, Vol. 4, pp. 658–64; Hobsbawm, *Industry and Empire*, p. 137.
24. Hobsbawm, *Age of Capital*, pp. 220–21.
25. Polanyi, *The Great Transformation*, pp. 77–86.
26. Ibid., p. 102.
27. Hobsbawm, *Industry and Empire*, pp. 82–83.
28. Hobsbawm, *Age of Capital*, pp. 230–50.
29. Hobsbawm, *Industry and Empire*, pp. 156–57.
30. Derry, *Short History of England*, pp. 114–19.
31. Ibid., pp. 297–302; Mitchell, *European Historical Statistics*, p. 8.
32. Mitchell, *European Historical Statistics*, pp. 297–302.
33. Woodruff, "Emergence of an International Economy," pp. 708–709.
34. Mitchell, *European Historical Statistics*, pp. 344–48.
35. Skidmore and Smith, *Modern Latin America*, pp. 324–25; Webster, "British, French and American Influences," in Humphreys and Lynch, *Origins of Latin American Revolutions*, pp. 75–83.
36. Hobsbawm, *Industry and Empire*, p. 147.
37. Curtin, *Image of Africa*, pp. 432–56; Derry, *Short History of England*, pp. 184–86.
38. Spear, *India, A Modern History*, pp. 215–88.
39. Wolf, *People Without History*, pp. 247–52.
40. M. Morris, "Reinterpretation of Indian Economic History," pp. 606–18.
41. Purcell, *Boxer Uprising*, pp. 65–80; Wolf, *People Without History*, pp. 252–58; Beeching, *Chinese Opium Wars.*
42. Marlow, *History of Anglo-Egyptian Relations*, pp. 30–137; Webster, *Foreign Policy of Palmerston*, Vol. 2.
43. E. Weber, *Peasants Into Frenchmen.*

44. Taylor, *Hapsburg Monarchy.*
45. Stearns, *1848: Revolutionary Tide in Europe.*
46. Hamerow, *Restoration, Revolution, Reaction,* pp. 33–37, 102–106; Calhoun, *Question of Class Struggle.*
47. Eyck, *Bismarck and the German Empire.*
48. Craig and George, *Force and Statecraft,* pp. 28–47.
49. Langer, *Encyclopedia of World History,* pp. 788–871; Darby and Fullard, *Cambridge History Atlas,* pp. 242–46, 253, 264–65, 275, 282–83.
50. Lenin, *Imperialism.*
51. Woodruff, "Emergence of an International Economy," p. 708; Mitchell, *European Historical Statistics,* pp. 408–16.
52. Lenin, *Imperialism,* p. 63.
53. Woodruff, *Impact of Western Man,* pp. 154–55.
54. Cited in Fieldhouse, "Imperialism," in Boulding and Mukerjee, *Imperialism and Colonialism,* p. 120.
55. Minchinton, "Patterns of Demand," in Cipolla, *Fontana Economic History,* Vol. 3, p. 106; Bureau of the Census, *Historical Statistics (to 1957),* p. 718. Calculations for the United States are based on actual growth of military spending, not just for armaments.
56. J. Schumpeter, *Imperialism.*
57. Juglar, *Des crises commerciales,* pp. 390–93.
58. Fels, "American Business Cycles," in Clark and Cohen, *Fluctuations, Growth, and Stabilization,* pp. 168–91.
59. Gourevitch, "Trade, Coalitions, and Liberty," pp. 281–313; Landes, *Unbound Prometheus,* pp. 231–37; Mitchell, *European Historical Statistics,* pp. 407–16.
60. Wolf, *People Without History,* pp. 296–353.
61. Gourevitch, "Trade, Coalitions, and Liberty."
62. Landes, *Unbound Prometheus,* pp. 242–43.
63. Hobsbawm, *Industry and Empire,* p. 159.
64. Mitchell, *European Historical Statistics,* pp. 40–43; Bureau of the Census, *Historical Statistics (to 1970),* p. 57.
65. Mitchell, *European Historical Statistics,* pp. 407–16, 424; Bureau of the Census, *Historical Statistics (to 1970),* p. 224.
66. Mitchell, *European Historical Statistics,* pp. 397, 400; Bureau of the Census, *Historical Statistics (to 1970),* pp. 368, 383.
67. Landes, *Unbound Prometheus,* pp. 269–76.
68. Lilley, "Progress and the Industrial Revolution," in Cipolla, *Fontana Economic History,* Vol. 3, pp. 243–49.
69. Ibid., p. 246.
70. Landes, *Unbound Prometheus,* pp. 249–69.
71. Mitchell, *European Historical Statistics,* pp. 223–25.
72. Ibid., pp. 290–91.
73. Bureau of the Census, *Historical Statistics (to 1970),* p. 828; Landes, *Unbound Prometheus,* pp. 281–90.
74. Bureau of the Census, *Historical Statistics (to 1970),* pp. 667, 692–94; Mitchell, *European Historical Statistics,* pp. 179–81, 223, 271.
75. Wallerstein, "Semiperipheral Countries," in Wallerstein, *Capitalist World-Economy,* pp. 95–118.
76. Chirot, *Social Change in the Twentieth Century,* pp. 45–47.

Chapter 5
1. Kuznets, *Growth of Nations,* pp. 11–40; for Russia, see Crisp, "Russia," in Cameron, *Early Stages of Industrialization,* p. 184.
2. Kuznets, "Quantitative Aspects of Economic Growth," Pt. 2, pp. 82–95; Cipolla, *History of World Population,* p. 29.
3. Love, "Raul Prebisch and Unequal Exchange," pp. 45–72.

4. Emmanuel, *Unequal Exchange.*
5. Furtado, *Economic Growth of Brazil,* pp. 193–203.
6. Bairoch, *Development of the Third World,* pp. 111–34.
7. See note 1, this chapter.
8. Mitchell, *Statistics: Africa and Asia,* pp. 39–43; McEvedy and Jones, *World Population History,* pp. 201, 227, 287, 306, 314; Cipolla, *Fontana Economic History,* Vol. 4 (various articles), pp. 392, 398, 412, 446, 672–74, 676, 747–48; W. A. Lewis, *Tropical Development,* pp. 103, 148, 209, 258; Rostow, *World Economy,* pp. 423, 468; Bureau of the Census, *Historical Statistics (to 1970),* pp. 8, 138, 889, 898; Miller, *Economic Development of Russia,* pp. 60–76. For sources of GNP/capita figures, see note 1, this chapter. For percent of the labor force in agriculture, see note 2, this chapter. For Indonesia the assumption has been made that GNP/capita in 1960 was not significantly higher than in 1900. See Geertz, *Agricultural Involution,* pp. 130–43.
9. Mitchell, *Statistics: Africa and Asia,* p. 486.
10. Coes, "Brazil," in Lewis, *Tropical Development,* pp. 106–107.
11. Harbison, "Colombia," in Lewis, *Tropical Development,* p. 85.
12. A. Smith, *Theories of Nationalism,* pp. 109–50; Ragin, "Social Bases of Political Regionalism," pp. 438–50.
13. Gellner, *Nations and Nationalism;* Kedourie, *Nationalism.*
14. Minchinton, "Patterns of Demand," in Cipolla, *Fontana Economic History,* Vol. 3, pp. 114–115; Lampman, "Top Wealth-Holders," in Zeitlin, *American Society, Inc.,* p. 100.
15. Bureau of the Census, *Historical Statistics (to 1957),* p. 74.
16. Wolf, *Peasant Wars,* p. 23; Wilkie, *Mexican Revolution,* pp. 24, 193, 203.
17. For a typical example see Chirot, *Change in a Peripheral Society,* pp. 89–154.
18. Wolf, *Peasant Wars,* pp. 3–25.
19. H. Fei, "Peasantry and Gentry," p. 14.
20. Moore, *Dictatorship and Democracy,* p. 176.
21. On the Chinese in Southeast Asia, see Myrdal, *Asian Drama,* pp. 133, 164, 169–70, 388, 402, 447, 464, 578, 813, 841; on the Jews in Eastern Europe, see Chirot, *Change in a Peripheral Society,* pp. 107–109, 144, 146, 150; on Indians in East Africa, see Dobson and Dobson, "Indians and Coloureds," in van den Berghe, *Africa: Change and Conflict,* pp. 267–73; on the Caribbean, see Despres, "The Implications of Nationalist Politics," in Bendix, *State and Society,* pp. 502–28.
22. Wolf, *Peasant Wars,* p. 15.
23. Moore, *Dictatorship and Democracy,* pp. 251, 341–53.
24. Wolf, *Peasant Wars.*
25. Broomfield, "Regional Elites," in Bendix, *State and Society,* pp. 552–61.
26. Wilkie, *Mexican Revolution,* pp. 45–47.
27. Woodruff, *Impact of Western Man,* p. 112.
28. Coleman, *Nigeria,* pp. 11–35.
29. Wallerstein, *Africa: Politics of Independence,* pp. 31–34; Warriner, *Land Reform,* pp. 3–10.
30. Hobsbawm, *Primitive Rebels,* pp. 57–92; Wolf, *Peasant Wars,* pp. 226–302.
31. Lenin, *Development of Capitalism in Russia,* pp. 549–55.
32. Von Laue, "Imperial Russia," in Bendix, *State and Society,* pp. 427–45.
33. Gerschenkron, *Economic Backwardness,* p. 131.
34. Ibid., p. 130.
35. Ibid., pp. 119–42.
36. Moore, *Dictatorship and Democracy,* pp. 228–313.
37. Gross, "Habsburg Monarchy," in Cipolla, *Fontana Economic History,* Vol. 4, pp. 228–78; Jelavich, *Habsburg Empire,* pp. 150–72.
38. D. North, "Economic Structure of the South," in Genovese, *The Slave Economies,* Vol. 2, pp. 111–15; Key, *Southern Politics,* pp. 160–61, 533–618.
39. Moore, *Dictatorship and Democracy,* pp. 413–83.

Chapter 6

1. Ward and Gooch, *Cambridge History*, Vol. 3, pp. 470–508.
2. Tuchman, *Guns of August*, pp. 33–157.
3. Taylor, *First World War*, pp. 13–24.
4. Bunle, *Le mouvement naturel*, pp. 110–12; Gilbert, *World War Atlas*, p. 158.
5. Gorce, *French Army*, p. 103; Bunle, *Le mouvement naturel*, p. 112.
6. Gilbert, *World War Atlas*, pp. 130, 158.
7. Ibid., pp. 144–55.
8. Hughes, *Contemporary Europe*, pp. 149–58.
9. Kindleberger, *World in Depression*, p. 292.
10. R. Parker, *Europe 1919–1945*, p. 102; R. Morris and Irwin, *Harper Encyclopedia*, p. 707.
11. Woodruff, *Impact of Western Man*, pp. 277–79.
12. Kindleberger, *World in Depression*, pp. 83–107; Burck and Silberman, "What Caused the Depression?" in Clark and Cohen, *Fluctuations, Growth, and Stabilization*, pp. 192–205.
13. Friedman and Schwartz, *Monetary History of the United States*, pp. 411–19.
14. Bureau of the Census, *Historical Statistics (to 1957)*, pp. 73, 179; R. Parker, *Europe 1919–1945*, p. 116; Kindleberger, *World in Depression*, p. 240; Kirk, *Europe's Population*, p. 197.
15. Woodruff, *Impact of Western Man*, p. 272.
16. Rostow, *World Economy*, pp. 210–11.
17. Karl Marx states the egalitarian position in *The Communist Manifesto*. The most notable racist inegalitarians were Joseph de Gobineau (*The Inequality of Human Races*) and Houston Chamberlain (*Foundations of the Nineteenth Century*). Though the monarchist writings of someone like Joseph de Maistre no longer seemed suitable for the capitalist bourgeoisie of the late nineteenth century, more modern anti-egalitarianism could be found in the theories of social Darwinists such as William G. Sumner (*The Challenge of Facts and Other Essays*).
18. For the classic statements about the nature of the state, see Jean-Jacques Rousseau, *Discourse on the Origin of Inequality*, and Thomas Hobbes, *Leviathan*.
19. Lenin, "What Is To Be Done?" in Lenin, *Selected Works*, Vol. 1, Pt. 1, pp. 203–409; Carr, *October Revolution*, pp. 58–86.
20. Woodcock, *Anarchism*.
21. Schmitter, "Century of Corporatism," pp. 85–131; Manoilescu, *Le siècle du corporatisme*; E. Weber, *Varieties of Fascism*.
22. Hartz, *Liberal Tradition in America*.
23. Von Laue, *Why Lenin? Why Stalin?*, pp. 5–122; Bonnell, *Roots of Rebellion*, pp. 390–455.
24. Von Laue, *Why Lenin? Why Stalin?*, pp. 123–85; Schapiro, *Communist Party*, pp. 178–266.
25. Schapiro, *Communist Party*, pp. 286–308; Deutscher, *Prophet Unarmed*.
26. Erlich, *Soviet Industrialization Debate*; Campbell, *Soviet Economic Power*, pp. 7–27; Carr, *October Revolution*, pp. 110–28; Kennan, *Russia and the West*, pp. 241–59. On the fate of the original Bolsheviks, see Haupt and Marie, *Makers of the Revolution*.
27. Eason, "Demography," in Mickiewicz, *Handbook of Soviet Data*, p. 58.
28. R. Parker, *Europe 1919–1945*, p. 102; Campbell, *Soviet Economic Power*, p. 48.
29. Eason, "Demography," in Mickiewicz, *Handbook of Soviet Data*, p. 55.
30. Field, "Health," in Mickiewicz, *Handbook of Soviet Data*, pp. 101–18; Pool et al., "Education," in Mickiewicz, *Handbook of Soviet Data*, pp. 137–58.
31. Carr, *October Revolution*, pp. 95–109. This, according to Schapiro, *Communist Party*, p. 386, is what Stalin told Churchill.
32. Fainsod, *How Russia Is Ruled*, pp. 531–32.
33. Laird, "Agriculture," in Mickiewicz, *Handbook of Soviet Data*, pp. 70–71.

34. Morton, "Housing," in Mickiewicz, *Handbook of Soviet Data,* p. 122.
35. Medvedev, *Let History Judge,* p. 239, and for a more thorough account, pp. 192–239.
36. Rosefielde, "Excess Mortality," pp. 385–409. For more details, see Antonov-Ovseyenko, *Time of Stalin.*
37. Carr, *Studies in Revolution,* pp. 152–65.
38. Kogan, Organski, and Sole-Tura, "Fascism and the Polity," in Woolf, *Nature of Fascism,* pp. 11–61.
39. Schapiro, *Communist Party,* pp. 353–54; Kennan, *Russia and the West,* pp. 273–74, 308–13.
40. Carsten, *Rise of Fascism,* pp. 55–62, 142–43; Lombardini, "Italian Fascism," in Woolf, *Nature of Fascism,* pp. 155–56; Linz, "From Falange to Movimiento-Organización," in Huntington and Moore, *Authoritarian Politics,* pp. 140–42, 175–85.
41. E. Weber, "Romania," in Rogger and Weber, *The European Right,* p. 532; Carsten, *Rise of Fascism,* pp. 143–44; Schapiro, *Communist Party,* pp. 559–60; Chirot, "The Corporatist Model," pp. 363–81.
42. R. Parker, *Europe 1919-1945,* p. 222.
43. Shirer, *Rise and Fall,* pp. 322–596.
44. Reischauer, *Japan,* p. 164.
45. Ienaga, *The Pacific War,* pp. 129–52.
46. Ienaga, *The Pacific War,* pp. 97–128; Reischauer, *Japan,* pp. 142–85; Gay, *Weimar Culture;* E. Weber, *Varieties of Fascism,* pp. 79–87.
47. Carsten, *Rise of Fascism,* pp. 230–36.
48. Dahrendorf, *Society and Democracy,* pp. 381–96. Ienaga traces similar developments in Japan in *The Pacific War* but considers them entirely negative.
49. Budd, "Inequality," in Zeitlin, *American Society, Inc.,* p. 144.
50. Bureau of the Census, *Historical Statistics (to 1957),* pp. 139, 718.
51. Schlesinger, *Age of Roosevelt,* pp. 166–83.
52. Kuznets, "Quantitative Aspects of Economic Growth," pp. 60–62.
53. Means, "Economic Concentration," in Zeitlin, *American Society, Inc.,* p. 12.
54. Weir and Skocpol, "State Structures and Keynesianism," pp. 4–29.
55. Kennan, *Russia and the West,* pp. 314–30.
56. Kennan, *American Diplomacy,* pp. 74–75.
57. See passages of Hitler's book, *Mein Kampf,* cited in Shirer, *Rise and Fall,* pp. 82–85. On the contradictions between the strictly rational exploitation of conquered territories and Nazi racial theories, see Milward, *War, Economy and Society,* pp. 164–65.
58. Milward, *War, Economy and Society,* pp. 132–68.
59. Ienaga, *The Pacific War,* pp. 153–80.
60. Ibid., pp. 181–202. Ienaga gives various numbers of Japanese civilians killed outside Japan that would alone more than double the Japanese deaths reported in the table.
61. Milward, *War, Economy and Society,* pp. 55–59.
62. Ibid., pp. 329–65; Darby and Fullard, *Cambridge History Atlas,* p. 61.
63. Woytinski and Woytinski, *World Population,* pp. 44, 47; R. Parker, *Europe 1919-1945,* p. 345; Bureau of the Census, *Historical Statistics (to 1957),* p. 735; Milward, *War, Economy and Society,* pp. 210–11; Rosefielde, "Excess Mortality"; "War's End Stirs Memories for China," *New York Times,* 20 August, 1985, p. 3.
64. W. Parker, *Europe and the Wider World,* pp. 233–34.

Chapter 7

1. Issawi, "Egypt Since 1800," in Issawi, *Economic History of the Middle East,* p. 373.
2. Baer, "Evolution of Private Landownership," pp. 79–90; Issawi, "Egypt Since 1800," p. 373; Issawi, "Land Policy 1906," p. 497, all in Issawi, *Economic History of the Middle East.* Also, Saab, *Egyptian Agrarian Reform,* p. 9.
3. Kuznets, *Growth of Nations,* p. 31.
4. Kuznets, "Quantitative Aspects of Economic Growth," p. 78.
5. Moore, *Dictatorship and Democracy,* pp. 354–55.

6. Thorner, "Long-term Trends in Output," in Kuznets, Moore, and Spengler, *Economic Growth*, pp. 121–23.
7. Kuznets, *Growth of Nations*, p. 31.
8. Balandier, "Colonial Situation," in van den Berghe, *Africa: Change and Conflict*, pp. 36–57.
9. B. Lewis, *Emergence of Turkey*, p. 444.
10. Ibid.
11. Ibid., p. 447.
12. Ibid., p. 350.
13. Myrdal, *Asian Drama*, p. 1396; Omran, "Population of Egypt," in Omran, *Egypt*, p. 13; Woytinski and Woytinski, *World Population*, p. 44.
14. Mitchell and Deane, *British Historical Statistics*, p. 6; Bureau of the Census, *Historical Statistics (to 1957)*, p. 7.
15. Lindman and Domrese, "India," in Lewis, *Tropical Development*, p. 314; Kuznets, "Quantitative Aspects of Economic Growth," p. 77.
16. Warriner, *Land Reform*, pp. 373–92.
17. Shils, "Intellectuals in Political Development," in Kautsky, *Political Change*, p. 198.
18. Benda, "Non-Western Intelligentsia," in Kautsky, *Political Change*, pp. 239, 243.
19. Rustow, "Ataturk," in Rustow, *Philosophers and Kings*, pp. 208–47.
20. Moore, *Dictatorship and Democracy*, pp. 188–89; Johnson, *Peasant Nationalism*, pp. 31–32.
21. Hutchins, *India's Revolution*.
22. Fall, *Reflections on a War*, pp. 59–60.
23. Fall, *Hell in a Small Place*.
24. Huntington, *Political Order*, p. 316.
25. Wolf, *Peasant Wars*, pp. 31–37.
26. Wilkie, *Mexican Revolution*, pp. 64–65.
27. Ibid., pp. 72–79.
28. Wolf, *Peasant Wars*, pp. 32–37.
29. Wilkie, *Mexican Revolution*, pp. 208, 236, 262, 264.
30. But recently, Mexico's performance has not been good. See Chapter 9 of the text for a discussion of more recent developments.
31. Johnson, *Peasant Nationalism*, p. 23.
32. Ibid., p. 24.
33. Schwartz, *Chinese Communism*.
34. Johnson, *Peasant Nationalism*, p. 31.
35. North and Pool, "Kuomintang and Communist Elites," in Lasswell and Lerner, *Revolutionary Elites*, pp. 381–82.
36. Moore, *Dictatorship and Democracy*, pp. 198–99.
37. Ibid., p. 378.
38. Myrdal, *Asian Drama*, pp. 257–303.

Chapter 8
1. Branson, "Trends in International Trade," in Feldstein, *American Economy in Transition*, p. 185.
2. Yergin, *Shattered Peace*.
3. Block, *Origins of Economic Disorder*, pp. 32–69.
4. Ibid., pp. 70–118.
5. Yergin, *Shattered Peace*, pp. 179–272.
6. Cumings, *Origins of the Korean War*, Vol. 1.
7. Yergin, *Shattered Peace*, pp. 388–90.
8. Gilpin, *War and Change*, pp. 173–74.
9. Horowitz, "Alliance for Progress," and Alavi and Khurso, "Burden of U.S. Aid," in Rhodes, *Imperialism and Underdevelopment*.
10. Bureau of the Census, *Statistical Abstract (1984)*, pp. 827–28.

11. Ibid., pp. 827–28; *Economic Report (1984)*, pp. 227–28, 253. The average figures are based on population and inflation data in the middle year of each period.

12. Bureau of the Census, *Statistical Abstract (1984)*, p. 824; *Statistical Abstract (1974)*, pp. 781–82; *Historical Statistics (to 1970)*, pp. 870–71.

13. Same sources as note 12.

14. *Economic Report (1984)*, p. 316.

15. Ibid., p. 332.

16. Bureau of the Census, *Statistical Abstract (1984)*, p. 873; *Economic Report (1984)*, p. 267.

17. Summers and Heston, "Improved Comparisons," pp. 207–62. Gross Domestic Product is equal to Gross National Product minus net receipts from abroad from trade or investments. In the case of an economy with a net deficit in its foreign accounts, this amount is subtracted from GDP to equal GNP. Real Gross Domestic Product per capita has been adjusted for changing terms of trade for each country. For details of this calculation, see the text of the article cited above, pp. 208–15. This adjustment permits more realistic comparisons of real purchasing power.

18. M. Morris, *Condition of the Poor*, pp. 41–59.

19. Ibid., pp. 102, 138–45.

20. Baran, *Political Economy of Growth*; Frank, *Underdevelopment in Latin America*.

21. Wheatcroft, *Atlas of Revolutions*, contains brief summaries of most of these events.

22. Keddie, "Iranian Revolution," pp. 13–26. For more details see Keddie, *Roots of Revolution*.

23. *Economic Report (1984)*, p. 338.

24. World Bank, *Development Report (1984)*, p. 171.

25. *Economic Report*, p. 335.

26. Thomas, *Suez*.

27. Wallerstein, *Africa: Politics of Independence*.

28. Chaliand, *Guerrilla Strategies*, pp. 186–215. See also Chaliand, *Revolution in the Third World*.

29. Wheatcroft, *Atlas of Revolutions*, pp. 164–69.

30. For an Arab viewpoint see Khalidi, "Palestinian Problem," pp. 1050–63; Said, *Palestinians*.

31. Keddie, "Iranian Revolution."

32. Bureau of the Census, *Statistical Abstract (1974)*, p. 781; *Statistical Abstract (1973)*, p. 769; *Statistical Abstract (1976)*, p. 523.

33. Modelski, "Performance Among Corporations," in Modelski, *Transnational Corporations*, pp. 46–47.

34. See the essays in Modelski, *Transnational Corporations*.

35. Gilpin, "Three Models," in Modelski, *Transnational Corporations*, pp. 359–61.

36. *The Economist*, December 25, 1982, p. 66; January 29, 1983, pp. 11, 58; October 15, 1983, pp. 72, 84; September 1, 1984, p. 47; October 27, 1984, pp. 16–17; January 5, 1985, pp. 53–54; February 2, 1985, pp. 57–58; July 6, 1985, pp. 17–22; World Bank, *Development Report (1981)*, p. 35; Bureau of the Census, *Historical Statistics (to 1970)*, p. 593.

37. Levy, "Decline of the West," pp. 999–1015.

38. Gilpin, "Three Models," in Modelski, *Transnational Corporations*, pp. 359–61.

39. *Economic Report (1984)*, pp. 87–95.

40. Mansfield, "Technology and Productivity," in Feldstein, *American Economy in Transition*, pp. 566–68; Scott, "Mechanization of Women's Work," pp. 167–87.

41. Olson, *Rise and Decline of Nations*.

42. Bureau of the Census, *Statistical Abstract (1984)*, p. 425; Bureau of the Census, *Historical Statistics (to 1970)*, p. 137.

43. *Economic Report (1984)*, p. 232.

44. Bureau of the Census, *Statistical Abstract (1984)*, pp. 613, 617, 789; Bureau of the

Census, *Historical Statistics (to 1970),* pp. 692–93, 716; *The Economist,* March 2, 1985, p. 10 of the special report on the automobile industry.

45. Bureau of the Census, *Statistical Abstract (1984),* p. 775.
46. Ibid., p. 874.
47. *Economic Report (1984),* p. 91.
48. *Economic Report (1984),* pp. 112–14; Rasmussen, "Mechanization of Agriculture," pp. 88–89; *The Economist,* May 21, 1983, pp. 107–108; *The Economist,* April 6, 1985, pp. 83–84.
49. Bureau of the Census, *Statistical Abstract (1984),* pp. 162, 597, 600.
50. *The Economist,* March 2, 1985, pp. 13, 63–64; *Economic Report (1983),* pp. 61–76; *Economic Report (1984),* pp. 35–41.
51. Cline, *International Debt and the Economy,* pp. 22–26.

Chapter 9

1. Bureau of the Census, *Statistical Abstract (1984),* pp. 865, 875–76.
2. Wallerstein, "Dependence in an Interdependent World," in Wallerstein, *Capitalist World-Economy,* pp. 69–70.
3. Mills, *The Power Elite;* Kolko, *Wealth and Power* and *Roots of American Foreign Policy;* Zeitlin, *American Society, Inc.;* Magdoff, *Age of Imperialism.*
4. Bureau of the Census, *Statistical Abstract (1984),* p. 465; Budd, "Inequality in Income and Taxes," in Zeitlin, *American Society, Inc.,* p. 144; Bureau of the Census, *Statistical Abstract (1974),* p. 384.
5. Bureau of the Census, *Current Population Reports,* cited in *World Almanac 1985,* p. 255.
6. World Bank, *Development Report (1983),* pp. 200–201; *The Economist,* August 11, 1984, p. 52.
7. Bureau of the Census, *Statistical Abstract (1984),* p. 481.
8. Ibid., p. 540; Bureau of the Census, *Statistical Abstract (1974),* pp. 483–84, 487.
9. Domhoff, *Who Rules America?,* p. 57.
10. Bureau of the Census, *Statistical Abstract (1984),* p. 546.
11. Bureau of the Census, *Statistical Abstract (1984),* p. 439; Bureau of the Census, *Statistical Abstract (1972),* p. 230; Bureau of the Census, *Historical Statistics (to 1957),* p. 74.
12. Maier, "Preconditions for Corporatism," in Goldthorpe, *Order and Conflict,* pp. 39–59.
13. Bureau of the Census, *Statistical Abstract (1984),* p. 439; *The Economist,* February 9, 1985, special section on France; *The Economist,* February 16, 1985, pp. 19–26, 56.
14. *Economic Report (1984),* pp. 232, 308; Bureau of the Census, *Statistical Abstract (1984),* p. 425; Bureau of the Census, *Historical Statistics (to 1970),* pp. 224, 1120.
15. Francis, "American Millionaires," *The Christian Science Monitor,* 19 April 1975, p. 21.
16. *Economic Report (1984),* p. 305; Bureau of the Census, *Statistical Abstract (1984),* p. 353; Bureau of the Census, *Historical Statistics (to 1970),* p. 1141.
17. Schurman, *Logic of Power,* pp. 401–500.
18. Murakami, "*Ie* Society," pp. 279–364, particularly pp. 354–58; Nakane, *Japanese Society,* pp. 87–103.
19. Pascale and Rholen, "The Mazda Turnabout," pp. 219–64.
20. Johnson, *MITI,* p. 13.
21. Dore, *British Factory–Japanese Factory,* pp. 302–305.
22. Johnson, *MITI,* pp. 314–16.
23. World Bank, *Development Report (1983),* p. 201.
24. Johnson, *MITI,* pp. 14–15, 313–14.
25. Yasusuke, "Mass Politics," pp. 29–72.
26. Johnson, *MITI,* pp. 14, 17.
27. Summers and Heston, "Improved Comparisons," pp. 207–62. See note 17, Chapter 8, above, for explanations. Bureau of the Census, *Historical Statistics (to 1970),* p. 225.
28. Skidmore and Smith, *Modern Latin America,* pp. 165–81.
29. Evans, *Dependent Development,* pp. 236–49.

30. Skidmore and Smith, *Modern Latin America,* 86–112.
31. Summers and Heston, "Improved Comparisons." See note 27, this chapter.
32. Skidmore and Smith, *Modern Latin America,* 242–55.
33. Summers and Heston, "Improved Comparisons." See note 27, above.
34. Skidmore and Smith, *Modern Latin America,* pp. 142–44.
35. Pereira, *Development and Crisis,* p. 184.
36. Felix, "Income Distribution Trends," in Hewlett and Weinert, *Brazil and Mexico,* pp. 265–316, and particularly p. 268.
37. Pereira, *Development and Crisis,* pp. 56–57.
38. Evans, *Dependent Development,* pp. 288–89.
39. World Bank, *Development Report (1983),* p. 201.
40. Hsiao, *Agricultural Strategies,* pp. 261–83. For more information on Taiwan see J. Fei, Ranis, and Kuo, *Growth With Equity.*
41. World Bank, *Development Report (1983),* pp. 186–87.
42. Ibid.
43. Ibid., pp. 190–91.
44. Bates, *Markets and States in Africa.*
45. A theoretical explanation of the corruption associated with "charismatic" Third World leaders is given by Roth in "Personal Rulership and Empire-Building," pp. 194–206.

Chapter 10

1. Schapiro, *Communist Party,* pp. 231–85.
2. Population figures are from World Bank, *Development Report (1983),* pp. 148–49.
3. Jowitt, *Leninist Response to Dependency,* pp. 34–62.
4. Schram, *Political Thought of Mao.* (The new spelling is Mao Zedong.)
5. Ulam, *Titoism and the Cominform.*
6. Campbell, "The Economy," in Byrnes, *After Brezhnev,* pp. 108–21.
7. Schapiro, *Communist Party,* pp. 437–40; Connor, *Socialism, Politics, and Equality,* p. 71; Gardner and Idema, "China's Educational Revolution," in Schram, *Authority, Participation, and Change,* pp. 257–89. For a general account of the rule of the Khmer Rouge in Cambodia, see Chandler and Kiernan, *Revolution in Kampuchea.*
8. Mitchell, *European Historical Statistics,* p. 43.
9. Lapidus, "Social Trends," in Byrnes, *After Brezhnev,* pp. 215–16.
10. World Bank, *Development Report (1983),* pp. 192–93; Shoup, *Data Handbook,* pp. 66–67.
11. Summers and Heston, "Improved Comparisons," pp. 207–62. See note 17, Chapter 8, above, for explanations.
12. Campbell, "The Economy," in Byrnes, *After Brezhnev,* p. 69; Central Intelligence Agency, *USSR: Measures of Economic Growth,* p. 20.
13. World Bank, *Development Report (1983),* pp. 192–93; Mitchell, *European Historical Statistics,* p. 43; Mitchell, *Statistics: Africa and Asia,* p. 81; Bureau of the Census, *Historical Statistics (to 1970),* p. 57; Lapidus, "Social Trends," in Byrnes, *After Brezhnev,* p. 216.
14. Connor, *Socialism, Politics, and Equality,* pp. 217–19.
15. Ibid., chapter 3.
16. Lapidus, "Social Trends," in Byrnes, *After Brezhnev,* p. 203.
17. Shoup, *Data Handbook,* pp. 351–54; Bureau of the Census, *Historical Statistics (to 1970),* p. 139.
18. Lipset, "Stratification Research and Scholarship," in Yanowitch and Fisher, *Stratification and Mobility,* pp. 359–62.
19. Lapidus, "Social Trends," in Byrnes, *After Brezhnev,* pp. 200–203.
20. Ibid., p. 195.
21. Ibid., pp. 215–21.
22. Hirszowicz, *Bureaucratic Leviathan;* Zaslavsky, *The Neo-Stalinist State.*

23. Tumarkin, *Lenin Lives!*
24. Johnson, *Peasant Nationalism;* Schram, *Political Thought of Mao,* pp. 44–45.
25. Lardy, *Agriculture in Economic Development,* pp. 41–43, 150–52.
26. Skocpol, *States and Social Revolutions,* pp. 265–80.
27. Lardy, *Agriculture in Economic Development,* pp. 130, 158.
28. Lee, *Politics of the Cultural Revolution,* pp. 64–139.
29. Hinton, *Hundred Day War,* pp. 154–70.
30. Lardy, *Agriculture in Economic Development,* pp. 130, 155, 165; Schram, "Introduction," in Schram, *Authority, Participation and Change,* pp. 97–98.
31. Lee, *Politics of the Cultural Revolution,* pp. 226–30. On the consequences for the Red Guards, see Heng and Shapiro, *Son of the Revolution.*
32. Lardy, *Agriculture in Economic Development,* pp. 164–66, 176, 186–87.
33. Ibid., pp. 190–221; *The Economist,* February 2, 1985, p. 11; *The Far Eastern Economic Review,* April 11, 1985, pp. 74–75.
34. Remington, "Yugoslavia," in Rakowska-Harmstone and Gyorgy, *Communism in Eastern Europe,* pp. 218–20. For more details, see Denitch, *Legitimation of a Revolution.*
35. Tyson, "Investment Allocation," pp. 288–303; Knight, *Reform in Socialist Countries,* pp. 88–95.
36. Tyson, "Investment Allocation," pp. 298–302; Remington, "Yugoslavia," in Rakowska-Harmstone and Gyorgy, *Communism in Eastern Europe,* pp. 231–36.
37. Bauer, "The Hungarian Alternative," pp. 305–306; Knight, *Reform in Socialist Countries,* pp. 65–66.
38. Marrese, "Agricultural Policy," pp. 329–45.
39. Information from Vlad Georgescu, Director, Romania desk of Radio Free Europe; Chirot, "Change in Romania," pp. 457–99.
40. Shawcross, *Quality of Mercy,* p. 115. The Heng Sanrin regime claims 2–3 million deaths. No one knows the precise number.
41. H. Smith, *The Russians,* pp. 302–26; Jowitt, "Political Innovation," pp. 132–51; Schram, "Introduction," in Schram, *Authority, Participation and Change,* pp. 5–9; Griffith, *Albania,* pp. 174–76; A. Smith, *Nationalism in the Twentieth Century,* pp. 127–49.
42. Cumings, "Corporatism in North Korea," pp. 269–94; Chirot, "The Corporatist Model," pp. 363–81; Henderson and Cohen, *The Chinese Hospital;* Hirszowicz, *Bureaucratic Leviathan,* pp. 20–44, 189–90.
43. *The Economist,* April 20, 1985, special section on COMECON, p. 7.
44. Ibid.
45. Skidmore and Smith, *Modern Latin America,* p. 282.
46. Bunce, "Evolution of the Eastern Bloc," p. 20.
47. Ibid., pp. 5–16.
48. C. Jones, *Soviet Influence in Eastern Europe.*
49. C.I.A., *USSR: Measures of Economic Growth,* pp. 54, 123.
50. Bunce, "Evolution of the Eastern Bloc," pp. 34–44.
51. That, after all, is the main theme of Lenin, *Imperialism.*

Chapter 11
1. Chirot, "Social and Historical Landscape," in Skocpol, *Vision and Method,* pp. 24–29.
2. Marx, *The Communist Manifesto;* Wallerstein, *Capitalist World-Economy.*

BIBLIOGRAPHY

Alavi, Hamza, and Amir Khurso. "Pakistan: The Burden of U.S. Aid." In Robert I. Rhodes, ed., *Imperialism and Underdevelopment.* New York: Monthly Review Press, 1970.

Anderson, Perry. *Passages from Antiquity to Feudalism.* London: NLB, 1974.

———. *Lineages of the Absolutist State.* London: NLB, 1974.

Antonov-Ovseyenko, Anton. *The Time of Stalin: Portrait of a Tyranny.* New York: Harper & Row, 1983.

Ashtor, Eliyahu. *A Social and Economic History of the Near East in the Middle Ages.* Berkeley and Los Angeles: University of California Press, 1976.

Baer, Gabriel. "The Evolution of Private Landownership in Egypt and the Fertile Crescent." In Charles Issawi, ed., *The Economic History of the Middle East 1800–1914.* Chicago: University of Chicago Press, 1966.

Bairoch, Paul. *The Economic Development of the Third World Since 1900.* Berkeley and Los Angeles: University of California Press, 1977.

Balandier, Georges. "The Colonial Situation: A Theoretical Approach." In Immanuel Wallerstein, ed., *Social Change: The Colonial Situation.* New York: Wiley, 1966.

Baran, Paul A. *The Political Economy of Growth.* New York: Monthly Review Press, 1957.

Barnes, Donald G. *A History of the English Corn Laws from 1660 to 1846.* New York: August M. Kelley, 1965.

Barraclough, Geoffrey. *The Medieval Papacy.* New York: Harcourt Brace & World, 1968.

Bates, Robert. *Markets and States in Tropical Africa.* Berkeley and Los Angeles: University of California Press, 1981.

Bauer, Támás. "The Hungarian Alternative to Soviet-Type Planning." *Journal of Comparative Economics* 7 (1983): 304–16.

Beard, Charles A., and Mary R. Beard. *The Rise of American Civilization.* New York: Macmillan, 1930.

Beeching, Jack. *The Chinese Opium Wars.* New York: Harcourt Brace Jovanovich, 1975.

Benda, Harry J. "Non-Western Intelligentsia as Political Elites." In John H. Kautsky, ed., *Political Change in Underdeveloped Countries: Nationalism and Communism.* New York: Wiley, 1962.

Berlin, Isaiah. *The Age of Enlightenment.* New York: Mentor, 1956.

Bloch, Marc. *Feudal Society.* Chicago: University of Chicago Press, 1961.

Block, Fred L. *The Origins of International Economic Disorder.* Berkeley and Los Angeles: University of California Press, 1977.

Blum, Jerome. "The Rise of Serfdom in Eastern Europe." *American Historical Review* 52 (1957): 807–36.

Bonnell, Victoria E. *Roots of Rebellion: Workers' Politics and Organizations in St. Petersburg and Moscow 1900–1914.* Berkeley and Los Angeles: University of California Press, 1983.

Bovill, E. W. *Caravans of the Old Sahara.* London: Oxford University Press, 1933.

Boxer, Charles R. *The Dutch Seaborne Empire 1600–1800.* New York: Knopf, 1965.

———. *Four Centuries of Portuguese Expansion, 1415–1815.* Berkeley and Los Angeles: University of California Press, 1972.

Branson, William H. "Trends in United States International Trade and Investment Since World Warl II." In Martin Feldstein, ed., *The American Economy in Transition.* Chicago: University of Chicago Press, 1980.

Braudel, Fernand. *The Mediterranean and the Mediterranean World in the Age of Philip II.* 2 vols. New York: Harper & Row, 1972–1973.

Braun, Rudolf. "Taxation, Sociopolitical Structure, and State-Building: Great Britain and Brandenburg-Prussia." In Charles Tilly, ed., *The Formation of National States in Western Europe.* Princeton: Princeton University Press, 1975.

Briggs, Asa. "Technology and Economic Development." *Scientific American* 209 (1963): 52–61.

Bronowski, J. *The Common Sense of Science.* Cambridge: Harvard University Press, 1978.

Brooke, Christopher. *The Twelfth Century Renaissance.* New York: Harcourt Brace & World, 1973.

Broomfield, J. H. "The Regional Elites: A Theory of Modern Indian History." In Reinhard Bendix, ed., *State and Society.* Boston: Little, Brown, 1968.

Budd, Edward C. "Inequality in Income and Taxes." In Maurice Zeitlin, ed., *American Society, Inc.: Studies of the Social Structure and Political Economy of the United States.* Chicago: Markham, 1970.

Bunce, Valerie. "The Empire Strikes Back: The Evolution of the Eastern Bloc from a Soviet Asset to a Soviet Liability." *International Organization* 39 (1985): 1–46.

Bunle, Henri. *Le mouvement naturel de la population dans le monde de 1906 à 1936.* Paris: Institut national d'études démographiques, 1954.

Burck, Gilbert, and Charles Silberman. "What Caused the Great Depression?" In John J. Clark and Morris Cohen, eds., *Business Fluctuations, Growth, and Economic Stabilization.* New York: Random House, 1963.

Bureau of the Census. *Historical Statistics of the United States, Colonial Times to 1957.* Washington: U.S. Government Printing Office, 1960.

———. *Historical Statistics of the United States, Colonial Times to 1970.* Washington: U.S. Government Printing Office, 1975.

———. *Statistical Abstract of the United States* [for the years] *1972, 1973, 1974, 1976, 1984.* Washington: U.S. Government Printing Office [printed in those years].

Calhoun, Craig. *The Question of Class Struggle: Social Foundations of Popular Radicalism During the Industrial Revolution.* Chicago: University of Chicago Press, 1982.

Campbell, Robert W. *Soviet Economic Power: Its Organization, Growth, and Challenge.* Cambridge: Houghton Mifflin, 1960.

———. "The Economy." In Robert F. Byrnes, ed., *After Brezhnev: Sources of Soviet Conduct in the 1980s.* Bloomington: Indiana University Press, 1982.

Carr, Edward H. *Studies in Revolution.* New York: Grosset & Dunlap, 1964.

———. *The October Revolution: Before and After.* New York: Random House, 1971.

Carsten, F. L. *The Rise of Fascism.* Berkeley and Los Angeles: University of California Press, 1967.

Central Intelligence Agency. *USSR: Measures of Economic Growth and Development, 1950–1980.* Washington: Joint Economic Committee, Congress of the United States, U.S. Government Printing Office, 1982.

Chaliand, Gerard, ed. *Guerrilla Strategies.* Berkeley and Los Angeles: University of California Press, 1982.

Chamberlain, Houston. *Foundations of the Nineteenth Century.* New York: H. Fertig, 1968.

Chandler, David P., and Ben Kiernan, eds. *Revolution and Its Aftermath in Kampuchea.* New Haven: Yale University South East Asia Studies, 1983.

Chaunu, Pierre. *Conquête et exploitation des nouveaux mondes.* Paris: Presses Universitaires de France, 1969.

Chirot, Daniel. *Social Change in a Peripheral Society: The Creation of a Balkan Colony.* New York: Academic Press, 1976.

———. *Social Change in the Twentieth Century.* New York: Harcourt Brace Jovanovich, 1977.

————. "Social Change in Communist Romania." *Social Forces* 57 (1978): 457–99.

————. "The Corporatist Model and Socialism." *Theory and Society* 9 (1980): 363–81.

Chirot, Daniel, and Thomas D. Hall. "World System Theory." *Annual Review of Sociology* 8 (1982): 81–106.

Chirot, Daniel. "The Social and Historical Landscape of Marc Bloch." In Theda Skocpol, ed., *Vision and Method in Historical Sociology*. Cambridge: Cambridge University Press, 1984.

Cipolla, Carlo M. *Guns, Sails and Empires: Technological Innovation and the Early Phases of European Expansion 1400–1700*. New York: Minerva Press, 1965.

————. *The Economic History of World Population*. Baltimore: Penguin, 1967.

Cipolla, Carlo M., ed. *The Fontana Economic History of Europe*. 6 vols. Glasgow: Fontana/ Collins, 1973–   .

Cline, William R. *International Debt and the Stability of the World Economy*. Washington: Institute for International Economics, 1983.

Cobban, Alfred. *The Social Interpretation of the French Revolution*. Cambridge: Cambridge University Press, 1965.

Coes, Donald. "Brazil." In W. Arthur Lewis, ed., *Tropical Development 1880–1913*. Evanston: Northwestern University Press, 1970.

Cohen, I. Bernard. *The Birth of a New Physics*. New York: Anchor Books, 1960.

Cohn, Norman. *The Pursuit of the Millennium*. New York: Harper Torchbooks, 1961.

Coleman, James S. *Nigeria: Background to Nationalism*. Berkeley and Los Angeles: University of California Press, 1960.

Connor, Walter D. *Socialism, Politics, and Equality: Hierarchy and Change in Eastern Europe and the USSR*. New York: Columbia University Press, 1979.

Craig, Gordon A., and Alexander L. George. *Force and Statecraft: Diplomatic Problems of Our Time*. New York: Oxford University Press, 1983.

Crisp, Olga. "Russia 1860–1914." In Rondo E. Cameron, ed., *Banking in the Early Stages of Industrialization*. New York: Oxford University Press, 1967.

Crouzet, François. "Croissances comparées de l'Angleterre et de la France au XVIIIe siècle." *Annales E.S.C.* 21 (1966): 254–91.

Cumings, Bruce. *The Origins of the Korean War: Liberation and the Creation of Separate Regimes, 1945–1947*. Princeton: Princeton University Press, 1981.

————. "Corporatism in North Korea." *Journal of Korean Studies* 4 (1982–1983): 269–94.

Curtin, Philip D. *The Image of Africa*. Madison: University of Wisconsin Press, 1964.

————. *The Atlantic Slave Trade: A Census*. Madison: University of Wisconsin Press, 1969.

Dahrendorf, Ralf. *Society and Democracy in Germany*. Garden City: Doubleday/Anchor, 1969.

Darby, H. C., and Harold Fullard, eds. *The New Cambridge Modern History Atlas*. Cambridge: Cambridge University Press, 1970.

Davis, Ralph. "English Foreign Trade 1660–1700." *Economic History Review*, ser. 2, 7 (1954): 150–66.

Deane, Phyllis. *The First Industrial Revolution*. Cambridge: Cambridge University Press, 1965.

————. "Great Britain." In Carlo M. Cipolla, ed., *The Fontana Economic History of Europe*. Vol. 4, *The Emergence of Industrial Societies*. Glasgow: Fontana/Collins, 1973.

Denitch, Bogdan D. *The Legitimation of a Revolution: The Yugoslav Case*. New Haven: Yale University Press, 1976.

Derrett, J. Duncan M. "Die Entwicklung des indischen Rechts." In Wolfgang Schluchter, ed., *Max Webers Studie über Hinduismus und Buddhismus*. Frankfurt: Suhrkamp, 1984.

Derry, John W. *A Short History of Nineteenth-Century England 1793–1868*. New York: Mentor, 1963.

Despres, Leo A. "The Implications of Nationalist Politics in British Guiana for the Development of Cultural Theory." In Reinhard Bendix, ed., *State and Society*. Boston: Little, Brown, 1968.

Deutscher, Isaac. *The Prophet Unarmed. Trotsky: 1921–1929.* London: Oxford University Press, 1959.

De Vries, Jan. *The Economy of Europe in an Age of Crisis, 1600–1750.* Cambridge: Cambridge University Press, 1976.

Dobson, Floyd, and Lillian Dobson. "Indians and Coloureds in Rhodesia and Nyasaland." In Pierre L. van den Berghe, ed., *Africa: Social Problems of Change and Conflict.* San Francisco: Chandler, 1965.

Domhoff, G. William. *Who Rules America?* Englewood Cliffs: Prentice-Hall, 1967.

Dore, Ronald. *British Factory–Japanese Factory.* Berkeley and Los Angeles: University of California Press, 1973.

Eason, Warren W. "Demography." In Ellen Mickiewicz, ed., *Handbook of Soviet Social Science Data.* New York: Free Press, 1973.

Eberhard, Wolfram. *A History of China.* Fourth Edition. Berkeley and Los Angeles: University of California Press, 1977.

The Economist. Dec. 25, 1982; Jan. 29, 1983; May 21, 1983; Oct. 15, 1983; Sept. 1, 1984; Oct. 27, 1984; Jan. 5, 1985; Feb. 2, 1985; Feb. 9, 1985; Feb. 16, 1985; Mar. 2, 1985; Apr. 6, 1985; Apr. 20, 1985; Jul. 6, 1985.

Economic Report of the President 1983. Washington: U.S. Government Printing Office, 1983.

Economic Report of the President 1984. Washington: U.S. Government Printing Office, 1984.

Elliott, John H. *Imperial Spain 1496–1716.* New York: St. Martin's Press, 1964.

———. *The Old World and the New.* Cambridge: Cambridge University Press, 1970.

Elvin, Mark. *The Pattern of the Chinese Past.* Stanford: Stanford University Press, 1973.

———. "Chinese Cities Since the Sung Dynasty." In Philip Abrams and Edward A. Wrigley, eds., *Towns in Societies.* Cambridge: Cambridge University Press, 1978.

Emmanuel, Arghiri. *Unequal Exchange.* New York: Monthly Review Press, 1972.

Erlich, Alexander. *The Soviet Industrialization Debate.* Cambridge: Harvard University Press, 1960.

Evans, Peter. *Dependent Development: The Alliance of Multinational, State, and Local Capital in Brazil.* Princeton: Princeton University Press, 1979.

Eyck, Erich. *Bismarck and the German Empire.* London: George Allen & Unwin, 1958.

Fainsod, Merle. *How Russia Is Ruled.* Cambridge: Harvard University Press, 1965.

Fall, Bernard B. *Hell in a Very Small Place: The Siege of Dien Bien Phu.* Philadelphia: Lippincott, 1967.

———. *Last Reflections on a War.* New York: Doubleday, 1967.

The Far Eastern Economic Review. April 11, 1985.

Fei, Hsiao-tung. "Peasantry and Gentry." *American Journal of Sociology* 52 (1946): 1–17.

Fei, John C. H., Gustav Ranis, and Shirley W. Y. Kuo. *Growth with Equity: The Taiwan Case.* New York: Oxford University Press, 1979.

Felix, David. "Income Distribution Trends in Mexico and the Kuznets Curve." In Sylvia A. Hewlett and Richard S. Weinert, eds., *Brazil and Mexico: Patterns in Late Development.* Philadelphia: ISHI, 1982.

Fels, Rendigs. "American Business Cycles, 1865–79." In John J. Clark and Morris Cohen, eds., *Business Fluctuations, Growth, and Economic Stabilization.* New York: Random House, 1963.

Field, Mark G. "Health." In Ellen Mickiewicz, ed., *Handbook of Soviet Social Science Data.* New York: Free Press, 1973.

Fieldhouse, D. K. "Imperialism: An Historiographic Revision." In Kenneth E. Boulding and Tapan Mukerjee, eds., *Economic Imperialism.* Ann Arbor: University of Michigan Press, 1972.

Francis, David R. "Most American Millionaires Start With Inherited Wealth." *The Christian Science Monitor,* April 19, 1975, p. 21.

Frank, Andre Gunder. *Capitalism and Underdevelopment in Latin America.* New York: Monthly Review Press, 1967.

Friedman, Milton, and Anna J. Schwartz. *A Monetary History of the United States, 1867–1960.* Princeton: Princeton University Press, 1963.

Furtado, Celso. *The Economic Growth of Brazil.* Berkeley and Los Angeles: University of California Press, 1965.

Gardner, John, and Wilt Idema. "China's Educational Revolution." In Stuart R. Schram, ed., *Authority, Participation, and Cultural Change in China.* Cambridge: Cambridge University Press, 1973.

Gay, Peter. *Weimar Culture: The Outsider as Insider.* New York: Harper Torchbooks, 1970.

Geertz, Clifford. *Agricultural Involution: The Process of Ecological Change in Indonesia.* Berkeley and Los Angeles: University of California Press, 1963.

Gellner, Ernest. *Nations and Nationalism.* Ithaca: Cornell University Press, 1983.

Genovese, Eugene D. *The World the Slaveholders Made.* New York: Vintage Books, 1971.

Gerschenkron, Alexander. *Economic Backwardness in Historical Perspective.* New York: Praeger, 1965.

Gilbert, Martin. *First World War Atlas.* New York: Macmillan, 1970.

Gilpin, Robert. "Three Models of the Future." In George Modelski, ed., *Transnational Corporations and World Order.* San Francisco: W. H. Freeman, 1979.

———. *War and Change in World Politics.* Cambridge: Cambridge University Press, 1981.

Gobineau, Joseph Arthur de. *The Inequality of Human Races.* London: Heinemann, 1915.

Godinho, Vitorino M. "Création et dynamisme économique du monde atlantique (1420–1670)." *Annales E.S.C.* 5 (1950): 32–36.

Gorce, Paul-Marie de la. *The French Army: A Military-Political History.* New York: George Braziller, 1963.

Gourevitch, Peter A. "International Trade, Domestic Coalitions, and Liberty: Comparative Responses to the Crisis of 1873–1896." *Journal of Interdisciplinary History* 8 (1977): 281–313.

Griffith, William E. *Albania and the Sino-Soviet Rift.* Cambridge: MIT Press, 1963.

Gross, N. T. "The Habsburg Monarchy 1750–1914." In Carlo M. Cipolla, ed., *The Fontana Economic History of Europe.* Vol. 4, *The Emergence of Industrial Societies.* Glasgow: Fontana/Collins, 1973.

Hamerow, Theodore S. *Restoration, Revolution, Reaction: Economics and Politics in Germany, 1815–1871.* Princeton: Princeton University Press, 1958.

Hamilton, Earl J. "American Treasure and the Rise of Capitalism." *Economica* 9 (1929): 338–57.

Hampshire, Stuart. *The Age of Reason.* New York: Mentor, 1956.

Harbison, Ralph W. "Colombia." In W. Arthur Lewis, ed., *Tropical Development 1880–1913.* Evanston: Northwestern University Press, 1970.

Hartz, Louis. *The Liberal Tradition in America.* New York: Harcourt Brace & World, 1955.

Haupt, Georges, and Jean-Jacques Marie, eds. *Makers of the Russian Revolution: Biographies of Bolshevik Leaders.* Ithaca: Cornell University Press, 1974.

Hecksher, Eli F. *Mercantilism.* London: George Allen & Unwin, 1955.

Henderson, Gail E., and Myron S. Cohen. *The Chinese Hospital: A Socialist Work Unit.* New Haven: Yale University Press, 1984.

Heng, Liang, and Judith Shapiro. *Son of the Revolution.* New York: Random House, 1984.

Hinton, William. *Hundred Day War: The Cultural Revolution at Tsinghua University.* New York: Monthly Review Press, 1972.

Hirszowicz, Maria. *The Bureaucratic Leviathan: A Study in the Sociology of Communism.* New York: New York University Press, 1980.

Ho, Ping-ti. *Studies on the Population of China 1368–1953.* Cambridge: Harvard University Press, 1956.

Hobbes, Thomas. *Leviathan.* London: J. M. Dent & Sons, 1928.

Hobsbawm, Eric J. *Primitive Rebels.* New York: Norton, 1959.

———. *The Age of Revolution: Europe 1789–1848.* New York: Mentor, 1962.

———. "The Crisis of the Seventeenth Century." In Trevor Aston, ed., *Crisis in Europe 1560–1660.* Garden City: Doubleday/Anchor, 1967.

———. *Industry and Empire.* Harmondsworth: Penguin, 1969.

———. *The Age of Capital 1848–1875.* New York: Charles Scribner's Sons, 1975.

Hodgson, Marshall G. *The Venture of Islam.* 3 vols. Chicago: University of Chicago Press, 1974.

Horowitz, David. "The Alliance for Progress." In Robert I. Rhodes, ed., *Imperialism and Underdevelopment.* New York: Monthly Review Press, 1970.

Hsiao, Hsin-Huang Michael. *Government Agricultural Strategies in Taiwan and South Korea: A Macrosociological Assessment.* Taipei: Academia Sinica, 1981.

Hughes, H. Stuart. *Contemporary Europe: A History.* Englewood Cliffs: Prentice-Hall, 1961.

Huizinga, Johan. *Dutch Civilization in the Seventeenth Century.* New York: Frederick Ungur, 1968.

Huntington, Samuel P. *Political Order in Changing Societies.* New Haven: Yale University Press, 1968.

Hutchins, Francis G. *India's Revolution: Gandhi and the Quit India Movement.* Cambridge: Harvard University Press, 1973.

Ienaga Saburo. *The Pacific War, 1931–1945.* New York: Pantheon, 1978.

Issawi, Charles, ed. *The Economic History of the Middle East 1800–1914.* Chicago: University of Chicago Press, 1966.

Jelavich, Barbara. *The Habsburg Empire in European Affairs, 1814–1918.* Chicago: Rand McNally, 1969.

Johnson, Chalmers. *Peasant Nationalism and Communist Power: The Emergence of Revolutionary China 1937–1945.* Stanford: Stanford University Press, 1972.

———. *MITI and the Japanese Miracle: The Growth of Industrial Policy.* Stanford: Stanford University Press, 1982.

Jones, Christopher D. *Soviet Influence in Eastern Europe: Political Autonomy and the Warsaw Pact.* New York: Praeger, 1981.

Jones, Eric L. *The European Miracle.* Cambridge: Cambridge University Press, 1981.

Jowitt, Kenneth. "Political Innovation in Rumania." *Survey* 93 (1974): 132–51.

———. *The Leninist Response to National Dependency.* Berkeley: Institute of International Studies, 1978.

Juglar, Clément. *Des crises commerciales et de leur retour periodique en France, en Angleterre, et aux États-Unis.* New York: Gregg Press, 1968.

Keddie, Nikki R. *The Roots of Revolution: An Interpretative History of Modern Iran.* New Haven: Yale University Press, 1981.

———. "The Iranian Revolution and U.S. Policy." *SAIS Review* 2 (1981/1982): 13–26.

Kedourie, Elie. *Nationalism.* London: Hutchinson, 1960.

Kennan, George F. *American Diplomacy 1900–1950.* Chicago: University of Chicago Press, 1951.

———. *Russia and the West Under Lenin and Stalin.* Boston: Little, Brown, 1961.

Key, V. O. *Southern Politics in State and Nation.* New York: Knopf, 1944.

Khalidi, Walid. "The Palestinian Problem." *Foreign Affairs* 59 (1981): 1050–63.

Kiernan, Victor G. "Revolution." In Peter Burke, ed., *The New Cambridge Modern History.* Vol. 13, *Companion Volume.* Cambridge: Cambridge University Press, 1979.

Kindleberger, Charles P. *The World in Depression.* London: Allen Lane, 1973.

Kirk, Dudley. *Europe's Population in the Inter-War Years.* New York: Gordon and Breach, 1968.

Knight, Peter T. *Economic Reform in Socialist Countries: The Experiences of China, Hungary, Romania, and Yugoslavia.* Washington: The World Bank, 1983.

Kogan, N., A. F. K. Organski, and J. Sole-Tura. "Fascism and the Polity." In S. J. Woolf, ed., *The Nature of Fascism*. New York: Random House/Vintage, 1969.

Kolko, Gabriel. *Wealth and Power in America: An Analysis of Social Class and Income Distribution*. New York: Praeger, 1962.

———. *The Roots of American Foreign Policy: An Analysis of Power and Purpose*. Boston: Beacon, 1969.

Kuhn, Thomas S. *The Essential Tension*. Chicago: University of Chicago Press, 1977.

Kula, Witold. *Théorie économique du système féodal: pour un modèle de l'économie polonaise, 16e–18e siècles*. Paris and The Hague: Mouton, 1970.

Kuznets, Simon. "Quantitative Aspects of the Economic Growth of Nations." *Economic Development and Cultural Change*. "P. One," Vol. 5, no. 1 (1956): 5–94; "P. Two," Vol. 5, no. 4 (supplement) (1957): 3–111; "P. Eight," Vol. 11, no. 2 (supplement) (1963): 1–80.

———. *Economic Growth of Nations: Total Output and Production Structure*. Cambridge: Belknap Press of Harvard University, 1971.

Laird, Roy. "Agriculture." In Ellen Mickiewicz, ed., *Handbook of Soviet Social Science Data*. New York: Free Press, 1973.

Lampman, Robert J. "The Share of the Top Wealth-Holders in National Wealth, 1922–1956." In Maurice Zeitlin, ed., *American Society Inc.: Studies of the Social Structure and Political Economy of the United States*. Chicago: Markham, 1970.

Landes, David S. *The Unbound Prometheus: Technological Change and Industrial Development in Western Europe from 1750 to the Present*. Cambridge: Cambridge University Press, 1969.

Langer, William L. *The New Illustrated Encyclopedia of World History*. New York: Harry N. Abrams, 1972.

Lapidus, Gail W. "Social Trends." In Robert F. Byrnes, ed., *After Brezhnev: Sources of Soviet Conduct in the 1980s*. Bloomington: Indiana University Press, 1982.

Lardy, Nicholas. *Agriculture in China's Modern Economic Development*. Cambridge: Cambridge University Press, 1983.

Lee, Hong Yung. *The Politics of the Chinese Cultural Revolution*. Berkeley and Los Angeles: University of California Press, 1978.

Lefebvre, Georges. *The Coming of the French Revolution*. New York: Vintage Books, 1947.

———. *The Great Fear of 1789*. New York: Vintage Books, 1973.

Lenin, V. I. *Imperialism, The Highest Stage of Capitalism*. New York: International Publishers, 1939.

———. "What is To Be Done?" In *Selected Works in Two Volumes*. Moscow: Foreign Languages Publishing House, 1950.

———. *The Development of Capitalism in Russia*. Moscow: Foreign Languages Publishing House, 1956.

Letwin, William. *The Origins of Scientific Economics: English Economic Thought 1660–1776*. London: Methuen, 1963.

Levenson, Joseph R., ed. *European Expansion and the Counter-Example of Asia 1300–1600*. Englewood Cliffs: Prentice-Hall, 1967.

Levy, Walter J. "Oil and the Decline of the West." *Foreign Affairs* 58 (1980): 999–1015.

Lewis, Bernard. *The Emergence of Modern Turkey*. London: Oxford University Press, 1961.

Lewis, W. Arthur, ed. *Tropical Development 1880–1913*. Evanston: Northwestern University Press, 1970.

Lilley, Samuel. "Technological Progress and the Industrial Revolution 1700–1914." In Carlo M. Cipolla, ed., *The Fontana Economic History of Europe*. Vol. 3, *The Industrial Revolution*. Glasgow: Fontana/Collins, 1973.

Lindman, Russell, and Robert I. Domrese. "India." In W. Arthur Lewis, ed., *Tropical Development 1880–1913*. Evanston: Northwestern University Press, 1970.

Linz, Juan J. "From Falange to Movimiento-Organización: The Spanish Single Party and the Franco Regime, 1936–1938." In Samuel P. Huntington and Clement Henry Moore, eds., *Authoritarian Politics in Modern Societies: The Dynamics of Established One-Party Systems.* New York: Basic Books, 1970.

Lipset, Seymour M. "Commentary: Social Stratification Research and Soviet Scholarship." In Murray Yanowitch and Wesley A. Fisher, eds., *Social Stratification and Mobility in the USSR.* White Plains: International Arts and Sciences Press, 1973.

Lombardini, S. "Italian Fascism and the Economy." In S. J. Woolf, ed., *The Nature of Fascism.* New York: Random House/Vintage, 1969.

Love, Joseph L. "Raul Prebisch and the Origins of the Doctrine of Unequal Exchange." *Latin American Research Review* 15 (1980): 45–72.

McEvedy, Colin, and Richard Jones. *Atlas of World Population History.* Harmondsworth: Penguin, 1978.

McNeill, William H. *Plagues and People.* Garden City: Anchor Press, 1976.

Maddalena, Aldo de. "Rural Europe 1500–1750." In Carlo M. Cipolla, ed., *The Fontana Economic History of Europe.* Vol. 2, *The Sixteenth and Seventeenth Centuries.* Glasgow: Fontana/Collins, 1974.

Magdoff, Harry. *The Age of Imperialism: The Economics of United States Foreign Policy.* New York: Monthly Review Press, 1969.

Maier, Charles. "Preconditions for Corporatism." In John H. Goldthorpe, ed., *Order and Conflict in Contemporary Capitalism.* Oxford: Clarendon Press, 1984.

Manoilescu, Mihail. *Le siècle du corporatisme: doctrine du corporatisme intégral et pur.* Paris: F. Alcan, 1934.

Mansfield, Edwin. "Technology and Productivity in the United States." In Martin Feldstein, ed., *The American Economy in Transition.* Chicago: University of Chicago Press, 1980.

Marlow, John. *A History of Modern Anglo-Egyptian Relations.* Hamden: Archon Books, 1965.

Marrese, Michael. "Agricultural Policy and Performance in Hungary." *Journal of Comparative Economics* 7 (1983): 329–45.

Marx, Karl, and Friedrich Engels. "Manifesto of the Communist Party." In Lewis S. Feuer, ed., *Marx and Engels: Basic Writings on Politics and Philosophy.* New York: Doubleday/Anchor, 1959.

Means, Gardiner C. "Economic Concentration." In Maurice Zeitlin, ed., *American Society, Inc.: Studies of the Social Structure and Political Economy of the United States.* Chicago: Markham, 1970.

Medvedev, Roy A. *Let History Judge: The Origins and Consequences of Stalinism.* New York: Vintage Books, 1973.

Merton, Robert K. *Social Theory and Social Structure.* Glencoe: The Free Press, 1949.
———. *Science, Technology and Society in Seventeenth-Century England.* New York: Fertig, 1970.

Miller, Margaret S. *The Economic Development of Russia 1905–1914.* London: P. S. King and Son, 1926.

Mills, C. Wright. *The Power Elite.* New York: Oxford University Press, 1956.

Milward, Alan S. *War, Economy and Society 1939–1945.* Berkeley and Los Angeles: University of California Press, 1979.

Minchinton, Walter. "Patterns of Demand 1750–1914." In Carlo M. Cipolla, ed., *The Fontana Economic History of Europe.* Vol. 3, *The Industrial Revolution.* Glasgow: Fontana/Collins, 1973.

Mitchell, B. R. "Statistical Appendix 1700–1914." In Carlo M. Cipolla, ed., *The Fontana Economic History of Europe.* Vol. 4, *The Emergence of Industrial Societies.* Glasgow: Fontana/Collins, 1973.

————. *European Historical Statistics 1750–1970.* New York: Columbia University Press, 1978.

————. *International Historical Statistics: Africa and Asia.* New York: New York University Press, 1982.

Mitchell, B. R., and Phyllis Deane. *Abstract of British Historical Statistics.* Cambridge: Cambridge University Press, 1971.

Modelski, George, ed. *Transnational Corporations and World Order.* San Francisco: W. H. Freeman, 1979.

Moore, Barrington, Jr. *Social Origins of Dictatorship and Democracy: Lord and Peasant in the Making of the Modern World.* Boston: Beacon, 1967.

Morris, Morris D. "Toward a Reinterpretation of Nineteenth-Century Indian Economic History." *Journal of Economic History* 23 (1963): 606–18.

————. *Measuring the Condition of the World's Poor: The Physical Quality of Life Index.* New York: Pergamon Press, 1979.

Morris, Richard B., and Graham W. Irwin, eds. *Harper Encyclopedia of the Modern World.* New York: Harper & Row, 1970.

Morton, Henry W. "Housing." In Ellen Mickiewicz, ed., *Handbook of Soviet Social Science Data.* New York: Free Press, 1973.

Murakami Yasusuke. "The Age of the New Middle Mass Politics: The Case of Japan." *The Journal of Japanese Studies* 8 (1982): 29–72.

————. "*Ie* Society as a Pattern of Civilization." *The Journal of Japanese Studies* 10 (1984): 279–364.

Myers, Alec R. *Parliaments and Estates in Europe to 1789.* New York: Harcourt Brace Jovanovich, 1975.

Myrdal, Gunnar. *Asian Drama: An Inquiry into the Poverty of Nations.* New York: Pantheon, 1968.

Nakane, Chie. *Japanese Society.* Berkeley and Los Angeles: University of California Press, 1972.

The New York Times. "War's End Stirs Memories for China." August 20, 1985, p. 3.

North, Douglass C. "The Economic Structure of the South." In Eugene D. Genovese, ed., *The Slave Economies: Slavery in the International Economy.* New York: Wiley, 1973.

North, Robert C., and Ithiel de Sola Pool. "Kuomintang and Chinese Communist Elites." In Harold D. Lasswell and Daniel Lerner, eds., *World Revolutionary Elites: Studies in Coercive Ideological Movements.* Cambridge: MIT Press, 1966.

Olson, Mancur. *The Rise and Decline of Nations.* New Haven: Yale University Press, 1982.

Omran, Abdel R., ed. *Egypt: Population Problems and Prospects.* Chapel Hill: University of North Carolina Population Center, 1973.

Ortei, F. "The Economic Life of the Empire." In S. A. Cook et al., eds., *The Cambridge Ancient History.* Vol. 12, *The Imperial Crisis and Recovery A.D. 193-324.* Cambridge: Cambridge University Press, 1971.

Ostrogorsky, George. *History of the Byzantine State.* New Brunswick: Rutgers University Press, 1957.

Parker, Geoffrey. *Spain and the Netherlands 1559-1659, Ten Studies.* Glasgow: Fontana/Collins, 1979.

Parker, R. A. C. *Europe 1919-1945.* New York: Delacorte, 1970.

Parker, William N. *Europe, America, and the Wider World.* Vol. 1, *Europe and the World Economy.* Cambridge: Cambridge University Press, 1984.

Pascale, Richard, and Thomas Rholen. "The Mazda Turnabout." *The Journal of Japanese Studies* 9 (1983): 219–64.

Payne, Stanley G. *A History of Spain and Portugal.* Madison: University of Wisconsin Press, 1973.

Pereira, Luiz Bresser. *Development and Crisis in Brazil 1930-1983.* Boulder: Westview, 1984.

Poggi, Gianfranco. *The Development of the Modern State*. Stanford: Stanford University Press, 1978.

Polanyi, Karl. *The Great Transformation*. Boston: Beacon, 1957.

Pollard, Sidney. "Factory Discipline in the Industrial Revolution." *Economic History Review* 16 (1963): 254–71.

Pool, Jonathan A. et al. "Education." In Ellen Mickiewicz, ed., *Handbook of Soviet Social Science Data*. New York: Free Press, 1973.

Purcell, Victor. *The Boxer Uprising: A Background Study*. Cambridge: Cambridge University Press, 1963.

Ragin, Charles. "Class, Status, and 'Reactive Ethnic Cleavages': The Social Bases of Political Regionalism." *American Sociological Review* 42 (1977): 438–50.

Rasmunsen, Wayne D. "The Mechanization of Agriculture." *Scientific American* 247 (1982): 76–89.

Reischauer, Edwin O. *Japan: Past and Present*. Third Edition. New York: Knopf, 1965.

Remington, Robin A. "Yugoslavia." In Teresa Rakowska-Harmstone and Andre Gyorgy, eds., *Communism in Eastern Europe*. Bloomington: Indiana University Press, 1979.

Ronan, Colin A., and Joseph Needham. *The Shorter Science and Civilization in China*. Cambridge: Cambridge University Press, 1978.

Rosefielde, Steven. "Excess Mortality in the Soviet Union: A Reconsideration of the Demographic Consequences of Forced Industrialization 1929–1949." *Soviet Studies* 35 (1983): 385–409.

Rostow, Walt W. *The World Economy: History and Prospect*. Austin: University of Texas Press, 1980.

Roth, Guenther. "Personal Rulership, Patrimonialism, and Empire-Building in the New States." *World Politics* 20 (1968): 194–206.

Rousseau, Jean-Jacques. *Discours sur l'origine et les fondements de l'inégalité parmi les hommes*. Paris: Éditions sociales, 1954.

Rudé, George. "The Bread Riots of May 1775 in Paris and the Paris Region." In Jeffry Kaplow, ed., *New Perspectives on the French Revolution*. New York: Wiley, 1965.

Rustow, Dankwart A. "Ataturk as Founder of a State." In Dankwart A. Rustow, ed., *Philosophers and Kings: Studies in Leadership*. New York: George Braziller, 1970.

Saab, Gabriel S. *The Egyptian Agrarian Reform 1952–1962*. London: Oxford University Press, 1967.

Said, Edward W. *The Question of Palestine*. New York: Times Books, 1979.

Schapiro, Leonard. *The Communist Party of the Soviet Union*. New York: Random House, 1960.

Schlesinger, Arthur M., Jr. *The Age of Roosevelt: The Crisis of the Old Order*. Cambridge: Houghton Mifflin, 1957.

Schluchter, Wolfgang. *The Rise of Western Rationalism*. Berkeley and Los Angeles: University of California Press, 1981.

Schmitter, Philippe C. "Still the Century of Corporatism?" *Review of Politics* 36 (1974): 85–131.

Schram, Stuart R. *The Political Thought of Mao Tse-tung*. Second Edition. New York: Praeger, 1969.

Schumpeter, Elizabeth B. *English Overseas Trade Statistics 1697–1808*. Oxford: Clarendon Press, 1960.

Schumpeter, Joseph A. *Business Cycles*. 2 vols. New York: McGraw-Hill, 1939.

———. *Imperialism and Social Classes*. New York: Meridian Books, 1955.

Schurman, Franz. *The Logic of World Power: An Inquiry into the Origins, Currents, and Contradictions of World Politics*. New York: Pantheon, 1974.

Schwartz, Benjamin I. *Chinese Communism and the Rise of Mao*. Cambridge: Harvard University Press, 1951.

Scott, Joan W. "The Mechanization of Women's Work." *Scientific American* 247 (1982): 167–87.

Sée, Henri. *L'évolution commerciale et industrielle de la France sous l'ancien régime.* Paris: Marcel Giard, 1925.

Shawcross, William. *The Quality of Mercy: Cambodia, Holocaust, and Modern Conscience.* New York: Simon & Schuster, 1984.

Shils, Edward A. "The Intellectuals in the Political Development of the New States." In John H. Kautsky, ed., *Political Change in Underdeveloped Countries: Nationalism and Communism.* New York: Wiley, 1962.

Shirer, William L. *The Rise and Fall of the Third Reich.* New York: Simon & Schuster, 1960.

Shoup, Paul S. *The East European and Soviet Data Handbook.* New York: Columbia University Press, 1981.

Singer, Charles. "Historical Relations of Religion and Science." In Joseph Needham, ed., *Science, Religion and Reality.* New York: George Braziller, 1955.

Skidmore, Thomas E., and Peter H. Smith. *Modern Latin America.* New York: Oxford University Press, 1984.

Skocpol, Theda. *States and Social Revolutions.* Cambridge: Cambridge University Press, 1979.

Smith, Anthony D. *Theories of Nationalism.* New York: Harper & Row, 1971.

———. *Nationalism in the Twentieth Century.* Oxford: Martin Robertson, 1979.

Smith, Hedrick. *The Russians.* New York: Quadrangle/The New York Times Book Co., 1976.

Spear, Percival. *India, A Modern History.* Ann Arbor: University of Michigan Press, 1961.

Stearns, Peter N. *1848: The Revolutionary Tide in Europe.* New York: Norton, 1974.

Stephenson, Carl, and Frederick G. Marcham, eds. *Sources of English Constitutional History.* New York: Harper & Row, 1972.

Summers, Robert, and A. Heston. "Improved International Comparisons of Real Product and its Composition, 1950–1980." *The Review of Income and Wealth,* ser. 30, no. 2 (1984): 207–62.

Sumner, William G. *The Challenge of Facts and Other Essays.* New Haven: Yale University Press, 1914.

Sweezy, Paul M. *The Theory of Capitalist Development: Principles of Marxian Political Economy.* New York: Oxford University Press, 1942.

Taylor, A. J. P. *A History of the First World War.* New York: Berkeley Medallion, 1969.

———. *The Hapsburg Monarchy 1808–1918.* Chicago: University of Chicago Press, 1976.

Thomas, Hugh. *Suez.* New York: Harper & Row, 1967.

Thomson, Edgar. *Plantation Societies.* Durham: Duke University Press, 1975.

Thorner, Daniel. "Long-term Trends in Output in India." In Simon Kuznets, Wilbert E. Moore, and Joseph J. Spengler, eds., *Economic Growth: Brazil, India, Japan.* Durham: Duke University Press, 1955.

Thrupp, Sylvia. "Medieval Industry." In Carlo M. Cipolla, ed., *The Fontana Economic History of Europe.* Vol. 1, *The Middle Ages.* Glasgow: Fontana/Collins, 1976.

Tilly, Charles. *As Sociology Meets History.* New York: Academic Press, 1981.

Tocqueville, Alexis de. *The Old Regime and the French Revolution.* Garden City: Doubleday, 1955.

Tuchman, Barbara. *The Guns of August.* New York: Macmillan, 1962.

Tumarkin, Nina. *Lenin Lives! The Lenin Cult in Soviet Russia.* Cambridge: Harvard University Press, 1983.

Tyson, Laura D'Andrea. "Investment Allocation: A Comparison of the Reform Experience of Hungary and Yugoslavia." *Journal of Comparative Economics* 7 (1983): 288–303.

Ulam, Adam B. *Titoism and the Cominform.* Cambridge: Harvard University Press, 1962.

Ullman, Walter. *A Short History of the Papacy.* London: Methuen, 1972.

Von Laue, Theodore H. "Imperial Russia at the Turn of the Century: The Cultural Slope and the Revolution From Without." In Reinhard Bendix, ed., *State and Society.* Boston: Little, Brown, 1968.

————. *Why Lenin? Why Stalin?: A Reappraisal of the Russian Revolution.* New York: Harper & Row, 1971.

Wallerstein, Immanuel. *Africa: The Politics of Independence.* New York: Vintage Books, 1961.

————. *The Modern World-System: Capitalist Agriculture and the Origins of the European World-Economy in the Sixteenth Century.* New York: Academic Press, 1974.

————. *The Capitalist World-Economy.* Cambridge: Cambridge University Press, 1979.

————. *The Modern World-System II: Mercantilism and the Consolidation of the European World-Economy, 1600–1750.* New York: Academic Press, 1980.

Ward, Adolphus W., and George P. Gooch. *Cambridge History of British Foreign Policy, 1783–1919.* Cambridge: Cambridge University Press, 1922–1923.

Warriner, Doreen. *Land Reform in Principle and Practice.* Oxford: Clarendon Press, 1969.

Weber, Eugen J., ed. *Varieties of Fascism.* New York: Van Nostrand Reinhold, 1964.

————. "Romania." In Hans Rogger and Eugen J. Weber, eds., *The European Right.* Berkeley and Los Angeles: University of California Press, 1966.

————. *Peasants Into Frenchmen: The Modernization of Rural France 1870–1914.* Stanford: Stanford University Press, 1976.

Weber, Max. *The Protestant Ethic and the Spirit of Capitalism.* New York: Scribners, 1958.

————. *Economy and Society.* New York: Bedminster Press, 1968.

Webster, Charles K. *The Foreign Policy of Palmerston, 1830–1841.* London: G. Bell, 1951.

————. "British, French, and American Influences." In R. A. Humphreys and John Lynch, eds., *The Origins of the Latin American Revolutions 1808–1826.* New York: Knopf, 1965.

Wedgwood, Cicely V. *The Thirty Years War.* Garden City: Doubleday/Anchor, 1961.

Weir, Margaret, and Theda Skocpol. "State Structures and Social Keynesianism: Responses to the Great Depression in Sweden and the United States." *International Journal of Comparative Sociology* 24 (1983): 4–29.

Wheatcroft, Andrew. *The World Atlas of Revolutions.* New York: Simon & Schuster, 1983.

Wilkie, James W. *The Mexican Revolution: Federal Expenditures and Social Change Since 1910.* Berkeley and Los Angeles: University of California Press, 1970.

Wilson, Charles. *The Dutch Republic.* New York: McGraw-Hill, 1968.

Wolf, Eric. *Peasant Wars of the Twentieth Century.* New York: Harper & Row, 1969.

————. *Europe and the People Without History.* Berkeley and Los Angeles: University of California Press, 1982.

Woodcock, George. *Anarchism: A History of Libertarian Ideas and Movements.* Cleveland: Meridian Books, 1962.

Woodruff, William. *Impact of Western Man: A Study of Europe's Role in the World Economy 1750–1960.* New York: St. Martin's Press, 1966.

————. "The Emergence of an International Economy." In Carlo M. Cipolla, ed., *The Fontana Economic History of Europe.* Vol. 4, *The Emergence of Industrial Societies.* Glasgow: Fontana/Collins, 1973.

World Almanac 1985. New York: Newspaper Enterprise Association, 1985.

The World Bank. *World Development Report 1981.* New York: Oxford University Press, 1981.

————. *World Development Report 1983.* New York: Oxford University Press, 1983.

Woytinsky, W. S., and E. S. Woytinski. *World Population and Production: Trends and Outlooks.* New York: The Twentieth Century Fund, 1953.

Wright, Arthur. *The Sui Dynasty.* New York: Knopf, 1978.

Wright, Gordon. *France in Modern Times, 1760 to the Present.* Chicago: Rand McNally, 1960.

Yergin, Daniel. *Shattered Peace: The Origins of the Cold War and the National Security State.* Boston: Houghton Mifflin, 1977.

Zaslavsky, Victor. *The Neo-Stalinist State: Class, Ethnicity and Consensus in Soviet Society.* New York: M. E. Sharpe, 1982.

INDEX

A 6
B 7
C 8
D 9
E 0
F 1
G 2
H 3
I 4
J 5